T0330599

ROUTLEDGE LIBRARY EDITIONS:
ACCOUNTING HISTORY

Volume 25

FORERUNNERS OF REALIZABLE VALUES ACCOUNTING IN FINANCIAL REPORTING

FORERUNNERS OF REALIZABLE VALUES ACCOUNTING IN FINANCIAL REPORTING

Edited by
G.W. DEAN AND M.C. WELLS

LONDON AND NEW YORK

First published in 1982 by Garland Publishing, Inc.

This edition first published in 2021
by Routledge
2 Park Square, Milton Park, Abingdon, Oxon OX14 4RN

and by Routledge
52 Vanderbilt Avenue, New York, NY 10017

Routledge is an imprint of the Taylor & Francis Group, an informa business

British Library Cataloguing in Publication Data
A catalogue record for this book is available from the British Library

ISBN: 978-0-367-33564-9 (Set)
ISBN: 978-1-00-304636-3 (Set) (ebk)
ISBN: 978-0-367-50749-7 (Volume 25) (hbk)
ISBN: 978-1-00-305109-1 (Volume 25) (ebk)

Publisher's Note
The publisher has gone to great lengths to ensure the quality of this reprint but
points out that some imperfections in the original copies may be apparent.

Disclaimer
The publisher has made every effort to trace copyright holders and would welcome
correspondence from those they have been unable to trace.

Forerunners of Realizable Values Accounting in Financial Reporting

edited by
G. W. Dean
M. C. Wells

Garland Publishing, Inc.
New York & London   1982

Library of Congress Cataloging in Publication Data
Main entry under title:

Forerunners of realizable values accounting in financial
   reporting.

   (Accountancy in transition)
   1. Accounting—Addresses, essays, lectures.
2. Current value accounting—Addresses, essays, lectures.
3. Cost accounting—Addresses, essays, lectures.
I. Dean, G. W.   II. Wells, M. C.   III. Title: Realizable
values accounting.   IV. Series.
HF5629.F6   1982   657'.73   82-82486
ISBN 0-8240-5334-6

The volumes in this series are printed on acid-free,
250-year-life paper.

Printed in the United States of America

Contents

Cognate Disciplines

Recent Contributions

ACKNOWLEDGMENTS

Berle, A A and Fisher, F S Jr, "Elements of the Law of Business Accounting," *Columbia Law Review*, October 1932, pp. 573–593, has been reprinted by permission of the editor of the *Columbia Law Review*.

Chambers, R J, "Accounting for Inflation," *Exposure Draft*, has been reprinted by permission of the author.

Corbin, D A, "Comments on the Accretion of Income," *The Accounting Review*, October 1963, pp. 742–744, has been reprinted by permission of the author and the editor of *The Accounting Review*.

Correspondence in *The Accountant*, as listed, has been reproduced by permission of the editor of *The Accountant*: F W Pixley, "Question of Audit," 4 December 1909, pp. 699–700; Editorial, "Balance Sheet Values," 4 December 1909, pp. 676–677; E M Carter, "Balance Sheet Values," 1 January 1910, pp. 12–13; Editorial, "Balance Sheet Values," 15 January 1910, pp. 75–77; Anon, "Balance Sheet Values," 15 January 1910, pp. 81–82; Editorial, "Balance Sheet Values," 22 January 1910, pp. 115–117; E M Carter, "Balance Sheet Values," 22 January 1910, pp. 126–127.

Haig, R M, "The Concept of Income—Economic and Legal Aspects" in R M Haig (Ed.), *The Federal Income Tax*, Columbia University Press, 1921 has been reprinted by permission of the Columbia University Press.

Lee, T A, "Reporting Cash Flows and Net Realisable Values," *Accounting and Business Research*, Spring 1981, pp. 163–170 has been reprinted by permission of the author and the editor of *Accounting and Business Research*.

Moss, A G, "Treatment of Appreciation of Fixed Assets," *Journal of Accountancy*, September 1923, pp. 161–179, has been reprinted by permission of the editor of the *Journal of Accountancy*.

Paton, W A and Stevenson, R, *Principles of Accounting*, 3rd Ed. Macmillan & Co., 1916, pp. 103–105, has been reprinted by permission of the authors.

Phillips, G E, "The Accretion Concept of Income," *The Accounting Review*, January 1963, pp. 14–25 has been reprinted by permission of the author and the editor of *The Accounting Review*.

Simons, H C, "The Definition of Income," *Personal Income Taxation*, University of Chicago Press, 1938, has been reprinted by permission of the University of Chicago Press.

Sterling, R R, "Companies are Reporting Useless Numbers," *Fortune*, 1980, pp. 105–107, has been reprinted by permission of the author and the editor of *Fortune*.

Stephens, Hustcraft, *Italian Book-Keeping*, 1735, pp. 1–5, has been reprinted by permission of the Registrar of the Institute of Chartered Accountants in England and Wales.

Viner, J, "Taxation and Changes in Price Levels," *Journal of Political Economy*, August 1923, pp. 494–504, has been reprinted by permission of the editor of the *Journal of Political Economy*.

INTRODUCTION

G W DEAN & M C WELLS

Editorial: Realizable Values in Perspective

Current selling prices are commonly found in all forms of, and proposals
for, accounting for external reporting. Sales are recorded at their
current sales price, and the sales prices of inventory items establish
the debit to debtors and the receipt of cash. Even depreciation calculations are based upon the presumption that the accounting records will
show how the asset value was taken from a current value upon acquisiton
to a current selling (salvage) value upon disposal.

Given the role of selling prices or realizable values within extant
accounting systems, the usual adverse reaction to proposals to value all
stocks of assets at their realizable value is surprising. If the aim of
all accounting systems is to record all assets, fixed and current, at
current prices upon acquisition and disposal, the use of realizable values,
while the assets are in stock does not seem to be very radical. Criticisms
of the proposals of Chambers and Sterling suggest otherwise.

Chambers' theory of Continuously Contemporary Accounting is the most
elegant, complete and rigorous theory of accounting ever developed. It
is based on the use of current selling prices for all assets at all
times, and on the contractual amounts of debt. All real increases in
wealth are counted as income in the period in which they occur. The
resulting system is designed to provide information necessary for people
and firms that conduct their affairs, and therefore adapt, continuously
in markets. Sterling's theory of income measurement was developed in the
limited context of a futures market for grain. Nevertheless, it has wider
application, as Sterling subsequently pointed out.

More recently, Lee has demonstrated that the current enthusiasm being
expressed by a number of academics and practitioners for cash flow
accounting also implies a position statement based on realizable values.
Similarly several of our present and former colleagues at the University
of Sydney have argued for the use of NRV's in a variety of contexts.

All of the work referred to above is of recent origin, and the impression might be given that suggestions for the use of NRV's were also solely a product of recent times. In terms of theoretical rigour within the accounting literature, that is undoubtedly true. There is no work comparable to Chambers' Accounting Evaluation and Economic Behavior in the accounting literature prior to 1960. But, in less rigorous or less complete form, there have been proposals and arguments for the use of realizable values in the accounting literature from the time of Pacioli. It is the aim of this collection to draw together some of the threads of arguments for valuing assets at their realizable value. In doing so, we hope to demonstrate the long and honourable history of those arguments, and the persistence with which they have been advanced, particularly in the last 100 years. For it is in that time that the historical cost system grew to its present dominance. That it is not, and never was, universally accepted is demonstrated in the pages which follow. In his commentary, Clarke provides further evidence of the pervasive nature of selling prices, as well as drawing together the threads of arguments provided by the Forerunners of proposals to base the financial reports of business entities upon the selling prices of assets.

To the best of our knowledge, there have not been any previous attempts to bring together a diverse literature of this sort. Some of the links with financial reporting are rather tenuous, some provide support by implication, others are clear and direct. Taken together, the papers presented here provide a perspective from which advocates of the use of selling prices in financial reporting will gain much support, and in the light of which those who are antagonistic to the use of selling prices might wish to reconsider the bases of their objections.

F L Clarke

Realizable Values: A Recurrent Theme*

A Matter of Perspective

Using selling prices in the valuation of physical assets has been a
recurrent theme in the accounting and related literatures. Much more so
than the current emphasis on replacement price valuations implies. For
although it might be conceded that the proposed use of replacement prices
has been the dominant theme from those proposing a departure from historical costs, it has been so primarily through their allegiance to a
'budgeting perspective' on financial reporting. The budgetary perspective
is manifest in the concern for maintaining the capacity of firms to
continue their present operations, to continue operating in their present
manner and in the concomitant retention of the composition and structure
of their present endowment of physical assets.

That perspective has persisted for over sixty years, under the generic
label of 'maintaining productive capacity'. In specific contexts that
perspective has been appropriate. It meshed neatly, for example, with
the compensatory ethic of public utility rate setting. A good enough
case can be made that the 'non-market' rates regulated by Government
agencies ought to allow for the replacement of capital consumed in
providing a public service according to prescribed specifications. In
those circumstances it is necessary to ensure the prolonged continuation
of the service to the consumer. And it is not unreasonable as a matter
of equity to investors that regulated rates at least partially simulate
those likely to emerge under those competitive (market) forces. For
whilst regulated firms are insulated against the viscissitudes of competition, they generally are prevented from exploiting. The productive
capacity perspective might likewise fit the private plans of managers
budgeting to continue a current mode of operation. But in neither
of those contexts, nor in others like them in which compensation or
indemnification is sought for property lost, sacrificed, or expropriated,

---

* F L Clarke is a Senior Lecturer in Accounting, University of Sydney.
This survey was commissioned for this volume. References accompanied
by an asterisk, eg Cournot (1838*, p.1) indicate articles reproduced
in and page numbers of this anthology.

or in which a decision to proceed in a specified way has been taken, is current wealth as a strict monetary measure a primary concern. They focus on the physical means of production and the cost of retaining or replacing them. Attention is directed away from the immediate financial consequences of those physical objects being part of a firm's asset endowment.

In contrast whenever wealth, per se, or the periodic monetary calculation of wealth or the changes in it over time, have been the object of enquiry and the perceived perspective of financial reporting, replacement price valuations have been far less prominent.

The wealth perspective has prevailed without equivocation in a number of settings; in the discussion by economists of wealth as an economic category; in explanations of its quantification in monetary terms and in explanations of calculations of changes in its quantification. There, contrary to the productive capacity perspective, selling prices of vendible physical assets have not been subordinated. Frequently they have been the dominant theme. Understandably so, for in the discussion of wealth, per se, the issues are what comprises wealth and which of those components an entity actually possesses; not whether specific items will be retained, maintained, or one day replaced. In the calculation of the monetary amount of wealth the primary issue has been the assessment of how much general purchasing power its possession endows on its owner, not what it would cost him to acquire his current wealth if he lost or was otherwise deprived of it. And in the calculation of changes in those amounts, the primary issue is whether the owner has more or has less wealth at one time relative to another, not whether it would cost him more, or cost him less, to acquire whatever is possessed at those different times. The wealth perspective therefore emphasises what unencumbered money an entity has, not what it will need to do this or that; and it empha- sises what money it possibly has access to by virtue of owning vendible physi- cal goods, not the amount of money it would need to have access to in order to acquire now, or in the future, items of wealth similar to those currently possessed. The wealth perspective has always implied that the financial significance entailed by the ownership of vendible physical goods is indicated by their current selling prices.

vi

The Wealth Perspective

Despite a subdued image in the accounting literature, the <u>wealth</u> <u>perspective</u> has been a persistent motivation underlying financial reporting (<u>Report of the Accounting Standards Review Committee</u>, chapters 2 and 3).

The subordination of selling price valuations for assets has been a casualty of the insouciant promotion of the budgeting and compensatory features of the productive capacity perspective. Selling price valuations have been viewed improperly as departures from primary ideas, rather than as conformity with the perspective imbedded in the legal motivation for financial reporting; creditor and investor protection, solvency monitoring, stewardship evaluation, wealth and progress assessment.

Achievement of broader social goals than investor protection likewise relies upon the wealth perspective: fiscal authorities assess and levy taxes on the basis of a taxpayer's wealth (or at least periodic changes in it), insolvency Courts assess wealth and its shortfall relative to a bankrupt's debts, fines and penalties imposed by Courts and other tribunals require satisfaction through the forfeiture of wealth, and public appeals for financial assistance to various causes are invariably for gifts of portions of donors' wealths. In each case, wealth as a monetary quantum is the object of attention. And where the taxpayer, bankrupt, defaulter and even the donor, are <u>short</u> of sufficient ready cash to meet the call upon them, then it is the money's worth of physical property, the cash obtainable for it, its selling price, upon which attention is focussed. Vendible property is confiscated to satisfy unpaid taxation assessments, debts and penalties established in the Courts, on the basis of its approximate selling prices. A donation of vendible property often is attributed the same significance as a gift of cash. As such, the <u>wealth perspective</u> pervades the foundations and daily functioning of ordinary commerce.

From antiquity, the <u>wealth perspective</u> has pervaded and persisted in simple accounting mechanisms: in accounting for the voyages of the merchant adventurers - essentially cash (or money's worth) in and cash (or money's worth) out; in the simple accounts of individual merchants operating upon a 'voyage' or 'venture' basis; in past and modern partnership arrangements and in the operation of joint ventures. The wealth perspective and its employment of selling prices also underly some other conventional accounting techniques imbedded in the so-called historical cost system; in the imposition of the 'lower of cost or net realizable value inventory rule; in the requirement (under British type corporate law) that 'current assets' not be stated above the 'amount they are likely to realise'; in the operation of the Courts adjudicating on the propriety of schemes for the reduction and return of 'capital' to corporate shareholders and in the progression of straight-line and reducing balance depreciation techniques towards estimated future scrap (selling price) values of property.

This anthology draws together, from diverse sources, illustrations of those manifestations of the wealth perspective and of the unequivocal use of selling price valuations it entails.

From the Economists

Curiously the numerous descriptions of wealth and its monetary quantification which support the selling price case attract little attention in the accounting literature. The common ploy is to refer only to those descriptions which refer to capital goods as physical agents of production and thereby highlight the physical characteristics of capital, rather than its monetary quantification with which financial reporting is concerned. Frequently, no distinction is drawn between the capital stock 'of society' and that of individual entities; no distinction is drawn   between macro and micro analyses by economists. Smith's (1776) reference to 'the acquired and useful abilities of all the inhabitants or members of the society' (p.265) as 'capital stock' is picked up by other authors to promote the productive capacity perspective, but his description of the quantification of individual entities' wealth is not:

> Every man is rich or poor according to the degree
> in which he can afford the necessaries, conveniences,
> and amusements of human life [Cantillon, Essai,
> pp.1,2]

> Wealth is power ... the power of purchasing ...
> labour ... product of labour ... the exchangeable
> value of everything must always be precisely equal
> to the extent of this power which it conveys to
> its owner. (p.31)

Only selling prices are indicative of the 'power of purchasing' which the possession of vendible physical wealth items endows. Cournot (1838*) is equally explicit that wealth is measured by the value in exchange. Note that he uses wealth as a synonym for value in exchange or what Smith described as power to purchase, to distinguish it from notions such as <u>utility</u> and <u>scarcity</u>, the causes of changes in the amount of one's wealth:

> ... to form an intelligible theory we ought to identify the sense of the word wealth with that which is presented to us by the words <u>exchangeable values</u> [selling prices] ... the proprietor of a great forest is only rich [wealthy - possessing great exchange value] on the condition ... of not glutting the market with his timber [forcing its selling price down] (p.5)

Thereafter Cournot reinforces those implied references to selling prices in his discussion of how wealth increases or decreases as prices vary (pp. 6-9), and the explicit synonymity of <u>wealth</u> and <u>value in exchange</u>, 'the idea of <u>wealth</u> or of <u>value in exchange</u>' (pp.6,7 and 13).

The same ideas permeate Mill's discourse (1848*). The 'preposterous' idea that only 'money is synonymous with wealth' (p.16) is corrected by Mill putting money in its proper place as the unit in which wealth is calculated:

> In common discourse, wealth is always expressed in money. If you ask how rich a person is, you are answered that he has so many thousand pounds ... [but] It is true that in the inventory of a person's fortune are included, not only the money in his actual possession, or due to him, but all other articles of value. These, however <u>do not enter in their own character, but by virtue of the sums of money [the prices] which they would sell for</u>, and if they would <u>sell</u> for less, that owner is reputed less rich [wealthy], though the things themselves are precisely the same ... those who enrich themselves by commerce, do so by giving money for goods as well as goods for money ... (pp.16-17, emphasis added).

Others have pursued the same line, up to the present: Marshall (1890) 'A man's wealth ... [includes items which] serve directly as the means enabling him to acquire material goods' (p.56). Only selling prices could measure those 'means'; Fawcett (1883) 'Wealth [consists] of every commodity which has an exchange value [has a selling price] (p.6); Walker (1896), 'Wealth comprises all articles of value ... value is the power which an article confers upon its possessor ... value is power in exchange' (p.5); Hobson (1906) restricted capital and wealth to 'marketable matter' (p.26) excluding those items for which no market and no price existed; Von Mises (1949) noted that capital or wealth 'is the sum of the money equivalent of all assets minus the sum of all liabilities' (p.262) and to Shackle (1970) 'a company's wealth, capital or 'fortune'

comprises the market value ... of all material objects ... legal rights
... plus the money it has ... [less] the debts owed' (p.28). The
significance of selling prices in the calculation of wealth which
accounting might be expected to achieve is indisputable according to
those economists.

From Early Accountants

Contrary to the historical cost paradigm, reference to market prices,
market values and present values have peppered the accounting literature
up to the present. And whereas replacement price valuations have been
prominent, the wealth perspective and recommendations for the use of
selling prices have been frequent enough to avoid the illusion that they
are radical ideas. Stephens [1735*] set the pattern by noting that 'By
the acceptance of this money', inter-personal comparisons of individual's
'Estates' (wealths) were possible:

> ... thus, such a thing of my own is <u>worth</u> 20/-.
> That is, people will give so much for it; and
> such a thing of another Man's is <u>worth</u> 20/-,
> consequently mine is equal to his <u>in Value</u> ...
> for Men's Abilities in purchasing things, are
> only said to be great or small by comparison
> ... (p.27 emphasis added)

Market (selling) prices were 'usual' with merchants, when they made a
general balance of their books, according to Hayes (1741), and Wardhaugh
Thompson (1777) explained that an 'exact state of our affairs' was
calculable from assessments of 'what payments we have to make, and
what cash <u>we can command</u>; (vol.11, pp.1-2). The immediate command of
cash resulting from the possession of physical goods is limited to and
indicated by their selling prices. Thompson's 'assessments' imply the
use of selling prices. Likewise Branford (1903*), the balance sheet
valuation of proprietor's capital, he explains, is to equal '... that
proportion of the value of property which would accrue to the proprietor
on realization'. A calculation of what 'would accrue ... on realization'
in respect to physical assets can only be according to their known or
or approximated selling prices. The same sentiments might be implied
from the anonymous reference in the <u>Encyclopaedia of Accounting</u> (1903*)
to the necessity that balance sheets 'state the assets at their <u>real</u>
value as a going concern' (p.49), and in the discussion of 'bank'
balance sheets showing not only 'financial position ... but ... assets
... in the order or realisability'. The juxtaposition of 'real' and
'realisation' is a reasonable basis for inferring that the use of 'real'

x

was in its economic sense as relating to money or money's worth and the entailed general purchasing power.

In The Appreciation Debate

Debate over the correct basis for 'balance sheet values' (in the United Kingdom) and whether 'appreciation' ought to be booked and whether depreciation ought to be charged (in the United States) gave 'market values' for physical assets a confusing airing. Whilst most of the debate in that form occurred prior to 1930, the trail of its wreckage has survived to the present. For the debate contributed greatly to the loose common reference to 'market values' or 'current values',with little or no distinction drawn between current selling prices and current or future replacement prices. Moreover, the debate appeared to cloud the necessity that such distinctions should be made.

The cross talk between Pixley (1909*),Carter (1910*), the anonymous (1910*) contribution to the debate in The Accountant and the editorial comments(1909* and 1910*),illustrate the British accountants' penchant for discussing selling price valuations, yet their extreme reluctance to actually name them as such. This is evidenced by Pixley's references to 'value', 'value of the asset' and 'too high a value' (p.54); and by the Editorial comment on 'opinions on values' (1909, p.52), 'Balance Sheet Values' (1910, pp.57, 61), 'values so arrived at' and 'values for Balance Sheet Purposes' (1910, p.63) in reference to Carter's strong allusions to the wealth perspective and selling price valuation according to Carter:

> ... the correct basis of value for assets is
> their market value ... when capital is distributed
> among shareholders it is paid in cash, and assets
> have to be sold at their market value in order to
> provide cash ... Market value [and by implication,
> selling prices] is the object in view throughout.
> (1910, p.55)

Debate on appreciation in the United States generally pursued the line that changes in replacement prices were appreciation. But, nonetheless the emphasis was on market values, as a departure from historical costs. And the line of reasoning was always that appreciation was indicative of an enhancement in the worth of an entity's assets - that somehow, because of asset appreciation the entity was richer. No explanation was forthcoming as to how an increase in replacement prices made a firm worth more.

The recourse by Paton and Stevenson (1916*) to vague descriptions of changes in 'property values', 'value changes' (p.72) and to 'market prices' (p.73) avoided the necessity to identify the prices to which reference was being made. But the 'fit' of selling price valuations into their argument is unambiguous. They allude to appreciation as the opposite of depreciation (p.72), and since depreciation techniques proceed towards the ultimate selling price of the asset as scrap, we might infer that appreciation booked in the accounts is also intended to approximate selling prices; they allude to fluctuations in security prices being indicative of market price (value?) changes (p.73), which implies that selling price changes are in mind, for selling prices are habitually referred to when the 'market prices' of securities are discussed; and finally the description of booked appreciation in land as a 'surplus' (p.75), is unequivocal when it represents a realizable gain such as increased market (selling) prices represent. Paton and Stevenson's exposition (perhaps unwittingly) fitted the selling price case perfectly. Fisher's 'actual value' (1907*, p.67) likewise invokes notions of selling prices, for lenders can be expected to look to the selling prices of property pledged as an indication of their security, not to the replacement prices. Bauer's (1913*) rejection of Leake's 'pretty rigid cost theory of value' (p.70) also fits the selling price mould. Note the familiar reference to amortisation down to the amount of the 'scrap value $100', even though Bauer's main point was to press home the replacement fund notion of depreciation. This is further illustrated by Moss' (1923*) exposition. The point is that whilst the general mode of argument at the time is good cause to suspect that replacement prices were uppermost in the price hierarchy according to those authors, their tone was more in keeping with the wealth perspective.

The wealth perspective is clear when simple, but complete, commercial scenarios are considered. MacNeal's (1939*) 'Three Fables' illustrate that. The worth of William's factory was not the $20,000 he paid for it, but said to be the $5,000 for which he could sell it. Because William 'was stupid' we might expect it would have cost him $20,000 (or more) to replace it (pp.97-8). The worth of Bill's and Henry's wheat inventories turned upon selling prices (99-101) and so did the worth of the portfolios held by the American and the National trusts (pp.102-8). MacNeal had no doubt how selling prices entered those calculations and others similar to them. The wealth perspective was the dominant theme of MacNeal's

common sense situations.

In Cognate Disciplines

Engineers, fiscal authorities and the Courts have drawn upon argument
implying selling price valuations when forced by the circumstances
to consider a firm's wealth and progress. The significance of 'market
values' is discussed by Main (1897*) in upholding the view of the 'court
in Massachusetts' that:

> the true value of a property is its market
> value ... such a sum as one party who has
> the capital, and who desires to purchase, is
> willing to pay for a plant, the owner being
> willing, but not forced, to sell. (p.117)

Clearly, for the owner the worth of property is seen to be the current
price for which he could sell it. 'Worth' is considered by Main as an
engineering valuation in a variety of ordinary commercial circumstances
employing items of wealth:

> buying or selling, raising money upon or bonding
> a property, rental, taxes, insurance, adjustment
> of losses by fire or accident, and condemnation ...
> (p.117)

And with respect to the resulting statement of financial position
reflected in balance sheets (Burton, 1901*) notes:

> it must always be remembered that it is the
> market, that is, the selling value ... which
> is being sought. (p.127)

The place of market values in taxation calculations has been a contentious
issue, for in the end taxes are satisfied with the payment of money,
wealth in its most concrete form. Viner (1923*) argues that distortions
arise in the tax base and in the perceived significance of taxes levied
when changes in the purchasing power of money are ignored (pp.165-8).
Yet, curiously, he implies that replacement price valuations for
assets ought to be imputed for taxation purposes, even though such are
never indicative of the general purchasing power to which the taxpayer
has access. In contrast Haig (1921*) explicitly adopts the wealth
perspective

> ... our definition demands the taxation of the
> net accretion of one's power measured in money
> or money-worth. (p.158)

Exclusion of changes in the 'money-worth' of assets according to Haig
'[is] illogical and the cause of much erosion'(p.159); 'the most acceptable
concept of income..is the money-value of the net accretion to economic
power between two points of time' (p.161). Income was thereby perceived
to be:

> the result obtained by adding consumption
> during the period to 'wealth' at the end of
> the period and then subtracting 'wealth' at the
> beginning. The sine qua non of income is
> gain ... estimated in a common unit by appeal
> to market prices. (Simons, 1938* , emphasis
> is added, p.183)

'Market prices', that is, for property consumed and for property possessed b
the taxpayer as part of his current wealth, not the prices he faces to
acquire his present asset endowment.

Such notions filter through legal judgements. In Re Spanish Prospecting
Co Ltd (1911*) the 'fundamental meaning of profits' was deemed to be
based upon a comparison of the 'total value of assets' at the beginning
and the end of a period - that is, by the comparison of market prices
(Fletcher Moulton, L J. p.201). Appreciation in the market value of assets
is acknowledged, '.. appreciation in value could properly be set off against
losses' (Ammonia Soda Company Limited v Chamberlain, 1918*), Peterson, J p.2
But even in the law 'appreciation' is less than definitive. Berle and
Fisher (1932*) allude to the use of current 'market values' for the
valuation of inventories, marketable securities and fixed assets in their
review of the elements of the 'law of business accounting'. The 'owners
of a fund in a business ... may be entitled both to the fund and to all
accretions from it' (p.226); how may 'accretions' emerge 'from' a fund,
except in cash? And how may they be measured, except by reference to the
selling prices of those items comprising 'the fund' which are not already i
a 'liquid' state? Liquidity is perceived to be a particular 'quality' of
assets in a 'business position'.

> For many business purposes (peculiarly for the
> banker who proposes to lend money at short term),
> interest is focussed on the business position of
> the body of assets. Can any of it be swiftly
> turned into cash? [Is it vendible, has it a
> selling price and if so what is it?] What
> proportion is fixed [physical in form, non-vendible]
> and non-liquid? ... much of our industrial life
> is built upon this assumption of
> liquidity (p.227).
>
> ... If we were to endeavour to make the whole process
> extremely clear ... there would be a series of
> running appraisals or values (p.228).

We might expect that the appraisals are intended to reflect the 'liquid'
or 'business position' of assets to which Berle and Fisher refer. And
later it might be inferred that 'appreciation' is used by them to describe

xiv

increases in market selling prices:

> ... the real valuation [of merchandise] ought
> to be the selling price at the time of accounting.
> This might be a fair guide for the owner ... [but]
> accountants commonly disregard it as a basis of
> valuation.
> ... Unrealized appreciation ... is not normally
> included in an account. (p.233)

> ... a primary question arises: to what extent must
> the value [selling price] of a particular item be
> reduced to cash before it may properly be included
> in the income statement? (p.242)

> ... there would seem little ground for giving any
> indication whatsoever of an unrealized appreciation
> to current assets - let the [frequent] deed of
> conversion [into cash] tell its own story -,
> whereas in the case of a fixed asset, the increase
> may well be the result of the community's
> revaluation of the potential productivity and
> utility of the property, which, as it is not designed
> for sale, may [unless booked] escape record
> indefinitely. In such a case, the recognition on
> the balance sheet of an unrealized appreciation of a
> fixed asset ... presents a somewhat truer picture.
> (p.243, emphasis added)

In Recent Contributions

Over the past twenty years the seeds of ideas regarding the use of
market prices in general, and selling prices in particular, for the
valuation of physical assets, have been propagated in explicit expositions
on the issue.

The propositions perceived to underlie the 1909-1910 UK debate on appreciation and the firmer discussions in the US literature during the 1920s
filtered through the accounting and engineering literature. They are
seen in the debate on appreciation, the dilemma over the 'proper' basis
for taxation and in the Courts' deliberations on the use of accounts, the
distributality of profits and the 'depreciation' question. By the 1960's
they were no longer vague. The inclusion of asset appreciation in both
balance sheet valuations and the income account are quite explicit in
Philips' 'The Accretion Concept of Income' (1963*).

The use of market selling prices as the best approximation of the 'current
cash equivalent' of assets argued by Chambers in his Accounting, Evaluation
and Economic Behavior (1966), is made explicit in his Accounting for
Inflation exposure draft (1975*) explaining the method of 'Continuously
Contemporary Accounting' (CoCoA). Sterling's exposition on '... Useless

Numbers' (1980*) is indicative of the support he has given to the selling price case and to the necessary practical distinction between replacement prices and selling prices. Both authors emphasise the serviceability of market selling price data for the ordinary, every day, purposes accounting reports are intended to satisfy. Serviceability is a central theme in Chambers' exposition on CoCoA. It is the overriding criterion in his exposure draft (pp.294-6) of the 'Evaluation' of competing accounting systems, 'The practical superiority of CoCoA is demonstrated' is his last word (p.296), 'The approach I'm proposing would do for asset values what McKesson & Robbins did for honest quantities', is Sterling's (p.305).

The monetary characteristic of the wealth perspective and its related cash flow and purchasing power implications surface in Lee's exposition of the cash flow/net realizable value nexus (1981*), 'CFA [Cash Flow Accounting] and NRVA [Net Realizable Value Accounting ... are] incomplete without each other'. The significant proposition is that cash flows are predicated on market selling price valuations for physical assets:

> ... [CFA] being concerned with the way in which
> cash has been generated ... and [NRVA] with the
> availability and accessibility of cash for future
> activity and needs (p.307).

Those 'concerns' had been shown by Gray and Wells (1977*) to be in fact the underlying emphasis in the thinking of the Commission of the European Communities on financial disclosure. The emphasis was on 'liquidity and exchangeability':

> It is, of course, no coincidence that the best
> indication of liquidity is also given by the face
> value of 'monetary assets and the availability of
> market selling prices of non-monetary assets.
> (p.299)
>
> ... An approach which is directly useful to readers
> of balance sheets is a system of measurement and
> classification based upon the ease with which
> assets can be exchanged [sold]
> ... Such an approach is consistent with the
> purpose of discovering corporate liquidity and
> more likely to provide useful insights into the
> capacity for business survival. (p.301)

The papers collected in this book contain numerous messages about market price valuations capable of different interpretations. Many give quite explicit support for the selling price case. Others are incapable of reasonable interpretation other than in support for selling price

valuations. And still others are not inconsistent with the selling
price case. The temporal and disciplinary diversities which they are
subjected to prevent the identification of any articulated development
of ideas. There is little evidence of inter-disciplinary influences.
In itself, that is important. For it means that the survival of the
case for market price valuations in financial reports, the recurrent
emphasis on and recourse to the wealth perspective, and the explicit
refernece to, and implicit 'fit' of, selling price valuations in diverse
contexts, is all the more compelling.

REFERENCES

Company Accounting Standards, Report of the Accounting Standards Review Committee (R J Chambers, Chairman) NSW Government Printer, 1978.

Fawcett H, _Manual of Political Economy_, Macmillan and Co 1883.

Hayes, Richard, _The Gentleman's Complete Book-keeper_, London, 1941.

Hobson, J A, _The Science of Wealth_, Williams and Norgate, 1906.

Marshall A, _Principles of Economics_, MacMillan and Co, 1890.

Shackle, L G S, _Expectation Enterprise and Profit: The Theory of the Firm_, George Allen and Unwin, London, 1970.

Smith, A, _The Wealth of Nations_ (1776), _The Modern Library_ edition, New York, 1936.

Thompson, Wardhaugh, _The Accomptant's Oracle_, New York, 1777.

Von Mises, L, _Human Action_, William Hodge and Company Limited, 1949.

Walker, F A, _Political Economy_, Macmillan and Co Limited, 1896.

NOTIONS OF WEALTH

A. COURNOT

RESEARCHES

INTO

THE MATHEMATICAL PRINCIPLES

OF

THE THEORY OF WEALTH

——◦◦✚◦◦——

CHAPTER I

OF VALUE IN EXCHANGE OR OF WEALTH IN GENERAL

1. The Teutonic root *Rik* or *Reich*, which has passed into all the Romance languages, vaguely expressed a relation of superiority, of strength, or of power. *Los ricos hombres* is still used in Spain for distinguished noblemen and eminent men, and such is also the force of the words *riches hommes* in the French of de Joinville. The idea which the word *wealth* presents to us to-day, and which is relative to our state of civilization, could not have been grasped by men of Teutonic stock, either at the epoch of the Conquest, or even at much later periods, when the feudal law existed in full vigour. Property, power, the distinctions between masters, servants and slaves, abundance, and poverty, rights and privileges, all these are found among the most savage tribes, and seem to flow necessarily from the natural laws which preside over aggregations

3

of individuals and of families; but such an idea of wealth as we draw from our advanced state of civilization, and such as is necessary to give rise to a theory, can only be slowly developed as a consequence of the progress of commercial relations, and of the gradual reaction of those relations on civil institutions.

A shepherd is in possession of a vast pasture ground, and no one can disturb him with impunity; but it would be vain for him to think of exchanging it for something which he might prefer; there is nothing in existing habits and customs to make such an exchange possible; this man is a landholder, but he is not rich.

The same shepherd has cattle and milk in abundance; he can provide for a numerous retinue of servants and slaves; he maintains a generous hospitality towards poor dependents; but he is neither able to accumulate his products, nor to exchange them for objects of luxury which do not exist; this man has power, authority, the enjoyments which belong to his position, but he has not wealth.

2. It is inconceivable that men should live for a considerable time near together without effecting an exchange of goods and services; but from this natural, and we may even say instinctive, action, it is a long step to the abstract idea of *value in exchange*, which supposes that the objects to which such value is attributed *are in commercial circulation*, *i.e.* that it is always possible to find means to exchange them for other objects of equal value. The things, then, to which the state of commercial relations and civil institutions permits a value in exchange to be attached, are those which in the language of to-day are characterized by the word

wealth; and to form an intelligible theory we ought to absolutely identify the sense of the word *wealth* with that which is presented to us by the words *exchangeable values.*

Under this conception, *wealth* has doubtless only an abstract existence ; for, strictly speaking, of all the things on which we set a price, or to which we attribute a value in exchange, there are none always exchangeable at will for any other commodity of equal price or value. In the act of exchange, as in the transmission of power by machinery, there is friction to be overcome, losses which must be borne, and limits which cannot be exceeded. The proprietor of a great forest is only rich on condition of managing his lumbering with prudence, and of not glutting the market with his lumber ; the owner of a valuable picture gallery may spend his life in the vain attempt to find purchasers ; while, on the other hand, in the neighbourhood of a city the conversion of a sack of grain into money will only require the time necessary to carry it to the grain market ; and at great commercial centres a stock of coffee can always be sold on the exchange.

The extension of commerce and the development of commercial facilities tend to bring the actual condition of affairs nearer and nearer to this order of abstract conceptions, on which alone theoretical calculations can be based, in the same way as the skilful engineer approaches nearer to theoretical conditions by diminishing friction through polished bearings and accurate gearing. In this way nations are said to make progress in the commercial or mercantile system. These two expressions are etymologically equivalent, but one is now taken in a good and the other in a bad sense, as is generally the case, according to Bentham, with the names of things that involve advantages and evils of a moral order.

5

We will not take up either these advantages or these evils. The progress of nations in the commercial system is a fact in the face of which all discussion of its desirability becomes idle; our part is to observe, and not to criticise, the irresistible laws of nature. Whatever man can measure, calculate, and systematize, ultimately becomes the object of measurement, calculation, and system. Wherever fixed relations can replace indeterminate, the substitution finally takes place. It is thus that the sciences and all human institutions are organized. The use of coin, which has been handed down to us from remote antiquity, has powerfully aided the progress of commercial organization, as the art of making glass helped many discoveries in astronomy and physics; but commercial organization is not essentially bound to the use of the monetary metals. All means are good which tend to facilitate exchange, to fix value in exchange; and there is reason to believe that in the further development of this organization the monetary metals will play a part of gradually diminishing importance.

3. The abstract idea of *wealth* or of *value in exchange*, a definite idea, and consequently susceptible of rigorous treatment in combinations, must be carefully distinguished from the accessory ideas of utility, scarcity, and suitability to the needs and enjoyments of mankind, which the word *wealth* still suggests in common speech. These ideas are variable, and by nature indeterminate, and consequently ill suited for the foundation of a scientific theory. The division of economists into schools, and the war waged between practical men and theorists, have arisen in large measure from the ambiguity of the word *wealth* in ordinary speech, and the

confusion which has continued to obtain between the fixed, definite idea of *value in exchange*, and the ideas of utility which every one estimates in his own way, because there is no fixed standard for the utility of things.*

It has sometimes happened that a publisher, having in store an unsalable stock of some work, useful and sought after by connoisseurs, but of which too many copies were originally printed in view of the class of readers for whom it was intended, has sacrificed and destroyed two-thirds of the number, expecting to derive more profit from the remainder than from the entire edition.†

There is no doubt that there might be a book of which it would be easier to sell a thousand copies at sixty francs, than three thousand at twenty francs. Calculating in this way, the Dutch Company is said to have caused the destruction in the islands of the Sound of a part of the precious spices of which it had a monopoly. Here is a complete destruction of objects to which the word *wealth* is applied because they are both sought after, and not easily obtainable. Here is a miserly, selfish act, evidently opposed to the interests of society; and yet it is nevertheless evident that this sordid act, this actual destruction, is a real creation of *wealth* in the commercial sense of the word. The

---

* By this we do not intend that there is neither truth nor error in opinions on the utility of things; we only mean that generally neither the truth nor the error is capable of proof; that these are questions of valuation, and not soluble by calculation, nor by logical argument.

† I have heard it said by a very respectable surveyor, that one of the greatest griefs which he had felt in his youth had been to learn that the publisher Dupont had done thus with the valuable collection of the Memoirs of the old Academy of Sciences.

publisher's inventory will rightly show a greater value for his assets ; and after the copies have left his hands, either wholly or in part, if each individual should draw up his inventory in commercial fashion, and if all these partial inventories could be collated to form a general inventory or balance sheet of the wealth in circulation, an increase would be found in the sum of these items of wealth.

On the contrary, suppose that only fifty copies exist of a curious book, and that this scarcity carries up the price at auction to three hundred francs a copy. A publisher reprints this book in an edition of a thousand copies, of which each will be worth five francs, and which will bring down the other copies to the same price from the exaggerated value which their extreme scarcity had caused. The 1050 copies will therefore only enter for 5250 francs into the sum of wealth which can be inventoried, and this sum will thus have suffered a loss of 9750 francs. The decrease will be even more considerable if (as should be the case) the value of the raw materials is considered, from which the reprints were made, and which existed prior to the reprinting. Here is an industrial operation, a material production, useful to the publisher who undertook it, useful to those whose products and labour it employed, useful even to the public if the book contains valuable information, and which is nevertheless a real destruction of wealth, in the abstract and commercial meaning of the term.

The rise and fall of exchange show perpetual oscillations in values, or in the abstract wealth in circulation, without intervention of actual production or destruction of the physical objects to which, in the concrete sense, the term *wealth* is applicable.

It has been long remarked, and justly, that commerce, properly so called, *i.e.* the transportation of raw materials or finished products, from one market to another, by adding to the worth of the objects transported, creates value or wealth in just the same way as the labour of the miner who extracts metals from the bowels of the earth, or the workman who adapts them to our needs. What ought to have been added, and what we shall have occasion to develop, is that commerce may also be a cause of destruction of values, even while making profits for the merchants who carry it on, and even when in every one's eyes it is a benefit to the countries which it connects in commercial intercourse.

A fashion, a whim, or a chance occurrence may cause a creation or annihilation of values without notable influence on what is regarded as public utility or the general welfare ; it can even come about that a destruction of wealth may be salutary, and an increase detrimental. If chemists should solve the problem of making diamonds, jewellers and the ladies who own sets of jewellery would suffer heavy losses : the general mass of wealth capable of circulation would experience a notable decrease, and yet I can hardly think than any sensible man would be tempted to consider it a public calamity, even though he might regret the individual losses involved. On the contrary, if the taste for diamonds should decline, if wealthy people should stop devoting an important part of their fortunes to this idle vanity, and if, in consequence, the value of diamonds in commerce should decrease, wise men would gladly commend this new depart ure of fashion.

4. When any event, accounted favourable to a country, as improving the condition of the majority of its inhabitants (for what other basis can be taken to estimate utility?), has nevertheless for its first effect the diminution of the mass of values in circulation, we are tempted to suppose that this event conceals the germ of an increase in the general wealth by means of its remote consequences, and that it will in this way turn out to the advantage of the country. Experience unquestionably shows that this is true in most cases, since, in general, an incontestable improvement in the condition of the people has kept pace with an equally incontestable increase in the sum total of wealth in circulation. But in consequence of the impossibility of following up analytically all the consequences of such complex relations, theory is unable to explain why this usually happens and is still less able to demonstrate that it must always continue to occur. Let us avoid confounding what is in the domain of accurate reasoning with what is the object of a more or less happy guess; what is rational with what is empirical. It is enough to have to guard against errors in logic on the first score; let us avoid encountering passionate declamations and insoluble questions on the other.

5. From a standpoint of mere etymology, whatever appertains to the organization of society belongs to the field of Political Economy; but it has become customary to use this last term in a sense much more restricted and by so much less precise. The Political Economist, being occupied principally with the material wants of mankind, only considers social institutions as far as they favour or interfere with labour, thrift, commerce, and population; and as far as they

affect the subdivision between the members of society of the gifts of nature and the rewards of labour.

This subject is still far too vast to be properly grasped by any one man. It affords inexhaustible material for unripe systems and slow investigations. How can we abstract the moral influences which enter into all these questions and which are entirely incapable of measurement? How are we to compare what may be called the material welfare of the Alpine shepherd with that of the Spanish idler or of the Manchester workingman; the convent alms with the poor rates; the drudgery of the farm with that of the workshop; the pleasures and expenditures of a Norman noble in his feudal manor, with the pleasures and expenditures of his far-away descendant in a house in London or on a tour through Europe?

If we compare one nation with another, by what invariable tokens shall we determine the progress or decay of their prosperity? Shall it be according to population? In that case China would far excel Europe. According to the abundance of coin? The example of Spain, mistress of the Peruvian mines, turned the world away from this gross error long ago, and, in fact, before even the first crude notions of the true rôle of coin were developed. According to business activity? Then inland peoples would be very unfortunate compared with those whom proximity to the sea invites to a mercantile career. According to the high price of goods or of wages? Then some miserable island would surpass the most smiling and fertile countries. According to the pecuniary value of what economists call the annual product? A year when this value increases greatly may easily be one of great distress for the greatest number.

11

According to the actual quantity of this product reckoned in the appropriate unit for each kind of goods? But the kinds of goods produced and the relative proportions are different for each country. How can comparisons be made in this respect? According to the rate of movement up or down whether of population or of annual product? Provided that the reckoning covers a sufficient time this is, to be sure, the least equivocal symptom of the welfare or misery of society; but how can this symptom help us except to recognize accomplished facts, and facts which have been produced, not only by economic causes in the ordinary meaning of the words, but also by the simultaneous coöperation of a multitude of moral causes.

We are far from wishing to depreciate the philanthropic efforts of those who seek to throw some light on social economy. It is characteristic only of narrow minds to decry medical science because physiological phenomena cannot be calculated as accurately as the planetary movements. Political Economy is the hygiene and pathology of the social system. It recognizes as its guide experience or rather observation; but sometimes the sagacity of a superior mind can even anticipate the results of experience. We only seek to make clear, that Political Economy fails to make progress by theory, towards its noble object of the improvement of the lot of mankind, either because the relations which it has to deal with are not reducible to fixed terms, or because these relations are much too complicated for our powers of combination and analysis.

6. On the other hand, as the abstract idea of wealth according to our conception constitutes a perfectly deter-

minate relation, like all precise conceptions it can become the object of theoretical deductions, and if these deductions are sufficiently numerous and seem important enough to be collected into a system, it will presumably be advantageous to present this system by itself, except for such applications as it may seem proper to make to those branches of Political Economy with which the theory of wealth is ultimately connected. It will be useful to distinguish what admits of abstract demonstration from what allows only of a questionable opinion.

The Theory of Wealth, according to the idea we are trying to give, would doubtless only be an idle speculation, if the abstract idea of *wealth* or *value in exchange*, on which it is founded, were too far from corresponding with the actual objects which make up wealth in the existing social status. The same would be true of hydrostatics if the character of ordinary fluids should be too far removed from the hypothesis of perfect fluidity. However, as we have already said, the influence of a progressive civilization constantly tends to bring actual and variable relations nearer and nearer to the absolute relation, which we attain to from abstract considerations. In such matters everything becomes more and more easily valued, and consequently more easily measured. The steps towards finding a market resolve themselves into brokerage, losses of time into discounts, chances of loss into insurance charges, and so on. The progress of the gregarious tendency and of the institutions related to it, and the modifications which have taken place in our civil institutions, all coöperate towards this mobility, which we would neither apologize for nor detract from, but on which the application of theory to social facts is founded.

J. S. MILL

PRINCIPLES

OF

POLITICAL ECONOMY

PRELIMINARY REMARKS

In every department of human affairs, Practice long precedes Science : systematic enquiry into the modes of action of the powers of nature is the tardy product of a long course of efforts to use those powers for practical ends. The conception, accordingly. of Political Economy as a branch of science is extremely modern ; but the subject with which its enquiries are conversant has in all ages necessarily constituted one of the chief practical interests of mankind, and, in some, a most unduly engrossing one.

That subject is Wealth. Writers on Political Economy profess to teach, or to investigate, the nature of Wealth, and the laws of its production and distribution : including, directly or remotely, the operation of all the causes by which the condition of mankind, or of any society of human beings, in respect to this universal object of human desire, is made prosperous or the reverse. Not that any treatise on Political Economy can discuss or even enumerate all these causes ; but it undertakes to set forth as much as is known of the laws and principles according to which they operate.

Every one has a notion, sufficiently correct for common purposes, of what is meant by wealth. The enquiries which relate to it are in no danger of being confounded with those relating to any other of the great human interests. All know that it is one thing to be rich, another thing to be enlightened, brave, or humane ; that the questions how a nation is made wealthy, and how it is made free. or virtuous, or eminent in literature, in the fine arts, in arms, or in polity, are totally distinct enquiries. Those things, indeed, are all indirectly connected, and react upon one another. A people has sometimes become free, because it had first grown wealthy; or wealthy, because it had first become free. The creed and laws of a people act powerfully upon their economical condition; and this again, by its influence on their mental development and social relations, reacts upon their creed and laws. But though the subjects are in very close contact, they are essentially different, and have never been supposed to be otherwise.

It is no part of the design of this treatise to aim at metaphysical nicety of definition, where the ideas suggested by a term are already as determinate as practical purposes require. But, little as it might be expected that any mischievous confusion of ideas could take place on a subject so simple as the question, what is to be considered as wealth, it is matter of history, that such confusion of ideas has existed—that theorists and practical politicians have been equally and at one period universally, infected by it, and that for many generations it gave a thoroughly false direction to the policy of Europe. I refer to the set of doctrines designated, since the time of Adam Smith, by the appellation of the Mercantile System.

While this system prevailed, it was assumed, either expressly or tacitly, in the whole policy of nations, that wealth consisted solely of money; or of the precious metals, which, when not already in the state of money, are capable of being directly converted into it. According to the doctrines then prevalent, whatever tended to heap up money or bullion in a country added to its wealth. Whatever sent the precious metals out of a country impoverished it. If a country possessed no gold or silver mines, the only industry by which it could be enriched was foreign trade, being the only one which could bring in money. Any branch of trade which was supposed to send out more money than it brought in, however ample and valuable might be the returns in another shape, was looked upon as a losing trade. Exportation of goods was favoured and encouraged (even by means extremely onerous to the real resources of the country), because, the exported goods being stipulated to be paid for in money, it was hoped that the returns would actually be made in gold and silver. Importation of anything, other than the precious metals, was regarded as a loss to the nation of the whole price of the things imported; unless they were brought in to be re-exported at a profit, or unless, being the materials or instruments of some industry practised in the country itself, they gave the power of producing exportable articles at smaller cost, and thereby effecting a larger exportation. The commerce of the world was looked upon as a struggle among nations, which could draw to itself the largest share of the gold and silver in existence ; and in this competition no nation could gain anything, except by making others lose as much, or, at the least, preventing them from gaining it.

It often happens that the universal belief of one age of mankind— a belief from which no one *was*, nor, without an extraordinary effort of genius and courage, *could* at that time be free—becomes to a subsequent age so palpable an absurdity, that the only difficulty then is to imagine how such a thing can ever have appeared credible. It has so happened with the doctrine that money is synonymous with wealth. The conceit seems too preposterous to be thought of as a serious opinion. It looks like one of the crude fancies of childhood, instantly corrected by a word from any grown person. But let no one feel confident that he would have escaped the delusion if he had lived at the time when it prevailed. All the associations engendered by common life, and by the ordinary course of business, concurred in promoting it. So long as those associations were the only medium through which the subject was looked at, what we now think so gross an absurdity seemed a truism. Once questioned, indeed, it was doomed ; but no one was likely to think of questioning it whose mind had not become familiar with certain modes of stating and of contemplating economical phenomena, which have only found their way into the general understanding through the influence of Adam Smith and of his expositors.

In common discourse, wealth is always expressed in money. If you ask how rich a person is, you are answered that he has so many thousand pounds. All income and expenditure, all gains and losses, everything by which one becomes richer or poorer, are reckoned as the coming in or going out of so much money. It is true that in the inventory of a person's fortune are included, not only the money in his actual possession, or due to him, but all other articles of value. These, however, enter, not in their own character, but in virtue of the sums of money which they would sell for ; and if they would sell for less, their owner is reputed less rich, though the things themselves are precisely the same. It is true, also, that people do not grow rich by keeping their money unused, and that they must be willing to spend in order to gain. Those who enrich themselves by commerce, do so by giving money for goods as well as goods for money; and the first is as necessary a part of the process as the last. But a person who buys goods for purposes of gain, does so to sell them again for money, and in the expectation of receiving more money than he laid out : to get money, therefore, seems even to the person himself the ultimate end of the whole. It often happens that he is not paid in money, but in something else ; having bought goods to a value equivalent, which are set off against those he sold. But he accepted these at a money valuation, and in the belief that they would bring in more money eventually than the price at which they were made over to him. A dealer doing a large amount of business, and turning over his capital rapidly, has but a small portion of it in ready money at any one time. But he only feels it valuable to him as it is convertible into money : he considers no transaction closed until the net result is either paid or credited in money : when he retires from business it is into money that he converts the whole, and not until then does he deem himself to have realized his gains : just as if money were the only wealth, and money's worth were only the means of attaining it. If it be now asked for what end money is desirable, unless to supply the wants or pleasures of oneself or others, the champion of the system would not be at all embarrassed by the question. True, he would say, these are the uses of wealth, and very laudable uses while confined to domestic commodities, because in that case, by exactly the amount which you expend, you enrich others of your countrymen. Spend your wealth, if you please, in whatever indulgences you have a taste for; but your wealth is not the indulgences, it is the sum of money, or the annual money income, with which you purchase them.

While there were so many things to render the assumption which is the basis of the mercantile system plausible, there is also some small foundation in reason, though a very insufficient one for the distinction which that system so emphatically draws between money and every other kind of valuable possession. We really, and justly, look upon a person as possessing the advantages of wealth, not in proportion to the useful and agreeable things of which he is in the actual enjoyment, but to his command over the general fund of things useful and agreeable ; the power he possesses of providing for any exigency, or obtaining any object of desire. Now, money is itself that power; while all other things, in a civilized state, seem to confer it only by their capacity of being exchanged for money. To possess any other article of wealth, is to possess that particular

17

thing, and nothing else : if you wish for another thing instead of it, you have first to sell it, or to submit to the inconvenience and delay (if not the impossibility) of finding some one who has what you want, and is willing to barter it for what you have. But with money you are at once able to buy whatever things are for sale : and one whose fortune is in money, or in things rapidly convertible into it, seems both to himself and others to possess not any one thing, but all the things which the money places it at his option to purchase. The greatest part of the utility of wealth, beyond a very moderate quantity, is not the indulgences it procures, but the reserved power which its possessor holds in his hands of attaining purposes generally ; and this power no other kind of wealth confers so immediately or so certainly as money. It is the only form of wealth which is not merely applicable to some one use, but can be turned at once to any use. And this distinction was the more likely to make an impression upon governments, as it is one of considerable importance to them. A civilized government derives comparatively little advantage from taxes unless it can collect them in money : and if it has large or sudden payments to make, especially payments in foreign countries for wars or subsidies, either for the sake of conquering or of not being conquered (the two chief objects of national policy until a late period), scarcely any medium of payment except money will serve the purpose. All these causes conspire to make both individuals and. governments, in estimating their means, attach almost exclusive importance to money, either *in esse* or *in posse*, and look upon all other things (when viewed as part of their resources) scarcely otherwise than as the remote means of obtaining that which alone, when obtained, affords the indefinite, and at the same time instantaneous, command over objects of desire, which best answers to the idea of wealth.

An absurdity, however, does not cease to be an absurdity when we have discovered what were the appearances which made it plausible ; and the Mercantile Theory could not fail to be seen in its true character when men began, even in an imperfect manner, to explore into the foundations of things, and seek their premises from elementary facts, and not from the forms and phrases of common discourse. So soon as they asked themselves what is really meant by money—what it is in its essential characters, and the precise nature of the functions it performs—they reflected that money, like other things, is only a desirable possession on account of its uses : and that these, instead of being, as they delusively appear, indefinite, are of a strictly defined and limited description, namely, to facilitate the distribution of the produce of industry according to the convenience of those among whom it is shared. Further consideration showed that the uses of money are in no respect promoted by increasing the quantity which exists and circulates in a country ; the service which it performs being as well rendered by a small as by a large aggregate amount. Two million quarters of corn will not feed so many persons as four millions ; but two millions of pounds sterling will carry on as much traffic, will buy and sell as many commodities, as four millions, though at lower nominal prices. Money, as money, satisfies no want ; its worth to any one, consists in its being a convenient shape in which to receive his incomings of all sorts, which incomings he afterwards, at the times which suit him best, converts into the forms in which they can be useful to him. Great as the difference would be between a country with money, and a country altogether without it, it would be only one of convenience ; a saving of time and trouble, like grinding by water power instead of by hand, or (to use Adam Smith's illustration) like the benefit derived from roads ; and to mistake money for wealth is the same sort of error as to mistake the highway which may be the easiest way of getting to your house or lands, for the house and lands themselves.[1]

Money, being the instrument of an important public and private purpose, is rightly regarded as wealth ; but everything else which serves any human purpose, and which nature does not afford gratuitously, is wealth also. To be wealthy is to have a large stock of useful articles, or the means of purchasing them. Everything forms therefore a part of wealth, which has a power of purchasing ; for which anything useful or agreeable would be given in exchange. Things for which nothing could be obtained in exchange, however useful or necessary they may be, are not wealth in the sense in which the term is used in Political Economy. Air, for example, though the most absolute of necessaries, bears no price in the market, because it can be obtained gratuitously : to accumulate a stock of it would yield no profit or advantage to any one ; and the laws of its production and distribution are the subject of a very different study from Political Economy. But though air is not wealth, mankind are much richer by obtaining it gratis, since the time

---

[1] [See Appendix A. *The Mercantile System.*]

and labour which would otherwise be required for supplying the most pressing of all wants, can be devoted to other purposes. It is possible to imagine circumstances in which air would be a part of wealth. If it became customary to sojourn long in places where the air does not naturally penetrate, as in diving-bells sunk in the sea, a supply of air artificially furnished would, like water conveyed into houses, bear a price : and if from any revolution in nature the atmosphere became too scanty for the consumption, or could be monopolized, air might acquire a very high marketable value. In such a case, the possession of it, beyond his own wants, would be, to its owner, wealth ; and the general wealth of mankind might at first sight appear to be increased, by what would be so great a calamity to them. The error would lie in not considering, that however rich the possessor of air might become at the expense of the rest of the community, all persons else would be poorer by all that they were compelled to pay for what they had before obtained without payment.

This leads to an important distinction in the meaning of the word wealth, as applied to the possessions of an individual, and to those of a nation, or of mankind. In the wealth of mankind, nothing is included which does not of itself answer some purpose of utility or pleasure. To an individual anything is wealth, which, though useless in itself, enables him to claim from others a part of their stock of things useful or pleasant. Take, for instance, a mortgage of a thousand pounds on a landed estate. This is wealth to the person to whom it brings in a revenue, and who could perhaps sell it in the market for the full amount of the debt. But it is not wealth to the country; if the engagement were annulled, the country would be neither poorer nor richer. The mortgagee would have lost a thousand pounds, and the owner of the land would have gained it. Speaking nationally, the mortgage was not itself wealth, but merely gave A a claim to a portion of the wealth of B. It was wealth to A, and wealth which he could transfer to a third person ; but what he so transferred was in fact a joint ownership, to the extent of a thousand pounds, in the land of which B was nominally the sole proprietor. The position of fundholders, or owners of the public debt of a country, is similar. They are mortgagees on the general wealth of the country. The cancelling of the debt would be no destruction of wealth, but a transfer of it : a wrongful abstraction of wealth from certain members of the community, for profit of the government, or of the tax-payers. Funded property

20

therefore cannot be counted as part of the national wealth. This is not always borne in mind by the dealers in statistical calculations. For example, in estimates of the gross income of the country, founded on the proceeds of the income-tax, incomes derived from the funds are not always excluded: though the tax-payers are assessed on their whole nominal income, without being permitted to deduct from it the portion levied from them in taxation to form the income of the fundholder. In this calculation, therefore, one portion of the general income of the country is counted twice over, and the aggregate amount made to appear greater than it is by almost[1] thirty millions. A country, however, may include in its wealth all stock held by its citizens in the funds of foreign countries, and other debts due to them from abroad. But even this is only wealth to them by being a part ownership in wealth held by others. It forms no part of the collective wealth of the human race. It is an element in the distribution, but not in the composition, of the general wealth.

[2]Another example of a possession which is wealth to the person holding it, but not wealth to the nation, or to mankind, is slaves. It is by a strange confusion of ideas that slave property (as it is termed) is counted, at so much per head, in an estimate of the wealth, or of the capital, of the country which tolerates the existence of such property. If a human being, considered as an object possessing productive powers, is part of the national wealth when his powers are owned by another man, he cannot be less a part of it when they are owned by himself. Whatever he is worth to his master is so much property abstracted from himself, and its abstraction cannot augment the possessions of the two together, or of the country to which they both belong. In propriety of classification, however, the people of a country are not to be counted in its wealth. They are that for the sake of which its wealth exists. The term wealth is wanted to denote the desirable objects which they possess, not inclusive of, but in contradistinction to, their own persons. They are not wealth to themselves, though they are means of acquiring it.

It has been proposed to define wealth as signifying "instruments:" meaning not tools and machinery alone, but the whole accumulation possessed by individuals or communities, of means for the attainment of their ends. Thus, a field is an instrument,

[1] [1st ed. (1848) " about "; 5th ed. (1862) " almost."]
[2] [Paragraph added in 6th ed. (1865).]

21

because it is a means to the attainment of corn. Corn is an instrument, being a means to the attainment of flour. Flour is an instrument, being a means to the attainment of bread. Bread is an instrument, as a means to the satisfaction of hunger and to the support of life. Here we at last arrive at things which are not instruments, being desired on their own account, and not as mere means to something beyond. This view of the subject is philosophically correct ; or rather, this mode of expression may be usefully employed along with others, not as conveying a different view of the subject from the common one, but as giving more distinctness and reality to the common view. It departs, however, too widely from the custom of language, to be likely to obtain general acceptance, or to be of use for any other purpose than that of occasional illustration.

Wealth, then, may be defined, all useful or agreeable things which possess exchangeable value ; or, in other words, all useful or agreeable things except those which can be obtained, in the quantity desired, without labour or sacrifice. To this definition, the only objection seems to be, that it leaves in uncertainty a question which has been much debated—whether what are called immaterial products are to be considered as wealth : whether, for example, the skill of a workman, or any other natural or acquired power of body or mind, shall be called wealth, or not : a question, not of very great importance, and which, so far as requiring discussion, will be more conveniently considered in another place.* [1]

* Infra, book i. chap. iii.
[1] [See Appendix B. *The Definition of Wealth.*]

22

ACCOUNTING ANTECEDENTS

Italian Book = Keeping,

Reduced into an ART:

BEING

An Entire New and Compleat

Syſtem of Accompts
In General.

Demonſtrated in a Chain of CONSEQUENCES from Clear and Self-evident PRINCIPLES.

To which is added,

The greateſt Variety of MERCHANTS ACCOUNTS, with an Explanation of all the Terms of Art, which have commonly been made uſe of. Together, with proper Reflections on the whole.

By *HUSTCRAFT STEPHENS*, Accomptant.

———— *Si quid noviſti rectius iſtis,*
Candidus imperti : Si non, his utere mecum. HOR.

With a *Preface*, ſhewing the Nature and Uſefulneſs of this ART, by JAMES WEIR, Gent.

LONDON:

Printed for W. MEARS, at the *Lamb* on *Ludgate-Hill.*

MDCCXXXV.

THE
INTRODUCTION.

IMMEDIATELY after the Diviſion of the World into Propertie
the exchanging of Things came into Uſe; for Men, not being ſufficient
ſtock'd with all Things neceſſary themſelves, were oblig'd to procu
from others, what they ſtood in Need of; and by the great Law of Righ
every one having it in his Choice, whether or no he wou'd ſupply his Neig
bours, to give ſomething as acceptable in return, was found the ſure
Means of obtaining what happen'd to be another Man's Property. Th
one having Drink enough without Bread, while another perhaps had Brea
without Drink, were each in a Capacity to furniſh themſelves with wh
they had Occaſion for, by an Exchange of Commodities: Whereas ha
either ſtood in Need of what the other poſſeſs'd, having nothing to give t
Way of Retalliation, then muſt the Neceſſitous have lain at his Neighbou
Mercy for what out of mere Charity might have been beſtow'd.

The Conſideration of which made Men value what they were on
Maſters of (over and above what they had an immediate Uſe for themſelve
more or leſs, as they thought it able to purchaſe from their Neighbou
ſuch Things as they wanted, and induced every prudent Man carefully an
exactly to compare what he had with what he might have Occaſion
purchaſe from others, that he might the better provide againſt the Want
Neceſſaries, and the many Inconveniencies that commonly attend that M
fortune.

For this Reaſon even thoſe who had the largeſt Poſſeſſions were neverth
leſs highly concern'd thus to examine them, that being ſo warn'd, they mig
the more wiſely regulate their Expences within the Bounds of their Abi
ties, for none could have ſo much, but Miſmanagement might impair,
not totally deſtroy and confound it.

And for this Reaſon likewiſe, thoſe of inferiour Ranks were oblig'd often
compare what they had with the Things that belong'd to their Neighbou
in Order to make a right Judgment to the beſt Advantage, that by goo
Conduct they might in ſome Meaſure ſupply the Defects of their ſcanti
Portions.

Now the vaſt Variety of Things render'd it impoſſible for any Man
compare what he had with what he might have Occaſion for without
Medium; that is, ſomething common to them all, which Neceſſity broug

B

The INTRODUCTION.

the Ufe of Money, univerfal Confent having determin'd it the Standard Meafure of the Value of all Things; every Government choofing their wn Way of Tale and Species of Coin, as in *England*, the Reckonings are ept by the nominal Sums of Pounds, Shillings, and Pence, &c. their oins Crowns, half Crowns, Shillings, &c. and in *Holland* they keep their eckonings in Pounds *Flemifh*, Skellens, Groots, &c. and Dalders, Skelns, Guilders, Stivers, &c. are the Coins they ufe.

By the Affiftance of this Money, every *one* might compare what he had ith the Things of his Neighbour, by firft applying it to the one, and then the other, thus; fuch a Thing of my own is worth 20*l.* that is, *People* ill give fo much for it; and fuch a Thing of another Man's is worth o*l.* confequently mine is equal to his in Value; and fo by taking the alue of all his Things together, and comparing them with thofe of o-her Men, he could make a Judgment of the Rank he held in the World, hich was the only certain Rule Men had to govern themfelves by; for len's Abilities in purchafing Things, are only faid to be great or fmall by Comparifon.

That Portion of Things which a Man poffeffes, or has otherways belong-g to him, as a Security, taken all together, I call the Eftate, and the Worth of a Man's Eftate, confider'd abftractly from the Things which are alued, I call the computed Value or Extent of a Man's Eftate.

By which computed Value or Extent it being exactly made, a Man may ompare what he has with others, judge of the Rank he holds in the World, nd perfectly inform himfelf of what he is able to purchafe from his Neigh-our; for the Comparifon is, and can only be made in the Value, after it brought into a certain fettled Sum of the common Meafure, Money, as ppears from what has been faid above concerning a Medium.

Now notwithftanding it is neceffary for a Man to have fomething to give n lieu of what he intends to purchafe from others, yet the Price is not lways immediately paid, but People will part with their Goods, and truft o the Ability and Honefty of the Buyer for what they are to receive in Return. *Example,*

I buy from a Merchant 1000*lb.* of Tobacco, for which I agree to pay im 50*l.* perhaps three Months hence: I fay, by fuch Tranfaction, I have nore Effects than I had, and for a greater Value, being entirely Mafter of vhat I bought, fo foon as the former Owner transferr'd his Title to me, but n Regard I ftand bound to the Seller, for a Sum to be raifed from all my Effects or Securities promifcuoufly, I can reckon myfelf, in Refpect of my Rank of Riches among Men, only by the Remainder of the computed Value of my Eftate, after that Sum is deducted.

Suppofe I have at firft to the computed Value of 100*l.* and buy Effects rom *A. B.* for which I agree to pay him 20*l.* by adding thefe two Sums ogether, the computed Value of all will amount to 120*l.* of which Sum

there

there is only 100 *l.* clearly my own, for tho' all the Effects or Things charg
are equally my own, and equally at my Difpofal, fo that there is no D
ftinction with Relation to what Part of them I owe for from the reft, y
I am obliged to be accountable for, and pay to *A. B.* the Sum of 20
where-ever I get it ; which makes a Diftinction of the computed Value
my Eftate abfolutely requifite, in Order to a competent Knowledge of it
for if I confider the computed Value in general only, I fhall very muc
deceive myfelf, as to the Rank I hold among Men, becaufe all wou'd ap
pear to be mine, tho' at the fame Time I owed the largeft Share of it
other People ; as in the Example of *A. B.* above, it would appear I ha
120 *l.* whereas, indeed, 20 *l.* of it had another Proprietor ; befides, it fre
quently falls out that another's Property does not confift of any certain Sur
to be paid, but of fomething only valued by Money, becaufe it is th
common Meafure of Comparifon. *Example,*

Suppofe I owe a Man 50 *l.* payable only in Cafe of the Performanc
or Non-performance of certain Terms and Conditions, or of the occurrin
or not occurring of fome Contingencies ; then, I fay, feeing there is
Probability of my being releafed without paying all or any Part of th
Debt, imply'd in the very Nature of it ; I am not to reckon it as fo muc
of the common Meafure, but as valued at fo much of the common Mea
fure ; or if inftead of agreeing to pay *A B* 50 *l.* I had agreed to hav
given him 150 *lb.* Weight of Tobacco, the Value of which was 50 *l.* S
that I am oblig'd to know the Property as well as the Proprietor exactly
in Order to difcover whether my own clear Share of the Extent be goo
or bad : for it is faid to be good, when the Sum of any Man's Pro
perty is fufficient to difcharge it or more ; and bad, when it is not as i
the Cafe above. If the Tobacco be paid with 50 *l.* or lefs, then is my
clear Extent fo far good ; but if it cannot, then it is fo far bad, as it come
fhort of Payment : and in the former Cafe, my clear Share of the com
puted Value is better or worfe, as a greater or fmaller Share of the 50 *l*
happens to difcharge it. By all which it is very evident, that a genera
Knowledge of the computed Value of an Eftate is not fufficient ; but he
that would act wifely, muft endeavour to inform himfelf of fuch com
puted Value, as it is divided into feveral Properties or Parts ; and the
more fimple thefe are, the more exact and eafily attain'd the Knowledge of them will be.

But notwithftanding we efteem what we have, as it can purchafe
from others, and have moft exactly calculated the Sum of the Value of
all our Securities, or that which belongs to us ; yet by Reafon of the frequent Revolutions of Circumftances which almoft as frequently changes and
varies the Eftimate of them, makes it abfolutely neceffary, that we know
what Securities we have thus belonging to us ; or we can never clearly
and certainly perceive the Rank we hold among other Men. For *Ex-*
ample,

The INTRODUCTION.

mple, Suppofe I have Things whofe compound Value amounts to 1000 *l*. tho' by this Sum I can judge what I am able to purchafe from my Neighbour, yet it is only on Condition, that the Securities which I have valued, are now efteemed worth fo much. But when I know that *A. B.* wes me 100 *l.* and that the Remainder is 10,000 *lb*. Weight of Tobacco, worth 500 *l.* and 10,000 *lb*. Weight of Sugar worth 400 *l.* I can then tell whether thefe Securities are capable of fetching fo much or not, and fo determine whether my Eftate be good or bad; for it is faid to be the former, when the Securities by Appearance are able to procure as much or more s there is of the computed Value depending on them; and it is termed ad, when they are not capable in Appearance to purchafe what they tand charged with.

And when the Securities are confider'd after this Manner, with their efpective Sums depending on them, with no Regard to the computed Va-ue in general, this I call the Condition of my Eftate.

From hence appears plainly, that it is indifpenfably required of every prudent Man to know exactly the computed Value and Condition of his Eftate, in order to the well governing himfelf in the Management of his worldly Affairs: for without that Knowledge, he cannot make any one Step in them with Certainty; but muft grope blindly in the Dark, and by Chance fink or fwim; which is a Hazard no wife Man would willingly ruft his Fortune to.

But it is not fufficient at one Time only to underftand his Circum-ftances; but he ought always and at all Times to be acquainted compleat-y thro' the many Revolutions of them; he muft be able to trace them from the firft to the prefent Period, in a Chain of Confequences, or he never can judge of the prefent Circumftances exactly; whether he has not oft by Overfight of his own, or Impofition of his Neighbours; he cannot make any Judgment of the future from the paft, or juftly reflect upon his own former Conduct, whether good or bad.

Neither muft he neglect fo to regulate Matters, that this Knowledge of his may be tranfmitted as intire and perfect to others as he had it him-felf; for at a Man's Death his Heirs, Succeffors, or any concerned that Way are never the wifer; for his having been throughly acquainted with every Step of his own Bufinefs, unlefs he has left them Inftructions, whereby they may inform themfelves of the fame; or if on any Occafion one be intrufted to examine another's Affairs, the Matter muft be made known to him by the Principal, or it will not be poffible for him to perform t; for which Reafon it is a Duty incumbent on every one to make plain o the Underftandings of others, as well as his own, whatever is done in his Affairs, fo far as is requifite to the aforemention'd ufeful Knowledge, provided ftill fuch others are fufficiently skill'd properly to receive fuch nftructions, which is impoffible they fhould ever be, unlefs they are

acquainted

29

acquainted with his Method, and it were an endlefs Task for him to inftruct all the reft, who in any Event might come to be concerned after his Death or in his Abfence ; wherefore Men have endeavour'd to attain a certain Method to be ufed commonly by them all, and term'd it *Italian Book-keeping*, probably for that the firft Attempt made towards it happen'd in *Italy*.

Now what follows is a Treatife concerning Rules for attaining the faid Art, which will certainly anfwer thofe Purpofes, being deduced from felf-evident Principles, in a Chain of Confequences, until the Art of *Italian Book-keeping* is compleated from the firft Definition of it.

V. BRANFORD

Accounting in its Relation to Economics.—

Without necessarily agreeing that there are "at least two sciences and five arts" (J. S. Mackenzie, *Introduction to Social Philosophy*) which claim the title of Economics, one is bound to take note of the fact that the boundaries of Economics are very ill-defined. The significance to be attached to the words Accountancy and Accounting is also much wanting in precision. Our conception of the relation of Accountancy to Economics will thus be largely influenced by our understanding of the nature and scope of the two subjects.

In the short space available for this article, it is proposed to restrict the main inquiry to an investigation of their relationship under the head of Value, and only incidentally touch upon other points of contact between Accountancy and Economics.

The general plan of the article implies a consideration of the following amongst other elemental questions:—(1) Does the theory of value as expounded by contemporary economic authorities correspond to the theoretical assumptions implicit in the mind of the working accountant? (2) If the explicit theory of the economist (*i.e.* his verbally formulated doctrine) does not correspond to, but falls short of, the implicit theory of the accountant (*i.e.* his working hypotheses unexpressed and largely unconscious), then how can the accountant help the economist to make their correspondence more exact? (3) If the economic does exactly correspond to the accounting theory, then what future developments may be looked for in regard to both? (4) If the economic includes and transcends the accounting theory, then should the accountant endeavour to make his own theory conform to that of the economist, and thereafter or simultaneously try to modify his practice in the same direction, and if so, how is he to do it? These questions, and particularly the last, imply a consideration of the further questions—(largely educational ones)—Should the accountant try to make explicit and fully conscious in his mind the economic theory that underlies his practice? And if so, what advantages may be expected to accrue (*a*) to the accountant individually; and (*b*) to the society in which he is a working unit?

It is not pretended that definitive answers to these questions are attainable in the present state of formulated knowledge. Still less is it contemplated to provide satisfactory answers—or even any solutions at all—in the present article. But the putting of specific problems in the foreground is a useful means of focussing attention, and so of setting up a goal for thought. What will be attempted in the following pages will be the suggestion of fruitful lines of research in a field which hitherto has been very slightly cultivated, and not at all systematically, with an indication of sources of relevant knowledge, and as far as possible its summarisation.

ACCOUNTING IN ITS RELATION TO ECONOMICS

It is one of the historic instances of how wanting in philosophical perspective may be even the wisest among men, that John Stuart Mill should have introduced his discussion of value by saying, "Happily there is nothing in the laws of value which remains for the present or any future writer to clear up. The theory of the subject is complete." At the very time that this statement was appearing unmodified in edition after edition of Mill's *Principles of Political Economy*, certain obscure economists were trying to introduce new conceptions into the theory of value, which now that they have been recognised and are being developed, promise to effect profound modifications—even if they have not done so already—in that doctrine which the leading mid-century English economist affirmed to be finished and complete. "At first unnoticed, then for long but little thought of, worked out by men who for the most part did not know of each other, but yet agreed where so many had doubted and disagreed, came a new theory based on a new foundation." Thus in its origin the new theory of value was typical of the struggle with which most new ideas commence their career. As it is impossible to understand the working of a system without knowing something of its origin, so the essential features of the theory of value can only be grasped by tracing its development from the facts of experience and from the simpler ideas out of which it historically grew up by a process of gradually deepening analysis of those phenomena of the business world which the theory seeks to describe and explain. And first of all one must try to clearly realise what are these facts and processes of everyday business which the economist by means of his theory of value tries to make us comprehend in their hidden or half-disclosed bearings.

What are the practical tasks of everyday business out of which arise the theoretical problems of value? Consider, for instance, the question of income distribution—the apportionment of the national dividend amongst individuals and families. To produce the goods (using that word in the technical economic sense which covers commodities and services alike) which maintain and develop life, men co-operate with one another and with nature. In other words, the producing of goods is, in modern complex societies, all but universally a social or collective and not an individual process. The consuming or using of goods is, on the other hand, to a large extent a necessarily individual process. There are of course many goods, such as works of art, which can be "enjoyed" (*i.e.* "used" in the economic sense) by the public collectively; but by far the greater quantity of goods (including, of course, food and clothing), though collectively produced, must, by the very nature of man, be individually appropriated and used. Now, as a matter of observed fact, a certain amount of food, clothing, etc., does find its way into the hands of individuals for private ownership and use. This particular quantity of goods, for a given individual, we may, without any imputation of justice or injustice, call his economic share. In the course of ages, as societies have in one place and time grown in numbers, in complexity and in wealth, or in other places and times stagnated and decayed, the need for distributing amongst individuals their economic shares has in practice, of necessity, always worked itself out in greater or less degree of harmony with the general modes of life and thought in the given society at the time and place under consideration. Now if we concentrate attention—as most economists do—on western society, as it has been during the past few centuries and as it is to-day, we see that the actual distribution of economic shares amongst individuals has come to be effected in practice by an extremely complex set of arrangements constituting a piece of social

32

machinery which, though it works with much obvious friction and waste, yet works with a degree of efficiency which yields many excellent and even admirable results.

In practical life each person forms, with a greater or less degree of consciousness, an estimate of what he conceives to be his proper economic share, and seeks to secure it. In the interaction of these individual strivings, certain habits, customs, and laws are generated. These, regarded as a working system, may be said to constitute the social machinery by which the apportionment of economic shares is effected in practice. In regard to these habits, customs, and laws, we may ask among other questions —(1) What are they? (2) How do they work? (3) What is their origin and history? (4) In what relation do they stand to other human efforts and activities? (5) Whither do they tend? (6) In what way is it desirable to try and modify such tendencies? It is the business of a theory of value to answer these questions.

When an attempt is made to answer these questions it is soon found that a vast number of preliminary inquiries as to matters of fact, the use of words, the significance of events, the criteria of evidence, and so forth, have to be set on foot. Amongst these prior inquiries are questions as to the amount of income of persons or groups of persons (e.g., a business corporation, family, nation, etc.) during a given period of time, and as to the relationship of the money or nominal income to the real income in commodities and services, the consumption of which determines the customary standard of well-being. If, as a preliminary matter of fact, we ask—What is the total nominal income as estimated in money of a given society during a given time? and—What is the real income in goods and services of that society during the same time?—we cannot get a direct answer for want of available statistics. Yet every producer in point of fact is more or less constantly engaged in estimating what amount of goods and services it may be worth his while to contribute to the general income. And the same person as consumer is also more or less continuously engaged in estimating what amount of commodities and services his means enable him to extract and use out of the social fund of commodities and services existent at a given moment. Now as every one is a consumer and most people are producers, it is clear that the whole adult population (however unconsciously) is giving its attention to the problem of estimating social production and consumption. Each family assumes in its daily action that the total social income during a given period will, when fractionally divided, yield sufficient to provide for the family's wants, according to standards estimated by experience of the past, and varied according to calculations of the future. In other words, the aggregate of families assume that their total income will reach a certain level. In short, consumers, as a whole, make periodical valuations of the social income. But this gross valuation is nowhere explicit, is nowhere numerically expressed as a total. It is only implicit, in the actions and conduct, in the speech and thought of individuals. But the same group of individuals looked at as a whole are also the producers; that is to say, they are the persons responsible for ensuring that the total social income does not fall short of the valuation which they themselves as consumers implicitly put on it. As individuals responsible for production they are, therefore, concerned to ascertain the limits of their own productive contributions to the total fund. This implies an attempt on the part of producers to interpret those signs of social valuation which are implicit in the actions of consumers. But it also implies an estimation of the means available for producing that part of the social fund which the individual producer takes as the aim of his own business.

Arising out of the foregoing valuations, a certain scale of prices for commodities and services is seen, as a fact of experience, to emerge. These prices are of course what we call the current values of commodities and services expressed in money. Assuming certain limits of price, the consumer arranges the details of expenditure which express his standard of life. Assuming also a certain scale of prices, the producer determines the kind and quantities of products he is going to produce. Looking again at producers as a whole, we see that they have to calculate (1) the quantity of goods and services required during a given period, (2) the means available for the provision of these, (3) the manner of dealing with a possible excess or defect in production over the estimated quantity required. Here we have, therefore, stated in general terms from the point of view of valuation the problem of equilibrating the quantity of production and consumption in a given society. The fact that in the modern western world, life continues with as little economic disturbance as it does, shows that experience has taught men a considerable degree of proficiency in the art of equilibrating production and consumption. But the fact also of commercial crises recurring periodically, in the general form of economic disturbance throughout society, in the particular form of bankruptcies and liquidations in individual businesses, and in the disruption of families and the wreckage of individuals by severe or sudden depression of the standard of living—all these phenomena are for the most part describable as, in the first instance, errors of valuation, with inability to readjust incorrect valuations to new conditions without grave economic loss and waste of human life. Much, therefore, as has been achieved by practical experience in the equilibration of social demand and supply—in the harmonising of consumption and production—it is clear a great deal more remains to be done.

It is the aim of a theory of value to describe the means by which, in the course of long experience, practical men have learned to make their valuations, to elucidate the conditions and purposes of these valuations, and to suggest means for carrying to a higher degree of perfection the art of making them. In modern business the values of commodities and services are indicated by the money prices at which these are bought and sold. In a first superficial analysis, commercial values and money prices are thus interchangeable terms. The successful valuation is that estimate of price which is confirmed by the subsequent course of events. The comparison of estimates with the results is likely to be more or less accurate and exact in proportion to the fulness and accuracy of the record that is kept. The more perfectly the relevant facts and statements are recorded the more reliable will tend to be the inference drawn from the comparison of estimates and results, and the safer the guide thus derived for future valuations. The system of Accounting is historically the means which experience has devised for comparing anticipated with actual valuations. Accounting from this broad point of view is to be regarded as that specialised form of activity to which the private individual, the man of business, the family group, or the state government all have recourse in the record and computation of values. The treatment of values as money prices enables the accountant to apply to the analysis and synthesis of the highly complex phenomena of production and consumption those powerful instruments of thought which are called the rules of arithmetic—for values in becoming prices take on the form of arithmetical quantities. The aim of the accountant is thus to place at the disposal of all those responsible for making valuations (and that is practically every adult) such means of perfecting their valuations as the mathematical sciences afford. But to be able to do this the accountant must be (1) sufficiently master of mathematical science, to select from its vast resources such instruments of thought as are best applicable to the analysis and synthesis of values: he must also (2) be adequately familiar with the economic phenomena with which these values are concerned. This implies on the part of the accountant a working acquaintance with the economy of business, the economy of family life, and the economy of the State. The mere fact that the accountant, like every one else, grows up in the world of domestic, business, and national life ensures of course a certain practical acquaintance with the ordering of the details of economic livelihood in all these spheres. But this does not ensure that systematic and disciplined grasp of these affairs which it is the aim of economic science to impart. The accountant should then be competent not only in mathematical but also in economic science. It is true it is usually stated in text-books that accounting is applied mathematics. But since, as observed above, the accountant must of necessity, consciously or unconsciously, systematise his economic phenomena before or coincidently with the application of mathematical resources to quantitative economic measurement, the contention seems unassailable that the science of Accountancy, wherever else it may find a position in the classification of knowledge, must also be considered as a branch of Applied Economics.

The essential contribution of mental effort directed to the measurement and registration of economic quantities is embodied and focussed in specialised forms of thinking which are called Accounts. The word economy in phrases like domestic economy, business economy, national economy has come into use to signify the systematic effort made continuously to economise action in the consumption and the production of wealth. And while the effort to economise action in the satisfaction of one's wants is at first instinctive, yet in the course of the history alike of the race and the individual, it tends to become more conscious, more rational, more directed to a preconceived ideal. In this progress from more or less blind instinctive economy of effort towards rationalised action consciously seeking ideal achievement —in the course of this material progress, the mental processes, the states of mind which alternately as effect and cause accompany it, undergo a corresponding transformation. Dimly-perceived mental states pass into ordered and systematic thought. The same impulse that compels to economy of action also compels to economy of thought. But as sensation and movement are united on the lower planes, so on the higher, thought and action are always found in combination co-operating in different degrees towards a common purpose. And as primitive striving to satisfy wants develops into an ordered practical art of economy, so coincidently with the growth of these later stages of concrete activity there is developed a corresponding way of thinking called theory or science. Hence corresponding to the Art of Economy we have the correlative Science of Economics.

The relation of the practice of economy in action as business, to the science or theory of these processes as economics, is to be deemed similar to the relationship subsisting between accounting in practice as a necessary part of modern business, and the theory or science of accounting considered in relation to economics. What, then, are the implications in saying that the science of accounting is a branch of applied economics? (Though the custom is scarcely more than incipient, and local only in its incipience, it might be well, at any rate it would save considerable repetition, to use the word accountancy for the science or theory, and the word accounting for the practice or art of account-keeping.) If we say that accountancy is a branch of applied economics, we in the first place imply that accounting is a branch of business. Accounting being considered as a specialised occupation, the latter statement is of course obviously correct. But that is not the whole sense intended. If we consider business as the systematic endeavour to economise action in the use and provision of wealth, then business energy (except in its very simplest and most primitive manifestations) will always of necessity, and by reason of the very complexity of modern business, devote a portion of itself to account-keeping, because account-keeping itself is nothing but a device discovered and elaborated by racial experience for economising business energy.

The mere fact that so complex an art as is the most advanced accounting system of to-day, has in the course of centuries grown up out of the needs of business, attests a long series of interactions between doing and thinking. In the alternation and interweaving of thought and action which accompanies the continuous effort to adapt circumstances to human needs and needs to circumstances, a body of experience accumulates, and this stands in relation to the practical affairs with which it is correlated as theory to practice, and, when a certain degree of systematisation is reached, as science to art. The theory itself, in turn serving as a more rationalised basis for new experimental action, gives rise to the idea of applied science—this phrase, being used without sufficient discrimination both for the ensuing course of action (for which, however, consistency should reserve the title of art), and also for the scientific knowledge on which it is based. Thus in calling accountancy a branch of applied economics several different though not necessarily exclusive standpoints have to be kept in view. And in particular we have to remember that reference may be intended to that knowledge of economic principles which is implicit in the mind of the business man, or on the other hand to the more fully systematised science of economics which has been made explicit by professed scientists. How far accountants have, as a matter of fact, made principles borrowed from the science of economics serve as a ground of action is a question of history. How far they might do so is a question of policy.

It is well to try to realise as clearly and fully as possible what implications as to thought are conveyed by the statement that accountancy is applied economics. The main issue, however, is not with controversial contentions as to whether accountancy is or is not applied economics, nor whether it is applied economics or applied mathematics. The important question is as to what extent and degree have the resources of all other knowledge and experience been pressed into the service of account-keeping, and to what extent and degree are there untapped resources available for promoting the further progress of account-keeping. The onus or rather the privilege that rests upon the accountant is to exploit to the utmost for the benefit of his own special work the instruments of thought and action accumulated by all other workers, no matter in what field. But in the vast universe of human knowledge the accountant, even if he do not altogether lose his way, will inevitably waste much effort in futile attempts at discovery, unless his explorations are directed by expert guides. It is here where there arises an appropriate demand for the services of a group of investigators who would make it their special though not their sole occupation to cultivate the science as distinct from the practice of account-keeping. It has been noted above that progress lies in successive stimulations of theory by the needs of practice, and applications of theory to the improvement of practice. In this series of interactions it is impossible to say where practice ends and theory begins. Progress is an unfolding web in which both are interwoven. It belongs to the very constitution of man that he is unable to demarcate thought from action. But it is equally an element of his constitution that he should deal with the complexities of life by a temporary isolation or abstraction of various elements, for he cannot otherwise in the perpetual flux of things give the necessary concentration of attention to detail. But on pain of either merely wasting the effort given to the temporary process of abstraction, or of incurring the worse danger of positive error, the various elements temporarily and provisionally isolated in thought must be brought together again, in order that the result of the thinking may serve as a basis for action.

Just as a certain crude theory of economics was implicit in the minds of practical men before the conscious elaboration of it by economists into a systematic body of thought or science,—so the theory or science corresponding to the practice of account-keeping has up to the present been for the most part implicit in the minds of practical men, but now requires corresponding elaboration and explicitness. As the development of account-keeping proceeds, there is bound to occur a similar subdivision of labour in accounting, by which specialists will cultivate that department which, for purposes of order and convenience, will be isolated as science. That this subdivision is already incipient and growing at a considerable pace is attested not only by the expanding efforts of the text-book writers to construct a systematic theory of their subject, but even more by the commencing recognition of the universities. One English and several American universities have up to the present year (1902) admitted the study of account-keeping to their list of professional and, therefore, presumably also cultural or semi-cultural studies. The merits of this line of advance are obvious. The peril to be avoided is the insidious tendency to isolation of the men of action and the men of thought into two separate and even hostile camps—a state of things that leads to the sterilisation and stereotyping of both science and art—a process which, if sufficiently protracted, means the negation and consequent decay of both.

It has been stated above that a first preliminary analysis identifies commercial values with prices. But every reflective man of business will recognise that a deeper analysis is required—that, in fact, there is an important element not only in values, but even in commercial values, which differentiate them from prices. It will probably be agreed that "price" does, as a matter of fact, tend more and more to be restricted in its use to expressing the money equivalent of the current market unit of a particular kind of commodity or service. To ask the price of pig-iron, of consols, or of dock labour means to ask the current quotation for a ton of pig-iron, for £100 nominal of consols, or for one hour of dock labour. On the other hand, it is a growing commercial usage to restrict the term value to the money equivalent not of a current market unit, but of some larger and less conventionalised unit—some stock or fund of varying dimensions, and regarded as a distinct totality by itself. Thus the value of a particular stock of iron would be the quantity of that stock multiplied by its current quoted price per unit. The value of a given investment in consols would be the quantity of nominal hundreds of stock multiplied by the current price. These growing tendencies to greater precision in commercial nomenclature, corresponding to improvements in the practical conduct of business, are examples of that double growth of more systematised thought or science and more ordered and disciplined action or art, which arises out

37

of the needs of everyday life, in obedience to the dictates of accumulated experience in which thought and action are not yet differentiated. The impulse to the extra initial trouble involved in more exact quantitative measurement and more definitive precision in language comes, of course, from the discovery which experience makes that this extra initial trouble is more than compensated by the greater economy made possible by the more orderly and systematic use of commodities and services in the present, and the greater certainty with which future wants can be estimated and provided for.

Past experience, which has ever been straining after increased exactitude of measurement and precision of nomenclature in business, is resumed and summarised in those two highly-specialised forms of thought—the Profit and Loss Account and the Balance Sheet. Here is to be found the highest expression of the empirical art of account-keeping, and implicit in the formulæ of these two accounts must be sought the most generalised expression of the ideas evolved by business men in the quantitative handling of business. It is here, then, and through these two most highly-developed accounting forms, that one might naturally expect a contact to be established between the theory of account-keeping and the special science of economics.

An examination of the profit and loss account and the balance sheet enables us to see how far practical experience has succeeded in measuring and defining the economic aspects of the realities of action corresponding to such elemental conceptions as wealth, value, capital, property, price, income, profits, interest, rent, wages, etc.—conceptions which, to be sure, are the very stuff of economic science. The balance sheet is a form for the summary of a series of inventories and valuations which are all supposed to be taken simultaneously at a given moment of time. Either by an effort of abstraction the processes of industry are momentarily arrested (or in some businesses where abstract thinking is not highly cultivated, by an actual stoppage of machinery and cessation of business), and the commercial world, or at least that part of it comprised in the business under consideration, is conceived as a stationary body at rest in all its parts. Under these static conditions exhaustive inventories of all the economic goods concerned are taken and their values computed. The accuracy with which this can be done will depend, amongst other things, on the perfection with which the goods can be classified and divided into units for comparison with other goods whose competition or co-operation conditions their value. The first aim, then, of the processes leading up to and culminating in the balance sheet, is the classification of goods and the valuation of each of these classified groups or stocks. Where, as in nearly the whole range of wholesale trade in staples, experience has evolved a highly perfected system of classification of kinds of goods and grading of qualities, the valuation of the groups or stocks may be made by an almost mechanical reference to the current market price of the customary unit and the multiplication of this price expressed in money by the number of units in the stock. As we descend from the staples like wheat, iron, cotton, timber, etc., whose price is fixed in the great organised world markets down to the valuation of such difficult accounting quantities as, say, dilapidated machinery or goodwill, we encounter problems of valuation which are, speaking generally, difficult in proportion as experience has not succeeded in generically classifying and grading the goods to be valued and building up an organised market for their sale and purchase. The resources of the accountant are taxed to the utmost in those cases—and they constitute the great majority of his higher tasks—

38

where only a more or less remote indirect reference can be made to market prices. Valuations have to be made and put upon commodities in all stages of completion from raw materials to finished products, upon machinery at all stages of its life from the time when it is new till the time when it is "scrapped," upon buildings at any phase of their rise and decline, upon patents and copyrights at any moment of their fluctuating career. What is the response which the accountant makes as his particular contribution towards the solution of these problems and tasks of valuation? What are the means which accounting experience has devised for the solution of these practical problems of everyday life? To answer that question one must refer back to those preliminary accounts whose balances at various degrees of remove are carried forward to the final account or balance sheet. If the system of factory account-keeping which begins with the registration of attendance made by the timekeeper as the employees file past him on entering the factory, and which ends with the closing entries in the private ledger of the proprietor, be regarded as one single process, the aim of all this long process may be regarded as the provision of means whereby the proprietor of the business may ascertain what proportion of value in the finished products turned out by the factory has been contributed by the respective agents (generically spoken of as land, labour, and capital) concerned in the production. By the manufacturer these agents must be analysed with that degree of fulness and detail which his business instincts dictate as advisable; and to each of these elements he must be able to allocate its respective amount of contribution to the final value. Even when he works to order, the manufacturer either has to quote an estimate; or even if not asked for an estimate, he has to assign a due proportion of various general expenses to the cost of the order, for the sake of charging a fair price. In either case a clear analysis of contributory values is a necessity of successful business. But of course, in the great majority of instances, the manufacturer does not work to order, but on what might be called speculative account. In other words, it is true that the great mass of economic goods is produced more or less in advance of the needs of mankind. Thus the manufacturer has to face and provide against the contingency of the fluctuations in the value of his products, which the future may contain. Hence the burden rests upon him as a producer of utilising to the utmost such past experience as is available for an index and guide to the movement of values in general and of those of his special products in particular. For the manufacturer past experience as to the values of products is very largely stored and embodied in the value of the means and instruments which have produced these products. Hence the great importance to the producer of keeping an accurate record of the values of all his means and instruments of production and the changes which these values undergo in the course of time. Looking to the value of the finished products as the aim which is constantly before the producer, we see how it behoves him to anticipate these future values; and experience shows that the most effective way of doing so is to assume that in the growth of these future values the various factors or agents in production will contribute their respective shares in certain ascertainable proportions. The system of accounts is devised for the purpose of recording such facts as may enable the producer to test with the maximum of accuracy his various assumptions, and to modify them wherever experience dictates. ¶ The accountant is, as it were, the specialised eye-piece through which the producer sees how the value of his products is reflected back in detail all along the lines of production that diverge from the finished goods back towards cost of raw material, price of labour, rent of land and buildings, interest on capital, and all the other items which are factors in price. The ideal which the accountant has to set before himself is the perfecting of the instruments of quantitative measurement by means of which the values of goods are—in Professor Smart's convenient phraseology—conducted back and distributed over all the various factors and agents which the most exhaustive business analysis of the day may consider as contributory agents in production.

Into what degree of detail it may be advisable to analyse the productive agents in a given business for the purpose of discovering their respective contributions of value must be determined by the particular requirements of the business as conceived and estimated by the managing authority; but in every case a limit will be set to the scope and extent of the analysis by the resources which the contemporary art of account-keeping is capable of affording. The more intimate the co-operation of the accountant and the manager, the further back will this limit be pushed—assuming the utmost capacity of business organisation and administration on the part of the manager, and a complete mastership of his art on the part of the accountant.

But in all productive business, whatever may be its speciality, there must always be an increasing tendency to emphasise and extend the analysis of cost. For do not changes in the methods of production, the improvement of old processes, and the invention of new ones all go on at an accelerating pace as industry more and more passes under the ordered dominion of applied science? In this ceaseless change the producer may at any moment be called upon to consider and decide as to the advisability of introducing some novelty in machinery, in labour, in power, in lighting, in heating, and what not. And if every such case is, as of course it ought to be, decided on grounds of scientific evidence, one of the first questions to be asked will be that addressed to the accountant—in regard to that item or factor which it is proposed to modify, what economic part did it play in the cost account; what was its particular contribution to the value of the commodity it helped to produce; and what is the estimated difference attributable to the proposed modification?

Here would be the place to introduce a consideration of the principles on which different managers and accountants rely in their calculation and allocation of fixed or relatively fixed charges, such as rent, interest, taxes, insurance, depreciation, and administrative expenses. In assigning a portion of these charges to the cost of a particular product, as also in calculating rates of dilapidation and depreciation, different accountants appeal to different economic principles; and though the slow growth of experience can alone be trusted to select the best methods, yet it would not be difficult to show that very considerable assistance could be derived by the practitioner from a knowledge of the relevant theoretical studies made by scientific economists. It would perhaps be not less easy to show that economists lose something by not paying more attention to the manner in which accountants handle these same phenomena.

But passing on to the consideration of the balance sheet as a summation of the values of productive agents and other economic factors concerned in a particular business, we have still to discover the significance and special interpretation which various elemental conceptions of economic science take on in the formulæ of the balance sheet. Take, for instance, the conceptions wealth, capital, and property; and see how the realities behind these terms are dealt with in the typical balance sheet. In regard to each of these

ACCOUNTING IN ITS RELATION TO ECONOMICS

terms, the two questions are customarily asked, What is it ? and What is it worth ? The balance sheet answers the first question directly or indirectly by an inventory which enumerates particular kinds of goods. In simple cases each separate item in the inventory may be found specifically enumerated or symbolised in the balance sheet. In a more complex state of affairs classified groups of goods only will be indicated in the balance sheet, the detailed enumeration of the items composing these several groups being discoverable by reference to the auxiliary accounts which are resumed in the balance sheet. The list of assets in the balance sheet we may assume to indicate the quantity of the property, and the value of the assets measures the value of the property, whether or not the property be unencumbered. If there are claims on the property the value of these claims is measured by the amount of the liabilities, and the deduction of this amount from the value of the assets gives that proportion of the value of the property which would accrue to the proprietor on realisation. And this particular value is also the value of the capital as defined by the accounting formula—Assets – Liabilities = Capital. Here, then, is the answer to the question, What is the value of the particular capital at a given moment of time ? But what is this capital ? In what does it consist ? The actual goods which correspond to this capital value will be found enumerated in the inventory of assets. But if we want to specify the particular goods whose value precisely corresponds to capital value, we shall be met in the great majority of cases with the difficulty that some of the goods are under lien for claims defined and summarised in the liabilities. Hence we are compelled to admit that no precise definition of capital goods is deducible from the formulæ of accounting—at least so far as the balance sheet is concerned. All the accountant can supply with exactitude is a measure of the value of capital goods. There would seem, however, to be implicit in the mind of the accountant, as a reflex from the tacit assumption of ordinary language and business, an idea that all the items included in the inventory of assets are to be considered as capital goods. On this view, then, all economic goods of whatever kind or of whatever degree of completion in existence at any given moment of time constitute capital ; and the corresponding assumption would have to be made that the value of these specified goods is the value of the capital at that moment of time. But this particular conception of capital value is not necessarily coincident with, and, as we have seen above, would in the great majority of cases be different from, the specific capital item in the balance sheet. To reconcile the conflict between the two points of view, we have to imagine a distinction, implicit in the interpretation of the balance sheet, between the individual capital of a business conceived as the unencumbered property of the proprietor, and the social capital of the business, the latter including items of capital that may at the time be under lien.

The word Wealth has no technical use in the nomenclature of accounting. The popular question as to wealth is, How wealthy, or how rich, is a man ? and the question is usually held as satisfactorily answered if either the amount of the income is given, or the amount of the capital value of his property after deduction of all claims against it—the latter measure being supplied by the balance sheet. One of the most recent noteworthy attempts of economic science to gain precision in the definition of its elemental concepts has resulted in the definition of capital as the stock of wealth in existence at a given moment of time ; and this was held to be deducible from the usage of account-keeping. The argument on which it was based might be set forth and extended somewhat as follows. Assuming that every

41

owner of wealth in a community keeps accounts on the same double-entry system, and assuming that none of the wealth owned outside the community enters into these accounts, then if every balance sheet is drawn up at the same moment of time we shall have in the integration of these balance sheets a complete and exhaustive measure of the total capital wealth of the community at the given moment of time. Taking all accounts together, the total of liabilities cancels an equivalent amount of assets as between one individual and another; and it only remains to subtract the total of liabilities from the total value of the assets to arrive at the total value of the capital wealth of the community at the given moment of time. The same result would of course be reached by the direct summation of the specific valuation of capital in all the several balance sheets.

In this ideal integration of balance sheets for the hypothetical measurement of social capital, it will of course be understood that the accounts of legal corporations are neglected, since the property provisionally held by these is in ultimate analysis distributable amongst the individual shareholders. Alternatively, to be sure, the hypothetical case can be imagined in which all production of goods which are valued in money be undertaken wholly by legal corporations; and obviously in that case the amount of social capital at a given moment of time could be estimated by neglecting private accounts, and merely integrating the accounts of the legal corporations.

Practically speaking, such ideals in which private and individual accounting merges into social accounting, are doubtless highly hypothetical, but they need not on those grounds be deemed wanting in reality for science. Though here and there a possible direct stimulus to action, yet these speculative efforts of ordered thought find their chief use and justification in the development of scientific theory, and so serve as an indirect aid in the improvement of practice. The accountant whose scientific conceptions (that is to say, whose theoretical thinking) are limited to the immediate horizon of the few businesses or even groups of businesses with whose affairs he happens to be associated will certainly not adequately meet all the demands that will be made upon his powers. Only will he succeed in minimising the risk of error in the larger issues of his work if it is part of his habitual mental outfit to conceive of certain matters of cost and valuation as dependent upon ever-widening conditions, until it may be the whole process of world production has to be taken into practical consideration.

And here it may be remarked that the uses to the accountant of a training in economic science include, but do not stop short at, an endowment of systematised knowledge, and a facile access to sources of knowledge beyond the range of immediate acquisition. An adequate economic training eventuates in the development of higher powers which utilise positive knowledge merely as a tool. Economic education should be the organised means of equipping the accountant with a certain habit of mind, a certain way of handling economic phenomena, which, carried into practical business life, does not rest satisfied with superficial or customary views, but pushes on to ever-deepening analysis, which, again successively alternating with synthesis, gives at once the clearest attainable view of a situation in its detailed parts and in its widest totality. And if the acquired analytic habit of mind tends (as so often is the case) to the paralysing and not to the strengthening of the will, the defect is to be sought either in the native character of the student or in the incompleteness of his science; for it is the very end and purpose of science to prompt to appropriate action. To be practical means to have a clear knowledge of what details may in action be omitted as irrelevant to the business in hand, and to know at what point to stop the investigation of causation, the search for operating factors. But it also means something more positive than this. If business is to be treated as an art based on its correlative science or group of sciences, then it must be held that theoretical study is inadequate if it stops short of providing not only a sanction for the main principles of action, but also a positive command for their performance. If the position be maintained, as is so commonly done to-day by economists, that economic science is merely descriptive and analytical, and terminates at the indicative mood, then it is a consequence of this doctrine that the study of economics, whether as training for business or for general culture, is incomplete, and that its necessary complement is such a study of ethics as would enable the student to pass from the sterile indicative to the fruitful imperative mood. It is only as a temporary device that economics can be isolated; for the scheme of labour subdivision by which a group of men make it their special occupation to search for greater economies of thought is in order that these, when discovered, may eventuate in corresponding economies of action. Thus the labour of science is wasted unless—it may be at many removes—it returns to and fulfils itself in practical art.

ANON

Balance Sheets.

DEFINITION.—A balance sheet is a concise statement compiled from the books of a concern which have been kept by double entry, showing on the one side all the assets and on the other side all the liabilities of the concern at a particular moment of time. A similar statement when not prepared from books kept by double entry is called a statement of affairs, a state of affairs, or a statement of assets and liabilities. The distinction is important. The balance sheet of a business is prepared for the purpose of showing the financial condition of the concern at a particular moment of time, and should be so classified and arranged as to give the clearest and fullest idea of the financial position of the business. The balances shown by the trial balance having been adjusted by the closing entries giving effect to the valuations of stock, unexpired charges, reserves, and other particulars, the balances remaining are assets so far as they are debit balances, and liabilities so far as they are credit balances. The amounts due by customers and the amounts due to creditors, and other particulars involving many items, are not given in the balance sheet in detail, but are contained in separate schedules or lists, or in a balance book kept for the purpose. If the assets exceed the liabilities the balance sheet shows a surplus, which is due to the owner or owners of the business, and forms the capital of the concern. Capital is therefore the surplus of assets over liabilities, or the measure of the indebtedness of a business to the owners in respect of money invested in the business and accumulated profits. It is the principal sum invested or remaining in the business. Book-keeping is so complete and thorough that even the owner of a business is looked upon as an outsider, and his account, called the Capital Account, is credited with what he puts into the business, as he means to get back again what he puts in, he becomes a creditor of the business for it, and he also gets credit for any profit the business earns, as he is entitled to that also. The Capital Account was formerly sometimes called the Stock Account, but this use of the word "stock" is now almost obsolete, and it is as well, to prevent confusion, to keep the word "stock" for goods and merchandise.

In the case of a company, as for example one registered under the Companies Act of 1862, where the capital is fixed, the surplus of assets over liabilities may consist of the capital, of a reserve created for the benefit of the shareholders and the stability of the company, and of the unappropriated or undivided profit.

If the liabilities exceed the assets the balance sheet shows a deficiency, and the amount of the deficiency is the measure of the insolvency of the concern, or the indebtedness of the owners to the business for losses incurred.

A balance sheet may thus be defined as a statement of the liabilities of a concern (credit balances as taken from the ledger), including the capital, reserve, and unappropriated profit, on the one side, and the assets of the concern (debit balances as taken from the ledger), including any deficiency, on the other.

The main distinction between a Profit and Loss Account and a balance sheet is that the Profit and Loss Account shows the progress of the business during a period, while the balance sheet shows its position at a particular moment.

ON WHICH SIDE OF THE BALANCE SHEET THE ASSETS SHOULD BE PLACED.—When a book-keeper has completed those entries known as "closing" entries, including the preparation of the Profit and Loss Account, and has balanced off all the Ledger Accounts, carrying down the balances to begin the accounts for the next year, he usually prepares a statement of the ledger balances, arranging all the debit balances in the left money column, and all the credit balances in the right money column, in some such form as the following :—

STATEMENT OF LEDGER BALANCES as at 31st December.

	Dr.	Cr.
CUSTOMERS' LEDGER :—		
J. Collins	£300 0 0	
W. Simpson	650 0 0	
	£950 0 0	
CREDITORS' LEDGER :—		
Jack and Co.		£370 0 0
Scott and Tait		230 0 0
		£600 0 0
GENERAL LEDGER :—		
Bills payable		280 0 0
Bills receivable	300 0 0	
Goods	700 0 0	
Rent		20 0 0
Capital		1210 0 0
DUE BY BANK	95 0 0	
CASH ON HAND	65 0 0	
	£2110 0 0	£2110 0 0

45

It will be observed that in the foregoing statement all the balances of the accounts appear just as they are in the ledger after the balances have been carried down, that is, the debit balances are entered in the debit column, and the credit balances in the credit column. The particulars above given in the statement of ledger balances, if thrown into the form of a balance sheet, would appear as follows :—

(Correct Form.)

BALANCE SHEET as at 31st December

Assets.			Liabilities.		
Due by Customers . . .	£950	0 0	Due to Wholesale Houses .	£600	0 0
Bills Receivable . . .	300	0 0	Bills Payable	280	0 0
Goods on Hand . . .	700	0 0	Rent accrued to date .	20	0 0
In Bank	95	0 0		£900	0 0
Cash on Hand . . .	65	0 0	Capital	1210	0 0
	£2110	0 0		£2110	0 0

In the above balance sheet it will be observed that the assets appear on the left side, and the liabilities on the right side of the statement, just as they appear in the ledger. It will be observed, further, that the contractions *Dr.* and *Cr.*, for debtor and creditor, are not used as part of the heading. This is because the balance sheet is not an account, but is a statement of ledger balances. In a set of books kept completely by double entry, and in which even the balancing of the accounts is done through the medium of the journal, an account is used entitled the "Balance Account," into which all the balances are transferred at the close of the year, and in which the Ledger Accounts would appear as they are given in the above statement of ledger balances. For the opening entries a Balance Account would also be used, but the items would necessarily appear on opposite sides from the closing Balance Account. The balance sheet, if given in the form above shown, is thus practically a copy of the closing Balance Account. From this point of view the assets should undoubtedly be placed on the left side of the balance sheet, which corresponds to the debit side of the closing Balance Account. Further, all balances which represent assets are debit balances, and accountants and bookkeepers naturally come to associate assets with the debit or left side of either an account or a statement. Theoretically, therefore, the left side is the side upon which the assets should appear in the balance sheet. In practice in the United Kingdom, however, the assets are usually to be found upon the right side, and it may prove interesting as well as instructive to investigate the matter further. The fundamental idea of a balance sheet is that it is a statement showing how the Ledger Accounts of a concern stand at a particular moment of time. It would be unnecessary if we could see and comprehend at one view the contents of a set of ledgers. As we are unable to do this we prepare a balance sheet, but why in the process the assets which are on the debit side and the liabilities which are on the credit side, as according to the principles of accounting they ought to be, should change places, it is impossible to justify. The custom seems to have arisen through the influence of the forms given in Acts of Parliament, chiefly the Companies Act, 1862, which must have been prepared by those unacquainted with the theory of accounts. The Profit and Loss Account is taken from the ledger without the sides being transposed.

and there is no logical reason why the sides in the balance sheet should be reversed when the items in it are the balances remaining in the ledger after certain other balances have been taken to the Profit and Loss Account. In the accounts of public undertakings, such as railways, formed under the sanction of Acts of Parliament, when the receipts and expenditure on account of capital must be published, the Capital Account, in the form prescribed, has the items as they appear in the ledger, but the balance sheet, the form of which is also prescribed, has the items reversed. The form of balance sheet in which the assets appear upon the left side is both theoretically the correct form and in practice is the more convenient form to use. It is the form adopted on the Continent, in America, and, in fact, throughout the world, with the exception of the United Kingdom. Until recent years it was the form almost universally adopted in Scotland. Prior to about the passing of the Companies Act 1862, it was the form chiefly adopted in England, but is so no longer. It is known by the name of the Continental or Scotch form. The form of balance sheet prescribed by Table A of the Companies Act 1862 has the liabilities on the left side, and this is the form now generally adopted throughout the United Kingdom. The Scotch form, however, is still largely used in Scotland, even for companies under the 1862 Act which applies to Scotland. The practice is so diverse that there are firms of accountants in which one of the partners invariably uses one form and the other partner as invariably the other. It is certainly most desirable that the form of balance sheet with the assets on the left side, which is founded on correct principles, should become universal, but this could now, in view of existing statutes where the form which is contrary to the true principles of accounting is prescribed, only be brought about by an Act of Parliament. Such an Act would, no doubt, cause a little temporary inconvenience, but this would be nothing to the advantage of having all balance sheets uniform, and conforming to the best traditions and the accepted practice of the rest of the world.

The reason given for putting the liabilities on the left side of the balance sheet is that the balance sheet is a statement showing the position of the business in relation to the owner and to other persons. The business is the creditor for the assets, and is the debtor for its liabilities. This is, however, begging the question. Whichever form is used, the contractions "Dr." and "Cr." should never be put upon a balance sheet, because, as already stated, it is not an account.

Several banks and large financial concerns adopt neither of the methods under discussion, but have the assets placed underneath the liabilities. This is called the report form of balance sheet.

The following statement shows how the assets and liabilities were treated by authors of works on book-keeping prior to 1859. After that date the authors of works on book-keeping published in the United Kingdom in most cases adopt the method of placing liabilities on the left side :—

Mode of Placing Assets and Liabilities in Balance Sheets

Author.	Date.	Title of Work.	Description of Statement or Account.	Method of Placing.	
				Left-hand Side.	Right-hand Side.
S. Monteage . .	1708	Debtor and Creditor made Easy	Balance	Assets	Liabilities
A. Malcolm . .	1718	Arithmetick and Book-keeping	Balance	Assets	Liabilities
William Webster	1721	Essay on Book-keeping	Balance	Assets	Liabilities
A. Malcolm . .	1731	Book-keeping	Balance	Assets	Liabilities
John Mair . .	1800	Book-keeping Modernised	Balance Account	Assets	Liabilities
T. Dilworth . .	1801	The Young Book-keeper's Assistant	Balance	Assets	Liabilities
W. Lorrain . .	1807	Book-keeping by Double Entry	Balance	Assets	Liabilities
Chas. Hutton .	1810	A Complete Treatise on Book-keeping	Balance	Assets	Liabilities
Rees Cyclopedia.	1819	Article on Book-keeping	Balance	Assets	Liabilities
J. Morrison . .	1820	Practical Book-keeping	Balance Account	Assets	Liabilities
P. Kelly . . .	1821	The Elements of Book-keeping	Balance	Assets	Liabilities
J. P. Corg . .	1839	Practical Treatise on Accounts	Balance Account	Assets	Liabilities
C. Morrison . .	1843	Practical Book-keeping	Balance Account	Assets	Liabilities
J. Caldecott . .	1850	Practical Guide to Book-keeping	Balance Account	Assets	Liabilities
B. F. Foster . .	1852	Double Entry Elucidated	Balance Sheet	Assets	Liabilities
G. H. Boulter .	1857	A Course of Book-keeping by Double Entry	Balance	Assets	Liabilities
W. Inglis . . .	1858	Book-keeping	Balance Sheet	Liabilities	Assets
James Haldon .	1859	Rudimentary Book-keeping	Balance Account	Assets	Liabilities

A Full and Fair Balance Sheet. — The Companies Act of 1862 does not specially state how the balance sheet of a company is to be prepared, but the following regulations are given in Table A appended to the Act, and these regulations apply to all companies limited by shares, unless they are excluded or modified by the Articles of Association adopted by the company. The following are the regulations relating to the balance sheet :—

Regulation No. 81.—A balance sheet shall be made out in every year, and laid before the company in general meeting, and such balance sheet shall contain a summary of the property and liabilities of the company arranged under the heads appearing in the form annexed to this table, or as near thereto as circumstances admit.

Regulation No. 94.—The auditors shall make a report to the members upon the balance sheet and accounts, and in every such report they shall state whether, in their opinion, the balance sheet is a full and fair balance sheet, containing the particulars required by these regulations, and properly drawn up so as to exhibit a true and correct view of the state of the company's affairs, and in case they have called for explanations or information from the directors, and whether they have been satisfactory ; and such report shall be read, together with the report of the directors, at the ordinary meeting.

The 94th Regulation from the Act 1862, given above, is now superseded by the Companies Act 1900, sec. 23, which is as follows :—

23.—Every auditor of a company shall have a right of access at all times to the books and accounts and vouchers of the company, and shall be entitled to require from the directors and officers of the company such information and explanation as may be necessary for the performance of the duties of the auditors ; and the auditors shall sign a certificate at the foot of the balance sheet stating whether or not all their requirements as auditors have been complied with, and shall make a report to the shareholders on the accounts examined by them, and on every balance sheet laid before the company in general meeting during their tenure of office ; and in every such report shall state whether, in their opinion, the balance sheet referred to in the report is properly drawn up so as to exhibit a true and correct view of the state of the company's affairs as shown by the books of the company ; and such report shall be read before the company in general meeting.

The balance sheet, whether of a company or of a private concern, should be, as mentioned above, "full and fair." The necessity of a balance sheet being "full and fair" is evident when the uses for which a balance sheet is prepared are considered. A private trader prepares a balance sheet first of all for his own satisfaction and guidance in order to see exactly his financial position at a given date. The trader, however, may be desirous of obtaining a partner, and a balance sheet would require to be prepared as at the date of the assumption of a new partner. This balance sheet, it is evident, must state the assets at their real value as a going concern, allowances being made for depreciated property, and it must also contain all the liabilities at the date of the assumption. The capital of the old partner is ascertained from this balance sheet, and if it showed the assets at figures in excess of their real value, or if the liabilities were understated, the new partner would be prejudiced. Cases have occurred where a partner has been assumed, and after he had sunk his capital in a concern on the basis of a false balance sheet, it has been discovered upon investigation that the business at the time of the assumption of the partner was hopelessly insolvent. A balance sheet is often used when a trader is negotiating a loan, and in this case the balance sheet is used by the bank or other lender for his information, and everything depends upon the care and honesty with which it has been prepared. When a private trader or firm is being converted into a limited company, a balance sheet is made up, but this balance sheet is very seldom used as the basis of valuation. Separate valuations of the property, plant, etc., are in most cases made, and it is at these figures that the assets are taken over.

THE BALANCE SHEET OF A BANK not only shows its financial position at the date at which it is prepared, but it is so framed as to show the assets in the order of realisability, and thus enable its depositors and customers to judge of its ability to meet all possible demands. The assets should be arranged so as to show the liquid or easily realisable assets distinct from the others. The form on p. 209 may be taken as the balance sheet of a bank as published at the present time.

The balance sheet of a limited company shows the shareholders the financial position of the company; but the balance sheet also shows to a creditor, who is contemplating giving the company credit, the total assets, including the uncalled capital, which are available for payment of his debt.

In a balance sheet everything depends upon the character of the various assets and liabilities. Thus, if the liabilities are of such a nature that the owner of the business may be called upon to pay them within short notice, then the assets must be such as to be realisable in the same time. Otherwise, while the business may be thoroughly solvent, that is, may have a surplus of assets over liabilities, the owner may be rendered bankrupt through being unable to meet some liability which can be legally at the time enforced against him.

All the assets included in a balance sheet should be stated at their fair value, and the liabilities should be fully shown. The balance sheet should not conceal any weakness in the financial position of the concern, but should give the fullest information to the shareholders and the general public, consistent, of course, with the proper conduct of the business. In some cases it might be advisable not to reveal too much, in consequence of the competition of similar concerns, but what is really the failing of balance sheets is that they reveal too little and not too much. The balance sheet formerly given in the Scotch form is now given in the English form, but it has been varied slightly to show a better method of grouping the assets,

BALANCE SHEET as at 31st December 19

Liabilities.

I. To the Public:—
Notes in Circulation	£500,000	0 0
Deposits and Credit Balances	4,000,000	0 0
Balances Due to Banking Correspondents	6,000	0 0
Drafts Issued, Payable on Demand	32,000	0 0
	£4,538,000	0 0

II. To the Partners:—
Capital Authorised and Subscribed—100,000 Shares of £20 each . . . £2,000,000 0 0

viz.—
£4 per Share Paid up	£400,000	0 0		
4 ,, Callable	400,000	0 0		
12 ,, Reserved	1,200,000	0 0		
£20	£2,000,000	0 0		

Reserve Fund	200,000	0 0
Profit and Loss Account	50,000	0 0
	650,000	0 0
	£5,188,000	0 0

Assets.

Gold and Silver Coin at Head Office and Branches	.		£400,000	0 0
Cash at Call with London Bankers	.		200,000	0 0
Do. with other Banking Correspondents, Exchangeable Notes and Cheques on other Banks	.		150,000	0 0
			£750,000	0 0

Consols and other Securities of the British Government	£200,000	0 0		
Colonial Government, Bank of England, and British Corporation Stocks	300,000	0 0		
Debenture and Preference Stocks, other Stocks, Shares, and Securities	500,000	0 0		
Temporary Loans on Stocks and other Marketable Securities	200,000	0 0		
			1,200,000	0 0
			£1,950,000	0 0

Bills Discounted, Advances on Cash Credit Bonds and on other Accounts and Securities	2,500,000	0 0
Bank Buildings, Furniture, and Fittings, at Head Office and Branches	738,000	0 0
	£5,188,000	0 0

and it has further been assumed that the balance sheet is that of a company with a paid-up capital of £700.

BALANCE SHEET as at 31st December.

(*English Form.*)

Liabilities.				Assets.				
DUE TO CREDITORS :—				DUE BY CUSTOMERS :—				
On Open Accounts	.	. £600	0 0	On Open Accounts	.	. £950	0 0
On Bills Payable .	.	280	0 0	On Bills Receivable	.	. 300	0 0
		£880	0 0			£1250	0 0
RENT ACCRUED TO DATE .	.	20	0 0	GOODS ON HAND	.	. 700	0 0
DUE TO SHAREHOLDERS :—				CASH :—			
Capital . . £700 0 0				In Bank . . £95 0 0			
Undivided Profit 510 0 0				On Hand . . 65 0 0			
		1210	0 0			160	0 0
		£2110	0 0			£2110	0 0

The following might have been the Profit and Loss Account of this company for the year :—

PROFIT AND LOSS ACCOUNT for the Year.

Expenditure.				Income.			
To Cost of Goods	.	. £2200	0 0	By Sales .	. . .	. £3000	0 0
,, Rent .	. .	. 70	0 0				
,, Wages :	.	. 200	0 0				
,, Discount	. .	. 20	0 0				
,, Profit for Year	.	. 510	0 0				
		£3000	0 0			£3000	0 0

If the balance sheet in the English form and the Profit and Loss Account of this company were printed in the annual report to the shareholders, as is usually the case, it will be observed that the net profit of £510 would appear on the left side of the balance sheet, and also on the left side of the Profit and Loss Account. It is more in keeping with our ideas of book-keeping by double entry that these items should appear on opposite sides, as they would do if the Scotch form of balance sheet were adopted,

EDITORIAL

Balance Sheet Values.

IN another column of the present issue we reproduce a letter written by Mr. F. W. PIXLEY, F.C.A., to the editor of *The Financial Times*, which is of interest not merely on its own account, but also, as it seems to us, by reason of its bearing on our last week's article entitled "A Question of Values."

Mr. PIXLEY very properly points out in the course of this letter that auditors are not qualified valuers, and that, therefore, necessarily they are not competent to express expert opinions on values, whether for Balance Sheet purposes or otherwise. But his explanation as to what a Balance Sheet really is, or ought to be, is one that, it seems to us, will be taken exception to. We are told that a Balance Sheet is in very few instances, save those of bankers, finance and insurance companies, a statement of liabilities and assets. Why, it may be asked, are bankers, finance and insurance companies thus separated from other concerns? If the distinction exists in fact, the man in the street may well inquire what (if any) principle underlies it; and unless the principle is one that satisfies him as being reasonable he will most likely decline to recognise the distinction. For our own part we think that the Balance Sheets of bankers, finance and insurance companies are no more statements of liabilities and assets than are the Balance Sheets of most other concerns. They do, however, belong to the class of undertaking that naturally, for the purposes of its business,

keeps all its reserves in a very liquid form. The basis on which the assets are valued does not differ, or should not, from the basis on which similar assets would be valued by other undertakings. The essential difference is, that in the one case the assets are almost entirely liquid, whereas in the other case they will be for the most part fixed.

So regarded, it becomes simple to reduce the whole business to a principle that will be readily intelligible to the general public and equally acceptable to specialists. Liquid assets are necessarily valued for Balance Sheet purposes having regard to their realisable values, because their realisation in the near future has, naturally, to be contemplated. Fixed assets, on the other hand, are held not for the purpose of realisation in the ordinary course of business, but to be used in their existing form. So regarded, they represent—for Balance Sheet purposes at least - not so much tangible property capable of being sold for a stated sum, as expenditure, which, for the time being at least, may properly be capitalised instead of being charged at once against profits.

We take it that the primary rule of all sound accounting must be that *primâ facie* all payments are proper revenue charges unless the contrary can be established. The contrary can, of course, be established with regard to payments that are pure revenue payments in so far as it can be shown that they are payments in advance, and that it is therefore equitable that they should be charged against the profits of a series of years rather than against the profits of any one year—upon the assumption, as Mr. PIXLEY very properly puts it, that each company is a permanent institution. This principle, that expenditure ought in fairness to be charged against the profits benefited by that expenditure, applies not merely to purely revenue items, but equally to all capital expenditure. It is, indeed, as it seems to us, the sole justification for capitalising any expenditure whatever. Such expenditure will, in practically all instances, last not for ever, but for a more or less limited period of time, after which it will have to be renewed if the undertaking is to be maintained as a permanent institution. Whether one regards the original expenditure as a revenue payment spread over a term of years, or the ultimate cost of renewal as a revenue payment chargeable against the profits of the same series of years, is a matter of little practical importance, inasmuch as it would involve precisely the same figures so long as prices remained constant, and is, therefore, not likely to produce any important difference of figures over an extended period of time.

The advantage of regarding all so-called capital expenditure, or expenditure upon fixed assets, as expenditure that will eventually have to be written off against revenue, apportioned equitably over a series of years, is that it provides a quite intelligible reason for disregarding fluctuations in realisable values at intermediate periods. It is a plan that can be easily understood by all persons of ordinary intelligence, and has, moreover, the merit of stating the requirements of the situation without the necessity of imposing confusing exceptions.

It may be, and possibly will be, objected that our argument is for all practical purposes one for the universal double-account system in fact, if not in form. That is hardly the case, however, for we contemplate all expenditure being sooner or later charged against revenue; but there can be little doubt that from many points of view most commercial Balance Sheets would be far clearer if re-cast into double-account form. And we may indeed venture the suggestion that the double-account form would be very much more largely employed in practice, were it not the fact that the influence exercised by merchants on accounting forms even in the present day is out of all proportion to the relative importance of trading undertakings, as compared with those connected with industry or finance. The merchant (like the banker, who is, after all, himself only a merchant) of course possesses but few fixed assets, and these are relatively unimportant in amount. That being so, it is little short of absurd that those engaged in industry should have swallowed whole what the merchant had to tell them as to the best methods of accounting. But the circumstances are perhaps the less surprising when one remembers that even now most merchants think they know all that can be known about accounts, whereas all intelligent manufacturers know that there is a great deal about accounts with which they are entirely unacquainted. In the first instance therefore, while manufacturing was in its infancy, it seems perfectly natural that it should have modelled its accounting systems on those of the merchant ; but why it should continue to be satisfied with this very unsuitable model is, it seems to us, little short of marvellous. Perhaps the true explanation is, that the typical manufacturer is, as a rule, an exceedingly bad hand at office work of all descriptions.

F. W. PIXLEY

Company Law Reform.

The Question of Audit.

[The following letter, which appeared in a recent issue of *The Financial Times*, is referred to in a leading article this week. —Ed. *Acct.*]

To the Editor of *The Financial Times*.

Sir,—Mr. W. H. Terry, Barrister-at-Law, who is writing an interesting series of articles on Company Law Reform, makes some remarks in his article in your issue of to-day on "Accounts and Audit" which must meet with the approval of members of the legal and accountancy professions as well as of the general public.

He is correct in stating that Balance Sheets are frequently so drawn up that it is impossible for even an expert accountant, unless behind the scenes, to gauge the position of a company from the mere study of the returns submitted at general meetings, and it was to enable the uninitiated to deal with this difficulty that I allowed a paper I read on the subject of "How to read the Balance Sheet of a Commercial Concern" to be lately reprinted.

It is also satisfactory to notice, as Mr. Terry points out, that the shareholder auditor is rapidly becoming a thing of the past. It is, nevertheless, astonishing what a number of highly respectable and otherwise intelligent people there are who, without training or knowledge, are still prepared to shoulder the onerous and responsible duties of an auditor.

I must, however, join issue with Mr. Terry on two points. One is his suggestion of throwing greater responsibilities upon auditors. The responsibilities fixed upon auditors a few years ago by one of the Judges were so great that many well-known Chartered Accountants reluctantly came to the conclusion that it would not be right for them to bring their sons into the profession and so expose them to the risk of entire ruin for a single error of judgment or oversight. The Court of Appeal fortunately took a more business-like view of the matter, but even as it is the responsibilities of auditors of companies are absurdly great having regard to the fees paid them.

The other point on which I join issue with Mr. Terry is his statement that "Audits which ignore the question of the value of assets, for instance, are of little use." Now although Mr. Terry admits that an auditor is not paid to discharge, and, presumably, is not competent to discharge the duty of a valuer, he submits that auditors ought to take responsibility for the value placed upon the items in the accounts, or companies should have valuers. Let me here repeat what has been so often stated, not only by myself in my writings, but by other well-known Chartered Accountants, in their papers addressed to Students' Societies and others, that a Balance Sheet is in very few instances, such as those of banks, finance and insurance companies, a statement of liabilities and assets. It is nothing but a collection of the debit and credit balances of the Ledgers, subject to this qualification—that the debit balances of the Ledgers, which are placed on the credit side of a Balance Sheet, are supposed to be reduced, when necessary, by what is known as "depreciation," before such balances are taken out, leaving them at an amount which is considered to be their value, having regard to the fact that the company is a going concern.

As an example:—Supposing a company fits up a factory with entirely new machinery of the best description at cost, including fitting, of £100,000, in a Balance Sheet prepared the day after the completion of this work the company can surely take credit for this property at £100,000—its cost price. This, however, cannot be called the value of the asset, as, if it had to be disposed of the very day—that is, the day after the completion, before it has been used—it would probably not fetch £50,000. No one conceive of a company being obliged to deal with its assets upon this basis of valuation, it might be impossible for it to pay a dividend for ten or fifteen years.

Balance Sheets can only deal with Ledger balances except in the case of stocks, shares, and stocks-in-trade, and a Chartered Accountant, in going into the question as to the amount which shall finally be placed on the credit side of a Balance Sheet in respect of any Ledger balance, investigates by means of a cross-examination of the officials of the company each balance, and requires the proper amounts to be written off for depreciation or for wear and tear, or else in his report comments upon the fact that the Ledger debit balances are taken credit for in the Balance Sheet at too high a value.

It must be assumed—unless it is a known fact that at the end of a certain period a company must come to an end—that each company is a permanent institution, and consequently, each item on the credit side of the Balance Sheet must be taken credit for on the basis that the company is a going concern.—I am, &c.,

FRANCIS W. PIXLEY.

58 Coleman Street, E.C.

E. M. CARTER

8

Balance Sheet Values.

(To the Editor of The Accountant.)

SIR,—Mr. Pixley's letter, in your issue of the 4th inst. Balance Sheet values, raises a question of the utmost importance to auditors—in fact, it is one on which the whole structure of company audits depends; but it is a difficult and elusive question, and, as far as I know, has never been studied as it ought to be, so that we are without any guiding principle to help us in deciding what is a true and correct Balance Sheet.

I am inclined to agree to some extent with Mr. Pixley's conclusions, but I disagree absolutely with the way he appears to arrive at them. Your article on the subject is, to my mind, much more practical and instructive, but I think we get the clearest view of the question by looking at it from exactly the opposite point to that which you choose, and, as you invite further discussion, I will as briefly as possible explain this point of view.

In your leading article you indicate how the transactions that occur in a business should be dealt with in the accounts in order to arrive at a reasonable and intelligible result. I, on the other hand, propose to look at the question from the outside investor's point of view. Our conclusions are very similar, but I think my point of view shows more clearly the principle involved. I will begin by stating two propositions.

I.—*Profit is Increase of Capital.*—The profit or loss of a joint-stock undertaking in any period is commonly understood to be the increase or decrease of capital in that period, due allowance being made for capital paid or withdrawn.

II.—The capital of the undertaking is for this purpose taken to mean the excess of the total value of its assets over its total liabilities, and the value of the assets must be based on their *market values* as far as practicable.

If these two main propositions are admitted, everything else is simplified. It must, however, be clearly understood that, in consequence of the impossibility of ascertaining market values in some few cases, and the inconvenience which would arise if we did use them in a few others, by common consent the rule has been modified in certain instances, hence the words "as far as practicable" at the end of my second rule. I maintain that, by stating the question in this way, we get a far clearer view of it. We first of all make up our minds what is correct in theory, and then decide how far we are justified in departing from it in practice, so it brings debatable questions within a restricted area, and affords a clear basis for discussing them.

To return to my two propositions, I do not see how anyone can deny that in theory *profit* is synonymous with *increase in capital*; if it were possible for capital to diminish while it produced profits, then the expression "profit" would lose all tangible meaning. Also, in practice, if we are to look on profit as not connected

with capital, then it follows that Balance Sheet figures are mere balances of accounts strung together so as to balance when such a so-called profit figure is brought into account, and this makes a Balance Sheet mere nonsense. In the mathematical theory of interest, capital or principal is always assumed to remain intact; without this assumption the whole theory falls to the ground, and so it must be with other more complex forms of capital and profit, and, roughly, this is how the man in the street looks at it.

The only debatable point in my second proposition is the assertion that the correct basis of value for assets is their *market value*. It will be said that plant and machinery have an intrinsic value to an undertaking quite apart from their market value; this, in a way, is quite true, but it must be remembered that when profit or capital is distributed among shareholders it is paid in cash, and assets have to be sold at their market value in order to provide the cash. Plant and machinery when first acquired are taken at what they cost, which is assumed to be their market price, and it is a proof of good accounting if, when a machine is finally sold, it has been written down to its then market value. Market value is the object in view throughout; but in the long interval between the original purchase of a machine and its final sale a hypothetical value has of necessity to be attached to it based on well-understood rules, including the assumption that the undertaking remains a going concern. But the main thing to observe is that market value is taken to be the proper basis of value as far as practicable.

Goodwill is another asset (if it may be called an asset) which cannot be given its market value. A large sum may be paid for goodwill and yet in a year or two its value may have vanished, and perhaps in another few years a new goodwill of greater value may be built up again. Its market value can only be proved on the sale of the business itself. By universal consent it has been decided that fluctuations in the value of an asset so vague and unstable as goodwill may be ignored in Balance Sheets. It would not be practicable to state its market value. Each shareholder of a company forms his own opinion on the subject, and the market value of the company's shares are settled by their opinion.

Apart from plant, machinery, and goodwill, there are comparatively few important exceptions to the general rule that assets should be stated in a Balance Sheet at their market value, and it would not be difficult to lay down general rules which would cover all possible cases that are generally considered permissible exceptions. Theoretically they are not justifiable, but for practical purposes, in order to avoid difficulty and inconvenience, such exceptions must exist. To look at the question in this way has been most useful to me, and I cannot help thinking that most auditors from the back of their minds really regard it from the same point of view; anyhow, I offer it for what it is worth.

One other point mentioned by Mr. Pixley I should like to say a word on—namely. the remark that auditors are not qualified valuers. In a general sense that is true, but we are valuers of a particular sort, who go about our work in a particular way. We cannot, by looking at machinery and plant, tell what their value is, but, by being acquainted with the records connected with them and the opinions of those responsible for them, we are in many respects in a better position to judge of their value than a professional valuer would be.

Yours truly,

ERIC M. CARTER.

Birmingham, 21st December 1909.

EDITORIAL

Balance Sheet Values.

WE must confess to some little disappointment that the exceptionally able letter from Mr. ERIC M. CARTER, F.C.A., which appeared in our issue of the 1st inst., has not so far been productive of more discussion on this most interesting and important subject. The question of Balance Sheet Values, and of the duties of the Auditor in connection therewith, is one that lies at the very root of all accountancy matters, and the practical utility of the accountancy profession to the community generally depends, as it seems to us, entirely upon the ability with which this question is solved. Hence we cannot help regarding with feelings somewhat akin to dismay the apparent apathy of our readers with regard thereto, more particularly in view of the statement put forward by Mr. CARTER, which can hardly be gainsaid, that we are without any guiding principle to help us in deciding what is a true and correct Balance Sheet.

The difficulty of the outsider in judging as to the truth or correctness of the Balance Sheet put forward by the directors of any particular company must, it is to be feared, always remain while the principle of maintaining Secret Reserves is sanctioned by the Courts and the general sense of the business community. But the difficulty to which Mr. CARTER draws attention is not so much that of the outsider as of the auditor, who has a statutory right of access to all books and documents tending to throw any light upon the matter, and the right to interrogate directors and other officers of the company in respect of their dealings with regard to its affairs. To suggest, therefore, that we are without any guiding principle to help us in deciding what is a true and correct Balance Sheet, in the face of all this information, is to suggest a condition of affairs that can hardly fail to prove startling to the man in the street; yet the exceedingly diverse opinions that have been expressed with regard to the matter from time to time show that this is no mere exaggeration. They do, however, as it seems to us, go far towards making out an overwhelming case in favour of a really exhaustive discussion of the matter, so that the necessary guiding principles may be evolved. That such guiding principles actually exist can hardly be doubted by those who honestly believe that there is any real future for the accountancy profession.

Mr. CARTER, while expressing the view that the conclusions he arrives at with regard to the whole matter are very similar to those expressed by us in our article of the 4th ult., prefers to take exactly the opposite point of view to that which we selected, as being in his opinion that by which very much the clearest insight into the whole question may be gathered. We are not prepared to say that much may not be said in favour of this contention, and indeed our chief reason for selecting the particular standpoint that we did was that it is one which we believe has. so far, been almost totally ignored. At the same time we had another reason for our selec-.ion—a desire to be practical, and to recognise that while there is much to be desired concerning the way in which the Courts review decisions affecting the position and profits of companies, the real question at issue in the vast majority of cases is not so much the determining of the economic or theoretical profit that has been earned, as the profit earned that is—rightly or wrongly—legally divisible among shareholders in the form of dividend.

It is here, of course, that the standpoint selected by Mr. CARTER breaks down completely. We are quite prepared to concede that in theory capital, or principal, must always be assumed to remain intact before profit or interest can even be thought of; but in practice —that is to say, in law—it is recognised, and we think all practical auditors must recognise, that there may be divisible profits where there have been no economic profits; and *per contra* that there may have been an economic profit and increase of capital without there having been any profit legally available for distribution among shareholders.

By deliberately selecting as his basis for determination of profits the computation of the excess of the total value of assets over the total liabilities, Mr. CARTER effectively debars himself from distinguishing in any way between the causes that have affected the aggregate values of assets and liabilities respectively; and he necessarily compels himself to judge in each individual case—often a matter of exceeding difficulty—when the rule that he has laid down as to the valuation of assets is to be regarded as a binding principle, and when it is to be regarded as an exception that may safely be disregarded. We entirely agree that, however profits have been computed in the first instance, it is desirable that a Balance Sheet based upon this computation of profits should subsequently be reconsidered from the point of view of seeing whether the figures it incorporates can be justified, or whether they are not "mere balances of accounts strung together so as to balance when such a so-called profit is brought into account"; but this, it seems to us, is a point that is not likely to be overlooked by any thoughtful practitioner. Our reason for selecting the more unusual point of view was that by that means—and, as it seems to us, by that means alone—can one distinguish between economic profits that are legally capable of distribution and economic profits that are not. Mr. CARTER tells us that, apart from plant, machinery, and goodwill, there are comparatively few exceptions to the general rule that assets should be stated in a Balance Sheet at their market value, and that it would not be difficult to lay down general rules which would cover all possible cases that are generally considered permissible exceptions. We were in hopes that our article of the 4th ult. might have thrown some light upon these permissible exceptions, which, after all, are really the most difficult and the most important part of the whole problem—difficult because *primá facie* it seems astounding that there should be any reason for departing from actual market values, important because a blind adherence to market values may quite as easily result in a belittlement of divisible profits as in their exaggeration. To mention only one point, Mr. CARTER suggests that, apart from plant, machinery, and goodwill, exceptions to his general rule would be comparatively few and unimportant ; but surely land is one of the most obvious and one of the most usual ? If land be added to his list, it for all practical purposes comes back to what we described in our article of the 4th ult. as " capital expenditure."

Shortly stated our article was, in effect, a plea for the more general recognition of the basis and the principles involved in the double-account system. Mr. CARTER, on the other hand, prefers apparently to rely upon the single-account system, but admits that there must be exceptions to its strict application, although for what reason he does not very clearly explain. It is undoubtedly most satisfactory to find that so able an authority as Mr. CARTER, investigating the problem from an entirely different point of view, arrives at very similar conclusions to our own ; but we cannot help thinking, much as we appreciate his contribution to the discussion, that it is chiefly valuable as confirming these conclusions. From the point of view of a useful and practical guide to the average practitioner, the real solution lies, we think, in the direction of intelligently applying the principles of the double-account system, and subsequently reviewing the application of these principles with the view to making sure that the Balance Sheet thereby evolved is not mere nonsense, but rather capable of justification as a statement of items rightly held in suspense because their ultimate solution may properly be regarded as belonging to a subsequent financial period.

ANON

Balance Sheet Values.
(To the Editor of The Accountant.)

SIR,—The limited liability principle is no longer new. Since 1862 some hundred thousand companies have been registered, of which many thousands still survive to publish Balance Sheets. There are 1,216 practising Chartered Accountants in London alone, mostly engaged in certifying year by year that Balance Sheets are "true and correct." Nevertheless, an accountant of eminence says in your last issue that "we ar "without any guiding principle to help us in deciding "what is a true and correct Balance Sheet." Were this so, a discreet silence would best become the profession. Happily it is not so. Neither are Mr. Carter's two propositions likely to be accepted without demur. In fact, I respectfully submit that the first proposition is unsound, and the second, far from luminous.

Surely the root-principle, which should guide the auditor, existed long before the creation of limited companies, and is to be found in any well-kept Trust Accounts, in which gain or loss of capital is always most carefully distinguished from ordinary income or expenditure, and is added to or deducted from Capital Account. Trustees cannot ordinarily make income payments out of capital, but the loss of part of the capital does not compel the trustees to starve the beneficiary out of existence while the loss is made good out of income. No more does the loss of part of the capital compel the directors to starve the shareholders. In short, if all charges proper to be charged against profits, including a reasonable allowance for wear and tear, are charged, the balance is clear profit available for dividend. Capital losses are a thing apart, requiring exceptional treatment, simply because the share capital of a company is a fixed figure. If exceptional losses of a distinctly capital nature have been made, is it not simply a matter of prudence, not of law, how far they should be made good out of profits by building up a reserve before dividing the profits.

If, on the other hand, through a windfall, there be an accretion to capital, sound accountancy would carry that accretion to a Reserve Fund, though sound law might, in the case of a company, permit of its being divided as a dividend.

As regards Balance Sheet values, is the question so difficult and elusive as Mr. Carter modestly thinks it to be?

Balance Sheet values may be classed as fixed, floating, and nominal assets. The distinction is so well known that one need not enlarge upon it. All are equally essential, directly or indirectly, or should be, to the main object of the company, which, though it may not be stated quite so bluntly in the memorandum of association, is to make money. Floating assets are the subject of annual valuation which an auditor can usually test, even if only roughly.

The auditor will mentally classify the fixed assets roughly as follows :—

(1) Directly remunerative and realisable.
(2) Not directly remunerative, but realisable.
(3)   "   "   " unrealisable.

He will also consider which are subject to depreciation by reason of wear and tear ; how far they are liable to supersession through obsolescence ; or are what is known as "wasting" assets. He must see that depreciation by reason of wear and tear is duly provided for out of profits, or, if need be, report the omission to the shareholders, and if necessary he will use his powers of persuasion to convince the directors that as a question of sound accountancy and finance, though not necessarily of law, reserves should be made in respect of the other assets, according to the category into which they fall. If it is clear that the Balance Sheet fixed or nominal values are over-stated, that is a matter for judicious comment in the auditor's report but it does not necessarily affect the question of divisible profits, since the decreased values may be due to capital losses, which can only be dealt with by a reduction of capital.

Is there any reason why the accounts of a limited company should not be prepared as prudently as those of a private trader, always bearing in mind that just as traders do write capital losses off Capital Account, so a company may reduce its capital (albeit by a somewhat cumbrous process), or may even carry the capital losses to a Suspense Account. As a matter of fact, the ordinary provisions for a surrender of shares would meet the whole difficulty in most cases, and may have been originally devised for that purpose, but unfortunately they have been rendered nugatory, owing to the atmosphere of obscurity which usually envelops matters of account when brought into the Law Courts.

I submit, Sir, that the "guiding principle" of the great body of accountants is a thorough knowledge of bookkeeping and accounts, particularly of the distinction between capital and revenue, which, combined with a serious purpose and a clear head, has furnished us with many a "guiding *principal*," of whom not the least is Mr. Carter.

Yours faithfully,

6th January 1910.   ANON.

EDITORIAL

Balance Sheet Values.

A S we understand our correspondent "Anon," whose letter under the above heading we reproduced last week, his contention is that the question of Balance Sheet values, which Mr. CARTER, in agreement with ourselves, has described as a difficult and an elusive one, is really perfectly straightforward to the man who has thoroughly mastered the principles of book-keeping and accountancy. Inasmuch as it is an accountancy question, this is, of course, in one sense a mere truism, but in another sense it is an assertion which furnishes, perhaps, the most complete justification we could have for the space that we have thought it worth while to devote to the matter.

It seems to us, with all respect to our correspondent—who, although he prefers to remain anonymous, is doubtless an able accountant—that he does not really appreciate the full significance of the issues at stake, or realise how very little he has contributed towards their solution.

His view apparently is, that there is not the least difference between the distinction between capital and income in connection with the accounts of a trust, and capital and revenue in connection with the accounts of an ordinary business concern. The assertion is easily made, but not nearly so easily proved. There are, it is true, a certain number of decisions, doubtless well-known to all qualified accountants, the effect of which is to declare that in certain stated circumstances certain losses need not be charged against revenue before dividing profits, but these decisions can hardly be said to enunciate any general principle. In so far as any questions of principle have been decided in the matter, it seems to us that they are rather :—

(1) That the capital of a company cannot be divided as profit.

(2) That the Court will not ordinarily interfere with the decision come to by a company as to the allocation of its profits.

(3) That all kinds of profits are not divisible profits.

(4) That there is nothing whatever to prevent a company from applying the whole of its divisible profits towards the reinstatement of capital.

These principles are, doubtless, as interesting as they are important, but they afford singularly little practical assistance to the auditor in endeavouring to arrive at a fair conclusion as to whether a Balance Sheet submitted for his approval is properly drawn up so as to exhibit a true and correct view of the state of the company's affairs. It seems to us, moreover, that our correspondent reads a good deal more into these decisions than is really there. The analogy between business accounts and trust accounts is doubtless both interesting and instructive up to a point, but it can, we think, easily be carried too far—first, because there is no definite legal authority for declaring that the two kinds of accounts must invariably rest upon the same basis ; secondly, because the best business practice is undoubtedly opposed to the somewhat archaic rule adopted in trust accounts (which is reasonably practicable only in those cases by reason of the great care with which all capital has been invested) ; and, thirdly, because if it were the real intention of the Legislature that the trust account analogy should be followed without the least qualification, the all-important account for the auditor to examine and report upon would undoubtedly be the Revenue Account rather than the Balance Sheet, yet it is the Balance Sheet that is especially referred to in the Companies Acts.

If our correspondent's dictum is to be accepted in its entirety it would seem to follow that the published accounts of a company might quite properly ignore all conceivable kinds of losses on Capital Account without there being any necessity for the auditors to report specially with regard to the facts; for his suggestion, as to the opening of a Suspense Account to deal with capital losses, is evidently intended to be optional. It is, however, exceedingly difficult to reconcile this view with the wording of Section 113 (2) of the Companies (Consolidation) Act, 1908, for it cannot, by any stretch of imagination, be said that a Balance Sheet, which entirely ignores variations of capital value, has been drawn up so as to exhibit a true and correct view of the company's affairs.

But even supposing, in spite of all the manifest difficulties in the way, we accept our correspondent's dictum, that all that is really necessary is to see that the Revenue Account is a correct record of the working results, including due provision for depreciation ; even then we are as far off as ever from arriving at any practical hints as to the course to be pursued, for we are entirely without a clue

as to the proper method of assessing depreciation, save that our correspondent appears to suggest that only depreciation by way of wear and tear is a revenue charge, and that depreciation by obsolescence is a capital charge. It is, we think, fairly obvious that our correspondent cannot really mean what he undoubtedly suggests under this heading, for the depreciation (say) of leases is clearly depreciation by obsolescence rather than by wear and tear. What he probably intended to suggest was, that a sudden loss arising through unforeseen obsolescence need not necessarily be treated as a revenue charge. There is, doubtless, in many cases a good deal to be said in favour of this proposition; but it is one that must, in practice, be accepted with very considerable reservations, for, as applied to plant and machinery, it would certainly not be overstating the case to say that a large number of these assets become obsolete before they are worn out, and that therefore the obsolescence cannot be regarded as unforeseen. If our correspondent desires us to accept his assertion that foreseen losses by way of obsolescence need not be charged against revenue before arriving at divisible profits, he must expect to be called upon to produce his arguments before the statement can be accepted unconditionally.

But, leaving on one side for the moment the vexed question of obsolescence (as we have already left upon one side the question of capital losses), we may ask, What sort of practical advice is it to the auditor to tell him that he must see that due provision has been made for depreciation by wear and tear, when no suggestion whatever is made as to how he is to compute whether the provision for

depreciation is adequate, inadequate, or
excessive? In the article which appeared in
these columns on the 1st inst. we endeavoured
to initiate a principle on this point which we
thought could be abundantly justified in
practice, although it would really result in
Balance Sheet values coinciding with realisable values. And we even went further, and
stated that, in our opinion, values so arrived at
were preferable to realisable values for Balance
Sheet purposes from every point of view, and
that a Balance Sheet so framed could honestly
be said to exhibit a true and correct view of
the state of a company's affairs as a going
concern; but, so far as we can see, our correspondent has suggested no criteria to enable
the auditor to distinguish between capital
values that are true or false, sound or unsound.
The sort of Balance Sheet that he advocates
might, it seems to us, very well be a mere list
of balances of accounts strung together so as to
balance—the sort of Balance Sheet which Mr.
ERIC M. CARTER has, we think, very properly
described as " mere nonsense "—and that, even
although the provision made for depreciation
against the current year's profits was unexcep-
tionable. The whole problem, we think, calls
for more careful and more clear-headed investigation than our correspondent has apparently
deemed necessary; and it is probably because
it is so often dealt with in a slipshod way
that audited Balance Sheets fail to command
that respect from the business community which
they ought at all times to be entitled to.
Another reason for the unsatisfactory nature of
many Balance Sheets is the prevalence of
Secret Reserves, which undoubtedly has a very
important bearing on the matter.

attach any other meaning to "profit" the expression becomes meaningless. There can be no such thing as profit while capital is being lost. If profit is made, it must be over and above the original capital, which must remain intact. This is the underlying principle which is the foundation of all Balance Sheets and Trading Accounts.

In practice, however, we find it is impossible always to adhere to this principle, not only because of the difficulty of computation, but also because of the inconvenience which would arise, but we do try to adhere to it as nearly as practicable.

During the last fifty years thousands of accountants have concentrated their thoughts more or less unconsciously on the question of how nearly it is practicable to conform to the principle I have enunciated in the accounts of joint-stock companies. Their work has been watched by hundreds of thousands of investors, and the Law Courts have made suggestions now and again, with the result that at the present time a definite understanding has been arrived at in some directions but not in others.

The investing public are our employers in this work, and we accountants have to meet their requirements as far as practicable. Now, what an investor wants to see in a Balance Sheet is not only what profit has been made, but also whether his original invested capital remains intact, and accountants try to meet this want as nearly as possible. This object can only be carried out by accepting the fundamental conception that profit is increase of capital; accountants and the public thus being united in an attempt to arrive at what is theoretically correct. The difficulties that lie in our path can only be appreciated by experts.

Our first difficulty is to know how to measure capital with its increases and decreases. In discussing this difficulty, we must see clearly how capital, such as we take it to be, is represented on a joint-stock company's Balance Sheet. For our purpose, the capital of a joint-stock company must be not only the paid-up capital, but also the accumulated reserves and the balance of Profit and Loss Account, since profit, according to definition, is increase of capital. Capital may therefore be stated to be the excess of the value of assets over liabilities. So that, to measure capital, we must measure the values of assets and liabilities.

The values of assets and liabilities cannot be measured until we can agree on a basis of value. The *market value* of an asset is a thing we can understand.

E. M. CARTER

Balance Sheet Values.
(To the Editor of The Accountant.)

Sir,—The fact that you appreciate the great importance of the question of Balance Sheet Values encourages me to hope that you will not think another long letter from me out of place, even though I repeat myself to some extent.

The confusion of ideas shown in the letter from an anonymous correspondent in your issue of the 15th inst. is, as you say, a usual one. He asserts that "a thorough knowledge of bookkeeping and accounts" is a "guiding principle." Bookkeeping and accounts are, of course, mere methods of recording and modes of expression, nothing more. One might just as reasonably say that a thorough knowledge of the English language is a "guiding principle." As long as accountants are content with this confused and superficial way of looking at things, so long will they fail to realise the existence of underlying principles, and they will continue to muddle along and dogmatise.

Yet all the time there is an underlying principle so simple and obvious that it is a marvel to me that it has never been recognised before. This principle I will now attempt to state more clearly than I did in my previous letter.

Theoretically, the fundamental idea of *Profit* is *increase of capital* and *Loss* is *decrease of capital*. If we attempt to

When an asset is first acquired by an undertaking its cost price can fairly be taken to be its market value at the date it is acquired, and when an asset is eventually sold, what it sells for is its then market value. So in valuing the assets of a company we start with their cost price and aim at bringing their values to what they will eventually realise ; thus we have a definite object in view which harmonises with theory and which meets the wishes of our investor, because he finds that, when the time for realising assets arrives, his capital remains intact, which is his main desire. Practice varies to some extent as to how this is done, and as to how far a general Reserve Fund in a limited company's Balance Sheet may be looked on as providing for the diminishing values of wasting assets. Some people may object to the market value basis, they assert that an asset has an *intrinsic* value to a company apart from its market value, but to apply this argument only leads to confusion.

There is, however, one very important exception to taking the realisable value as a basis for valuing assets. Everyone agrees that goodwill is far too fluctuating and uncertain an asset for any notice to be taken of changes in its value. The usual attitude towards it is a wish to get rid of it altogether from a Balance Sheet, and its realisable value is ignored. To treat goodwill as if it were an ordinary asset would be most inconvenient, shareholders form their own opinions of its value, and the market prices of shares depend on those opinions.

There are well-recognised rules which custom has established for valuing most assets on the basis of what they will ultimately realise, though it would take up too much of your valuable space to state them here. There are differences of opinion in regard to certain other assets, especially those more or less analogous to goodwill, such as licences and other rights and powers, and material assets which have in them an element of goodwill. The number of these moot points, however, is getting less.

The conclusion I arrive at from the foregoing considerations is that profit must be increase of capital and nothing else, and that the value of capital is mainly based on the realisable values of assets. At the same time there are certain more or less recognised exceptions to this principle which are adopted in joint-stock companies' Balance Sheets merely for the sake of convenience. Perhaps in the not distant future a common understanding may be arrived at in regard to these exceptions, but this can never be the case unless some underlying principles can be agreed on, such as I have attempted to explain.

It must not be supposed, however, that a Balance Sheet can ever be correct in a mathematical sense. Its values are a good deal dependent on forecasts of the uncertain future, and the labour and difficulty of bringing together the mass of details which make up the values are so great that at best a Balance Sheet can only be an estimate and an approximation worked out on defined lines. At present the lines are not sufficiently defined, each man being too much a law unto himself.

Yours truly,

ERIC M. CARTER.

Birmingham, 17th January 1910.

13

I. FISHER

Over-Capitalization Deceitful.

There seem to be two opposite notions abroad as to the over-capitalization of railroads. One is that it does not matter what the capitalization is—that it·is " merely a matter of bookkeeping "; the other is that over-capitalization is responsible for all abuses of railway administration, including the regulation of freight charges.

To my mind, both of these views are in error. It is true that the capitalization of a railroad company, or of any other company, is " merely a matter of bookkeeping "; but honesty requires that bookkeeping should record fact and not fiction. There can be no object in a false capitalization except the object behind any false statement, namely, deceit. Of course, if everyone knows that a railroad is over-capitalized, and knows in what particulars the assets and liabilities are stretched in order to admit of such bookkeeping, no harm is done, for there is no deceit. But it seldom happens that such knowledge exists. The books of a company are *prima facie* evidence of the condition of the company. If the capitalization is swollen, there must be an equal exaggeration of the other side of the capital account—the assets side. The railroad, or its rolling stock, or its franchises, or some other of its assets, must be entered at a value above the true value. This gives an exaggerated appearance of strength, and is calculated to beguile the unwary investor into buying the bonds of the railroad, by causing him to believe that the security on which they are based is more valuable than it actually is. The case is parallel to that of an individual who wishes to mortgage his house for $100,000 when its actual value is $50,000. He may succeed if he can mislead some lender into believing that his property is worth $200,000.

But while over-capitalization may deceive investors and the public and create for a time false selling prices on both bonds and stocks, it would be absurd to attribute to this cause all the evils connected with the present railway management. These evils are far broader and deeper than juggling with accounts. A reduction of capitalization to a true statement would not necessarily affect freight and passenger rates at all. It is one of the most mischievous and yet persistent fallacies, that the value of a property determines the prices which can be charged for the use of it. The precise opposite is the truth—the value of a property is determined by the price that can be charged for the use of it. It is not because an orchard is valuable that it yields apples. On the contrary, it is because it yields apples that it is valuable. It is not because a railway is valued at one figure or another that it charges high or low rates and makes large or small earnings. On the contrary, it is the estimated earning power of the railroad which determines the value of the road.

The revaluation of railroad property would be of much utility if it would reveal the facts exactly as they are. We cannot have too many facts, or record them too accurately. Every compilation of statistics on railroads will help to solve the railroad problem, by supplying the data on which any sane judgment must be based. If uniformity of accounts could be secured for railroads, as at present for national banks and insurance companies, a great step in advance would be taken. The ordinary man could then tell at a glance the approximate status of any company. The capital should be entered ordinarily on the basis of the original actual investment, and any accretions (not due to new investments, but due to appreciation of railroad property from whatever cause) should be entered as surplus or undivided profits. The capital accounts of such a company, taken at different points of time, would exhibit a true history of the value of its property. The sum of the capital and the surplus would then roughly represent the capitalization of earning power belonging to the stockholders, although conservative bookkeeping would ordinarily place this somewhat below the total market value of the shares.

Those who discuss a revaluation of our railroads should not forget that an important step has already been made in this direction in Bulletin 21 of the Department of Commerce and Labor, entitled "Commercial Valuation of Railway Operating Property in the United States, 1904." It contains the most elaborate and painstaking compilation of railway valuations ever attempted. These valuations are based entirely on market values. It was found impracticable to appraise railway properties on the basis of their valuation by state officials for purposes of taxation or other purposes. It would probably be found impracticable likewise to assess the value of railway property on the basis of its cost of replacement. Such a revaluation could never include the real estate. It would seem that the best which could be expected of a new federal census of railway property would be to trace the history of the value of that property, including in that history a complete statement of the original cash invested by stockholders. If the results of this history could be put in a simple summarized form, contrasting the original investment with the subsequent commercial valuations from time to time, and if in addition the accounting could by law be made hereafter uniform, we should then be in a position of vantage with reference to the railroad problem which has never yet been attained. We should not have solved it, but we should be in possession of exact facts, the knowledge of which would help solve it.

J. BAUER   14

Depreciation and Wasting Assets and Their Treatment in Assessing Annual Profit and Loss. By P. D. LEAKE. (London: Henry Good and Son. 1912. Pp. xi, 195. 10s. 6d.)

The author is a well-known English accountant. He has written extensively on accounting subjects, especially on depreciation, and his writings have been marked by common sense and clearness of expression. The same characterization should be made of the present volume. It presents a discriminating and clear discussion of a technical and rather slippery subject. It should be read not only by accountants but especially by managers of large business.

The book consists of twelve chapters. In chapters 1 to 4 the author explains the nature of depreciation and to what kind of assets it applies; in 5 and 6 the methods by which annual depreciation may be determined; and in chapter 7 he makes a special application to the industrial plant and shows how detailed records of depreciation may be kept. Through chapters 8 and 9 he shows how depreciation applies to special kinds of assets: natural raw materials (coal and ore deposits) and recurring crops; purchased terminal annuities; purchased terminal concessions, leaseholds, copyrights, patent rights, good-will and trade-marks. The last chapter applies especially to England, urging that depreciation should be allowed before the income tax is levied upon annual business profits. Finally, there is an appendix with depreciation tables.

The author holds that "capital outlay on wasting assets consists merely of payments made in advance on revenue account" (p. 19), *i.e.*, capital is prepaid expense. To correspond with this view, he considers depreciation "expired capital outlay" (p. 12), the part of original prepaid expense that has been used up. He holds to the straight-line method of calculating depreciation, *i.e.*, applying a fixed annual rate to the original cost value of the assets. This he compares especially with the method of applying a fixed annual rate to the balance of cost value. He prefers the straight-line method because it approximates more closely to the facts of production (*i.e.*, he believes that the plant produces very nearly in equal annual instalments), and because it is simplest in application and most easily understood by managers.

For many concerns the author's method is as good as any, or better. Simplicity for managers is a strong argument! On the point of theory, however, there is little real support for the method; but there is not space to argue the matter. As for ease of application, why should it be harder to apply a given rate to the *balance* than to the *original cost* of an asset value? Moreover, the original-cost basis probably requires more individual calculations and entries for the detailed plant records than does the balance-of-cost basis.

Like most accountants the author holds to a pretty rigid cost theory of value. Thus, he argues, the book values of wasting assets should not be marked up whatever the market price; likewise the amount of annual depreciation should not be affected by any fluctuations in the market value of the assets in question (p. 11). Is not this rather an extreme position? Besides keeping track of cost elements, should not the accounts also show the real standing and real changes in the business? Cost values and real values are certainly not the same thing. Moreover, unless changes in market prices are regarded, not enough or too much depreciation may be allowed. Thus, suppose a given machine cost $1100, with expected life ten years, and scrap value $100: then, according to the author, depreciation of $100 a year must be allowed to replace the machine in ten years. But suppose in five years the market price of such machines has advanced to $1500. Then, obviously, the $100 allowance will not be enough to replace the machine and the real capital of the business will suffer encroachment. Of course, temporary price fluctuations cannot very well be recorded. But, to disregard changes that appear reasonably permanent is not to tell the whole truth about the business.

On matters of accounting theory, the author's contentions on many points may well be disputed. But his plea for systematic provision for depreciation in plant is strongly presented—and his principal object in the book is just that plea.

JOHN BAUER.

Cornell University.

15

W. A. PATON & R. STEVENSON

APPRECIATION AND DEPRECIATION

As was stated in Chapter II property values may either increase or decrease. A property item may receive an increase in value because of physical additions or because of an advance in the level of prices. *Appreciation* is the term applied to the second type of value increase; whenever the value of an asset increases, without the addition of new units, it is said to have appreciated. Decreases in property value are of three kinds: (1) A property item may decrease in value because of the withdrawal of specific units; (2) A property may decrease in value because of a fall in the level of prices; (3) properties may decrease in value because of physical decay in business operation and expirations due to the passage of time. (1) and (3) are similar, but the withdrawals in the latter case are such that they cannot be conveniently measured. *Depreciation* is the term applied to the second and third types of value expirations.

The question arises: to what extent should these value changes be shown by the accounts? According to the view already developed, the accounts, if they are to be scientifically accurate, should record *all* these changes, and immediately. That is, the accounts should be as sensitive as possible to all price and value changes.

72

However, it is not possible in all cases to determine value changes as they occur; and even if this were possible it would not be feasible to record all changes in the accounts. For example, such property items as merchandise, raw materials, etc., which move rapidly through the business process, are subject to current fluctuations in price. It is not expedient to follow all these changes in the accounts. It is considered good practice to leave such commodities on the books at cost, unless there is a significant change in price. This rule is sometimes given: use cost prices unless market prices are lower, in which case use market prices. Such a rule is unreasonable. If it were practically possible all changes in either direction should be registered by the accounts. Since this is not the case, the rational procedure is to use cost prices unless market prices fall or rise considerably or a long interval is involved; in which case use market prices. Assets such as securities are often subject to daily fluctuations. It would not be wise to attempt to follow these changes in the accounts. Often security prices fluctuate because of minor causes, and in such cases their prices do not accurately reflect the value of the enterprises represented. Here as in the case of materials and the like, the reasonable course is to use cost prices unless market prices are widely divergent and for a long period, in which case securities should be valued at the market.[6]

The value changes which affect property items of a permanent character, such as buildings, machinery, etc., are usually *decreases*. Any possible appreciation in such cases is normally more than offset by depreciation. An important exception is land. In general all land properties increase in value with the growth of the community. As far as it can be definitely ascertained this appreciation should appear in the accounts. Both public and private interests wish to know what economic resources are being devoted to a particular end. It is sometimes objected, that if a factory site, for example, appreciates, it does not add anything to the physical efficiency of the site for manufacturing purposes; hence it should not be considered in the accounts. This objection is not valid. If all similar factory sites have risen in value, an advance in the price of the product in question will follow. If only the value of a particular site has increased, due to conditions entirely outside of the industry involved, this fact should be recognized in the accounts in order that the entrepreneur realize the situation, and either make more efficient use of the property or move the enterprise as soon

---

[6] Banking institutions are compelled to recognize current changes in the prices of the securities which they hold as assets.

as feasible to a cheaper site. For it is evident that a piece of land is being devoted to a purpose for which it is too valuable, either from the standpoint of public or private interest. There are practical difficulties in the way of recognizing such appreciation in the accounts. In the first place if land appreciation is countenanced by good practice, unwarranted estimates may be used; as there is no test of purchase and sale, and values are determined from the prices of contiguous property. Further, there is a tendency to credit these increases to current revenue in lean years, which is illegitimate. Increases in land value should not be used in inflate current income, but should be credited to accumulated surplus; thus:

Land $10,000
    Surplus $10,000

If, however, increases in land value are conservative estimates, and are not used to juggle the current Income sheet, there is no valid reason for keeping such items out of the accounts.

The principles of depreciation accounting will be fully discussed in Chapter VIII.

16

A. G. MOSS

Treatment of Appreciation of Fixed Assets
IN THE ACCOUNTS AND BALANCE-SHEET
AND FOR INCOME-TAX PURPOSES*

At first thought this subject appeared simple enough to be briefly and clearly covered in a single paper. However, upon investigation it was found that the subject is rather broad, has a number of interesting angles and diligent study will lead one into the realm of economics as well as accounting.

We are not here to discuss the propriety of recognizing the appreciation of fixed assets but only its treatment in the book account, the balance-sheet and for income-tax purposes. As a matter of fact the question of whether the appreciation of fixed assets should or should not be recognized is passée. This question has already been answered in the affirmative. It is now considered proper to recognize the appreciation of fixed assets and, under certain conditions, it is absolutely necessary.

The advent of the world war and the resulting appreciation of values (or the decline of the purchasing value of the dollar, if you prefer) to such heights as were not thought of ten years ago, coupled with the high income-tax laws, have brushed aside the old and much respected orthodox accounting rule that fixed assets should not be valued in excess of cost. It is interesting, however, to contrast the old rule with the new, as laid down by those whom we recognize as authorities. Seymour Walton, in the November, 1918, JOURNAL OF ACCOUNTANCY, stated the old rule in the following language:

There is no point in accounting upon which there is more settled opinion than that an unrealized appreciation of fixed assets should not be taken into account. The fact that market increases in the cost of reproduction seem to indicate an increased value of an asset does not make the asset

*A paper read before the Texas chapter of the American Institute of Accountants, June, 1923.

of any greater value to the manufacturing plant, because of the fact that it is a fixed asset, not a current one. The value of a manufacturing plant lies in its productive power, not in its market value. If the plant were to be sold, the profit might be realized, but as long as the plant is to be retained for productive purposes, the profit cannot be realized. In any event it could be realized only by a sale and not by a mere fluctuation. If the appreciation is taken into account, it means that the asset account will be increased and hence a larger amount of depreciation will necessarily be written off in order to reduce the asset to scrap value at the time when it will be discarded.

In the long run, therefore, no advantage will be gained because of the fact that the credit passed to surplus at the time the appreciation is put on the books will be offset by the larger charges to manufacturing cost on account of depreciation, and the consequent reduction in the apparent profits from operations. Hence at the very best, the writing up of a fixed asset is merely an anticipation of operating profits, and at the worst it is an anticipation of profits which may prove to be fictitious ones. There are many cases on record where property has risen in value on the market and been written up, only to decline again and have to be written down. If the credit to surplus of such increases in value is used as a basis of a dividend, there is no better established point in legal accounting than the rule that the directors would be liable for the payment of dividends out of surplus which really resulted in an impairment of the capital.

But at the time the above article was written, Mr. Walton evidently realized that appreciation was a fact and must be dealt with in accounts, because in the concluding paragraph of this article he says:

As a sop to the managers who insist upon placing the appreciated value on the books, some accountants allow the increase to be placed in the asset account but to be offset by a credit to a reserve for unrealized profit on appreciation of fixed assets. This reserve must be rigorously kept out of the surplus. The depreciation reserve can then be built up by the same additions that have heretofore been made, so that when the asset is discarded, the sum of the depreciation reserve and the reserve for unrealized profit on fluctuation of fixed assets will be sufficient to take care of the loss in capital incident to the discarding of the plant.

Robert H. Montgomery, *Auditing, Theory and Practice,* 1921 edition, page 173, states the new rule as follows:

When appraisals are made in which appreciation is included, there is no objection to setting up appraised values in balance-sheets, provided the valuation is qualified by an explanation and provided the excess of the appraisal above book value is credited to special or capital surplus and is not merged in earned surplus.

And again on page 323 Mr. Montgomery says:

Capital assets should be carried at cost values and until some change occurs which justifies a revaluation. In a going business, the ownership or control of which does not change, revaluations may be made at any time provided the changes between original costs and revaluations are clearly shown.

There are many reasons which prompt business men to set up appreciation of fixed assets, some of which are the following:

1. As the basis for stock dividends.

2. For the consolidation of two or more corporations.

3. As a matter of policy in the conservation of funds for replacements at the appreciated values.

As to reason 1, it appears quite logical (at least to those who wish to do so) to make appreciation of fixed assets the basis of a stock dividend. For example: Assume the par value of the capital stock of corporation A to be $1,000,000; its plant has a sound value (that is, reproduction cost less depreciation) of $500,000 in excess of book value; its dividend rate is 15 per cent. per annum, based on the par value of its stock. Stockholder Y owns one-tenth of the outstanding stock and wishes to dispose of it at $150.00 a share, a value clearly indicated by the earning power of the corporation. But, because many investors are opposed to paying more than the par value for stock, he cannot find a ready buyer. The result is that upon application to the secretary of state and submission of proof of the present value of the plant, the corporation is authorized to increase its capital stock to $1,500,000, and thereupon stockholder Y offers his stock for sale at the par value, and it is easily disposed of, because its earning power is 10 per cent. per annum. This procedure is not recommended.

As to reason 2, appreciation of fixed assets frequently results from the revaluation of the assets which are transferred upon consolidation. For example: Corporations B and C are manufacturers. Corporation B's plant was built in 1914 and corporation C's plant was built in 1920. In 1920, corporation D was organized for the purpose of acquiring the properties of corporations B and C. The stockholders of corporations B and C exchange their stock for new stock in corporation D. The sound value of corporation B's plant in 1920 was twice the book value; consequently, in order to equalize the values of the contributions to the new corporation, the plant of corporation B is entered on the books of the new corporation at its sound value. and stock therefor is issued to the former stockholders of corporation B.

As to reason 3, the setting up of appreciation of fixed assets and the consequent increase in the annual depreciation charge permit the accumulation, in part, of the necessary funds for replacements at the appreciated values.

It seems to be apparent that the proper treatment in accounts of appreciation of fixed assets will be a matter to be dealt with by accountants for some years to come. Regardless of our past convictions, we must acknowledge appreciation and find a prominent place in our procedure for its treatment. Like Bolshevism and other social and economic strangers, it is all wrong; but, it is here and cannot be ignored. Such being the case, the question to be answered by accountants is this: How shall it be treated in accounts? In a general way, the answer would appear to be the following: Proper accounting requires that accounts shall reveal the truth and they must continue so to function, even after they have embraced appreciation. Accordingly, appreciation must be properly labeled and should not be permitted to lose its identity.

The specific application of this general principle to particular cases may best be brought out by the use of an example. In order that the length of this paper may be kept within reasonable limits, let us take, for example, a typical manufacturing plant, the raw materials for which are and always will be available, thus excluding the timber, oil and mining industries, which are subject to depletion.

The plant of the X Y Z Company was erected in 1910, at a cost of $300,000.00, exclusive of land, which cost $25,000.00. The estimated life of the plant as a whole is twenty-five years. For the purpose of this example, depreciation is computed from January 1, 1911. With the exception of ordinary repairs and renewals, no replacements were made for the nine-year period ended December 31, 1919. At that time an appraisal was made of the plant showing the replacement value and accrued depreciation as of March 1, 1913, and December 31, 1919, respectively. To simplify the example, actual depreciation, as disclosed by the appraisal, is set down at the same rate per annum as the book rate, namely, four per cent. The valuations, both cost and appraisal, as of the several dates were stated as follows:

As of March 1, 1913

Cost of plant	$300,000.00
Less: depreciation (2 1/6 years @ 4%)	26,000.00
Net book value of plant	$274,000.00
Add: cost of land	25,000.00
Total book value of property	$299,000.00

Reproduction cost of plant $360,000.00
   Less: depreciation (2 1/6 years @ 4%) 31,200.00

Sound value of plant $328,800.00
Add: appraised value of land 25,000.00

Total appraised value of property $353,800.00

As of December 31, 1919

Cost of plant $300,000.00
   Less: depreciation (9 years @ 4%) 108,000.00

Net book value of plant $192,000.00
Add: cost of land 25,000.00

Total book value of property $217,000.00

Reproduction cost of plant $900,000.00
   Less: depreciation (9 years @ 4%) 324,000.00

Sound value of plant $576,000.00
Add: appraised value of land 75,000.00

Total appraised value of property $651,000.00

For fear that the reproduction costs as above set forth may cause some surprise, it should be explained that the March 1, 1913, increase of 20 per cent. is an arbitrary percentage; however, the December 31, 1919, increase of 300 per cent. is in accord with a chart appearing in the *American Appraisal News,* issue of January, 1923, which indicates that a typical manufacturing property arose in value from 100 per cent. in 1914 to 280 per cent. in 1919. The increase of 20 per cent. from 1910 to 1914, plus the subsequent increase of 280 per cent., equals the increase of 300 per cent. used in the example.

The company desires to adjust its books so as to give effect to the appraised values of its property as of March 1, 1913, and December 31, 1919, respectively, the former date being for income-tax purposes. The company also desires to claim a depreciation allowance for 1917 and subsequent years, based on the March 1, 1913, valuation. On the assumption that the bureau of internal revenue has agreed to accept the March 1, 1913, valuation, the entries suggested are shown on page 164.

Similar entries at the end of 1918 and 1919 would also be necessary. The effect of the entry to record depreciation for 1917 is, of course, to decrease the taxable income in the sum of $2,400.00. The setting up of the March 1, 1913, value over cost does not affect invested capital for tax purposes. However, the transfer at the end of each year from "revaluation surplus" to "earned surplus" of the amount of the March 1, 1913, value charged to operations during the year is necessary in order to restore "earned surplus" to the figure at which it would have appeared had the March 1, 1913, increased value not been taken into the accounts at all. This procedure has the effect of permitting taxpayers to eat their cake and have it too. As regards federal taxes, authority for the foregoing procedure may be found in article 844 of regulations 45 and regulations 62.

After giving effect to the foregoing entries and to the subsequent entries for the years 1918 and 1919, the property accounts would show the following as of December 31, 1919:

As of January 1, 1917

DEBIT	Plant value as of March 1, 1913, over cost ..:................	$60,000.00	
CREDIT	Reserve for depreciation of March 1, 1913, plant value increase		$14,400.00
CREDIT	Surplus arising from revaluation of plant as of March 1, 1913..		45,600.00
	To record the excess of the March 1, 1913, plant value over cost and the accrued depreciation thereon from January 1, 1911, to December 31, 1916		

As of December 31, 1917

DEBIT	Depreciation on cost of plant...	$12,000.00	
DEBIT	Depreciation on March 1, 1913, increase ....·....	2,400.00	
CREDIT	Reserve for depreciation on cost of plant		$12,000.00

CREDIT Reserve for depreciation on March 1, 1913, increase		2,400.00
To record depreciation for the year 1917.		
DEBIT Surplus arising from revaluation of plant as of March 1, 1913	2,400.00	
CREDIT Earned surplus		$ 2,400.00
To record appreciation of plant, as of March 1, 1913, realized by depreciation charged to operations for 1917		
Cost of plant	$300,000.00	
Less: depreciation (9 years @ 4%).	108,000.00	
Net book value of plant		$192,000.00
Plant value of 3/1/13, over cost	$ 60,000.00	
Less: depreciation (9 years @ 4%).	21,600.00	
Net 3/1/13 value over cost (which, also, is the surplus arising from revaluation)		$ 38,400.00
Total March 1, 1913, value of plant		$230,400.00
Cost of land (which, also, is the March 1, 1913, value)		25,000.00
Total March 1, 1913, value of property		$255,400.00

It will be seen that the total net value of the property as carried on the books as of December 31, 1919, is $255,400.00, and that the total net appraised value of the property as of that date is $651,000.00. To record this latter valuation, the entries suggested are shown as follows:

DEBIT Land value as of December 31, 1919, over cost	$ 50,000.00	
CREDIT Surplus arising from revaluation of land		$ 50,000.00
To record the excess of the December 31, 1919, value of land over cost.		

DEBIT   Plant value as of December 31, 1919, over March 1, 1913, value $540,000.00

CREDIT Reserve for depreciation of December 31, 1919, plant value increase $194,400.00

CREDIT Surplus arising from revaluation of plant as of December 31, 1919 ....   345,600.00

To record the excess of the December 31, 1919, plant value over the March 1, 1913, value and the accrued depreciation thereon from January 1, 1911, to December 31, 1919.

After giving effect to the foregoing entries the property accounts would show the following as of December 31, 1919:

Cost of plant	$300,000.00	
Less: depreciation (9 years @ 4%)	108,000.00	
Net book value of plant		$192,000.00
Plant value as of March 1, 1913, over cost	$ 60,000.00	
Less: depreciation (9 years @ 4%)	21,600.00	
Net March 1, 1913, value over cost		$ 38,400.00
Plant value as of December 31, 1919, over March 1, 1913, value	$540,000.00	
Less: depreciation (9 years @ 4%)	194,400.00	
Net December 31, 1919, value over March 1, 1913, value		$345,600.00
Total December 31, 1919, value of plant		$576,000.00
Cost of land	$ 25,000.00	
Land value as of December 31, 1919, over cost	50,000.00	
Total December 31, 1919, value of land		75,000.00
Total December 31, 1919, value of property		$651,000.00

Having thus entered the appreciation of fixed assets on the books, the next step is to provide a scheme for the writing off of such appreciation during the remaining life of the plant. Much has been written on this subject during the past four years and the opinions of the writers on this subject differ. Both sides of the question, however, are well worth considering, and the following digests of several articles on this subject are submitted:

John Bauer, in the December, 1919, JOURNAL OF ACCOUNTANCY, page 413, says that charges to operations for depreciation should be based on renewal costs. He further states that all recognized methods for handling depreciation charges result in charging to operating account the original cost of property retired, but that this policy, in view of the present level of prices, is wrong and will not maintain physical capital in the face of rising prices. He further says:

> The purpose of management certainly must be to maintain the physical plant, and to keep up production without drawing upon capital funds. If this be true, then, when the price level has risen, the charge to operations for renewals should not be the original cost of the property retired, but the cost of new property which, in function and capacity, is required to replace the old.
>
> To the extent that the present high prices are permanent, or that prices will not return to the former level, operating costs are everywhere understated by an amount equal to the difference in the amortization of original cost of property retired and the cost of actual renewal. Understatement of operating costs means a corresponding understatement of profits and, except in case of very conservative management, excessive payment of dividends or withdrawal of earnings. The dividend payments then become private income and result in unjustified feeling of personal prosperity, and in excessive private expenditures for luxuries or services which are not justified by actual industrial conditions.

Mr. Bauer thinks the present generation should pay for renewals at the increased cost, based upon the theory that the present generation is using high-value equipment regardless of the original cost of such equipment.

J. Hugh Jackson, in the June, 1920, JOURNAL OF ACCOUNTANCY, page 452, in answer to the question "What is true cost?" says in part:

> The cost of doing work or of producing commodities includes the loss due to the physical and functional depreciation of fixed assets, and this wearing out and this obsolescence are incurred during the life of the equipment. Hence this expense is chargeable against the product turned out during the life of the assets, and not against any product turned out after their life-time. The original cost of the equipment, less any salvage value, is the depreciation expense chargeable to the total output of a plant during its economic life. The fact that the plant cannot be replaced at the same cost, but only at much more, has nothing to do with the cost of its product but only with the cost of future product turned out by the

subsequent plant. True cost, therefore, can be obtained only by including as total depreciation the loss based on the original cost of the equipment.

At the same time, Mr. Jackson recognizes that this matter involves business policy as well as accounting, and that while correct accounting demands that depreciation be based on original cost, business policy is not so exacting, and he further says:

On the other hand, the fact that true cost can only be obtained by using a depreciation charge based on the original cost of the plant does not mean that prices must be fixed on the cost figures so found. This would mean that the customer gets the use of low-cost plant in the days of high-cost plant. It is not a question of accounting, but of business policy, whether the manufacturer or the customer is to get this advantage. Most equipment now in use has been purchased when prices were lower than at the present time. True costs are considerably lower than they would be if the depreciation charge to operations were made on the basis of replacing the present physical plant, so, unless a somewhat greater percentage is added to the cost to obtain selling price, the customer will have the benefit of the fact that most equipment was purchased when prices were lower than now. Actual cost, however, is a fact, whatever policy is adopted; cost cannot change so far as the depreciation expense is concerned.

Mr. Jackson believes that in the case of a public utility, the amount it is permitted to charge for services should be based on cost determined by the use of a depreciation charge based on actual cost of plant, and not on renewal cost. In the case of an industrial organization, the principle is the same, but, as the obtaining of additional capital is on a somewhat different basis from that of a public utility with its assured return, it would seem only just that the customer pay enough to compensate the manufacturer for the use of his equipment at whatever the market price may be and without considering at all what the manufacturer may have paid for that equipment.

Ernest S. Rastall, in the February, 1920, JOURNAL OF ACCOUNTANCY, page 123, also thinks that depreciation based on renewal cost of plant would be incorrect accounting. In part, he says:

To set up a replacement reserve or even an enlargement reserve by a debit to surplus and a credit to reserve would be permissible, but it would not be correct procedure to charge it to surplus via the operating route.

When prices are seen to be rising, prudent stockholders will, of course, reserve from earnings enough for replacement needs, but this should not all be charged to operation.

The fabricated production department of the Chamber of Commerce of the United States, in a pamphlet on *Depreciation* issued in October, 1921, maintains that "depreciation for cost purposes is not concerned with resale or replacement values but aims to recover the cost of assets, less any salvage." Also:

> The replacement theory substitutes for something certain and definite, the actual cost, a cost of reproduction which is highly speculative and conjectural and requiring frequent revision. It, moreover, seeks to establish for one expense a basis of computation fundamentally different from that used for the other expenses of doing business. Insurance is charged on a basis of actual premiums paid, not on the basis of probable premiums three years hence; rent on the amount actually paid, not on the problematical rate of the next lease; salaries, light, heat, power, supplies are all charged at actual, not upon a future contingent, cost.

W. A. Paton, in an article on *Depreciation, Appreciation and Productive Capacity,* appearing in the July, 1920, JOURNAL OF ACCOUNTANCY, discusses at length, the propriety of increasing the depreciation charge to provide for high-cost renewals, but it appears rather difficult to understand exactly where Mr. Paton stands on the subject. As to whether or not depreciation should be based on cost or replacement value, Mr. Paton says:

> The solution of the matter lies in the revision of orthodox accounting policies with regard not to depreciation methods but to closing valuations. The values which the accountant uses in closing the books and preparing statements ideally should be based upon economic conditions at the moment of closing. If plant and equipment assets were valued at the close of each period on the basis of costs of replacement—effective current costs— depreciation charges would be increased in a period of rising prices and the other concomitant effects would be registered in the accounts in a rational manner.

To illustrate this procedure, Mr. Paton takes the case of a machine purchased January 1, 1915, for $5,000.00 The machine has a life of five years, and from 1915 to 1920 the replacement cost advances twenty per cent. each year. By revaluing the machine at the end of each year for depreciation purposes, the annual depreciation charge would range from $1,200.00 in 1915 to $3,283.34 in 1919, the total of all charges amounting to $10,000.00, which would be the replacement cost as of January 1, 1920.

Having advanced the foregoing theory, which appears to be original, Mr. Paton then proceeds to muddy the water when he says:

> Revised as has been outlined, so as to provide for concurrent adjustments of assets, expense and proprietorship, the writer believes that there is considerable merit in Mr. Bauer's contention. There is still room for argument, however, that this whole matter is one of no real consequence. The two alternatives discussed above, it may be urged, lead to the same results for the entire period involved; for, if proprietary income be conceived broadly as the net credits to proprietorship outside of investments and withdrawals, then the $5,000 credit to capital as appreciation exactly offsets the additional $5,000 charges to expense; and the effect upon the statement of net earnings throughout the five years is consequently nil.

85

In other words, is it not folly to write assets up, crediting proprietorship for the amount of appreciation, since this will mean merely that a like increase must be charged to depreciation expense during the life of the property? If the entire net income in this broad sense of increased proprietorship were withdrawn from the business the final status of assets and capital would be the same if cost of replacement were charged to expense as if only original cost were so charged.

By way of conclusion, Mr. Paton says in part:

It is not intended here to argue that appreciation of fixed assets should be recognized in the accounts. From the standpoint of management (which is interested in effective current costs and not in costs five years ago) and from the standpoint of the various interests which would like to see the balance-sheet really exhibit what it purports to show, viz., a correct statement of the assets, liabilities and proprietorship of a business on a given date, there is much to be said in favor of such recognition.

In view, on the other hand, of the conjectural character of asset values at best and the consequent importance of conservatism, the difficulties in the way of determining effective replacement costs in the case of complex assets, the constant fluctuation of such costs and the fact that having once made an investment the management is often thereby committed to a policy for a considerable period regardless of the movement of prices, probably most accountants would feel that original cost is the best basis upon which to value fixed assets. A management, for example, cannot scrap a $3,000,000 plant in order to take advantage of the appreciation of a $100,000 site. The site in such circumstances is virtually removed from the market for a period of several years at least.

An elaborate argument can be made on either side of this proposition. It has been the purpose of this paper merely to point out the limitations inherent in accounting as a means of showing comparative economic well-being; to show that cost of replacement cannot be charged to expense except as the conventional method of valuation is abandoned and antecedent charges and credits are made to assets and proprietorship, respectively, so that all elements of the balance-sheet are made to reflect concurrently the changes in prices in so far as they affect the specific situation; and, finally, to indicate that such a revision of valuation policies could be adopted without the distortion of any accounting fact, and, in that it would tend to maintain the physical extent of the plant in any case, would have much to commend it from the standpoint of management.

All the articles mentioned are extremely interesting and no doubt most accountants have read them. However, the digests made of the articles may not be all that their authors intended and for this reason readers are respectfully referred to the entire articles.

Many of us will find ourselves in complete accord with the definition of true cost so admirably expressed by J. Hugh Jackson, namely: "True cost . . . can be obtained only by including as total depreciation the loss based on the original cost of the equipment."

As to whether depreciation on original cost or replacement cost should be used in fixing prices, it is believed most emphatically that depreciation on replacement cost is the proper basis. Depreciation ordinarily constitutes only a small proportion of the entire cost of manufactured products. For example, assume that material, direct labor and burden represent ninety-five per cent. of the cost of a finished article and that depreciation, based on the original cost of plant, represents the remaining five per cent. For the sake of argument, assume that the first three mentioned elements of cost have doubled in price since the plant was built. Is it not splitting hairs, then, to say that the fourth element, which also has doubled in value, but the increased value has not been actually realized by conversion into money, should be included at only half its real value? In other words, why should the manufacturer, in fixing prices, ignore the increased value of the thing he produces due to the element of appreciation of fixed assets, simply because fixed assets do not circulate rapidly, when he is forced to recognize appreciation of the other elements of cost because they are beyond his control? Did you ever hear of a producer of petroleum, lumber or coal refusing to increase prices during an advancing market merely because the oil well, timber tract or coal mine was acquired during a low-cost period? Certainly not. But when the producer of any of the products mentioned advances prices on a rising market he includes unrealized appreciation as an element of cost for price fixing purposes, and no one questions his right to do so. It does seem rather far-fetched, then, to say to such producers that unrealized appreciation of your petroleum, timber or coal is a proper factor to be included in fixing prices, but unrealized appreciation of your plants should not be so included, because you should not burden the present generation with costs that should be borne by future generations, or words to that effect.

As a matter of fact, in actual practice the appreciation of plant is being brought into actual production costs continuously. Manufacturing plants are rarely allowed to depreciate to the extent that they must be replaced in their entirety. Renewals, in part, are constantly being made. The machine which cost $5,000.00 fifteen years ago is replaced today with one costing $10,000.00. Thus, the unrealized appreciation of yesterday becomes the original cost of today.

Furthermore, all of us cannot bring ourselves to believe that in fixing prices the employment of a depreciation charge based on replacement cost would have no effect on the earnings of the manufacturer. It is only human to think that if the depreciation charge should be doubled, the selling price would be increased at least to the extent of the increased depreciation charge and perhaps a slight bit more, and thus an increased inflow of dollars into the treasury of the manufacturer would result. Moreover, if this increased inflow of dollars is treated in the accounts of the manufacturer in a manner that prevents distribution of the additional profits as dividends, so much the better.

Reverting to the foregoing example which shows the property accounts of the X Y Z Company as of December 31, 1919, after giving effect to the appraisal valuation, it is seen that (a) the original cost of the plant was $300,000.00; (b) the increase as of March 1, 1913, was $60,000.00 over cost; the increase as of December 31, 1919, was $540,000.00 over the March 1, 1913, value; and (d) the aggregate of the three mentioned amounts is $900,000.00, which is the replacement value of the plant as of December 31, 1919. The annual depreciation charge, based on the assumed rate of four per cent. per annum, amounts to $36,000.00. To dispose of this amount for the year 1920, the following entries are suggested:

DEBIT	Depreciation on cost of plant.	$ 12,000.00	
DEBIT	Depreciation on March 1, 1913, value	2,400.00	
DEBIT	Surplus arising from revaluation of plant as of December 31, 1919	21,600.00	
CREDIT	Reserve for depreciation on cost of plant		$ 12,000.00
CREDIT	Reserve for depreciation on March 1, 1913, increase		2,400.00
CREDIT	Reserve for depreciation on December 31, 1919, increase To record depreciation for the year 1920.		21,600.00
DEBIT	Surplus arising from revaluation of plant as of March 1, 1913	$ 2,400.00	

CREDIT Earned surplus .... $ 2,400.00
      To record depreciation of
      plant as of March 1, 1913,
      realized by depreciation
      charged to operations for
      1920.

In explanation of the apparently inconsistent disposition of the depreciation charge on the March 1, 1913, increase as compared with the disposition of the depreciation charge on the December 31, 1919, increase, it will be remembered that the depreciation charge on the March 1, 1913, increase is an allowable deduction for income-tax purposes, whereas the depreciation charge on the December 31, 1919, increase is not an allowable deduction. It is deemed advisable to charge the amount to operations to comply with section 212 of the revenue act of 1921, which provides, in substance, that the method of accounting employed by the taxpayer shall clearly reflect the income. If this amount were charged direct to the surplus account, as in the case of the December 31, 1919, item, it could be said that the method of accounting does not clearly reflect income for income-tax purposes.

It might be argued that the foregoing is a violation of the rule cited, namely, that depreciation on appreciated value should not be charged to surplus via the operation route. It is a technical violation of the rule, but not an actual violation, because after first charging operations with the amount in the guise of depreciation, and thus reducing "earned" surplus by the amount of the charge, the procedure calls for the immediate transfer of a like amount from "appreciation" surplus to "earned" surplus. Consequently, the net effect on "earned" surplus is nil.

It will be seen, also, that the suggested treatment of the depreciation on the December 31, 1919, increase does not affect the "earned" surplus, but merely results in the reduction of the "appreciation" surplus with a corresponding increase in the depreciation reserve for the appreciated value. This procedure does not provide one dollar for replacements, but if the owners of the plant have taken the increased depreciation charge into account in fixing prices, and if the profits were thereby increased, good business policy demands that the amount of the increase in profits be transferred to a reserve for replacements and not distributed as dividends.

Attention is again directed to the property accounts of the X Y Z Company as of December 31, 1919. For balance-sheet purposes, let it be assumed that the capital of the company amounts to $325,000.00 (the original cost of the land and plant) and that, with the exception of its property accounts, it has no assets except an amount of current assets equal to the reserve for depreciation on the original cost of the plant. The following statement, then, would appear properly to reflect the accounts:

ASSETS

CURRENT ASSETS			$108,000.00
FIXED ASSETS:			
Land at cost		$ 25,000.00	
Plant at cost	$300,000.00		
Less: reserve for depreciation	108,000.00	192,000.00	
Total net cost of property..		$217,000.00	
Appraised value of land as of December 31, 1919, over cost		$ 50,000.00	
Appraised value of plant as of December 31, 1919, over cost	$600,000.00		
Less: reserve for depreciation	216,000.00	384,000.00	
Total net appraised value of property over cost (per contra)		$434,000.00	
Total book value of property			651,000.00
Total assets			$759,000.00

LIABILITIES

CAPITAL STOCK	$325,000.00	
Surplus arising from revaluation of fixed assets (per contra)	434,000.00	
Total liabilities		$759,000.00

At the end of each year, the net appraised value of the property over cost and the surplus arising from revaluation of fixed assets would be reduced by the amount of the depreciation charge until such time as that part of the appreciation on the plant had been written off entirely. The appreciation of land and the surplus resulting from the writing up would remain constant from year to year, unless values declined or increased and the effect thereof was entered in the accounts.

It is believed that no one should be deceived as to the real contents and meaning of the balance-sheet. However, the date of the appraisal should invariably be shown. The importance of this suggestion can best be illustrated by again referring to the chart appearing in the *American Appraisal News*. As previously stated, this chart indicates that a typical manufacturing property rose in value from 100 per cent. in 1914 to 280 per cent. in 1919. The chart further shows that the value of a typical manufacturing plant declined from 280 per cent. in 1919 to 230 per cent. in 1920 and to 195 per cent. in 1921. On the basis of this chart, therefore, the reproduction cost of the X Y Z Company's plant declined from $900,000.00 at the close of 1919 to $750,000.00 at the close of 1920 and to $645,000.00 at the close of 1921. In such circumstances, the property accounts should be adjusted so as to give effect to the decline in value. Failing in this, the accountant should qualify the balance-sheet in such manner as will clearly bring out the decline in value.

Many plant owners are having appraisals made for insurance purposes, and if such appraisals are kept up to date by necessary revision of values, the matter of adjustment of the book property accounts from year to year will be much simplified.

The matter of issuing stock dividends against surplus arising from appreciation of fixed assets is, as already stated, not recommended. However, it is being done, and some difficult accounting problems are possible as the result. In the case of the X Y Z Company, for example, suppose it decided to increase its capital to $650,000.00, using $325,000.00 of the $434,000.00 "appreciation" surplus as the basis for a stock dividend. It would then be necessary to distinguish between paid in capital and capital created by revaluation of fixed assets. The credit side of the balance-sheet would then read as follows:

Capital stock paid in		$325,000.00
Capital stock issued against appreciated value of fixed assets		325,000.00
Total capital stock outstanding		$650,000.00
Surplus arising from revaluation of fixed assets	$434,000.00	
Less: amount used as the basis for stock issue	325,000.00	109,000.00
Total		$759,000.00

Assuming that the plant values do not require a revision, upward or downward, and that the only changes made therein are the annual depreciation entries, and recalling that the proposed scheme for handling depreciation of appreciated value would result in a decrease in "appreciation" surplus of $24,000.00 a year, the question arises as to what will become of the capital stock issued against the appreciated value of assets, after the aggregate annual charges for depreciation have wiped out the remaining balance of $109,000.00. The answer is not hard to find, for it would appear that the X Y Z Company must set aside sufficient earnings to take the place of the annual reductions of "appreciation" surplus. If this is done, the above classification of capital stock will, in time, need revision; the amount of paid-in capital will be increased and capital stock issued against appreciated value of fixed assets will be correspondingly reduced.

The treatment of appreciation for income-tax purposes is the last and least important of the three divisions of the subject of this paper. Appreciation is a meaningless word in so far as the existing income-tax law is concerned, and before the bureau of internal revenue it has absolutely no standing until realized by a closed transaction. According to regulation 62, "appreciation in value of property is not even an accrual of income to a taxpayer prior to the realization of such appreciation through sale or conversion of the property." Even in the revaluation of property as of March 1, 1913, for depreciation purposes, the resulting appreciation is not recognized for any income-tax purpose until it is charged against operations and then it is said to be "realized." Under the existing revenue act, appreciation cannot be given away for income-tax purposes. Only in the event of death is it possible to pass appreciation to others free of income tax, but even so, it is subject to the estate tax in the case of estates which, in value, exceed the legal exemption.

In view, however, of the rather liberal provisions of the existing revenue act, relative to gain or loss from exchanges of property, it may appear, in certain cases, that owners of property which has appreciated in value are permitted to exchange such property for stock of a corporation and thus benefit from appreciation at the time the corporation begins to compute its depreciation deductions based upon the increased value of the property. However, the legal doctrine that a corporation is an entity, separate from its stockholders, asserts itself, and, therefore, the benefit in the eyes of the law is only apparent and not real.

It is a well known fact that appreciation cannot be included as invested capital for tax purposes. All are familiar with the famous case of *La Belle Iron Works vs. United States*, in which the supreme court established the doctrine that invested capital cannot be based upon an appraisal showing the value of property as of any date subsequent to the date of acquisition. The exception to this rule occurred under the revenue act of 1917, in which appreciation for invested-capital purposes was recognized to a limited extent. In the case of tangible property paid in for stock or shares prior to January 1, 1914, the value for invested-capital purposes was either (a) the actual cash value of such property on January 1, 1914, or (b) the par value of the stock or shares specifically issued therefor, whichever was lower. It is not recalled, however, that many taxpayers ever received any great amount of comfort from this provision of the law.

93

K. MACNEAL

I

THREE FABLES

ACCOUNTING is the language of finance. Members of the accounting profession are interpreters upon whom the vast majority of people must rely for information relating to any business or project with which they are not intimately and personally familiar. If interpreters do not tell the truth, or do not tell the whole truth, or tell truths intermixed with half truths, many people may be deceived to their hurt.

Doubtless few accountants or business men would contend that present accounting principles are perfect, or that all financial statements prepared in accordance therewith state truly and without misrepresentation the facts that they purport to state. But it is to be doubted if many laymen, business men, or even accountants, realize how faulty present accounting principles are and how serious and far reaching are the evils for which they are responsible.

Not so long ago the truthfulness of the financial statements issued by a business was largely a matter that concerned only the owner of the business and its creditors. During the past twenty-five years, however, a great change has taken place in the ownership of business organizations. Almost every business of any magnitude now is incorporated, and it is extremely rare for a large corporation to be owned entirely by individuals active in its management. Such a corporation is very apt to be owned by hundreds, or

94

thousands, or even hundreds of thousands of small stockholders who know nothing at all about its affairs except the information contained in the financial statements issued periodically by its management.

In the quite recent past the owner of a business could not be deceived by an untruthful balance sheet or profit and loss statement pertaining to his own business because he ran the business himself and was familiar with every phase of it at first hand. But now an untruthful balance sheet or profit and loss statement may give stockholders a false impression which they have no means of correcting. If published financial statements overstate the assets or earnings of a business, hundreds of investors may be led into paying too much for its stock, or may be led into buying the stock of a company which is on the road to bankruptcy while under the impression that the company is really prosperous. On the other hand, if published financial statements understate the assets or earnings of a business, hundreds of disappointed stockholders may be led to sacrifice their holdings for only a portion of what such holdings are worth. Hence it can be seen that the truthfulness of financial statements has become an extremely important matter, not only to managements, creditors, and stockholders, but to the general investing public as well.

The following fables illustrate, in a very simple and purposely exaggerated fashion, a few of the situations that present accounting principles repeatedly cause to arise.

THE FABLE OF THE TWO FACTORIES. Once upon a time there were two little factories. These little factories were alike in all respects. Their design, condition, and equipment were identical. Both factories had just been built by a local builder and each was quite obviously worth the same amount, but only the builder knew exactly what it had cost to build them.

In this same locality lived a capable business man named John and a stupid business man named William. The builder of the two factories went to John and, by reason of skillful argument, succeeded in selling him one factory for $5,000. A few days later this builder went to William and, by reason of William's stupidity, succeeded in selling him the one remaining factory for $20,000.

John then formed a corporation so that he could sell stock to raise money for operating his factory. He sold his factory to this corporation for the same price that he had paid for it, namely, $5,000, and accepted stock to a par value of $5,000 in payment therefor. John then called in a reputable accountant and asked him to prepare a certified balance sheet for publication. The accountant found that John's company had bought a factory for $5,000, and prepared a certified balance sheet showing the factory to be worth $5,000. William, copying John, also formed a corporation so that he could sell stock to raise money for operating his factory. He sold his factory to this corporation for the same price that he had paid for it, namely, $20,000, and accepted stock to a par value of $20,000 in payment therefor. William also called in the reputable accountant and asked him to prepare a certified balance sheet for publication. The accountant found that William's company had bought a factory for $20,000, and prepared a certified balance sheet showing the factory to be worth $20,000.

Both John's company and William's company then sold

additional stock on the basis of their respective balance sheets. A banker put $5,000 cash into John's company in return for stock to a par value of $5,000. The banker thus acquired a one-half interest in John's company in return for his $5,000. A farmer invested his cash savings of $5,000 in William's company in return for stock to a par value of $5,000. The farmer thus acquired a one-fifth interest in William's company in return for his $5,000.

Now almost everybody in town, except the farmer, knew that John's factory and William's factory were identical and were worth the same amount, so it was not long before William found himself arrested on a charge of defrauding the farmer. William defended himself by putting the sole responsibility for the balance sheet upon the accountant, whereupon the accountant was arrested and put on trial.

The accountant defended himself by confessing that he did not know the value either of John's factory or of William's factory. He did not know what these factories could be sold for, nor indeed, if they could be sold at all. He did not know what it would cost to build and equip them. In the absence of any inkling as to what they could be sold for, or what they could be built for, he had used the original cost price to John's company as the value of its factory, and had used the original cost price to William's company as the value of its factory. He claimed that this was the best he could do and, while admitting that the difference between the values of the two factories was absurd, he maintained, nevertheless, that the makeshift of adopting original cost price as value was the only makeshift at hand. He spoke of these original cost prices as constituting "going concern values" and challenged the jurors to say what they would have done if they had been in his place.

When the jury retired to consider its verdict, it disagreed. Certain jurors thought that the accountant should have made numerous inquiries as to what the factories could be sold for, and should have adopted one of the resulting bids as the value of each factory. Some jurors thought that the accountant should have had a builder estimate what it would cost to build each factory, and should have used this amount as its value. Still others felt that the accountant did right in adopting the value of $5,000 for John's factory, and the value of $20,000 for William's factory because, they reasoned, no one could know what the factories could be sold for, and an accountant could hardly be expected to know what a factory could be built for. At the end of three days the jury was still in disagreement and the accountant was released.

But the farmer, nevertheless, because of his reliance on the accountant's balance sheet, received for his $5,000 only a one-fifth interest in the assets and earnings of William's company, whereas the banker, in reliance on the same accountant's balance sheet, had, for the same sum, received a one-half interest in John's company. Yet William's company had at no time been worth one penny more than John's company although the reputable accountant had certified one as having assets worth $20,000 and the other as having assets worth $5,000.

The accountant was anxious to do right but he himself did not know what to do. Therefore, although he was careful to keep away from twin factories in the future and was never arrested again, he continued to prepare balance sheets in the same manner that he prepared John's and William's. And reputable accountants still do the same down to this day.

THE FABLE OF THE TWO FLOUR MILLS. Once upon a time there were two corporations, each of which had just been formed. Each corporation had $150,000 cash in its treasury, had no other assets and had no liabilities. Thus the net worth of each corporation was exactly $150,000. All of the capital stock of one corporation was owned by a very competent business man named Henry. All of the capital stock of the other corporation was owned by a very incompetent business man named Bill.

Each corporation started operations on January 1 by leasing a small flour mill for an annual rental of $1,000, and each immediately paid one year's rent in advance in cash. Thus, at this point, each company had $149,000 cash remaining in its treasury.

On January 1, wheat was selling at $1.00 a bushel. Henry, who had studied the wheat market closely, decided that this was as low as wheat would be apt to go. Accordingly he invested $100,000 of his corporation's cash in wheat. Flour was then correspondingly cheap so he decided to hold the wheat until he could get a higher price for flour, after which he would convert the wheat into flour and sell it.

Bill, on the other hand, knew little about the flour business or about the wheat market. Accordingly he did not buy wheat in January when it was low but waited for it to go still lower. Meanwhile he put $100,000 of his corporation's cash out at 6% interest. Shortly thereafter wheat began to go up in price, but Bill left his money out at interest and waited for wheat to come down again. Finally a year passed and on December 31 wheat, which had risen steadily, sold at $2.00 a bushel. Then Bill became fearful that it would go still higher so he called in his money, amounting to $100,000 plus $6,000 interest, and put $100,000 into wheat at $2.00 a bushel. Of course Bill could only buy one-half as much wheat as Henry had bought because he paid twice as much per bushel for it.

Thus, on December 31, Henry and Bill each had $100,000 invested in wheat, but Henry had an unrealized profit of 100% on his $100,000, whereas Bill had earned only 6% interest on his $100,000.

At this point both Henry and Bill decided to sell one-half of their capital stock to the public. Henry employed the most reputable accountant in the town and asked him to prepare a certified balance sheet and profit and loss statement. The accountant prepared a balance sheet showing the remainder of Henry's original cash, namely, $49,000, and showing Henry's wheat at its original cost price of $1.00 per bushel, namely, $100,000. Thus Henry's balance sheet showed that his company now had assets valued at $149,000. The accountant also prepared a profit and loss statement showing that Henry's company had incurred, during the year, a net loss of $1,000 representing the rent which it had paid for its mill.

Then Bill employed the same accountant and asked him to prepare a certified balance sheet and profit and loss statement. The accountant prepared a balance sheet showing the remainder of Bill's original cash, namely, $49,000, and showing his wheat at its original cost price of $2.00 per bushel, namely, $100,000. In addition the accountant showed that Bill had $6,000 cash for the interest his money had earned during the year. Thus Bill's balance sheet showed that his company now had assets valued at $155,000. The accountant also prepared a profit and loss statement showing that Bill's company had, during the year, earned a net profit of $5,000 consisting of $6,000 interest less $1,000 rent.

Both Henry and Bill now mailed their certified financial statements to a wealthy farmer in a neighboring town. Henry offered to sell one-half of his $150,000 capital stock for $75,000 and Bill offered to sell one-half of his $150,000 capital stock for $75,000. The farmer knew very little about financial statements so he went to his bank for advice. The banker pointed out that a comparison of the net worths shown on the two balance sheets revealed that Bill's business was worth $6,000 more than Henry's business. The banker also pointed out that Bill's profit and loss statement disclosed that he had earned $5,000 during the year, whereas Henry's profit and loss statement disclosed that he had lost $1,000 during the year. The banker said that this indicated that Bill was a more capable business man than Henry. Accordingly the banker advised the farmer to purchase Bill's stock rather than Henry's stock. So the farmer bought Bill's stock and never ceased to regret it.

Of course the farmer and his banker were deceived because Henry's business was really worth $249,000 whereas Bill's business was worth only $155,000. Henry must therefore really have earned $99,000 during the year whereas Bill had earned only $5,000 during the year.

Henry converted his wheat into flour during January and sold it for $100,000 profit. Bill converted his wheat into flour during January and sold it for no profit at all.

Yet, when the reputable accountant was later questioned, he insisted that he had done right in refusing to "anticipate" the unrealized profit on Henry's wheat and in valuing both Henry's and Bill's inventories at "cost or market whichever is the lower." The accountant described his method of valuing these inventories as "conservative." And reputable accountants still value inventories in that manner down to this day.

THE FABLE OF THE TWO INVESTMENT TRUSTS. Once upon a time there was a small group of financiers. These financiers formed two investment trusts. One investment trust was called the American Trust and the other was called the National Trust. Each trust started business with a paid-in capital of one million dollars comprising its sole assets and net worth. Each trust had numerous small stockholders, but the management of each was controlled by the small group of financiers. Each trust proposed to operate by investing its capital in small amounts among a large number of listed securities, buying such securities when they were considered cheap and selling them when their market price had appreciated so much that they were no longer considered attractive. Dividends were to be immediately reinvested.

Very soon after the formation of the two investment trusts, a crash in the stock market gave each of them an opportunity to invest all of its capital in sound securities at low prices. This each did and the American Trust invested its capital in exactly the same securities at exactly the same prices as did the National Trust. The stock market then started up and continued to go up for the next four years.

Now the financiers who controlled each of these trusts not only understood the investment trust business but also understood accounting principles. They were keenly aware of the opportunities presented to financiers by modern accounting procedure and they decided to enrich themselves at the expense of the public by taking full advantage of these opportunities. They therefore laid their plans with this in view.

By December 31 of the first year of operation both the American Trust and the National Trust had fared exactly alike because their investments were the same. Dividends had not amounted to much because the securities purchased had very small yields, but the appreciation in the market value of these securities had amounted to an average of 20% of their cost. Accordingly on December 31 the American Trust was ordered to sell all of its securities in order to "realize" its profit and was ordered to reinvest the proceeds in other securities. The investment manager of the American Trust pleaded in vain that other securities could not be more desirable than those already owned, but the financiers were firm. The investment manager therefore had no choice except to obey orders, and the securities on hand were sold and other securities were purchased.

On January 1, the small group of financiers requested a well-known firm of certified public accountants to prepare a balance sheet and income statement for the past year for each of the two trusts controlled by it. This firm of certified public accountants was respected by everybody for its incorruptible integrity, and for the ability of its staff. Financial statements certified by it were accepted without question by bankers and individuals all over the world. This firm of certified public accountants made an audit of both trusts, and a certified balance sheet and a certified profit and loss statement for each trust were prepared by it and delivered to the financiers.

The profit and loss statement of the American Trust disclosed that it had earned $30,000 from dividends and had earned $200,000 from realized profits on the securities it had sold. This amounted to $230,000 or 23% on its capital stock. Its balance sheet disclosed that it had securities to a value of $1,230,000 and no liabilities. These securities were described as being valued at "cost or market whichever is the lower."

The profit and loss statement of the National Trust disclosed that it had earned $30,000 from dividends and that it had no other earnings whatever. Its earnings as certified therefore amounted only to 3% on its capital stock. Its balance sheet disclosed that it had securities to a value of $1,030,000 and no liabilities. These securities were described as being valued at "cost or market whichever is the lower." It is true that there was a footnote on the balance sheet stating that the present market value of these securities was $1,230,000, but most of the public did not pay much attention to this and looked chiefly at the total of the assets which was distinctly shown as $1,030,000 and at the surplus which was distinctly shown as $30,000. The few people who did see and understand the footnote disregarded it because, they said, the appreciation of $200,000 was only a paper profit and could not be considered until it had been realized by being converted into cash, because a decline in the security market might wipe it all out in no time. Also, earnings were clearly shown in the profit and loss statement as only $30,000 without any qualification whatever.

Now, of course, as soon as the certified financial statements of the American Trust and of the National Trust were mailed to stockholders and printed in the newspapers, everybody learned that the American Trust had earned 23% on its capital stock during the year whereas the National Trust had earned only 3% on its capital stock. The price of the American Trust stock therefore rose sharply as many investors rushed to buy it, and the price of the National Trust stock dropped sharply due to selling by disappointed stockholders.

But the small group of financiers knew that, although the American Trust had earned 23% on its capital stock, the National Trust had also really earned 23% on its capital stock. It was intelligent enough to see that a decline in the security market which would wipe out the 20% unrealized profit of the National Trust would also wipe out the 20% realized profit of the American Trust and that therefore the unrealized profit was just as safe as the realized profit. So the small group of financiers sold a large part of its holdings of American Trust stock at high prices and bought additional stock of the National Trust at very low prices.

By December 31 of the next year both trusts had earned an additional $30,000 from dividends and each had a further unrealized profit of $200,000 in its securities. So this time the National Trust was ordered to sell all of its securities and to invest the proceeds in the same securities that the American Trust owned. This was done and the profit of $200,000 for the current year plus the profit of $200,000 for the previous year was duly realized. The assets of the National Trust were now identical with those of the American Trust. The market value of each was $1,460,000. The two trusts were exactly alike and each owned exactly the same quantities of the same securities with a total market value of $1,460,000.

On January 1 the same widely known and trusted firm of certified public accountants was requested to prepare balance sheets and profit and loss statements for the past year for each of the two trusts. When this had been done the profit and loss statement of the American Trust disclosed that it had earned $30,000 from dividends and that it had no other earnings whatsoever. Its earnings as certified therefore amounted only to 3% on its capital stock. Its balance sheet disclosed that it had securities to a value of $1,260,000 and no liabilities. These securities were described as being valued at "cost or market whichever is the lower."

The profit and loss statement of the National Trust, however, disclosed that it had earned $30,000 from dividends and had earned $400,000 from realized profits on the securities it had sold. This amounted to $430,000 or 43% on its capital stock. Its balance sheet disclosed that it had securities to a value of $1,460,000 and no liabilities. These securities were described as being valued at "cost or market whichever is the lower."

Now, of course, as soon as the certified financial statements of the American Trust and of the National Trust were mailed to stockholders and printed in the newspapers, everybody learned that the American Trust had earned only 3% on its capital stock during the past year whereas the National Trust had earned 43% on its capital stock during the same period. The price of American Trust stock therefore dropped sharply due to selling by disappointed stockholders and the price of National Trust stock rose sky high as investors rushed to buy it.

But the small group of financiers knew that the American Trust had really earned 23% on its capital stock during the past year although its earnings were certified as only 3% and it also knew that the National Trust had earned only 23% on its capital stock during the past year although its earnings were certified as 43%. Also, it was intelligent enough to realize that a decline in the security market which would wipe out the 20% unrealized profit of the American Trust would also wipe out the same amount of the realized profit of the National Trust because each trust owned exactly the same quantity of exactly the same securities. Therefore the unrealized profit of the American Trust was obviously just as safe as the realized profit of the National Trust. In fact there was no difference whatever between them. It was clear to the small group of financiers that each trust now possessed exactly $1,460,000 of the same securities, and that each had started with exactly $1,000,000 in money two years ago. Neither trust had received anything except profits earned in the ordinary and usual course of its business. Therefore, each trust must have made exactly the same amount of money since its formation, and the practice of the accountants in recognizing realized profits as earnings but in refusing to recognize unrealized profits as earnings must have been pure hokum. So the small group of financiers bought back at low prices the American Trust stock it had sold at high prices a year ago and bought more in addition. Then it sold at high prices the National Trust stock it had bought at low prices a year ago and sold more in addition.

The profits to the financiers on these transactions were far greater than they could have hoped to make merely from dividends on their stock. So they continued the process year after year and never failed to make a killing because they knew that the accounting firm would always maintain that unrealized profits were not earnings. And they have become exceedingly wealthy and respected, and no one has ever ventured to criticize them because the trusted firm of accountants has certified every one of their financial statements and everyone is convinced that such a firm would never certify a fraudulent or deceptive profit and loss statement or balance sheet.

Yet it is obvious that year after year small stockholders were deceived and defrauded because of their confidence in the trusted firm of accountants. And down to this day this firm and other accounting firms still maintain that realized profits are earnings and that unrealized profits are not earnings and, of course, the small group of financiers and other groups of financiers enthusiastically agree.

FUTILITY OF SECURITIES LAWS. Business throughout the country is now laboring under the Amended Securities Act of 1933 and the Securities Exchange Act of 1934. It has been charged that these acts are contrary to American ideals of government because they invade the rights of the States and individuals and because the commission created by them acts, in a very practical sense, in the multiple rôle of law maker, prosecutor, witness, judge, and jury. However, quite apart from this, it is relevant to the design of this book to note that the chief purposes for which the acts were passed can probably never be more than partly realized as long as present accounting principles remain unchanged.

Virtually the entire purpose of the Securities Act of 1933, and at least an important part of the purpose of the Securities Exchange Act of 1934, is to exact reliable information from the issuers of securities so that investors may be enabled to form dependable opinions regarding the value of present or prospective investments. The most important exhibits in the required information, and indeed the only exhibits which pretend to give a comprehensive picture of the value of the securities offered, are the financial statements of the issuing company. If these financial statements are false and misleading, it must necessarily follow that many investors will be deceived, regardless of the multiplicity of other data furnished to them.

It seems a pity that the present complicated laws, with their vast and ramified government machinery and the great expense, delay, and uncertainty which they necessarily cause to business, should in a large part be so clearly futile from the outset. This is the more to be regretted because, if accounting principles were changed, perhaps most of the objectives of the Acts might be achieved without the Acts themselves, and without their intricate and expensive machinery, merely by permitting the preparation of truthful financial statements and by educating investors to demand them. Under such circumstances the laws governing fraud might alone be sufficient to cope with such dishonesty as might occur, entirely without the aid of the dozens of security laws now on the statutes of the individual states and also entirely without the numerous blue-sky commissions now functioning in the individual states.

Most of the machinery of government regulation of security issues, as typified by the numerous state blue-sky commissions, and finally by the enormously burdensome Federal Acts, has originated in the conviction of the public that it was not being treated fairly by the sellers of securities. The public knew that its purchase of securities was largely a hazardous gamble, and it quite naturally concluded that the cause of this was deliberate dishonesty on the part of business men. Accordingly, over a long period of years, blue-sky laws have been passed and blue-sky commissions have been set up in most of the forty-eight states. These commissions have passed upon new security issues after minute and onerous investigations without any noticeable reduction in the hazards of investing except as regards the most flagrant type of security crook. After the financial collapse of 1929 it was realized that these blue-sky commissions were of little value, but it was manifestly not realized where most of the fault lay. The Federal Government therefore superimposed upon the state blue-sky commissions a national blue-sky commission with the duty of regulating security issues throughout the entire country.[1] It was apparently hoped that this would serve the

[1] Originally the Federal Trade Commission. Later the Securities and Exchange Commission.

purpose which the state blue-sky commissions alone had failed so signally to perform.

The writer ventures to predict that the national commission will be scarcely more successful in safeguarding investors than have the individual state commissions. It seems evident that this must be so as long as the figures relating to the securities offered are false and misleading. What is needed is a revision of those figures, not a multiplication of administrative machinery. If the principles of accounting could be corrected so that accountants could prepare truthful balance sheets and profit and loss statements, then the figures presented would speak for themselves and no amount of verbal or written comment could effectively serve to deny them.

The problem is intellectual, not moral. The accounting profession is not corrupt. Its individual members are, on the whole, as honorable as any group of men in the country, and they are faithfully following principles that have been expounded and developed by accounting authorities over many years. Nor does bad faith on the part of business men, nor on the part of investment bankers, cause the trouble. For the most part these publish faithfully the figures prepared by independent accountants. The real difficulty lies in the sophistry, illogic, and untruth of accounting principles which produce figures deceiving accountants, business men, and the public alike.

WEIGHT OF AUTHORITY. Yet these faulty accounting principles are tenaciously defended by the overwhelming majority of contemporary accounting, banking, and business authorities. There is hardly a practicing accountant, banker, or business man in the country who does not regard them with respect or reverence. Unquestionably the weight of authority is on their side. The young business executive who may indulge in some clear thinking and attempt to question them finds himself immediately against a stone wall of opposition. His firm of certified public accountants will courteously refuse to be shown. His banker will question his business judgment. Older business men will smile at his impetuous ignorance.

COGNATE
DISCIPLINES

Engineers

C. T. MAIN **18**

DCCLIX.*

THE VALUATION OF TEXTILE MANUFACTURING PROPERTY.

THE engineer is called upon to place valuations upon manufacturing property for various purposes, as buying or selling, raising money upon or bonding a property, rental, taxes, insurance, adjustment of losses by fire or accident, and condemnation where private or corporate property is taken by the State or town for public improvements.

I shall confine my remarks to the valuation of textile manufacturing plants, and property usually connected therewith; but the same principles will hold good in the value of other properties, the application being made to suit the peculiar conditions of the business under consideration.

The court in Massachusetts has established that the true value of a property is its market value, and substantially that the market value is such a sum as one party who has the capital, and who desires to purchase, is willing to pay for a plant, the owner being willing, but not forced, to sell.

It would seem at the first glance that there should be but one value for a plant for any or all purposes, and that value should be its market value. This is the value which is most important of all, and upon which all other values largely depend.

MARKET VALUE.

Let us therefore consider, first, what is the "market value" of a plant, and what elements enter into the determination of such a value.

The Methods of Determining Value.—There are a great many who place more confidence in the off-hand estimate of the practical business man than in a careful estimate of value by an accountant or engineer; but if the latter combines with his careful

* Presented at the New York meeting (December, 1897) of the American Society of Mechanical Engineers, and forming part of Volume XIX. of the *Transactions.*

weighing of each element which enters into the whole plant a. general business knowledge and a large quantity of common sense, the result will be nearer the truth than the off-hand value which has considered these elements in a general way only. It is not unlikely that the results might agree very closely, thus confirming the opinions and judgment of both.

By whichever method the value is determined, there must enter into it, either consciously or unconsciously, certain fundamental elements which determine its value.

Comparison with Other Properties.—The prices brought for small pieces of property, as house-lots, houses, and such properties as are being sold frequently, are a measure of value for comparison of adjacent and similar pieces of property; but the sale of a large plant is not an every-day occurrence, in fact it is a very rare occurrence; and the conditions which have made the sale necessary, and which surround the sale, and of the plant itself, are usually such that the prices realized cannot be used as comparative in determining the actual value of another somewhat similar plant surrounded by other conditions.

Elements of Value.—Into the market value of a plant enters the broad element of location, with its varying hours and price of labor; skill and abundance or scarcity of operatives; cost of transportation of raw material, supplies, and finished product; cost of fuel or power; cost of construction and equipment; and rate of taxation. Also the narrower and more restricted element of the physical condition of the plant and its relative value to a new plant constructed upon modern principles, and constructed with all regard to the economical production of a finished product of the best quality of the goods manufactured. The standard of value should be a modern mill constructed as described above, and located so as to avail itself of as many combined advantages as possible.

The ultimate value of a plant is its capability of producing a profit, and into the possibility of producing a profit enter all of the above items and perhaps some not mentioned.

Management.—The question of management is a personal one, and must not enter into the problem, except so far as to make sure that with good management the business would be successful. The business of a large and valuable plant might be conducted in such a manner as not to realize a profit; but it might, nevertheless, have great value, and would bring a large amount if offered for sale. On the other hand, a plant not nearly so valuable might, with skilful and close management, yield a profit; but if offered for sale would bring very little. Although the past profits of a concern will have some influence in determining its value, they are not a measure of its value; because a purchaser might by different management reverse the profit or loss, or the changes, real or anticipated, in trade might do the same thing. We must therefore eliminate as far as possible all personal equations from the problem.

Choice of Location.—Textile manufacturing requires considerable power; the cost of labor is a large part of the value of the product; the labor must be skilled to produce a satisfactory product; and the cost of transportation of raw materials and finished products is considerable. All of these items require attention in estimating the value of a plant with reference to its location. If a new plant is to be built, all of these can be weighed approximately; but if an existing plant is to be valued, the relative cost and effect of the fixed location with that of the more favored one must be determined as nearly as possible.

It is the balance of the sum of these items in favor of the South which has caused the rapid increase of southern mills in the last two or three years, and which has caused the northern cotton manufacturers of a certain class of goods to locate their new mills there in preference to the North.

There exist there the following advantages: in some locations, less cost for transportation of raw materials and finished products, low-priced fuel, low rates of taxation, longer hours of labor at a less price than in the North. This last item of advantage may in time, if there is a great demand for labor, adjust itself, so that there will be no advantage in this particular over the northern mills.

The most skilful employees in the North are, as a rule, found in the large manufacturing centres, and, of course, are more numerous there, and the concern is not dependent upon a very limited few for its operation. The operatives enjoy living in a live, bustling place, where there is excitement and entertainment, rather than in some quiet country place. Whether it is better for them or not does not enter into the question. On the other hand, the smaller concerns, located in the country or in a small town, can hire their help at a somewhat lower price than at the larger manufacturing centres, and are freer from labor troubles.

119

On general principles, I should say that the balance would be in favor of the larger districts.

Transportation. — The cost of transportation is more definite and tangible. Although it varies somewhat from time to time, it is not very likely that there will be any radical change unless by the construction of new railroads or canals.

The weight of the raw materials and the finished product in a cotton mill are approximately the same, and in a woollen and worsted mill the weight of the finished product is less than the weight of the raw material, varying with the fineness of the product. It is desirable, then, that the mills be located so that the cost of freight on the raw material shall be as low as possible, other things being equal, and that the distance to the consumer in time and distance shall be small.

The item of carting is in some instances a very considerable expense. Unless the mill is located on a side or spur track, or on navigable water, it may be necessary to do a large amount of carting. This is usually one of the drawbacks connected with the development and use of a water power situated at a distance from the railroad. The difference in cost of teaming between a location on a branch track and a location at considerable distance is a definite amount, which, if known, can be used in the determination of the value of the plant, and the extra cost of transportation can also be treated in the same manner.

The effect upon the values of a property of excessive charges for carting and freight is to reduce its value, and the amount of reduction will vary somewhat, according to the return which a man or corporation is satisfied with. I should say that, taking into consideration the uncertainties of the future, one would be warranted in making an expenditure which promised a return of ten per cent. on his investment. That is, if a person is considering the purchase of a property, and finds that the extra cost of carting and freight would be $1,000 more a year at the fixed location of the mill than at many other locations which might be chosen for a new mill, with all other conditions equally as good, that he would say that he could afford to pay $10,000 more for a mill at the more favored location than for the one under consideration; or if the mill is to be purchased with this incumbrance upon it, that its value would be $10,000 less than if situated at the more favored location.

The situation is equivalent to the mill having a mortgage upon it which requires the payment of $1,000 a year for all time, and the net value of the property to a purchaser is its full value less the amount equivalent to the $1,000 tax.

Centres of Trades.—There are certain localities which have become centres for certain classes of work, where skilled workmen in their particular trades are in abundance, and which may have other distinct advantages. There may be a choice between several centres devoted to the same class of work, the balance of the sum of all the advantages being in favor of one particular place. Into this sum enter the items explained before, and some other items which can be determined quite closely in money value.

Taxes.—The rate of taxation and the method of valuation for taxes may afford a decided advantage to some particular location. This is a part of the fixed charges of the plant which is always visible, and which goes on whether the business goes on or stops; and the value of a plant to a person free to purchase and locate at the place under consideration, or in any other location, is affected by the amount of taxes levied upon the concern.

In the same way as for greater cost for transportation, the greater cost for taxes would warrant an expenditure of an amount which would return an income of about 10 per cent., and would therefore decrease the value to a prospective purchaser by that amount.

Municipal Government.—A more remote item, and one which cannot be figured in dollars and cents, is the general character of the municipal government and its attitude towards industrial enterprises. In most towns or cities at the present time there is an attempt to attract manufacturers by concessions direct or indirect. There are other places which do not care to have manufacturing establishments within their limits, and others in which there is an undercurrent towards crowding the various industries, and making them pay the largest amount of the taxes which they will stand, for which they, as corporations, receive very little direct benefit.

Cost of Construction.—The cost of construction in one place may be less than in another, and the purchaser having his choice of locations should consider the effect of this item. Clearly, if all other things are equal, one could not afford to pay any extra charge for construction and equipment of the mill more than the cost at the most favored location, and the value of an established plant must be diminished by an amount which represents the difference. This sum stands for itself, with no capitalization, and is probably as definite as any which goes into the sum total. The difference can be obtained by investigation of the costs of material and labor, and the costs of machinery and supplies, erected and ready to run.

Cost of Power.—The cost of power, which is another one of the fixed and general expenses of a mill, has always been a problem in the determination of a site. Cheap fuel is to be desired, especially where large quantities of steam are required for other purposes than power. The location in which coal can be purchased at a low cost has a distinct and definite advantage in this respect over the location in which the fuel cost is large. Between mills driven by steam power alone this item can be closely estimated and the proper deduction of value made to a purchaser, or the amount estimated which he can afford to expend for the sake of getting the cheaper fuel.

Water Power.—It very often happens that a mill whose value is under consideration is driven partially by water power—very rarely is it driven wholly by water power—and the approximate estimate of the value of the power must be made.

The value of a water power has been fully discussed by the writer in a paper before the American Society of Mechanical Engineers, vol. xiii., ccclxxi., and will not be treated in detail here ; but some portions will be repeated, with the conclusions drawn, and some further remarks made.

It is easier to determine the value for a specific business than in a general way.

The essential points which must be considered, as to whether an undeveloped power can be developed and used to a greater profit than any particular business or the general run of business could be conducted elsewhere with a different source of power, are as follows :

Quantity of water, uniformity of flow, head, conditions affecting the cost of construction, freight charges, use of exhaust steam, need of water for other purposes than power, and more uniformity of speed attainable from steam power than from water power.

The determination of the flow is not always easy. The flow can be measured at intervals, but a continuous record is needed to get at the flow with much exactness. In many places no records are kept which are of any value, and the only recourse is to estimate the flow from the rainfall and character of the watershed, and by comparison with existing records of similar streams.

The power which has the most value is one which has a flow during a dry year which is nearly constant, or which can be made so by storage basins, and which requires no augmentation from other sources. Its value can be determined by comparison with the cost of uniform power produced in a fairly economical manner, at any place or places equally convenient to the place at which the water power is located, for the transaction of the business under consideration.

The value of an undeveloped constant water power is such a sum as when put at a proper rate of interest, say 10 per cent., will pay the difference in cost between steam and water power, all items of cost being considered.

A power which is variable, and which cannot be depended upon throughout the year, has of course less value than one which is constant. In such a case the items for consideration are:

The maximum, minimum, and average quantity of water, and length of time when there is no water; all the other items which enter into the value of a uniform power; necessity in nearly all cases for a supplementary steam plant, with the expense of maintenance and running for a portion or all of the time.

The value of an undeveloped variable power is little or nothing if its variation is great, unless it is to be supplemented by a steam plant. It is of value then only when the cost per horse-power for the double plant is less than the cost of steam power under the same conditions as mentioned for a permanent power, and its value can be represented in the same manner as the value of a permanent power has been represented.

To determine the market value of such a power which has been developed, it will be necessary to consider the power by itself, independent of the plant; that is, to determine first the value of the power as though it were undeveloped, and then to determine the value of the improvements. The sum of both will represent the value of the power as developed.

It might happen in some cases that the value of the privilege would be a minus quantity, but that the value of the improvements more than offset that, thus making it of value in the developed state.

The cost of developing a power originally will not always represent the value of the improvements, except in so far as it relates

123

to the character of the work done. Considering the work properly and substantially done, the value of that work immediately after completion may not be represented by its cost. A certain power may cost to develop twice as much as another of equal power, the difference in cost being due to difference in head or some other natural cause; but, all other things being equal, the one which cost double has no more value than the other, because it produces no more.

The value would depend largely, however, upon the character of the work done and the condition of the dam, canal, and wheel plant. If any portion required renewing soon, the value would be lessened; and if a general renewal of all the plant were necessary, the value would then be practically the same as though it were undeveloped.

The actual value of a plant would depend upon the amount of depreciation which had taken place; or, better, upon the number of years which it would run without renewing.

The value of the plant will be its cost, less depreciation, up to the point where the cost of water power equals that of steam power; for it would be justifiable to make an expenditure up to an amount which would give as good financial returns as any other source of power. Beyond this point, when water power costs more than steam power, the value of the improvements would not be represented by their cost.

The value of a developed power is as follows: If the power can be run cheaper than steam, the value is that of the power plus the cost of the plant, less depreciation. If it cannot be run as cheaply as steam, considering its cost, etc., the value of the power itself is nothing; but the value of the plant is such a sum as could be paid for it new, which would bring the total cost of running down to the cost of steam power, less depreciation. That is, it is worth just what can be gotten out of the plant, and no more.

Although the water may have no value for power, it may have considerable value for dyeing and washing purposes, and its value for these purposes can be based upon the charges made for such water in manufacturing centres where the water is suitable for such purposes.

If low-pressure steam is required for heating purposes, and exhaust steam can be used, the heat thus saved should be credited to the cost of coal for running the substitute plant, and the cost of attendance should be proportioned between cost of power and cost of heating.

In order to have a standard of value for comparison of costs, it is necessary to estimate the cost of producing a constant power by water alone, if the water power is constant, such as that at Niagara Falls, on the present development for power, or by water power supplemented by steam power at such times as are necessary to produce a uniform power, and to compare this with the cost of producing a constant and equal amount of power by steam alone. There may be some exceptions to this rule where the power to be used is not required to be absolutely constant, as for a saw mill, grist mill, and certain kind of paper mills, where a large stock of pulp is ground up in the wet season and stored for use in summer.

In nearly all cases to be considered, the power is variable, and no true comparison of its value can be made until it is made constant by some supplementary power, at least for textile manufacturing, which requires a uniform power. It is the result of omitting this important factor in the value of a water power which causes the values given oftentimes to appear beyond reason.

In estimating the damages by reason of diversion of water power, it is customary to capitalize the difference in cost in favor of water or against steam power at about 5 per cent. This damage has been done against the owner's wishes, and he is entitled to a capitalization at a smaller rate than would be done in an investment where the purchaser is of his own free will assuming certain risks, as damages caused by freshets, which he will not assume for nothing. He is also basing his comparisons upon the steam plant with its present efficiency. For these reasons the difference in favor of water power should be capitalized at not less than 10 per cent.

It is not impossible that some cheaper source of power may be discovered, thus destroying our present standard for large powers. For small powers we already have the gas, gasoline, and oil engines, and in some places electric power can be bought. Any of these may be used as a standard of value if adapted to the work and circumstances.

PHYSICAL PROPERTIES AND VALUE OF A PLANT.

The valuation of property as made by different individuals will vary according to their ideas of the proper return to be obtained from such property, and upon their judgment as to the proper amount of depreciation to be allowed. In determining such a valuation, comparison must be made with the cost of a new and model plant, and between the costs of operating the old and new plants in so far as the organization of the old plant is detrimental to economical running, when such poor organization cannot be rectified. When it can be changed to a proper organization, the cost of making this change must be deducted from its value if such defects did not exist.

The value depends primarily, but not necessarily, on the first cost of the property under consideration, which might have been excessive at the time of its inception; nor necessarily upon the first cost to-day of a plant identical to the one under consideration; for a smaller plant, owing to improvements, might be installed to-day which would produce the same results as the one under consideration. The first cost to be used in comparison, then, is the cost to-day of a plant which will produce equal results in quantity and quality as the one under consideration.

ENGINEERING VALUATIONS.

VALUATIONS IN GENERAL.

THE Joint Stock Companies Act of 1862 has exerted an influence over English trade little contemplated by its authors at the time it passed. Not only has it permitted, and in part ministered to, a vast increase in volume of business and concentration of capital, but it has modified and changed the methods and ethics of commerce and manufactures, and called into existence a new profession. Nor does this influence at present exhibit any signs of decay; on the contrary, the tendency to organise private firms as limited liability companies seems to increase, and the advantages gained by this form of trading appear to be greater than the risk incurred of losses through fraudulent or reckless speculations. Recent legislative proposals and enactments accelerate this process, and it is frequently found that a number of small firms banded together as one moderately large company can effect insurances or make other provision to meet the onerous conditions now imposed, which, as separate firms, they would find impossible. This tendency to incorporation renders great care necessary on the part of engineers, lest they should, in the course of the evolution proceeding, be ousted from their management of the works on which they are employed, and transformed into technical assistants to financial experts. There is really no necessity for any such alteration of status, and we are convinced that it would not be for the ultimate advantage either of the purchasers of the machinery or works constructed, or of the investors in the constructing works, although it would undoubtedly benefit the financial authorities whose authority it increased. That there is danger of some such development, and that it has the friendly support of the official class, may be gathered from a reply made by the Inspector-General in Bankruptcy (Mr. John Smith, C.B.) to Lord Farrer, before the Select Committee of the House of Lords on the Bill to amend the Companies Acts. His Lordship had been pressing the witness with questions as to the valuation of assets, and the provision to be made against an imprudent, unskilful, or over-sanguine estimate of them. He continued, "1550. "Then the valuation will depend upon the character of the directors, and is therefore very indeterminate." Mr. Smith replied: "So far as regards many imprudent valuations, I do not think it is possible to provide by legislation against them, except by requiring an audit: to some extent that will check imprudent valuations." Translated into ordinary every-day language, this reply means that auditors who have not gained, in their ordinary professional character, any acquaintance with the technic of a business, of the variation in its markets, or the improvements introduced into its machinery or manufacture, can better value its assets than men who spend their lives working it, and whose incomes depend on its prosperity. The doctrine is a dangerous one, and if this hypothesis of "clerkism" is persisted in, it may seriously repress the prefecting of scientific and technical management.

The engineer, however, who desires to effectively control all departments of his factory or undertaking, and to supervise financial relations as well as mechanical processes, must carry into his office the same habits of careful research, and rigid adherance to facts which he observes himself, and requires from his assistants, in the shops. There is no insuperable difficulty in this. Bookkeeping, whatever its practitioners may say, is no secret art, and far less thought and application than is required for mastering the elements of trigonometry would enable the engineer to comprehend any set of books which are properly kept. They look formidable in the safe or on the desk, from their size and number, but they contain merely an accumulation of facts and figures invariably following the same routine, and acquaintance with the methods of a few of the entries is sufficient for the understanding of all. The continued repetition teaches no lesson but mechanical care, and there is no occasion to undertake this monotonous drudgery in order to appreciate their purport.

In dealing with engineering valuations, it is almost impossible to dissociate them from engineering accounts. The value of the works, whether for mere financial purposes on which dividends are based, for estimate for purposes of sale, or for comparison with other and competing factories, must be largely determined by these items of repairs, renewals, and depreciation which are recorded in the books of the firm. Table A of the Act of 1862 contains a form of balance-sheet, with very definite instructions for completing it, and, as it covers nearly all the items comprised at the present time in a private or company balance-sheet, it forms an excellent precedent, and we annex a copy of it. The debit side (capital and liabilities) may be disregarded as outside the limits of our present inquiry; and on the opposite side (property and assets) there is no occasion to consider the fourth and fifth items, i.e., debts owing to the company, and cash and investments, these being sufficiently and properly dealt with by the bookkeeping element of the firm. The third item (property held by the company), however, introduces us to the very essence of our subject, since the amounts to be inserted for property, immovable and movable, depend on valuations, which, to be correct and reliable, should be prepared by experts. It is well to bear in mind that the ordinary commercial use of the term "value" is the same employed by Mr. John Stuart Mill in the word "price," "to express the value of a thing in relation to money." Mr. Mill, however, adds: "Its money, therefore, or price, will represent, as well as anything else, its general exchange value, or purchasing power; and, from an obvious convenience, will often be employed by us in that representative power; with the proviso that money itself does not vary in its general purchasing power, but that the value of all things, other than that which we happen to be considering, remain unaltered." Although it is not essential, in a practical treatise, to discriminate so nicely between the ordinary and scientific use of particular words, as it is in a work on political economy, it is desirable to remember that econo-

BALANCE-SHEET OF THE SALTASH GOLD REFINING COMPANY, LIMITED, MADE UP TO DECEMBER 31, 1896.

Capital and Liabilities.					Property and Assets.				
I. Capital.		Showing :	£ s. d.	£ s. d.	III. Property held by the company.	7	Showing : Immovable property, distinguishing— (a) Freehold land (b) „ buildings (c) Leasehold	£ s. d.	£ s. d
	1	The number of shares ..							
	2	The amount paid per share ..							
	3	If any arrears of calls, the nature of the arrear, and the names of the defaulters							
	4	The particulars of any forfeited shares ..				8	Movable property, distinguishing— (d) Stock-in-trade .. .. (e) Plant .. .. The cost to be stated with deductions for deterioration in value as charged to the reserve fund or profit and loss		
II. Debts & liabilities of the company.		Showing :							
	5	The amount of loans on mortgage or debenture bonds ..							
	6	The amount of debts owing by the company, distinguishing (a) Debts for which acceptances have been given.. (b) Debts to tradesmen for supplies of stock-in-trade or other articles.. (c) Debts for law expenses (d) Debts for interest on debentures or other loans (e) Unclaimed dividends .. (f) Debts not enumerated above			IV. Debts owing to the company.	9	Showing : Debts considered good, for which the company hold bills or other securities ..		
						10	Debts considered good, for which the company hold no security ..		
						11	Debts considered doubtful and bad. Any debt due from a director or other officer of the company to be separately stated		
VI. Reserve fund		Showing : The amount set aside from profits to meet contingencies ..			V. Cash and Investments.	12	Showing : The nature of investment and rate of interest		
VII. Profit & loss		Showing : The disposable balance for payment of dividend, &c. ..				13	The amount of cash, where lodged, and if bearing interest		
Contingent liabilities		Claims against the company not acknowledged as debts Moneys for which the company is contingently liable ..							

mists place certain limitations on such expressions, and that we at present use them as generally accepted, and not under their various philosophical interpretations.

THE BOOKKEEPER'S VALUATION.

If we follow the balance-sheets in chronological order, it is evident that the amounts inserted, in the first one, as the values of (a) freehold land, (b) freehold buildings, (c) leasehold buildings, must be those paid either to the vendors, if purchased as a going concern, or as purchase money for land, for materials used, and wages expended in erection of buildings, if the works have been erected by the owing company ; or to the former landowner for the ground, and to a contractor for erection of the buildings. In like manner plant (e) will be valued at the amount paid to the vendors—that is, to the manufacturers who have built the machines, and erected them in place. The first method requires little consideration ; it is in its nature similar to the purchase of a load of hay or a sack of corn in the open market, and is essentially ruled by the law of supply and demand ; the vendor obtains the highest price he can, and the purchaser pays what he considers the place to be worth to him under the circumstances in which he will work it. In the second method there is a little apparent departure from the application of this law ; just as in the former case it rules the price paid for the material purchased, and the labour employed, but an additional factor of cost comes in which some accountants contend should not be charged against the initial value of the works, but be dealt with as preliminary expenses, to be written off within a very limited period after commencement of operations ; it is the cost of management and superintendence during erection, when such duties are performed by the company's own officials. It will, however, be apparent that, whether the works be purchased from a former owner or occupier, or be erected by a contractor for an agreed sum, this charge for superintendence in some way or other enters into the amount paid, and by analogy should therefore be included in the value when the owners or directors elect to perform the erection with their own employés' labour under the direction of their own staff. Care must, however, be taken that the salaries of officials are not charged to this account during such periods as they are engaged upon preliminary arrangements for the management of the concern, or for securing orders ; otherwise a fictitious value will be given to the buildings, which will not be got quit of by the ordinary methods of depreciation. In the third method the law of supply and demand is again reverted to, the contractors being, in this instance, in the place of the vendors, seeking by all means in their power to enhance the price for their contract, and this price when determined and paid being the value of the asset in the balance-sheet.

With the second balance-sheet, however, a new set of conditions arises. Land, buildings, and machinery will, in the ordinary course of business, be subject to a decrease in value, due partly to lapse of time and partly to user. This is rectified by accountants by the methods of writing off depreciation, which, however, it may be stated in the balance-sheet, invariably amounts to a reduction in the assumed value of assets. There is now a material difference between the two valuations ; a difference arising from the introduction of a new factor, usually, however, dependent on the original valuation for its amount, as it takes the form of a percentage. The manner in which this is arrived at by professional auditors may be gathered from a treatise by Mr. Lawrence R. Dicksee, F.C.A., on "Auditing : A Practical Manual for Auditors," of which a new edition has recently been published. Fluctuations, which may possibly involve appreciation of values, the author treats as "something wholly distinct from depreciation," the latter being "always a charge upon revenue, while the fluctuation (whether up or down) affects capital alone." With this explanation, Mr. Dicksee lays down the following general principles for depreciation :

"*Freehold Lands* may quickly be dismissed ; they suffer no depreciation.

"*Freehold Buildings* require depreciation to an extent varying greatly according to the quality of the workmanship and materials employed in their erection. If the instalment plan be adopted, from 1¼ to 3 per cent. of the original amount may be deducted annually ; or if the annuity method be preferred, such a sum may be set aside as will accumulate to the cost of the building in from 50 to 150 years. In each case all repairs will have to be borne by revenue in addition to the depreciation.

"*Goodwill* does not, properly speaking, depreciate. The amount at which goodwill is stated in a balance-sheet is never supposed to represent either its maximum or its minimum value ; no one who thought of purchasing a business would be in the least influenced by the amount at which the goodwill was stated in the accounts ; in short, the amount is absolutely meaningless.

"*Houses* invariably depreciate. The rate of depreciation will probably vary between 15 and 25 per cent. on the starting balance of the account. Revaluation is, however, recommended as the safer course.

"*Leasehold Land and Premises.*—The premium paid for leases may be regarded as the purchase money paid for a terminable annuity of the difference between the annual value of the property and the annual charges. In short-term leases the readiest method will be to charge a proportionate part of the term against each year's revenue ; but the method is too rough to be employed if the term exceeds, say, eight years. In the case of longer leases the annuity plan must be adopted.

"*Machinery* depreciates by wear and by becoming obsolete. In addition to charging all repairs and (partial) renewals to revenue, from 7½ to 12½ per cent. should be written off annually from reducing balances. Boilers, which depreciate more rapidly, should be reduced from 10 to 15 per cent. per annum. Tools are most conveniently dealt with by means of a revaluation.

"*Plant*, other than machinery, runs comparatively little risk of becoming obsolete, and a deduction of from 5 to 7½ per cent., will therefore usually suffice. Furniture and fittings should, however, be subjected to a somewhat higher rate.

"*Patents* are virtually leases of a monopoly, and although it is possible that some value—in the nature of goodwill—may remain after the patent has run out, it seems desirable that the cost of a patent should be written off within the course of its life. Where a patent has not been purchased, but remains the property of the original patentee, it is very undesirable that the item should be treated as an asset at all ; such a course would seem to be every bit as artificial as a similar treatment of good will, which *sans dire* is a latent asset in every paying concern."

The rates of percentage given by Mr. Dicksee are not invariably adopted by auditors ; indeed, they vary considerably according to the predilections of the auditor, the desires of the directors, and the prosperity of the business ; but the principle of estimation and adjustment thereof is usually that of annual percentages so lucidly laid down by him. By deducting the amount of this depreciation from the valuations of the previous balance-sheets, accountants and auditors arrive at the value of the assets for the current period. This value we may. for distinction, call the "bookkeeper's value." The term may not appear euphonious, but it seems to be a perfectly correct one, since the manner in which it is arrived at, and the knowledge and skill expended on it, are precisely what we might expect from an average bookkeeper ; and no more.

(*To be continued*)

ENGINEERING VALUATIONS.

(*Continued from page 2.*)

It will be patent to our readers that there are serious defects in this ordinary method of arriving at new valuations of fixed assets by writing off an arbitrary percentage depreciation from a previous valuation. Whether the use of a percentage is advisable or not, it is certain that it can only be fixed, if it is to make the slightest approach to accuracy, after careful consideration of all the circumstances affecting any particular case, and after allowance for many factors which are usually ignored by accountants. Whether this disregard arises from ignorance of technical matters on the part of the financial authorities, or the subordination thereof to the preparation of a balance-sheet easily understood by shareholders, it is unnecessary to inquire ; but the engineer who desires to be prepared to make, or to consider, proposals for purchase of his works, either by an actual cash payment or amalgamation with other companies, must provide himself with some more correct method of continuous valuation, and more accurate way of calculating the depreciation on which that valuation will be based.

It is absolutely necessary that the charges for maintenance should be debited against the revenue of the year, and not added to the value of the buildings or plant. In some few firms the cost of maintenance, repairs, and of renewals is added to the previous valuation standing in the books, and from the amount thus arrived at depreciation is written off ; and this course is justified on the plea that depreciation and maintenance cannot be separated from each other, and that the one should balance the other. The fallacy of this will be perceived when we consider the tendency of machinery to become obsolete through the introduction of improved types, and of buildings to become unsuitable through extensions of trade ; and that the most extensive repairs done to any machine or building cannot by any possibility do more than place it in as good and worklike form as it was in the first instance.

The repairs are a necessity incident to, and imposed by user ; depreciation may include this, as a form of account, but it includes much more in decay inevitable through lapse of time, and improvements developed by the ever-active human intellect. Even renewals will not in all cases fully compensate for the decline in value, and restore the assets to the amount at which they were taken in the original balance-sheet. If the renewed machine or building is an exact replica of the former one, it will be of less intrinsic value because of the years by which it will be nearer supersession; if it is of later or improved type, the money cost of it may be more or less than that of the original, being affected by the market prices at the time of purchase, which prices are in time affected, not merely by supply and demand, but in these present days by appreciation of gold. It must always be remembered that it is the market, that is, the selling value of the factory and its equipment, which is being sought, and not any estimation based on utility to the present owners. If, therefore, the amount written off for depreciation has to bear the burden of ordinary repairs necessary for the "up-keep" of the buildings and plant, without which they would speedily fall into decay, as well as renewals, and replacements, and loss through lapse of time, for which it was primarily intended, it is probable that it will be found inadequate. The scale will usually be adapted to the latter charge, but will be insufficient for the former, which will be looked upon fondly, but falsely, as increasing the value of the factory.

It is true that Parliament has recognised the combination of maintenance and renewal charges in railway accounts. In abstract A of the annual return directed by "The Regulation of Railways Act, 1871," the cost has to be stated of "maintenance and renewal of permanent way;" whilst abstract U has to contain the same information with respect to "repairs and renewals of carriages and wagons." But railways differ from most engineering undertakings, both in the permanence of their character, and more particularly in the factors which govern their sale and purchase. The primary considerations in acquiring a railway are the amount of traffic which it carries, the character of the country it passes through, and the assistance it will render to the purchasing company in the capacity of a feeder; these, much more than the exact past division of expenditure into capital and revenue, are the points looked at by a traffic manager. Former blunders may affect or prejudice the original shareholders, but they are probably remediable under the changed conditions of future management. Although, therefore, railways are required only to render statements of their expenditure under forms in which the cost of maintaining the road and rolling stock, and the payments for new rails or new wagons and carriages for renewal thereof, are mingled, yet the special conditions of this kind of enterprise are so different to those governing manufacturing establishments, that even the wisdom of Parliament will not justify the adoption of such a procedure generally.

When, however, provision is made, by the execution of ordinary repairs, for keeping the buildings and plant in good and sufficient working order out of revenue, it is necessary to ascertain some rate of depreciation which, by an accumulative fund, will prevent loss of capital to the shareholders. But here we are met with the difficulty of fixing a rate or scale which will apply to all classes of assets and under all conditions of time and user. Even Mr. Dicksee, writing only with the experience of an auditor, and without special reference to the variations of conditions in different trades and localities, was compelled to adopt different rates of depreciation, ranging from nothing in the case of freehold lands to 15 per cent. per annum for machinery, and 25 per cent. per annum for horses. Both for correctness and convenience his method was a wise one. It is desirable to divide the assets into classes for valuation and scale of depreciation, and to consider each class independently and on its own merits, and with reference to the special circumstances which may affect it. Even in the case of the purchase or sale of a factory as a going concern, this division is still necessary for the purpose of computation; the price agreed upon may be the aggregate sum, but the items must be separately estimated if the result is to approach correctness.

Freehold and Leasehold Land.—It is a generally accepted opinion with auditors that freehold land does not vary in value, and that it is quite unnecessary to write anything off the original cost price of it. This, however, is, under some circumstances, a delusion, although it may be true of the average district where trade continues prosperous. Mr. Herbert Spencer, in his "Principles of Sociology," says: "In England the first building containing many machines thus simultaneously driven was the well-known silk-throwing mill at Derby, erected early in the last century by Sir Thomas Lombe. The example he set was followed in cotton-spinning by Arkwright, Crompton, and Hargreaves. Their mills were of necessity erected on the banks of rivers yielding the requisite fall of water, a requirement which dispersed the manufacturers to scattered places, often to remote valleys. And here we are introduced to another of those great changes in industrial organisation which have been initiated by scientific discovery and resulting mechanical appliances. For the revolution which gave to the factory system its modern character arose from the substitution of steam power for water power . . . Another result was that wide distribution of factories was no longer necessitated by wide distribution of water power." Mr. Spencer uses the illustration to explain one portion of his general theory of evolution; and in admiration of his majestic generalisations he is apt to lose sight of some of the side-lights he throws on details which, rightly considered, have a practical value, and teach a practical workaday lesson. The great change which he indicates from water power to steam power deprived land in the neighbourhood of streams of the additional value conferred upon it by its adaptability for factory purposes; a value which was in the nature of a monopoly so long as water power was the only, or principal, motor available. When, however, this monopoly value was removed, and other competing conditions had free play, the trade gradually left the stream-served valleys and became fixed in large centres of population, where increased advantages arising from means of transport, and concentration of workpeople, could be obtained. But the buildings so abandoned would probably prove unsuitable for other trades; we can, in the Rossendale Valley and other remote corners of Lancashire, see ruined buildings, now unoccupied, which once were prosperous factories. They cannot be used as manufactories; it will hardly pay the cost of labour to remove the stones; and the cost of returning the land to agricultural purposes, even after the buildings have been pulled down, will be considerable. Here is a clear instance of depreciation in the value of land, not arising from lapse of time, but from change of conditions. It was probably purchased—in the majority of cases certainly would be purchased—at a price representing its value as the location of a manufactory; but at best it can only be sold for agricultural land, and that at an inferior price, since its dirty and uncultivated condition will render it unproductive, or less productive, than neighbouring land, for some considerable period. It will, in fact, be reduced to "prairie value," and in the absence of some special demand or fortuitous conditions in the district, will

only bring such a price when sold. Again, a fall
in the value of land, apart from the buildings
thereon, may occur in one part of a large town, in
consequence of the opening up of additional
facilities in a distant portion of the same town,
and the migration thereto of other offices and
manufactories. Such a process will probably
be a gradual one, but each additional removal
of a workshop from the decaying district to
the growing one will accelerate it, unless the
land can be utilised for other purposes, such as
workmen's dwellings, or further increase of re-
tailers' shops and stores. Or there may be throughout the whole town a depreciation in the value of
real estate, owing to depression in the principal
employments of the inhabitants, even though the
particular factory under consideration may have
been prosperous, or, at all events, paying its way,
during the recent period of its working. An instance of this character is quoted by Mr. Mellors,
a chartered accountant and estate agent in extensive practice, when giving evidence on July 17,
1896, before the Lords' Select Committee on the
Bill for the amendment of the Companies Acts.
The Earl of Leven and Molville had been enquiring
what would be the effect of stating in a published
balance-sheet the temporary market value of bills
held by a company, instead of their face value, in
the event of a panic like Overend and Gurney's
Black Friday. Mr. Mellors replied : "There is no
need to limit it to bills ; it will apply to real estate.
In Nottingham we have had a depression for 10
years, from 1884 to 1894. During that 10 years, if
real estate had had to be re-valued, it would have
had to be valued at 30 per cent. lower than either
now or previously to the time I have named. Then
with regard to machinery ; during seasons of depression of trade machinery goes for what is commonly called 'an old song ;' so that there is no
question that it would be very difficult to publish a
balance-sheet in such times in which the exact
market value of the assets was given fairly ; and it
would be a hardship upon a company to compel it
to write down its assets in that way." The question of machinery does not at present concern us ;
we are for the moment considering the land, and it
is evident that Mr. Mellors, from his own experience as an estate agent, knows that depreciation of
real estate may take place, even to the extent of 30
per cent. It is true a recovery in value has now
taken place, but during the 10 years of depression
the minds of owners must have been severely exercised by the reduced value in their assets ; and they
might possibly have been compelled to sell during
the period of these lower prices, when the prospective loss would have become an actual one. It
is not given to every prophet to foretell the succession of seven years of fat kine after the seven
years of lean ones.

The variation in the value of land may be in the
manner of an increase instead of decrease. Such
change will almost invariably follow on the transfer
of industrial enterprise, either from the watersides
of the valleys to larger towns, or from one portion
of the town to another ; the land in the district

which is in course of becoming congested will undoubtedly rise in price, and probably with more
certainty and greater rapidity than that of the
deserted portions will fall. The available quantity
of land is limited, and cannot be increased to meet
the demand, whereas the abandoned land may
possibly be used for other purposes. The opening
of a new railway, or the building of a new and
improved station, with increased siding accommodation, and facilities for junctions with private lines,
or the completion of a large and well-equipped canal,
like the Manchester Ship Canal, will cause a demand
for land for building purposes in the neighbourhood, which undoubtedly will produce a rapid rise
in prices.

Such variations in land values are undoubtedly
difficult to deal with, and the more so as such
changes, sometimes extending over a far larger
area than manufacturing districts, are very varied
in character, and, being subjected to other contingencies, do not always afford sufficient guidance
on which to formulate any absolute rule. Thus the
agricultural land in some of the southern and
eastern counties of England will not only fail to
sell at the prices ruling twenty or thirty years ago,
but is often unsaleable at any price ; whilst urban
land, suitable for villa residences or workmen's
cottages, in the same counties has actually appreciated during that time. Again, whilst land is of
increased value and almost unobtainable in a
prosperous town like Bury, it has shrunk in price
and become practically unsaleable in many of the
valleys near thereto, where successful mills were
once working. And yet correct estimation of the
financial position of the firm demands that in some
manner or other the depreciation or appreciation of
land shall be given effect to, unless it is undoubtedly
temporary in character. The first consideration,
therefore, for the engineer to determine is whether
it is permanent or temporary. And here it is
necessary to state that although many of the
determining causes, such as suitability of site,
are incident to his own particular trade, and
may be given effect to in his own individual
calculations, others are such as can only be
estimated by an estate agent as valuer, skilled in
the prospects of the property in that particular
district. The migration of one particular trade
does not necessarily involve lower prices for the
land on which the abandoned works are built. It
may possibly be utilised for other purposes outside
the engineer's ken, but the anticipation of which
will present itself instantly to the practising estate
agent.

Where the desertion of the district, or prospective desertion, arises from its becoming unsuited
for trade purposes, through changes in methods of
working such as that arising from transition from
water to steam power ; or through insufficiency of
railway and canal accommodation, thus involving
increased transit charges over competing districts ;
or through difficulties in providing housing for sufficient, and increasing numbers of workpeople,
without burdening them with toiling over long distances to their work ; then there is reasonable
probability that the fall in value will be perma-

nent, that not only will the buildings become valueless, save for such price as the old materials may bring, but the land itself will return to agricultural value, subject, however, to the expenditure thereon of a sufficient sum to bring it again into agricultural use. For it must be remembered that the correlation of trades at the present time is such that a district or town unsuited for one class of business will also be frequently found unsuited for allied but dissociated trades, and that the disadvantages under which it labours will be greater than the advantages which can be offered in reduced rents or cheaper land. No new trades have taken the place of the decaying industries of the Stroud or Rossendale valleys; and their inhabitants have to subsist on the fragments left them of those employments which find their fullest development elsewhere. That a revival may take place, and a return of prosperous trade be effected, even after such adverse straits, is undoubtedly possible, but the probabilities against such revival are so strong that no wise business man will anticipate it in preparing an estimate of his assets and liabilities.

It is, however, seldom that permanent fall in value of land is sudden in its operation. The instance of Nottingham, referred to by Mr. Mellors, is, indeed, an example to the contrary: the depreciation in the land values arose from temporary depression in the staple trades of the place, and from their transfer to other places; when trade revived, the selling price of land went up to its normal rate. There is thus an interval between the fat kine and the lean kine, of which advantage can, and ought to be, taken to write off from the revenue of the company a sufficient sum to compensate for the diminishing value of the land asset. The annual charge may be dealt with in any form most convenient to the circumstances of the company; the particular method does not concern us at the moment; but it must be adjusted so as to extinguish the loss in value by the time it comes into operation. To preintimate this date requires consideration of many factors, some of which are purely connected with the prospects of the trade, whilst others are dependent on the more varying moods of human emotion. It is a question of average, but withal one so complex that it will be found difficult to avoid errors in deciding it. Probably commercial experience, and knowledge of mankind, will be more serviceable than efforts after actuarial accuracy.

Although, on the one hand, there is a possibility of shrinkage in the value of land, there is, on the other, a strong probability that in other districts it will be increased; indeed, the very process of removal of works from less desirable localities to more desirable, will cause some increase, though not necessarily an exactly corresponding one, in the price of land in the latter places. The opening of the Manchester Ship Canal, and the increased transport facilities and reduced transit rates offered, or expected, in consequence, have caused an extension of new works into its neighbourhood; and this tendency will be accelerated, both by the proclivity to follow a leader, which is as pronounced among men as among sheep, and also by the aggregation of workpeople and workmen's dwellings, which speedily follow. The advantages which are expected are thus of a twofold character; reduced expenditure for carriage, and ready supply of labour within reasonable distance of the works. But as the transition from a prosperous manufacturing valley to an inferior sheep walk is a gradual process, requiring many years to accomplish, and affording time to provide against loss of capital by reducing the available distribution of net revenue, so the growth in value of a new district will be a gradual one, and afford to the earlier settlers opportunities of making profits which do not, strictly speaking, arise from their manufacturing business. The land when first purchased may have been agricultural land of more or less fertility, or waste moorland of little value, and the purchase price which appears in the first balance-sheet may have been a very low one. The cost of clearing and preparing the site, and of constructing roads and approaches, should appear under the head of land value, although by some accountants and auditors it is classified with buildings where land and buildings are placed in separate items; but whichever method is adopted, execution of this work in general increases the value of the premises to a greater extent than its actual cost. In like manner with the opening of a public railroad, tramway, or canal, though in a smaller degree; it has rendered land available for a variety of purposes for which it was previously unsuited, and increased the profit which may consequently be obtained from the sale of it in a ratio greater than the expenditure necessary for making the approaches. This would readily be perceived if the land were rented on yearly or short term tenancy: the rent demanded, and paid, for land properly levelled, and with good roads to it, would be more than for rough ground with no approaches, and the extra rent thus paid would, in most cases, be greater than the interest on the extra expenditure involved. It is perfectly right, and in accordance with sound business principles, to take account of this increased value of the land, at all events in the private records of the company, even if it should not be deemed advisable to exhibit such variations in the published balance-sheets whilst they remain merely approximations; when the profit or loss is fixed by actual sales, it must appear in the accounts submitted to the shareholders.

(To be continued.)

Taxation

W. B. FINLAY

The Income Tax Law and Farm Accounting Methods.

An interesting problem that has come up since the enactment of the income tax law bears upon the method of reporting income from farming operations. Many large ranches have excellent accounting systems designed upon approved double-entry principles, which for the present discussion may be designated as class (a); while others, which may be called class (b), have scarcely the scratch of a pen to enable them to compute their income, much less to enable them to make a return of income for the purpose of the tax. Both classes, of course, swear to the accuracy of the return, however it is made. Class (a) takes annual inventory of stock at a fair market value, likewise of produce raised and on hand, at what time all expenses incurred and accruals applicable to the year are taken into account, from which a report of operations and net gain or loss is made, and a balance sheet is prepared as in other properly conducted business enterprises. Class (b) has no such basis of comparing one year with another; but, when it has any method at all, it ordinarily prepares a report by setting up the actual money paid out, if it can be ascertained at all, against the amount of money received, if, also, that can be ascertained, and the remainder is the amount of gain for the year.

Form No. 1040, of the treasury department, which is the one upon which individual returns are made, gives the following instructions upon page 4, which are interesting in connection with this discussion:

Article 11—The farmer, in computing the net income from his farm for his annual return, shall include all moneys received for produce and animals sold, and for wool and hides of animals slaughtered, provided such wool and hides are sold, and he shall deduct therefrom the sums actually paid as purchase money for the animals sold or slaughtered during the year. When animals were raised by the owner, and are sold or slaughtered, he shall not deduct their value as expenses or loss. He may deduct the amount of money actually paid as expenses for producing any farm products, live-stock, etc. In deducting expenses for repairs on farm property the amount deducted must not exceed the amount actually expended for such repairs during the year for which the return is made (See page 3, item 6). The cost of replacing tools

135

or machinery is a deductible expense to the extent that the cost of the new articles does not exceed the value of the old.

Article 12—In calculating losses only such losses as shall have been actually sustained during the year covered by the return can be deducted.

The department of agriculture has issued a bulletin on farm bookkeeping which is also of interest at this time, inasmuch as it recommends the inventory method of determining annual profits on the farm. This is also the method advised by J. A. Bexell, of the Oregon agricultural college. While it is true that the farm that takes annual inventory and determines profits upon the basis of such inventory does not have to report its "income" upon that basis, yet it would be more convenient to do so, when all of its accounts have been arranged upon that basis.

The other class, (b), will report upon the basis of money received for livestock and produce sold and deduct costs and expenses paid, but the increase will not be reported until sales have been made and money collected for such sales. The following rates of depreciation are certainly a matter that cannot be overlooked: 5% on buildings (taking into consideration insurance and repairs); 10% on horses, above 5 years; 8% on milch cows, after the third year; 10% on machinery and tools (taking into account repairs and replacements). It would appear to the thinking person that some method of taking inventory of livestock and produce and other increases on the farm should be adopted, and that losses, by way of depreciation of animals used in farmwork, and also machinery, buildings, and losses of every kind, should be taken into consideration in arriving at "net profits."

The method of making returns for farming operations, as proposed by the treasury department, is, no doubt, the most practical method of securing approximate returns, but we must conclude that the increase of stock and produce on the farm is considered an accretion of capital and not subject to taxation unless expressly taken into the books by way of inventory. However, this certainly encourages poor business methods on the farm, where, of all places, there is great need of efficiency in operation. Personally, in the operation of a farm, I would want to know what my accrued profits were at the end of a fiscal period, which, according to the income tax law, is made

December 31, when most authorities agree that April 1 is a better time for taking an inventory upon the farm.

In connection with the subject of increment and income, Representative Hull, in his replies to questions asked by Representative Mann, said: " * * * in construing all these laws that I have observed * * * unless the unearned increment is expressly made income it is not considered income in any sense of the word, but simply increase of value or capital." While this expression, no doubt, had to do entirely with another matter —possibly the discussion of the value of real estate—still I do not see but that it applies to the increase of any capital asset.

It is my opinion that this ruling is a survival of that old difficulty: the confounding of two ideas of "income"— the one held by many lawyers and business men—that actual receipts of money constitute "revenue," when as a matter of fact "revenue" should be regarded as earned for the purpose of determining profits, whether it has been received or is receivable.

Notwithstanding the instructions of the treasury department, I still believe that livestock and farm products may be safely inventoried at market prices, and gross profit computed to include profits by increase figured on the same basis, otherwise it would seem difficult to provide a balance sheet "showing the condition of a business as at a given moment of time." If sales should not keep pace with increase, a large secret reserve would result in a number of cases under our observation. Omission of inventories on farms and ranches has a direct effect on general taxes, inasmuch as there is scarcely any way of verifying assessment lists, or at least confirming them. Some accounting practice should be definitely outlined upon the question of computing profits for this type of business, which up to this time seems to be a subject upon which very little accounting literature exists.

As these questions are constantly recurring in ranch accounting, I have taken this means of presenting these views on the subject, not thinking that this is the final word upon the subject, but hoping rather that some one may further elucidate the principles involved.

The following is illustrative of the two methods of making the income tax return by two farms having the same transactions, but different accounting methods:

(a)*

```
Gross income per operating account.........................$7,126.14
   Allowable deductions:
      Repairs  ....................................$  150.00?
      Interest  ....................................    350.00?
      Taxes  ......................................    600.00
      Wages  ......................................  1,000.00
      Deprec'n  ...................................    100.00?
                                                    ─────────
         Total deductions  ............................$2,200.00
                                                    ═════════
         Net income  ................................$4,926.14
   Less: Specific exemption.................................. 3,000.00
                                                    ─────────
         Taxable income  ...........................$1,926.14
                                                    ═════════
```

1% on $1,926.14 is $19.26, the amount class (a) will pay.

(b)†

```
Gross income (cash receipts from sales)  ...................$4,000.00
   (In addition to the above sales, there is $1,300 in accounts re-
   ceivable on the books representing sales made, but not yet
   collected, and which are not included in above "income.")

   Allowable deductions:
      Repairs paid for  .............................$  100.00
         (Balance $50 due but not paid for, hence not
         reported.)

      Interest paid  ................................    300.00
         ($50 accrued but not yet paid.)

      Taxes  ......................................    600.00
      Wages  ......................................  1,000.00
                                                    ─────────
         Total allowable deductions  ....................$2,000.00
                                                    ═════════
         Net income  ................................$2,000.00
                                                    ═════════
```

The following illustration is not based upon actual figures, but is simply prepared to show the two methods that have been used in making returns of income tax for 1913. Column 1 shows the figures for transactions on two farms, while column 2 shows the transactions which affect the report of class (b):

---

* Class (a) is making his report upon the basis of his books closed at the end of a fiscal period   Allowable deductions are shown in detail and not as required by schedule No. 1040, upon which individual returns are made.
† As the specific exemption is $3,000 in both cases, it will be noted that, (not taking into consideration the deductions of five-sixths of the income and five-sixths of the "specific exemption") class (b) has no tax to pay, while class (a) will have to pay $19.26.

		(1)	(2)
Dec. 31, 1912,	Inventory of grain ....$	507.86	
"	" of stock	1,966.00	
"	" of machinery	900.00	
1913,	Purchases of stock	400.00	$ 400.00
"	" of machinery (new)	200.00	
"	" " " (replacements) ..	100.00	100.00
"	" " " (repairs)	50.00	50.00
	Interest paid	300.00	300.00
"	" accrued (payable)	50.00	
	Taxes	600.00	600.00
	Wages	1,000.00	1,000.00
	Depreciation of machinery	80.00	
"	" of stock	20.00	
	Sales of grain	1,500.00	1,500.00
"	" " stock	3,800.00	3,800.00
	Grain fed to stock	700.00	700.00
Dec. 31, 1913,	Inventory of grain	4,400	
"	" of stock	300.00	

OPERATING STATEMENT

Class (a)

	Grain	Stock
Sales ....$	1,500.00	$3,800.00
Inventory	4,400.00	300.00
Grain fed	700.00	
	$6,600.00	$4,100.00
Grain fed ....$ 700.00		
Purchases 400.00		
Inventory ....$ 507.86 1,966.00	507.86	3,066.00
Gross trading profit	$6,092.14	$1,034.00

PROFIT & LOSS:

$6,092.14
1,034.00

Gross trading profit brought down $7,126.14

Expenses and losses:

Repairs and replacements ....$	150.00
Interest	350.00
Taxes	600.00
Wages	1,000.00
Depreciation of stock	20.00
" of machinery	8c oo

Total losses $2,200.00

Net profit, 12 months $4,926.14

R. M. HAIG

THE CONCEPT OF INCOME—ECONOMIC AND LEGAL ASPECTS

BY

ROBERT MURRAY HAIG, Ph.D.

The Sixteenth Amendment to the Constitution gives Congress power to tax "incomes, from whatever source derived." Acting under this grant of authority, Congress has, for eight years past, collected taxes upon what it has been pleased to term income. In no one of the three statutes passed during that time has Congress attempted to formulate definitely a positive definition of income. Moreover, eight years have proved insufficient to secure from the courts a fully adjudicated definition. It is true that certain important items, notably stock dividends, which Congress has sought to include within the scope of the term, have been eliminated by court decisions. Much more important items, however, await judicial consideration. Even such questions as the taxability of gains from appreciations of property values are still unsettled. Such decisions as have been handed down appear to be leading toward a definition of income so narrow and artificial as to bring about results which from the economic point of view are certainly eccentric and in certain cases little less than absurd. The unsettled status of the definition and the wide differences of opinion which exist as to what the term *income*, as used in the Sixteenth Amendment, did, does, or ought to mean justifies an examination of its content from the point of view of the economics of the problem and from the point of view of the practice elsewhere.

In this paper no attempt is made to evaluate or criticise the interpretation of the statutes or the Sixteenth Amendment by the courts from the point of view of general legal and constitutional principles involved. This will be done in other papers to follow. The approach here taken is the broader one of fundamental economics and equity.

First of all, consider what the economist means when he speaks of income. In this case, as in so many others, the economist uses a term in approximately the same sense as it is used in ordinary intercourse. It has merely been necessary for him to be more precise as to exact limits and distinctions. There has been no revolutionary contribution to economic thought on this topic since the passage of the Sixteenth Amendment. The economist and the man in the street both use the term now as they used it in 1913.

Modern economic analysis recognizes that fundamentally income is a flow of satisfactions, of intangible psychological experiences. If one receives a dollar he receives something which he ordinarily can and does spend—perhaps for a dinner. Is his income the dollar, or is it the dinner which he buys with the dollar, or is it, at bottom, the satisfaction of his wants which he derives from eating the dinner—the comfort and the sustenance it yields to him? If one spends his dollar for something more durable than a dinner—say a book or a pipe—is his true income the book or the pipe, or the series of satisfactions or "usances" arising from reading the book or smoking the pipe? There is no doubt as to the answer to these questions. A man strives for the satisfaction of his wants and desires and not for objects for their own sake.

How universal is the acceptance of this general view may be gauged from the following pronouncements of the writers of some of the most recent and widely used texts dealing with the principles of economics. Thus Professor Taussig, of Harvard, disposes of the question:

Now just as all production in the last analysis consists in the creation of utilities, so all income consists in the utilities or satisfactions created. Economic goods are not ends in themselves but means to the end of satisfying wants. . . Our food, clothing, furniture, may be said to yield psychic income. They shed utilities, so to speak, as long as they last.

Professor Irving Fisher, of Yale, in his book asserts most categorically that "Income consists of benefits," and, again,

¹ *Principles of Economics*, 1916, vol. I, p. 134.

that "A flow of benefits during a period of time is called income." [2]

Professor Ely, of Wisconsin, emphasizes the same point in these words:

Wealth refers to the stock of goods on hand at a particular time. Real income, on the other hand, has reference to the satisfaction we derive from the use of material things or personal services during a period of time.[3]

Finally, Professor Seligman, in his *Principles of Economics*,[4] declares that "We desire things at bottom because of their utility. They can impart this utility only in the shape of a succession of pleasurable sensations. These sensations are our true income."

The testimony of our leading economists on this point is unanimous. Even in England, where the concept of taxable income is different from our own in important respects, the modern economists recognize the validity of the analysis set forth above. Thus Professor Alfred Marshall, of Cambridge, states that:

. . . a woman who makes her own clothes, or a man who digs in his own garden or repairs his own house, is earning income just as would the dressmaker, gardener, or carpenter who might be hired to do the work. . . For scientific purposes, it would be best if the word income when occuring alone should always mean total real income.[5]

However, the economist, while recognizing all this, realizes that before he can proceed far with his analysis of economic phenomena he must arrive at something more definite and more homogeneous—less diaphanous and elusive than these psychic satisfactions. An individual, it is true, can compare the relative worth to him of a pipe or a book or a dinner and arrange his order of consumption without the use of any formal common denominator such as money. Yet this individual would have great difficulty in telling you exactly how much satisfaction he derived from his pipe or his book. How much more difficult would it be for a second person to measure those

[2] *Elementary Principles of Economics*, 1911, p. 34.
[3] *Outlines of Economics*, 1908, p. 98.
[4] 1914, p. 16.
[5] *Economics of Industry*, 1901, p. 51.

satisfactions for him without the aid of some common unit!
How impossible it is to compare one man's satisfaction with a
book with another man's satisfaction with his dinner! Thus Professor Taussig is led to conclude that:

> . . . for almost all purposes of economic study, it is best to content ourselves with a statement, and an attempt at measurement, in terms not of utility but of money income. . . The reason for this rejection of a principle which is in itself sound lies in the conclusion . . . regarding total utility and consumer's surplus: They cannot be measured.[6] .

The basis of comparison, the foundation upon which economic interaction and exchange take place is, of course, that of the common, universally-acceptable unit of value—money. The usances and satisfactions and the goods and services supplying them which are of significance to the economist in his analysis are those which are susceptible of evaluation in terms of money. This, of course, involves the element of scarcity, relative to demand. When one can express his wants and satisfaction in terms of dollars and cents he can use a language which other men can understand and which means something to the economic community generally.

It should be carefully noted, however, that, first, when one abandons "usances" and satisfactions and substitutes the goods and services yielding these satisfactions, he is taking a step away from the fundamentals, for two equal sets of goods and services may yield very different satisfactions; and second, if one takes the next step, as most income tax laws do in the main, and substitutes money received during a period in place of goods and services used, as the content of the term income, he has really moved a very appreciable distance from the fundamental conception, for not only does everyone receive goods and services of greater or less amount without buying them with money, but also everyone is, in effect, considered to be in receipt of his income when he gets the money with which to buy the goods and services which will yield the usances and satisfactions which go to make up his true income. Indeed, the purchase of the goods and ser-

[6] Taussig, loc. cit.

vices may, of course, be postponed indefinitely. In the words of Professor Ely:

> Money income should, perhaps, refer to the value of the goods consumed and the services enjoyed, although in popular speech and by many economists the word is used in the literal sense of the net amount of money that comes in, whether it is spent for enjoyable things or is saved.[1]

It is apparent from what has been said that when taxable income is identified with money received in a given period two approximations have been introduced, each of which involves anomalies and inequalities as between members of the same class ostensibly on equal terms. For example, two persons who receive precisely equal amounts of goods and services may derive therefrom very unequal "usances" and satisfactions. If "usances" and satisfactions are really the proper theoretical basis for apportioning the tax burden there is here an inequality. Certainly, everyone will agree that they constitute an entirely impracticable basis. Consequently, any theoretical injustice involved must necessarily be incurred if we are to have an income tax at all. But is there, after all, any theoretical injustice? Who, for instance, would seriously defend the proposition that taxes should be apportioned according to capacity for appreciation rather than according to the capacity to command the goods and services which are appreciated? The only economically significant goods are those which are susceptible of evaluation in terms of money.

In the next place, two persons who receive precisely equal amounts of money-income may receive very unequal amounts of goods and services, either because one has postponed spending a larger portion of his money than the other, or because one has received more income *in kind*. No great harm is done if the person who postpones spending his money is taxed upon it when he receives it rather than when he spends it. However, it is a different matter in the case of income *in kind*, such as the fire-wood the farmer cuts from his wood lot or the vegetables for his table which he gathers from his garden. Certainly, the fact that one man buys his fire-wood or

[1] Ely, *loc. cit.*

144

his vegetables, rather than receives them without the formality of a money sale, should not operate so as to increase the weight of his income tax. The economics of this situation is very clear. The statement made in the preceding paragraph is that the goods and services which are of significance are those which are susceptible of evaluation in terms of money. It is not necessary that they should actually have passed through the process of a sale. From the point of view of equity it is theoretically important that all goods [8] and services received without payment should be accounted for in case it is possible to value them in terms of money.

Perhaps it is clear, then, how and why the fundamental economic conception of income as a flow of satisfactions must undergo substantial modification to fit it for use in economic analysis generally and for use particularly as a basis for apportioning a tax burden. The satisfactions themselves become economically significant for the purpose only when they are susceptible of evaluation in terms of money. It is necessary as a practical proposition to disregard the intangible psychological factors and have regard either for the money-worth of the goods and services utilized during a given period or for the money itself received during the period supplemented by the money-worth of such goods and services as are received directly without a money transaction.

If the first option is taken, viz., the money-worth of the goods and services utilized during a given period, we arrive at a pure consumption tax, unless indeed we attempt an evaluation of the satisfactions arising from the consciousness of a saved surplus which is obviously an impracticable procedure. It is interesting to recall that this is the result which the English economist, John Stuart Mill, sought to establish a half-century ago, although the analysis underlying his conclusions was a quite different one. To tax saved income and then in future years to tax the income from those savings was, he contended, double taxation.[9] The same conclusion has

---

[8] For gifts, cf. infra., p. 26.

[9] The source of this and several other statements made in this paper with respect to the theories of foreign economists is an unpublished monograph by Mr. Clarence Heer, a former student in the seminar of Professor Seligman.

been reached by certain Italian writers, notably Einaudi.[10]

The second option, however, has been the one generally adopted as the definition of income in modern income tax acts. Under this conception, income becomes the increase or accretion in one's power to satisfy his wants in a given period in so far as that power consists of (a) money itself, or, (b) anything susceptible of valuation in terms of money. More simply stated, the definition of income which the economist offers is this: Income is the *money value of the net accretion to one's economic power between two points of time.*

It will be observed that this definition departs in only one important respect from the fundamental economic conception of income as a flow of satisfactions. It defines income in terms of power to satisfy economic wants rather than in terms of the satisfactions themselves. It has the effect of taxing the recipient of income when he receives the power to attain satisfactions rather than when he elects to exercise that power. This should do no violence to our sense of equity, however. The fact that a man chooses to postpone the gratification of his desires is no sufficient reason for postponing his tax.

It will be readily agreed that this definition, viz., that income is the net accretion to one's economic strength in a given period, constitutes, then, the closest practicable approximation of true income. It coincides very closely indeed with the flow of economic "usances" and satisfactions expressed in terms of money, which all economists agree constitutes the thing after all we are attempting to measure. Certainly this definition is scientific in the sense that it is broad enough to include everything of like nature. Anomalies are avoided by the very simple expedient of casting the definition in broad terms. On the other hand, is the definition so broad that it includes items fundamentally dissimilar? The test of similarity applied is power in terms of money to command goods and services yielding usances and satisfactions. Is it possible to add any other test without so restricting the definition as to exclude items which should be included and thus introduce

[10] Luigi Einaudi, *Corso di Scienza della Finanza*, 3rd Edition, Capitalo 4.

inequities and discriminations as between persons in substantially identical economic positions? Professor Seligman believes that in addition to the criteria of money-value, periodicity, and realization[7] included in the definition as stated above, there should also be applied the test of separation as a necessary attribute of income.[11] Much depends upon precisely what is meant by separation. Included in the test of "susceptibility of evaluation" is certainly the condition that the valuation attached to the accretion must be sufficiently definite to form the basis for a realization. The item must be realizable and separable, certainly. That there must be an actual physical separation, however, before economic income is realized, cannot, I believe, be conceded, for, with a definition so narrowed it is not possible, in the stock-dividend case, for example, to remove the inequity as between different classes of security holders. The adoption of the definition as developed above leads to the same conclusion as that reached by Professor Seligman, *viz.*, that stock-dividends are not income, but the reason is not that the income has not yet accrued to the shareholder when the stock-dividend is declared, but rather that, economically, it has accrued to the shareholder even before the stock-dividend was declared, *viz.*, if and when the improved economic position of the corporation was reflected in the holdings of the stockholder with sufficient definiteness to be susceptible of evaluation.

What more narrow definition than the one suggested will solve the problems presented by the following three questions?

1. Are stock-dividends income?
2. Is undistributed surplus income to the shareholder?
3. Are appreciations in property values income?

1. *Are stock-dividends income?* The Supreme Court has decided that stock-dividends are not income.[12] What is the effect of this decision upon the economic position of the three following persons, *A*, *B*, and *C*, who are shareholders in similar corporations, each owning ten per cent. of the stock? Assume

[11] Edwin R. A. Seligman, "Are Stock Dividends Income?" *American Economic Review* September, 1919.

[12] Towne *v.* Eisner, 245 U. S. 418; Eisner *v.* Macomber, 252 U. S. 189.

that each company makes $1,000,000 in the given accounting period. On the day of the directors' meeting when the question of the declaration of a dividend will be considered, the economic position of all three men is the same, and no one would deny that the economic strength of each had been increased by virtue of his ten per cent. interest in a corporation which has earned a million dollars net income. *A's* corporation declares a cash dividend of $1,000,000, *A's* share being $100,000 in money. *B's* corporation declares a stock-dividend of $1,000,000, *B's* share being $100,000 in stock. *C's* corporation declares no dividend, *C's* interest in the earnings of that year being reflected presumably in an increase in the market value of his stock. Before the stock dividend decision *A's* share and *B's* share were both considered taxable income. *C* was taxed only if and when the profits were distributed—unless in truth he were taxed indirectly in case he sold his stock at an appreciated value. *A* and *B* were together in one class. *C* was alone in a second class. As between the two classes there was a marked difference of treatment. The stock dividend decision disassociated *B* from *A* and placed him in the class with *C*. The line marking the difference of treatment is now no longer drawn between *B* and *C*. It is drawn between *A* and *B*. But the point is that the difference persists. Can justice be established in an income tax as among *A*, *B*, and *C* by any action short of making each of them subject to income tax upon the increase in his economic strength resulting from the earnings of the corporation in which he is interested? In this case *A* should account for the $100,000 cash dividend in his income tax return. *B* should account for the market value of his stock dividend on the last day of the year, minus any decline, if any, in the market value of his original block of stock during the year. *C* should be taxed on the increased market value of his block of stock. All of them, under the assumption, have received a net accretion of economic strength during the year definite enough to be susceptible of evaluation. Can a more narrow concept of income than this solve the problem here presented?

2. *Is undistributed surplus income to the shareholder?* The problem with respect to the taxation of undivided surplus may be presented best by a similar example. Assume that *A* owns ten per cent. of the stock of a corporation and that *B* owns a ten per cent. interest in a partnership, each of which earns $1,000,000 during a given accounting period. *B* must include in his individual income tax return his distributive share of the profits, $100,000, which item becomes subject to both normal and surtax rates. On the other hand, *A* includes in his personal income tax return his share of the profits in his corporation only if and when these profits are declared as dividends. If they are never distributed, they never become subject to the individual surtax rates. The corporation, it is true, pays the so-called normal tax at the time when the profits are earned, and *A* may take credit for part of this normal tax in his individual return when he receives the dividend. It is also true that the excess profits tax applies to corporate profits and not to partnership or individual profits and that for the present this has brought about a condition of poise which will be sadly disturbed if the excess profits tax should disappear. But what precise solution is there for this badly muddled situation short of the adoption of a concept of income broad enough to tax *A* on the increased market value of his stock which presumably results from ploughing the earnings back into the business of the corporation? In the absence of dependable market quotations, would not the accounts of the corporation, as to undistributed surplus, furnish light as to the increase in *A's* economic position?

3. *Are appreciations in property values income?* At the present time we consider appreciations of property values taxable income.[18] But we inventory nothing except stock-in-trade. In other words, we say in effect that nothing appreciates in value until it is sold. This, of course, is not in accord

---

[18] In a decision published after this paper was written, Judge J. D. Thomas, of the District Court of the United States, District of Connecticut, has decided, in the case of Brewster *v.* Walsh, Collector (No. 2133 at law), that the increase in the value of capital assets when realized by sale or other disposition, by one not a trader or dealer therein, is not income, and hence is not taxable as such. The Government has announced an appeal to the Supreme Court.

with economic facts, however perfectly it may synchronize with accounting practice. The truth is that certain so-called accounting principles have been evolved with other ends primarily in view than the accurate determination of relative taxpaying ability. The general result may be illustrated as follows: *A* and *B* each buy houses in 1914 for $10,000. Both houses appreciate in value until they are worth $20,000 each in 1916. *A* sells his house in 1916 and becomes taxable on the $10,000 profit. The highest surtax rates in 1916 were thirteen per cent. He holds his $10,000 uninvested. *B* retains his house, but after 1916 the value remains stationary. He sells in 1920 and realizes $10,000 profit. In 1920 the rates range as high as seventy-three per cent. Here are two men whose economic strength has varied in precisely the same manner. They are called upon to pay quite different amounts in federal income taxes. Can any proposal offer a satisfactory solution of this problem which does not assume a concept of income similar to that outlined above? To achieve exact justice the increased economic strength of the two men must be measured *period for period*.

The general conclusion from the foregoing discussion is this: That the economist when asked whether a particular item is income or is not income, must, in the opinion of the writer, make his reply depend upon whether the receipt of that item has increased the economic power of the recipient to command satisfaction-yielding goods or services. If it does, it is income; if it does not, it is not income. The answer would then be based on practically the bed-rock of economic principle—not quite, perhaps, because of the approximations already pointed out, but certainly on a level as near as is practicable to that bed-rock. If courts are to base their decisions on economic principle, the answer to their queries should be in terms of the most fundamental of principles.

These statements present nothing which is really novel. This same doctrine has long been taught by that faithful hand-servant of the practical business man—the accountant. When one examines the standard books dealing with the theory of accounting he finds the definition of the net profit of a business undertaking stated in almost the precise words used in the general definition given above. Thus, A. Lowes Dickinson in his *Accounting Practice and Procedure* [14] says:

In the widest possible view, profits may be stated as the realized increment in the value of the whole amount invested in an undertaking; and, conversely, loss is the realized decrement.

Again, Robert H. Montgomery in his *Auditing* remarks:

If an absolutely accurate balance sheet could be prepared at the beginning and the end of a period, the difference would constitute the net profit or the net loss for the term.

The economist and the accountant are also, of course, in complete accord as to the theoretical distinction between income on the one hand and capital, or property, or wealth on the other. The accountant's "absolutely accurate balance sheet," to use Montgomery's phrase,[15] is synonymous with the economist's "fund relating to a given instant,"[16] to use Professor Fisher's language, or, "accumulation of . . . utilities or income at an instant of time," [17] to use Professor Seligman's expression. The establishment of "net income," both agree, must not involve an impairment of the capital sum.

Confusion of thought is sometimes caused by the fact that the accountant usually speaks in terms of a business enterprise as a separate entity, while the economist usually speaks in terms of the individual person. The distinction between gross and net income—which occupies so large a part of the attention of the accountant—is summarily dismissed by the economist whose typical income receiver is the man whose expenditures are predominantly for purposes of personal consumption. The definitions and reasoning of the accountant, however, are very readily fitted to the case of this typical economic man if the accounting period is reduced to its true economic length, which in the case of the wage earner is a week and the salaried worker a month. In the typical business the period is, of course, a year, the net income not being determined and distributed until the end of that period.

[14] p. 67.
[15] 1916, p. 206.
[16] Fisher, *op. cit.*, pp. 56–57.
[17] Seligman, *loc. cit.*

The detailed technique of determining the precise deductions which should properly be made as business expenses, as contrasted with expenditures of a capital nature, has been developed by the accountants along lines entirely acceptable to the economist. Many interesting theoretical questions are involved, such, for example, as the degree to which risk may properly be insured against by means of various reserves, but a survey of this portion of the field—while germane to the topic—cannot be developed in the time available. Ordinarily the economist contents himself with the assertion that the income must be *net*, that all expenses connected with its production must have been met.

The problem of distinguishing sharply between business expense and personal expense is one which is the occasion of much practical difficulty and upon which wide differences of opinion exist. Certain German writers, *e. g.*, Weissenborn,[18] go so far as to classify all personal and family expenditures for food, clothing, and shelter as deductible expenses, rendering the income tax substantially a tax on merely saved income. This is a result diametrically opposite to that reached by the English and Italian economists referred to above [19]— and it is a conception which does not find any considerable response except in so far as the relief of a bare minimum of subsistence, under the various personal exemptions, may be conceived to be such a response.

It is often a long step, however, between the accountant's theory and his practice; between his abstract statement as to what net profit is and the actual figure certified as such on a balance sheet. It is an equally long step for the economist between his general definition of income and the content of the category which in his opinion forms the best basis for the imposition of an income tax. This is a practical, workaday world full of imperfections. Most economists, popular superstition to the contrary, are fairly conversant with the facts of modern business life and are fairly well aware of the practical difficulties of fitting abstract conceptions to the

[18] *Die Besteuerung nach dem Ueberfluss*, 1911.
[19] *Cf. supra*, pp. 6-7.

environment of the market-place. Certainly modifications—serious modifications—must be made in the general definition of income, as formulated above, to fit it for use as the item of net income entered on Form 1040 or Form 1120, and the scientific economist in advising the legislator would be the last to suggest an attempt to follow the implications of his analysis without regard to the limitations imposed by the actual conditions under which the law must function. Such a course would be anything but scientific. The point to be grasped very clearly, however, is this: Those modifications to which he would consent and which, indeed, he is among the first to urge, are, after all is said and done, merely modifications—merely concessions made to the exigencies of a given situation. For example, one might urge that no tax be placed on a gain arising from the appreciation of a fixed asset until it is actually sold. But the recommendation should not be urged on the ground that the appreciation is not income until it is sold. The economic fact is that the owner of that asset comes into possession of economic income whenever the increase in the value of that asset is sufficient in amount and definite enough in character to be susceptible of precise evaluation in terms of money. Again, one might urge that no tax be placed on the services which one actually enjoys when he lives in his own home rather than a rented one. But, again, that recommendation should not be supported by the assertion that this item is not income. It is income whenever it is susceptible of evaluation in terms of money. Neither the economist nor the courts should express their opinions in the form of an assertion that it is not income. That, it seems to the writer, is not the real question in either of the illustrations given. The real question is, rather: Is it justifiable to treat this item of income in some special way as compared with other items of income because of special circumstances surrounding its receipt? Thus, it may be futile and silly, from an administrative point of view, to attempt to include in the income tax return a money estimate of the income which the man receives when he lives in his own house. The Wisconsin authorities, after attempting to list such income for several years, have decided that the game is not worth the candle. Or, it may be impracticable as an accounting proposition, to reflect the varying worth of capital assets on the balance sheet. As the accountant, Dickinson, points out:

Inasmuch . . . as the ultimate realization of the original investment is from the nature of things deferred for a long period of years, during which partial realizations are continually taking place, it becomes necessary to fall back on estimates of value at certain definite periods, and to consider as profit and loss the estimated increase or decrease between any two such periods.[20]

If the difficulties of complete periodical revaluations are so great as to make it impracticable to tax appreciations as they accrue, they ought not to be so taxed, and the question is transformed into these new queries: "When may these appreciations best be taxed?" and "If they are taxed sporadically is the result so unjust that no attempt should be made to tax them at all?"

To the writer it seems unfortunate that the questions as to the constitutionality of the federal income tax on specific items are turning so largely on the question as to whether the items are or are not income. The items most controverted certainly fall within the definition of income established by the analysis of business facts made by both the economist and the accountant. Moreover, the concept of income is, after all, essentially an economic concept, and if the legal concept established by court interpretation under a particular constitutional provision or amendment departs in any very fundamental fashion from the economic concept, injustices may arise of such magnitude as to necessitate either the abandonment of the income tax or the adoption of a constitutional amendment which will give a positive and comprehensive definition of income. The difficulty could be avoided if the broad economic concept of income were frankly accepted with its single test as to whether the item resulted in an improvement in economic power capable of being evaluated. The questions which the courts would then be called upon to consider would be as to whether the modifications made by Congress and by the Treasury, in attempting to

[20] Loc. cit.

construct a concept of taxable income which will be at once workable and approximately just, are modifications which are reasonable and in conformity with the various constitutional guaranties.

It goes without saying that taxable income under an income tax law should approximate as nearly as practicable the true net income as defined by the analysis of the economist and the accountant. How close an approximation is possible depends upon the perfection of the environment in which the tax must live. No unnecessary departure from the true concept should be made. The imperfections of our present economic environment which are of most significance to this problem fall into three classes:

    1. The imperfections of the economic standard of value;

    2. The imperfections of accounting practice; and

    3. The imperfections of the administration.

A perfect income tax is unattainable so long as modifications must be made because of imperfections in our standard of value, our accounting, and our administration. These classes will be taken up in turn.

    1. *Imperfections of the economic standard of value.* That variations occur from time to time in the price level and in the value of money is well known to every person whose resources during recent years have been sufficiently limited to compel him to have any regard at all for his expenditures. If income is defined as the total accretion in one's economic strength between two points of time, as valued in terms of money, it is clear that his income will reflect every change in the value of money between those two points of time in so far as the items entered on the balance sheets at those times affect the computation. If the level of prices goes up ten per cent. the money value of my assets will ordinarily follow at a like rate. That particular increase in value does not really indicate an increase in my economic strength. My power to command economic goods and services has not increased, for the money-value of these goods and services has likewise increased. So long as we have a money standard which varies, we shall find that even a perfect accounting system will show a net income which is not

identical with the true accretion of economic power. Indeed, the more perfect the valuation and the accounting, the greater will this injustice be.

It must be borne in mind, however, that this is an evil which is with us under our present law. A man who sold an asset in 1920 which he had purchased in 1914, making an apparent profit of 100 per cent. and receiving his pay in fifty-cent dollars is, under our statute, subject to tax on his gain, although that gain is only apparent and not real. Moreover, the situation is particularly unjust under our present system. If complete periodical revaluations were used in determining income there would still be relative equality as between different taxpayers. But as the situation now stands, the transactions are closed in a haphazard and uneven fashion. A man who happens to sell out at the peak of the price curves, is taxed very unequally as compared with the man who continues his transaction until a period of lower price levels.

It should also be borne in mind that this element is of some influence even in an income tax such as that in force in Great Britain where appreciations in property values are not taxed, for an item of inventory included in one's accounts at the beginning of the year and sold in the course of the year will reflect the change in the prices during the period held.

If it were possible to modify the concept of taxable income so as to eliminate this variation it would certainly be desirable to do so. The prospect for a complete solution of the difficulty pointed out, however, is identical with the prospect for a perfect monetary standard. But an approximate solution might be realized if we were able to evolve a satisfactory index of the level of prices. If it were accurately known what the change in price level in a given year had been, it might be possible to qualify the results shown by a comparison of the balance sheets for the beginning and the end of the period in such a way as to eliminate the influence of the changing standard. But even this refinement is not likely to be introduced soon. Indeed, the desirability and urgency of its introduction is dependent largely upon the complete solution of the accounting problem, which solution is certainly not imminent.

2. *The imperfections of accounting practice.* The wide gap which stretches between theory and practice in the field of accounting has already been remarked. Until such time as everyone keeps accounts and the accounts furnish a perfect record of everyone's economic position, the concept of taxable income must be modified in order to meet the problem presented by the shortcomings of accounting practice. Dozens of illustrations of how the concept is modified in our statute because of the necessity of allowing for the imperfections and incompleteness of accounts will occur to everyone.

While the accounting ideal as stated by the leading theorists in the accounting field is in entire harmony with the economic analysis, it should be pointed out that many so-called accounting princip'es which are generally accepted are little more than rules of action formulated during an obsolete period when the use of accounts for tax purposes did not exist. So long as the chief purposes of the accounts were to provide a basis for applications for credit, and for the distribution of dividends, rules which tended toward a conservative statement of profits were certainly full of virtue. The increase in the tax burden has added a new primary use for the accounts, a use which demands certain qualities which are not important in the other cases. To form an entirely satisfactory basis for the imposition of income taxes the accounts must reflect the full, true, economic position of the taxpayer; and in so far as arbitrary rules of inventory valuations operate to build up hidden reserves, or other accounting practices tend to befog the picture, they must ultimately be eliminated and they have no place in truly scientific accounting.

3. *The imperfections of the administration.* A lively regard for the limitations of the administration is essential to the successful formulation of a tax statute. This is a factor which we have failed to recognize sufficiently in this country. Many of the modifications which our statute makes in the concept of income are obviously designed to simplify the problem of administration, but in spite of the number and character of these modifications there appears to be grave question as to whether they have been sufficient to reduce the administra-

tive task to manageable proportions. The British, with their splendid civil service, are appalled at the burden we place upon our inadequate treasury staff. Certainly such changes in the abstract definition of income as are necessary to make the statute practical and workable must be accepted, provided the cost in terms of equity is not so great as to make some available alternative tax a more attractive method of raising the revenue.

In addition to modifications on the above grounds, modifications of two additional types are often urged. Those who are convinced that taxation should be used for the furtherance of social ends often demand special modifications. For example, those who are deeply impressed with the desirability of increasing the amount of economic capital demand special treatment of the individual surplus of corporations, or reduced surtax rates upon that portion of individual incomes which are saved and reinvested. There are others who on social grounds believe in a differentiation between earned and unearned income.

Again, the fiscal necessities of the Government are sometimes urged as adequate ground for declining to bring the concept of taxable income into closer harmony with the concept of economic income, as in the case of the recent letter of the Secretary of the Treasury.

If time permitted it would be interesting to trace the historical evolution of the concept of economic income and of taxable income from the time these concepts became important down to the present. Only the barest summary, however, is here possible. The British income tax places very heavy stress upon the annual character of income. For an explanation of this conception, which results in the exclusion from taxable income of gains of an irregular nature, one must go back as far as the fifteenth century, when, with an agricultural society where few fortuitous gains developed, the idea of receipts as being annual in character became deeply impressed upon the minds of the people. It became the habit to think of one's regular receipts as his income, and to consider irregular receipts as additions to capital. Adam Smith spoke of income both as what remains free after maintaining the capital and as what people can consume without encroaching upon their capital. Ricardo accepted Adam Smith's conception of economic capital but protested vigorously against a concept of taxable income which would include legacies and even wages. McCulloch developed a theory of differentiated income under which income from personal services was to be fully insured in order to put it on a fair basis as compared with the income from a building from which depreciation allowances had been subtracted. Despairing of the practicability of such a proposal, he concluded that income taxation was fundamentally unfair. John Stewart Mill disapproved of McCulloch's theory of differentiation, but insisted upon exemption for savings. Because of the practical difficulties in the way of this he urged a remission of an arbitrary percentage of the income from "temporary" sources.[21] This is essentially the plan which has been incorporated into the Italian income tax of today. As has been noted, Marshall defines income in the broadest possible fashion.[22]

Just as the British income tax has served as the model for the various continental income taxes, so English writers have influenced the thought of the writers in other countries. Thus the German writers since Schmoller have broken away from the concept of yield and have emphasized the subjective concept. These Germans all agree that income includes all goods which are placed at the disposal of the individual for the satisfaction of his wants, but they disagree considerably as to the exact composition of that income and its relationship to the concept of capital. The idea of the durability of the source plays a considerable rôle in their discussions. Schanz calls income the net inflow of means during a given period, including all usances and services having a money value.[23]

To Roscher, income is a rather restricted category consisting of the aggregate of goods which, arising within a given period of time as the yields of durable sources of revenue, are at the

[21] Heer, op. cit.
[22] Cf. supra, p. 3.
[23] Heer, op. cit.

disposal of the individual for the satisfaction of his personal wants and those of his family. Wagner and his associates, including Cohn, Newman, and Philippovitch, emphasize both periodicity and permanency of source. Income to them is either the sum total of goods which at regularly recurring intervals flow into the treasury of the individual, or those commodities, valuable services of third parties, and usances which, as periodic fruits of permanent productive sources, flow into the possession of the individual and over which he has absolute control.[24] It should be noted that here again appears the idea of separation emphasized by Professor Seligman.[25]

If this is what the foreign writers say about the economic concept of income, what do the foreign legislators do about establishing the limits of the concept of taxable income? Both the British and the German statutes construct a concept much more narrow than ours. Both attempt to differentiate between regular and fortuitous gains. A British salaried man who dabbles in the stock exchange is not called to account for his gains or losses. The owner of a residence in Germany is not asked to include a profit realized on its sale. Gains and losses on property are recognized only when they accrue with respect to the stock-in-trade of a dealer. In Great Britain, if one sells his mine at a profit, that profit is not subject to income tax, but neither are depletion allowances deductible in making one's annual returns. The consideration paid for a lease is not taxed, but depreciation in the lease may not be deducted. The British do not tax gains from appreciation in the value of real estate, which reduces considerably the significance of the late-lamented British Increment Value Duty. As a matter of fact, the effect of this Duty was to operate as a fairly reasonable income tax on the profits from such transactions.

Having formulated a definition of economic income, having presented the broad grounds upon which modifications may properly be made in order to fit the concept to the necessities of the business situation, and having made a very brief survey

[24] *Ibid.*
[25] *Cf. supra,* p. 8.

of foreign theory and practice, let us examine the meaning of the term income as used in the Revenue Act of 1918 to ascertain how closely it approaches the ideal conception of income. Such a discussion will bring clearly to the fore the implications of the proposed definition; it will test the adequacy of that definition to resolve the anomalies of our present practice; and will raise questions as to the desirability of changes in our present statutory concept.

The Revenue Act of 1918 states that "there shall be levied, collected, and paid for each taxable year upon the *net income* of every individual (and corporation) a tax." [26] Net income is defined as gross income minus certain specific deductions.[27] Gross income, in turn, is described by specifying certain items which it shall include and exclude. This establishes the outer, the inclusive limits. But it is apparent that this merely describes certain specific sources, the income arising from which is taxed. In the familiar language of the statute, gross income "includes gains, profits, and income derived from salaries, wages or compensation for personal service . . ., of whatever kind and in whatever form paid, or from professions, vocations, trades, businesses, commerce, or sales, or dealings in property, whether real or personal, growing out of the ownership or use of or interest in such property; also from interest, rents, dividends, securities, or the transaction of any business carried on for gain or profit, or gains or profits, and income derived from any source whatever."

The first point which impresses one with respect to our statutory concept is its breadth as compared with the concepts used elsewhere. It attempts to draw no line between capital gains and gains of other types. It places no emphasis at all upon the permanence of the source or the regularity of the income. In its general scope it approaches almost to the point of complete identity the working concept of profit used by the accountant. It is by all odds the most theoretically perfect income tax law extant, from the point of view of its general scope. Whether it is, after all, the most scientific

[26] Secs. 210 and 230.
[27] Secs. 212 and 232.

law is another question, for that involves the degree of skill that has been used in modifying the theoretical concept to meet our actual conditions. In that we have not been strikingly successful.

It is interesting to note the dependence which our lawmakers are beginning to place upon the accountants and their standards of practice. The 1918 law, for the first time, specifically directs that certain results be reached by methods in accordance with accepted accounting procedure. This appears to be the modern tendency and is certainly a laudable one. Thus the German Excess Profits Law passed in 1915 is an exceedingly simple document which meets the whole problem of defining profits by stating that they shall be taken to be the "balance of profit duly reckoned in accordance with the legal prescriptions and recognized principles and methods of mercantile accounting." [28]

The net income which our 1918 Act attempts to reach is in the main money income. There are these exceptions: (1) There is a specific provision to the effect that income from personal services "of whatever kind and in whatever form paid" [29] shall be accounted for. (2) Stock dividends are declared taxable but this declaration is nullified by the recent decisions of the Supreme Court. [30] (3) In the case of exchanges, the property received in exchange is "treated as the equivalent of cash to the amount of its fair market value, if any," [31] with the qualification that in the case of reorganizations the transactions are not closed in case the par value of the securities received in exchange for the old securities is not in excess of the securities surrendered.

It will be recalled that our definition demands the taxation of the net accretion of one's power measured in money or money-worth. Should the statute go further than it does in taxing real income even when received in some form other than money? The problem is largely an administrative one. The specific case of the income one really receives when he

[28] *Reichs Gesetsblatt,* No. 187, Year 1915.
[29] Sec. 213.
[30] *Cf. supra,* p. 8.
[31] Sec. 202 (b).

lives in the house he himself owns has become rather acute, the favored position of such an owner being vigorously used by real-estate promoters, particularly those interested in the sale of high-class apartment buildings on the coöperative plan. Such real income should certainly be taxed if it is practicable to evaluate it. The present position is anomalous, particularly when one remembers that such owners, while they may not deduct insurance and upkeep, may, nevertheless, deduct the taxes on the property and the interest on any money they may have borrowed to carry the property. The way to remove the anomaly is to approach the definition of income more closely in practice.

The statute includes as taxable income appreciations of property values, whether those appreciations are in stock-in-trade, in capital assets, or in miscellaneous bits of property owned incidentally. In this it has the sanction of our definition. A distinct departure is made from the definition, however, by the practice of taxing those appreciations only irregularly as sales are consummated, and at the rates in force in the year during which the consummation occurs. This practice lies at the root of the present widespread dissatisfaction with the taxation of appreciations. Our definition demands their taxation whenever they become susceptible of a definite evaluation. A scheme of arbitrary apportionment of the gain over the period of accrual would be infinitely superior to the present practice. With rates varying as they have during the past few years, there has been a tremendous incentive to the business man to resort to methods of postponing the closing of his transactions. The tax on appreciations has in fact operated as a substantial force restraining the alienation of property.

So long as our accounting methods are not equal to the task of furnishing a complete revaluation of assets at the beginning and the close of each accounting period there is no complete solution to this problem. However, unless the administrative burden of the plan of arbitrary apportionment of gains actually made at times of sale is too great to be borne, that plan should certainly be given a trial.

Too much importance may easily be attached to British precedents in determining whether gains from appreciations in property values should or should not be included within the definition of income. The British concept of taxable income, which excludes such gains, is a product of a practical local situation which differs in essential respects from our own. The exclusion of such gains is acknowledged to be illogical and was the cause of much evasion of the Excess Profits Duty. In fact in the administration of that Duty it was found necessary to make important modifications in the direction of the acknowledgment of capital gains and losses as factors in the determination of income.[82] Finally the *Report of the Royal Commission on the Income Tax*, recently submitted, not only recommends the recognition of depletion to a limited extent but urges that, hereafter, gains from incidental business transactions, even where the property which appreciates is not worthy of the designation of "inventory," be included within the scope of taxable income.[83]

There is an interesting incidental point in connection with this problem. We have been accustomed to consider the income tax as one of our elastic taxes whose rates may be conveniently varied to meet the needs of a variable budget. Has not our recent experience with our income tax which taxes appreciation shown that with an income tax of this type variable rates must be avoided until the day of perfect accounting arrives? If the business man were certain that present rates would continue indefinitely, the present game of postponing realizations would quickly cease. On the other hand, it may be well to meet this problem by adopting the British procedure of taxing business profits on the basis of an average of previous years.

The present statute does not regard gifts received by individuals as taxable income. Ordinarily gifts may not be subtracted in arriving at the taxable income of the giver, but charitable contributions made to certain corporations may be deducted by an individual, subject to a fifteen per cent. limitation.

[82] *Cf.* Haig, *The Taxation of Excess Profits in Great Britain*, 1920, pp. 69–73 *et passim.*
[83] *Cmd. 615*, p. 20 *et seq.*, p. 41, *et seq.*

Until recently the Treasury permitted such an individual to deduct from his taxable income the value of the gift when made. This procedure, however, has been changed and he may now subtract merely the original cost or the value on March 1, 1913, if purchased before that date. Gifts to relatives of property upon which one wishes to realize are becoming a common method of evasion, for profit to the recipient is measured from the value of the gift at time of receipt.

In view of suggested legislative action with reference to gifts it is of interest to consider them in relation to the definition as developed above. Are gifts income? Under the terms of the definition, they are if they increase the economic strength of the recipient. But most gifts are either to relatives or to charitable institutions. With respect to family gifts a case may be made out for ignoring the transfer of title on the ground of the essential economic unity of the family. The family, as a matter of fact, is even now to a considerable extent the basic unit for income tax purposes. Gifts to charitable institutions are now, within the fifteen per cent. limit, deductible to the giver and exempt to the recipient. On the ground of public policy much can be said for continuing this practice although it is also true that, speaking in terms of economic fundamentals, the man who makes a gift to some person or corporation outside his immediate family deliberately chooses that way of spending his money because it yields him a greater satisfaction than some alternative use. In any case appreciations in the property given away would, under the proposed definition, become taxable gradually as they emerged in definite enough form to be susceptible of an evaluation.

In summary, then, it must be apparent that the differences among economists as to the definition of income are really more on questions of policy than on questions of principle. There is substantial agreement as to its fundamental character, but some disagreement as to how far the definition ought to be narrowed so as to make it useful for purposes of an income tax base.

The formal definition of *economic* income, which, in the opinion of the writer, provides the most acceptable concept of income, may be stated as follows: *Income is the money-value of the net accretion to economic power between two points of time.* This definition cannot be written into a statute in literal form because of the technical disadvantages in determining income as so defined, but so long as taxable income differs appreciably from this definition there will be anomalies and injustices in income taxation, and every step marking a closer approximation of this definition will result in the elimination of irregular and eccentric results.

The concept of *taxable* income is a living, mutable concept which has varied widely from time to time and from country to country with the conditions under which it has had to operate.

The concept as it stands in our own law is probably the closest approach to true economic income yet achieved by any country. The primary limiting factors are our varying level of prices, our inadequate accounting—including imperfections of valuation, and our incompetence of administration. Possibilities of further progress depend primarily upon our ability to improve our standard of value, our accounting, and our administration.

It is very undesirable from the point of view of economics and equity that the judicial definition of income should develop along narrow lines by the process of definitely eliminating from the concept certain items as not being income. The real question is not often "Is the item income?" but rather "Is the method used for reaching this class of income justified?" In other words, have Congress and the Treasury provided an equitable answer to the practical question as to how and when such income shall be taxed, taking into account the imperfections of the situation in which the tax must function? Under a given statute, is income taxed at such times and in such a manner as to bring about the necessary degree and the highest practicable degree of equity to the taxpayer and between taxpayers? The definition of income should rest on fundamental economic principles. The definition must be broad enough to iron out all the theoretical difficulties and solve all of the inequities and anomalies. The situation should be held in a mobile, flexible state which will permit the statutory definition of income to become progressively more precise and accurate with the improvement of the technique of our economic environment.

J. VINER

TAXATION AND CHANGES IN PRICE LEVELS

Changing price levels give rise to important theoretical and practical problems of taxation which have received no systematic treatment and only occasional mention in the economic literature on taxation and on price levels. The adequate theoretical presentation of the case for or against a particular tax often demands consideration of the special conditions resulting from the upward or downward swing of the general price level. Tax laws are almost invariably written in pecuniary terms. They may not operate in the manner intended by the legislators or they may even operate in a manner directly contrary to that anticipated by the legislators and productive of gross inequalities if provision is not made therein for changes in the value of the monetary unit. The relation of taxation to price levels is a problem of sufficient importance to merit a greater measure of attention from students of government finance than has been vouchsafed to it in the past. This article is an attempt to open up the subject in the hope that it will lead to further discussion of the general problem and its detailed manifestations.

INCOME TAXES

To take up first the bearing of fluctuating prices on income taxation, a careful reading of a number of current income-tax laws has not disclosed to the writer a single important instance of deliberate provision for adjustment to changing price levels. In a few instances, isolated provisions in these acts permit of some degree of adjustment, but this effect appears to be a happy coincidence not anticipated by the drafters of the acts.

Exemptions.—First, and most obviously, the specific amounts granted as exemptions to small incomes and for dependents have no rational basis unless they take into account the purchasing power of monetary incomes. The degree of adequacy for its intended purposes of a given exemption will vary inversely with fluctuations in the general price level.

Progression.—If the rates of an income tax are progressive the severity of the tax will increase as prices rise and will decrease as prices fall, even though the statutory rates remain unaltered, provided that monetary incomes in general vary in some degree of conformity with variations in the purchasing power of the monetary unit. The table presented below gives in Column I the schedule of rates of a hypothetical progressive tax, and in Columns II and III a series of incomes in the years 1915 and 1920, respectively, and the taxes payable thereon, constructed on the assumptions that between 1915 and 1920 there was a 100 per cent rise in the general price level and that monetary incomes were exactly adjusted to this rise in prices, so that real income for all individuals remained unchanged.

I	II			III		
Tax Rates on Amount of Income	Total Income, 1915	Tax	Percentage of Total Income	Total Income, 1920	Tax	Percentage of Total Income
Not exceeding $1,000—exempt $ 1,001–$ 10,000— 5 per cent $10,001–$ 20,000—10 per cent $20,001–$ 50,000—20 per cent $50,001–$100,000—40 per cent	A. $ 5,000 B. 10,000 C. 20,000 D. 50,000	$ 200 450 1,450 7,450	4.0 4.5 7.25 14.9	A. $10,000 B. 20,000 C. 40,000 D. 100,000	$ 450 1,450 5,450 27,450	4.5 7.25 14.9 27.45

The table demonstrates clearly enough that a rise in the price level increases the severity of a progressive scale of rates, even though the statutory rates are not increased. It can readily be demonstrated by arithmetical illustrations that, with a given progressive series of rates, the degree of increase in the severity of the rates will vary directly (although not necessarily in exact proportion) with the degree of rise in the price level, and that, with a given percentage of rise in the price level, the degree of increase in the severity of the rates will vary directly (although not necessarily in exact proportion) with the rate of progression in the tax law. In other words, the extent to which an increase in prices will increase the severity of progressive taxation depends upon both the percentage of increase in the price level and the rate of progression in the tax law. The greater the rise in prices and the greater the steepness in progression, the greater will be the increase in the severity of the tax. The reverse propositions also hold true: a fall in the general price level accompanied by a corresponding fall in money incomes will result in a decrease in the severity of a given progressive schedule of rates; the steeper the rate of progression in the tax and the greater the fall in prices, the greater will be the decrease in the severity of the tax. It follows that, assuming the national real income and its distribution to remain the same, the maintenance of a given progressive scale of rates in a general income tax during a period of rising prices will bring into the state treasury an increase in money revenue more than proportionate to the increase in the price level, and during a period of falling prices will result in a decrease in the money revenue more than proportionate to the fall in the price level. As a period of rising prices is probably also generally a period of increasing real income, and a period of falling prices a period of decreasing real income, the variations in the monetary revenue yield of a progressive income tax resulting from changing price levels will be still further accentuated.

A proportional income tax, on the other hand, aside from any exemption provisions it may contain, will not vary in its severity with changes in the price level to which money incomes adjust themselves, and the money revenue which it yields to the government will vary in exact proportion to the variations in the purchasing power of the monetary unit. This irregular and arbitrary variation in the severity and the productiveness of progressive income taxation during a period of changing price levels—from which proportional taxation is exempt—must be regarded either as a hitherto unnoticed objection to the progressive principle or as an argument for the frequent adjustment of the schedule of rates to allow for changes in the value of the monetary unit. Even if the latter alternative be chosen, it still remains true that such adjustment would be difficult to establish in practice, whether by statute or by administrative rule, and that it is not needed in connection with proportional taxation.

Capital gains.—One of the difficult problems in connection with income taxation is the propriety of including capital gains in taxable income. In general, writers on this topic definitely take either one position or the other, although logically the problem bristles with difficulties which should restrain the attempt to find in theory a categorical answer. Where the capital gain arises from the appreciation in value, as compared with the original cost, of an income-yielding asset, it can reasonably be argued in opposition to its taxation that such gain is the result of the capitalization of future income which will in due time pay its full measure of taxation. This argument does not hold, however, for those gains which are not reinvested by the recipients, but are used as current income. In such cases, failure to tax such gains either when they accrue or when they are realized results in the total escape from taxation of genuine income with full tax-paying ability. Since the income tax is assumed to be a general tax, it cannot be objected that the taxes on the future income yield of the sold capital asset were discounted in the sale price. There will normally be no shifting of a uniform tax upon all kinds of income. If there is a probability of lower tax rates in the future and if consideration is given to the difficulty of tracing the use to which the recipient of a capital gain puts the proceeds, there is ample justification for a compromise, such as is attempted in the American Revenue Act of 1921, between the full taxation of realized capital gains (as in the American Revenue Act of 1919) and the total exemption from taxation (as in the British income tax) by taxing capital gains more moderately than income in general.[1]

An additional reason for the more moderate taxation of capital gains is that apparent capital gains may merely represent

[1] The United States Revenue Act of 1921 provides that at the election of the taxpayer realized capital gains may be taxed separately from ordinary income at a rate of 12½ per cent. There is no justification in principle for restricting the relief from full taxation of capital gains to those whose taxable incomes are otherwise large enough to make them subject to rates higher than 12½ per cent. A more equitable method of granting relief would have been to permit a deduction for capital gains of a stated percentage, say 50 per cent, of the amount of tax to which they would have been subject in the absence of the relief provision. This principle holds, even though the object of the relief provision was not to afford a closer approximation of equity, but was to facilitate property deals.

the reappraisal of a capital asset in terms of a dollar of less purchasing power. No acceptable concept of income will include as income the rise in monetary value of a capital asset which represents merely the fall in the value of the monetary unit and is not indicative of increased purchasing power in general.[1] During a period of rising prices, a lower rate on capital gains than on ordinary income can be justified, therefore, as a rough attempt to offset the taxation of fictitious gains resulting from the fall in the value of the monetary unit. This conclusion remains valid even though it be admitted that, given a constant current interest rate, there will probably be a tendency of variations in the value of income-yielding capital assets to lag behind variations in their monetary yield. The owners or buyers of capital assets probably do not at once fully capitalize an increase or a decrease in monetary income, partly because of inertia, and partly on the logical ground that a rise or a fall in yield may prove to be of short duration. Another justification for the taxation of capital gains at specially low rates is suggested by the point made by Professor Powell, that, as capital gains are taxed only when realized, under progressive taxation a ten years' accumulated gain realized in one year will be subject to a greater tax than the same gain realized evenly year by year.[2]

During a period of falling prices, on the other hand, there may be a genuine capital gain, though the market value of the capital asset remains constant or even falls. In a period of rapid

---

[1] "A man who sold an asset in 1920 which he had purchased in 1914, making an apparent profit of 100 per cent and receiving his pay in fifty-cent dollars is, under our statute, subject to tax on his gain, although that gain is only apparent and not real. Moreover, the situation is particularly unjust under our present system. If complete periodical revaluations were used in determining income there would still be relative equality as between different taxpayers. But as the situation now stands, the transactions are closed in a haphazard and uneven fashion. A man who happens to sell out at the peak of the price curves is taxed very unequally as compared with the man who continues his transaction until a period of lower price levels."—R. M. Haig, "The Concept of Income," in *The Federal Income Tax* ("Columbia University Lectures," 1921), p. 17.

[2] Thomas Reed Powell, "Constitutional Aspects of Federal Income Taxation," in *The Federal Income Tax* ("Columbia University Lectures," 1921), p. 83.

deflation of a depreciated currency, a considerable measure of such capital gains may well be concealed by the general downward trend of prices.

Inventories.—In the taxation of business incomes, taxable income is generally measured by the increase in net worth between the beginning and the end of the fiscal period plus any intermediate distribution of earnings. Accounting practice generally demands that net worth be estimated on the basis of the cost price minus depreciation of fixed assets; the cost or market value, whichever is lower, of inventories; and the book value of other assets, adjusted, generally, by reserves for possible losses. During a period of rapidly rising prices, market values of inventory will generally exceed cost values, but if the "cost or market, whichever is lower" basis is used for valuing inventories, the rise in the market values of inventory will not affect the income as shown by the accounting records until the profit is actually realized through sale at the higher prices. The accountant's case for this method of valuing inventory rests mainly on the argument that the acknowledgment of losses as soon as they become prospective, and the admission of gains only when they are actually realized, promotes conservative business practice.

There are four possible basic methods of valuing inventories: at cost; at market; at cost or market, whichever is lower; or at cost or market, whichever is higher. Of these, the last-named is rarely, if ever, employed. It is sometimes held that for purposes of taxation it does not matter which method is used, since any loss or gain in market value not reflected in the inventory or any loss or gain in inventory valuation not reflected in market value will ultimately be offset by gains or losses shown by sales.[1]

[1] Cf. U.S. Revenue Act of 1916, Form 1031. "In case the annual gain or loss is determined by inventory, merchandise must be inventoried at the cost price, as any loss in saleable value will ultimately be reflected in the sales during the year when the goods are disposed of." Cf. also, A. A. Ballantine, "Inventories" in *The Federal Income Tax* ("Columbia University Lectures," 1921), p. 172: "The effect of admitting inventory losses, even wrongly, is *merely* to postpone profits from one year to another, while the effect of failure to admit them is to treat as income that which is really capital."

Under ordinary circumstances, however, and especially during a period of changing price levels, it does make a difference for taxation, even in the long run, whether one method or another of inventory valuation is used. To illustrate the significance of choice of method of taking inventories during a period of changing price levels, the following hypothetical cases are presented. Case A applies to conditions of rising prices followed by falling prices; Case B applies to conditions of falling prices followed by rising prices.

CASE A

Inventory of Stock Purchased in 1920, as of December 31, 1920	Sale Price in 1921, after Deduction of Selling Expenses, etc.
Cost, $100,000 Market, $150,000	$100,000

In Case A, if inventory were taken in 1920 at market value, or at cost or market, whichever was higher, there would have been admitted as income in 1920 a gain of $50,000, and there would have been deductible in 1921 a loss of $50,000. If the tax was proportional, if the rate was the same for both years, and if there was for the entire business in both years a net taxable income, then, and only then, would these two items offset each other for purposes of taxation. If there was a net loss for the entire business in 1921, there would be no opportunity in that year for the deduction of the tax paid in 1920 on what later proved to have been a fictitious gain.[1] If the tax was progressive, and if total net income in 1921 before deduction of the loss was not in the same taxable grade as total net income in 1920 after inclusion of the inventory gain, the deduction of the $50,000 loss in 1921 would either more than offset or would less than offset for taxation purposes the addition of $50,000 gain in 1920. In any case, the Treasury would have had the use for one year of the tax on the $50,000 temporary inventory gain. Valuation of inventory for taxation on the basis of market, or of cost or market, whichever is higher, tends to hasten the liability to taxation on gains during rising prices. If, as in the case given,

[1] The provision in the Revenue Act of 1921 (Sec. 204) which permits deduction of net loss in one year from net income of the next succeeding two years meets this problem in part, but only in part.

a rise in prices in one year is offset by a corresponding fall in the next year, valuation on the basis of market or of cost or market, whichever is higher, tends also to increase the total amount of tax paid in the two years, since taxable income is probably greater in the year of high prices. If the rise in prices continues, inventory valuation according to either of these two methods tends to advance the liability to pay taxes, ,ut under progressive taxation it probably operates to lessen the total amount of tax paid over a period of years, for rising prices generally bring increasing monetary incomes. When incomes are rising and taxation is progressive, the sooner the tax is paid on any particular item of gain, the lower will be the tax rate thereon. During a period of rising prices or rising tax rates, or both combined, these methods of inventory valuation would tend over a number of years to reduce the tax yield to the government.

In Case A, if cost, or cost or market, whichever was lower, was used as the basis of valuing inventory, there would be no taxable gain in 1920, and no loss in 1921. If prices continued to rise in 1921, however, either of these methods of valuing inventory would postpone taxation until the gain was actually realized. During a period of rising prices, if the tax was progressive, and still more if the tax rates were increasing, these methods of inventory valuation, by postponing liability to taxation to the years in which the rates were higher, and the net incomes greater, would tend to increase the tax yield to the government.

CASE B

Inventory of Stock Purchased in 1920, as of December 31, 1920	Sale Price in 1921, after Deduction of Selling Expenses, etc.
Cost, $100,000 Market, $50,000	$100,000

In Case B, if inventory were taken in 1920 at cost, or at cost or market, whichever was higher, no loss would be deductible in 1920, and there would be no taxable gain in 1921. If inventory were taken at market, or at cost or market, whichever was lower, a loss of $50,000 would be deductible in 1920, and there would be a taxable gain of $50,000 in 1921. As has been sufficiently demonstrated in connection with Case A. it would be highly improbable that for taxation purposes the loss in one year would be exactly offset by the equivalent gain in another year. If prices, instead of recovering in 1921, continued to fall, business incomes probably would fall also. Inventory valuation on the basis of market, or cost or market, whichever was lower, would tend to hasten the admission of losses. It would thus permit the appropriate tax deductions to be made in the years of higher incomes, and, therefore, of higher taxation.

The British income tax, in general, permits inventory valuations to be made only on the basis of cost or market, whichever is lower.[1] American federal income taxation started out with an attempt to determine income without reference to inventories, proceeded to the cost basis, and finally, when lower price levels were threatened, permitted, in the interest of the taxpayers, the use of the cost or market, whichever is lower, basis. As has already been pointed out, this basis of inventory valuation under progressive taxation tends to reduce the revenue yield during a period of falling prices, and this tendency is further accentuated if the period of falling prices is also marked by reductions in the statutory tax rates. This tendency, it should be noted, is independent of and additional to the similar tendency resulting from the decline in money incomes. On logical grounds this method of inventory valuation is open to criticism from the treasury point of view, inasmuch as under it inventory gains are reportable only when realized, whereas inventory losses are deductible as soon as they are reasonably certain to accrue. It is not practicable, however, to treat losses in any other manner. Many types of losses cannot be definitely proved to be such until long after they are written off the books, and this applies to inventory losses where the sale of the depreciated goods is indefinitely postponed in the absence of a market, or in the hope of a return of better times.

Depreciation.—A depreciation reserve which conforms to the standard accounting practice of distributing the original cost of

[1] R. M. Haig, "The Taxation of Excess Profits in Great Britain," *American Economic Review Supplement*, Vol. X, No. 4 (December, 1920), p. 45.

the property minus the ultimate salvage value over the useful life of the property will not be sufficient during a period of rising prices to provide for physical replacement unless replacement costs lag behind the upward trend of prices. Where accounting practice fails also to sanction the periodic re-appraisal of fixed assets during a period of rising prices so as to take account of appreciation, the maintenance of a depreciation reserve inadequate to take care of physical replacement, together with the failure to write up capital investment, will tend to give an exaggerated appearance of prosperity to the concern and will act as a stimulus either to increased distribution of earnings or to overexpansion of plant facilities.

	1915	1920
Capital.........................	$100,000	$100,000
Net income before depreciation....	15,000	30,000
Depreciation allowance...........	5,000	5,000
Net income after depreciation.....	10,000	25,000

In the foregoing illustration it is assumed that prices rose by 100 per cent between 1915 and 1920, that the fixed assets of the corporation remained unchanged physically except for full replacement of worn-out plant, and that whereas $5,000 was sufficient to provide for such physical replacement in 1915, $10,000 would be necessary in 1920. On the usual accounting basis the data in this illustration would indicate that the firm could distribute $25,000 as dividends in 1920 without encroachment on capital, as compared with $10,000 in 1915. In any case, under the usual income-tax law, the taxable income of the corporation would have to be reported as $25,000. After physical replacement, however, the money income in 1920 would be only $20,000, and in terms of real income there would have been no change from 1915. A fictitious profit to the amount of $5,000 would be taxed as income to the corporation and, if $25,000 was distributed as dividends, a distribution of capital assets to the amount of $5,000 would be taxed as income to the shareholder. There would be no offset when there was actual need of physical replacement at a money cost greater than the original cost and greater, therefore, than could be met from the depreciation reserve, since income-tax laws under such circumstances forbid a readjustment for taxation of earlier depreciation allowances proved in course of time to have been inadequate to provide for physical replacement. Such is specifically the case in the American federal income tax, where the Treasury regulations permit only of such deductions for depreciation as will suffice, with the salvage value, to provide at the end of the "useful life" of the property its original money cost and not its replacement cost.[1]

During a period of falling prices, if the cost of replacement of worn-out capital goods declines with the general price level, a depreciation allowance on the standard original-cost basis will enable the taxpayer to deduct each year from taxable income an amount greater than is necessary to replace his original physical investment. If the monetary income of the concern prior to depreciation falls *pari passu* with the fall in the general price level, the net monetary income after allowance for depreciation will fall more than proportionately with the fall in the price level, and the burden of taxation upon the concern will be lower, even under proportional taxation, in terms of purchasing power, although its real income remains the same. Allowance for depreciation on the original-cost basis tends, therefore, to increase the real burden of taxation during a period of rising prices and to decrease it during a period of falling prices.

[1] U.S. Treasury Department, *Income Tax Regulations 62*, 1922 ed., Art. 161.

H. C. SIMONS

CHAPTER II

THE DEFINITION OF INCOME

THE development of income taxes may be viewed as a response to increasingly insistent and articulate demand for a more equitable apportionment of tax burdens.[1] These taxes are the outstanding contribution of popular government and liberal political philosophy to modern fiscal practice. Thus, they may properly be studied in the light of considerations raised in the preceding chapter. Income taxation is broadly an instrument of economic control, a means of mitigating economic inequality. In what follows, we shall assume that moderation of inequality is an important objective of policy and proceed to consider income taxes as devices for effecting it. We shall be concerned, that is to say, largely with problems centering around that elusive something which we call "discrimination." Income taxes, in general, may seem peculiarly equitable; but serious problems arise when one proceeds to the task of describing, delimiting, and defining closely the actual tax base. Here, too, the problems may be dealt with largely in the light of considerations of justice.

We must face now the task of defining "income." Many writers have undertaken to formulate definitions.

[1] For stimulating development of this thesis see W. Moll, *Über Steuern* (Berlin, 1911), pp. 3–46. See also Bruno Moll, *Probleme der Finanzwissenschaft* (Leipzig, 1924), *passim*. The latter writer remarks (p. 99): "Vermögens- un Einkommensbegriff entspringen der gleichen Wurzel, dem Begriff des wirtschaftlichen Könnens, dem Vermögensbegriff im weitesten Sinne."

and with the most curious results. Whereas the word is widely used in discussions of justice in taxation and without evident confusion, the greatest variety and dissimilarity appear, as to both content and phraseology, in the actual definitions proposed by particular writers. The consistent recourse to definition in terms which are themselves undefinable (or undefined or equally ambiguous) testifies eloquently to the underlying confusion.

The fact that the term is widely used without serious misunderstanding in certain ranges of discourse, however, is significant. Since it is widely agreed that income is a good tax base, its meaning may be sought by inquiring what definition would provide the basis for most nearly equitable levies. At the same time we may seek to point out conflicts and contradictions in established usage and to discover the connotations of income which are essential and relevant for present purposes. Thus we may find those denotations which may best be accepted, to avoid ambiguity, and to minimize disturbance of terminological tradition.

What is requisite to satisfactory definition of income will appear clearly only as we come to grips with various problems. It may help, however, to indicate some general requirements—if only because their neglect has been responsible for so much careless writing in the past. Income must be conceived as something quantitative and objective. It must be measurable; indeed, definition must indicate or clearly imply an actual procedure of measuring.[2] Moreover, the arbitrary distinctions im-

---

[2] The importance of this requirement may be suggested by the following definition: "Net individual income is the flow of commodities and services

plicit in one's definition must be reduced to a minimum. That it should be possible to delimit the concept precisely in every direction is hardly to be expected.[3] The task rather is that of making the best of available materials; for no very useful conception in "social science," or in "welfare economics," will entirely satisfy the tough-minded; nor can available materials so be put together as to provide an ideal tax base. But one devises tools of analysis which are useful, if crude; and a tax base may be defined in such manner as to minimize obvious inequities and ambiguities. Such at least is the present task.

The noun "income" denotes, broadly, that which comes in. Thus, it may be used with almost any referent.[4] Even in the current usage of economics and business the term is commonly used in different contexts to denote several different things. It will suffice here to

---

accruing to an individual through a period of time and available for disposition after deducting the necessary costs of acquisition" (W. W. Hewett, *The Definition of Income* [Philadelphia, 1925], pp. 22–23). The author never undertakes to specify how this conception might be reduced to quantitative expression; he simply leaves the reader to guess how "the necessary costs of acquisition" might be deducted from "the flow of commodities and services accruing," or how either of these "quantities" might be arrived at separately.

[3] Kleinwächter, notably, endeavors to discredit the whole concept of income by pointing out that some arbitrary delimitations are unavoidable (*Das Einkommen und seine Verteilung* [Leipzig, 1896], pp. 1–16). He confounds himself and his reader with interesting conundrums having to do mainly with income in kind. See below, esp. chap. v.

[4] For discussion of the development of the income concept see Kleinwächter, *op cit.*, Introduction; also, Bruno Moll, *op. cit.*, esp. chap. xii; also Bücher, *Zwei mittelalterische Steuerordnungen* (Fests. z. Leipziger Hist. [1894]), pp. 138–39 (cited in B. Moll, *op. cit.*, p. 96).

note three or four distinct senses in which the term is employed.

There is, first, and most common in economic theory, the conception of what may be called *income from things*.[5] In this sense, income may be conceived in terms of services derived from things or, quantitatively, in terms of the market value of uses. Thus, we speak commonly of income from land, from produced instruments, or from consumers' capital. When used in this way, the term may have a merely acquisitive implication; for any property right, any mortgage against the community, has its yield.

The term is also frequently used to denote, second, *gain from transactions* or trading profit. If a share of stock is purchased for $100 and later sold for $150, it is customary to say that the venture has yielded an income of $50. The distinguishing feature of this conception is that it presupposes no allocation of income to assigned periods of time—that it does not raise the often crucial question as to when "income" accrues.[6] The period is merely the time between the first and last transactions in a complete and mutually related series. "Income" is imputed neither to preassigned time intervals nor to persons but merely to certain ventures, certain market operations.

There is, third, the familiar conception of *social or*

[5] This is nicely covered by the German *Ertrag*—which most writers distinguish (some, carefully and consistently) from *Einkommen*. The *Ertrag* conception is that commonly employed (e.g., by Irving Fisher) in analysis of the discounting process (see below, chap. iii, pp. 89 ff.).

[6] Actually, it is always misleading to talk about the accrual of income. See below, pp. 99–100.

182

THE DEFINITION OF INCOME

national income—which appears frequently in the literature and is often defined after a fashion.[7] Social income denotes, broadly, a measure of the net results of
economic activity in a community during a specified
period of time. This, of course, is no definition; indeed,
it is perhaps impossible to do more than indicate some
roughly synonymous, and equally ambiguous, expressions. While commonly employed as though it denoted
something quantitative, social income cannot be defined to any advantage in strictly quantitative terms.
Economics deals with economy; economy implies valuation; and valuation is peculiarly and essentially relative.
The prices with which rigorous economics deals are pure
relations; and relatives cannot be summated into meaningful totals. Market prices afford only the most meager
clues (or none at all) to the "value" of *all* goods produced and services rendered.

The concept of production, moreover, has itself a
strong ethical or welfare flavor. The social income might
be conceived in terms either of the value of goods and
services produced or of the value of the productive services utilized during the period (after deduction for depreciation and depletion).[8] On neither basis, however,

---

[7] "The aggregate money income of a country . . . . must equal the aggregate money value of all goods produced and services rendered during the
year" (R. T. Ely, *Outlines of Economics* [4th ed.; New York, 1923], pp. 100
and 105). One may remark upon the failure to introduce depreciation or depletion into the calculation. The necessity of such deduction is recognized in
Alfred Marshall, *Principles of Economics* (8th ed.), p. 81; but Marshall's conception of social income is nowhere made explicit.

[8] This view is developed especially in Cassel, *The Theory of Social Economy*, trans. Barron (New York, 1932), chaps. i and ii. See also the same
author's *Fundamental Thoughts on Economics* (New York, 1925).

is it possible to avoid the question as to whether all economic (acquisitive) activity may be deemed productive. The use of resources to establish monopoly control can hardly be thought of as adding to the income of the community as a whole; nor is it easy to include the cost of the more egregious frauds perpetrated upon consumers. The tough-minded economist may argue that advertising is merely a service demanded by consumers— that an advertised product is simply a different commodity from a physically identical article with no distinctive label on the container; and this may solve the difficulty for one interested in the mechanics of the pricing process. But even a person of such interests will hesitate to maintain that all selling devices, truthful, false, and ludicrous, contribute to the social income. Large amounts of resources are employed to conceal issues in elections and to secure favor with actual and prospective government officials. But the point need not be labored. Surely it is impossible to distinguish sharply between uses of resources which involve production, predation, and mere waste. Such distinctions, however, are implicit in the idea of social income.

In short, social income is merely a welfare conception. To say that it has increased is to say that things which must be economized are more abundant (or, perhaps, are utilized with greater "efficiency"). This manifests an ethical or aesthetic judgment. Increase in the social income suggests progress toward "the good life," toward a world better in its economic aspect, whatever that may be; and it is precisely as definite and measurable as is such progress.

If it be true that social income belongs far outside the realm of rigorous, quantitative concepts, the conclusion is important for the definition of *personal income*—a fourth sense in which the term is commonly used. Many writers imply or assert explicitly that personal income is merely a derivative, subordinate concept in the hierarchy of economic terminology. The view that personal income is merely a share in the total income of society is to be found in almost every treatise on economics; and some writers, forgetting even the distinction between a real and a personal tax (and that between *base* and *source*), insist that income taxes must bear—presumably by definition!—only on the net social income as it accrues to individuals.[9] On this view, gifts, capital gains, and other items must be excluded from the base of a personal tax because such items cannot be counted in the income of society as a whole!

Such notions derive, perhaps, from the central emphasis placed upon national income by Adam Smith and the mercantilists and from the central place of so-called distribution theory in classical economics. Economists have discussed the influence of trade policy upon the size of the national income; they have broken up that income curiously into functional elements; indeed, they have done almost everything with the income concept except to give it such definition as would make it eligible to a place among our analytical tools. As a matter of fact, traditional theory is concerned primarily not with *Einkommen* but with *Ertrag*—with the pricing of goods

[9] E.g., Walther Lotz, *Finanzwissenschaft* (1st ed.; Tübingen, 1917), pp. 444-50.

and productive services. Its acquaintance with *Einkommen* is tenuous, implicit, and largely incidental.[10] Social income is neither an indispensable analytical tool for relative-price theory nor a concept whose content must be specified implicitly by a sound system of theory. At all events, no writer, to our knowledge, has succeeded in giving any real meaning to the idea that personal income is merely a share in some undistributed whole. The essential point has been most happily phrased by Schmoller, who says in an early work, "Nach unserer Ansicht gehört der Einkommenbegriff aber überhaupt streng genommen nur der Einzelwirtschaft an, der Volkswirtschaft nur in bildlich analoger Ausdehnung."[11] Certainly much should be gained by cutting loose from a terminology ambiguous at best and inherited from the discussion of problems largely, even totally, irrelevant to those with which we are here concerned.[12]

[10] For discussion of this point see A. Ammon, "Die Begriffe 'Volkseinkommen' und 'Volksvermögen' und ihre Bedeutung für die Volkswirtschaftslehre," *Schr. d. Verein für Sozialpolitik*, CLXXIII, 19–26.

[11] G. Schmoller, "Die Lehre vom Einkommen . . . . ," *Zeitschrift für die gesamte Staatswissenschaft*, XIX (1863), 78. Schmoller himself actually defines national income as the sum of all individual incomes (*ibid.*, p. 20) but in such context that one may hardly charge inconsistency.

[12] Most of the innumerable German discussions of the meaning of income start with, and pretend to lean upon, Hermann, who was concerned primarily with the concept of social income, and who certainly did not write from the point of view of taxation (as do his "followers"). See Hermann, *Staatswissenschuftliche Untersuchungen* (2d [posthumous] ed.; München, 1870), esp. chap. ix.

In Germany the "correction" of Adam Smith's overemphasis upon the "accounting" conception of social income ("ausschliesslich in dem von Standpunkte des capitalistischen Unternehmers berechneten Ueberschusse das reine Einkommen zu erblicken," is Robert Meyer's characterization of

Although personal income is not amenable to precise definition, it has, by comparison with the concept of social income, a much smaller degree of ambiguity. Its measurement implies estimating merely the *relative* results of individual economic activity during a period of time. Moreover, there arises no question of distinction between production and predation. Social income implies valuation of a total product of goods and services; while personal income is a purely acquisitive concept having to do with the possession and exercise of rights.

Personal income connotes, broadly, the exercise of control over the use of society's scarce resources. It has to do not with sensations, services, or goods but rather with rights which command prices (or to which prices may be imputed). Its calculation implies estimate (*a*) of the amount by which the value of a person's store of property rights would have increased, as between the beginning and end of the period, if he had consumed (destroyed) nothing, or (*b*) of the value of rights which he might have exercised in consumption without altering the value of his store of rights. In other words, it implies estimate of consumption and accumulation. Consumption as a quantity denotes the value of rights ex-

Smith's "narrow" conception [*Das Wesen des Einkommens* (Berlin, 1887), p. 3]) is regarded as a major contribution of German economics. Schmoller and most writers after him give credit to Hermann for this contribution. Meyer (*ibid.*, chap. i) insists, however, that Schmoller has found in Hermann the opposite emphasis from what is really there and that credit for the contribution belongs really to Schmoller (and to Rodbertus). The controversy is hardly important for present purposes in any event, for the present writer's position implies, so far as concerns the definition of personal income, that Schmoller to some extent, and his followers especially, erred simply in getting away from Smith.

ercised in a certain way (in destruction of economic
goods); accumulation denotes the change in ownership
of valuable rights as between the beginning and end of a
period.

The relation of the income concept to the specified
time interval is fundamental—and neglect of this crucial
relation has been responsible for much confusion in the
relevant literature. The measurement of income implies
allocation of consumption and accumulation to specified
periods. In a sense, it implies the possibility of measuring the results of individual participation in economic relations *for an assigned interval* and without regard for
anything which happened before the beginning of that
(before the end of the previous) interval or for what may
happen in subsequent periods. All data for the measurement would be found, ideally, within the period analyzed.

Personal income may be defined as the algebraic sum
of (1) the market value of rights exercised in consumption and (2) the change in the value of the store of property rights between the beginning and end of the period
in question. In other words, it is merely the result obtained by adding consumption during the period to
"wealth" at the end of the period and then subtracting
"wealth" at the beginning. The *sine qua non* of income
is *gain*, as our courts have recognized in their more lucid
moments—and gain *to* someone during a specified time
interval. Moreover, this gain may be measured and defined most easily by positing a dual objective or purpose,
consumption and accumulation, each of which may be
estimated in a common unit by appeal to market prices.

This position, if tenable, must suggest the folly of describing income as a flow and, more emphatically, of regarding it as a quantity of goods, services, receipts, fruits, etc. As Schäffle has said so pointedly, "Das Einkommen hat nur buchhalterische Existenz."[13] It is indeed merely an arithmetic answer and exists only as the end result of appropriate calculations. To conceive of income in terms of things is to invite all the confusion of the elementary student in accounting who insists upon identifying "surplus" and "cash."[14] If one views society as a kind of giant partnership, one may conceive of a person's income as the sum of his withdrawals (consumption) and the change in the value of his equity or interest in the enterprise. The essential connotation of income, to repeat, is *gain*—gain *to* someone during a specified period and measured according to objective market standards. Let us now note some of the more obvious limitations and ambiguities of this conception of income.[15]

In the first place, it raises the unanswerable question as to where or how a line may be drawn between what is and what is not economic activity. If a man raises vege-

[13] Quoted by Schmoller (*op. cit.*, p. 54) from Schäffle, "Mensch und Gut in der Volkswirtschaft," *Deutsche Vierteljahrschrift* (1861).

[14] This point, with all its triteness, can hardly be overemphasized, for it implies a decisive criticism of most of the extant definitions of income. Professor Hewett, e.g., asserts and implies consistently that income is merely a collection of goods and services which may, so to speak, be thrown off into a separate pile and then measured in terms of money. He and others too, no doubt, know better; but, when one undertakes the task of definition, one may expect to be held accountable for what one literally says. For other instances of this fallacy see below, chap. iii.

[15] Most of the points raised in the following pages will be dealt with again in succeeding chapters as problems of income taxation.

189

tables in his garden, it seems clearly appropriate to include the value of the product in measuring his income. If he raises flowers and shrubs, the case is less clear. If he shaves himself, it is difficult to argue that the value of the shaves must also be accounted for. Most economists recognize housewives' services as an important item of income. So they are, perhaps; but what becomes of this view as one proceeds to extreme cases? Do families have larger incomes because parents give competent instruction to children instead of paying for institutional training? Does a doctor or an apothecary have relatively large income in years when his family requires and receives an extraordinary amount of his own professional services? Kleinwächter suggests[16] that the poorest families might be shown to have substantial incomes if one went far in accounting for instruction, nursing, cooking, maid service, and other things which the upper classes obtain by purchase.

A little reflection along these lines suggests that leisure is itself a major item of consumption; that income per hour of leisure, beyond a certain minimum, might well be imputed to persons according to what they might earn per hour if otherwise engaged. Of course, it is one thing to note that such procedure is appropriate in principle and quite another to propose that it be applied. Such considerations do suggest, however, that the neglect of "earned income in kind" may be substantially offset, for comparative purposes (for measurement of relative incomes), if leisure income is also neglected. For

[16] *Op. cit.*, Introduction. We have drawn heavily, in this and other passages, on Kleinwächter's conundrums.

income taxation it is important that these elements of income vary with considerable regularity, from one income class to the next, along the income scale.

A similar difficulty arises with reference to receipts in the form of compensation in kind. Let us consider here another of Kleinwächter's conundrums. We are asked to measure the relative incomes of an ordinary officer serving with his troops and a *Flügeladjutant* to the sovereign. Both receive the same nominal pay; but the latter receives quarters in the palace, food at the royal table, servants, and horses for sport. He accompanies the prince to theater and opera, and, in general, lives royally at no expense to himself and is able to save generously from his salary. But suppose, as one possible complication, that the *Flügeladjutant* detests opera and hunting.

The problem is clearly hopeless. To neglect all compensation in kind is obviously inappropriate. On the other hand, to include the perquisites as a major addition to the salary implies that all income should be measured with regard for the relative pleasurableness of different activities—which would be the negation of measurement. There is hardly more reason for imputing additional income to the *Flügeladjutant* on account of his luxurious wardrobe than for bringing into account the prestige and social distinction of a (German) university professor. Fortunately, however, such difficulties in satisfactory measurement of relative incomes do not bulk large in modern times; and, again, these elements of immeasurable psychic income may be presumed to vary in a somewhat continuous manner along the income scale.

If difficulties arise in determining what positive items

shall be included in calculations of income (in measuring consumption), they are hardly less serious than those involved in determining and defining appropriate deductions. At the outset there appears the necessity of distinguishing between consumption and expense; and here one finds inescapable the unwelcome criterion of intention. A thoroughly precise and objective distinction is inconceivable. Given items will represent business expense in one instance and merely consumption in another, and often the motives will be quite mixed. A commercial artist buys paints and brushes to use in making his living. Another person may buy the same articles as playthings for his children, or to cultivate a hobby of his own. Even the professional artist may use some of his materials for things he intends or hopes to sell, and some on work done purely for his own pleasure. In another instance, moreover, the same items may represent investment in training for earning activity later on.

The latter instance suggests that there is something quite arbitrary even about the distinction between consumption and accumulation. On the face of it, this is not important for the definition of income; but it must be remembered that accumulation or investment provides a basis for expense deductions in the future, while consumption does not. The distinction in question can be made somewhat definite if one adopts the drastic expedient of treating all outlays for augmenting personal earning capacity as consumption. This expedient has little more than empty, formal, legalistic justification. On the other hand, one does well to accept, here as elsewhere, a loss of relevance or adequacy as the necessary cost of an essential definiteness. It would require some temerity to propose recognition of depreciation or depletion in the measurement of personal-service incomes —if only because the determination of the base, upon which to apply depreciation rates, presents a simply fantastic problem. It is better simply to recognize the limitations of measurable personal income for purposes of certain comparisons (e.g., by granting special credits to personal-service incomes under income taxes).

Our definition of income may also be criticized on the ground that it ignores the patent instability of the monetary *numéraire*;[17] and it may also be maintained that there is no rigorous, objective method either of measuring or of allowing for this instability. No serious difficulty is involved here for the measurement of consumption—which presumably must be measured in terms of prices at the time goods and services are actually acquired or consumed.[18] In periods of changing price levels, comparisons of incomes would be partially vitiated as between persons who distributed consumption outlays differently over the year. Such difficulties are negligible, however, as against those involved in the measurement of accumulation. This element of annual income would be grossly misrepresented if the price level changed markedly during the year. These limitations of

[17] See Jacob Viner, "Taxation and Changes in Price Levels," *Journal of Political Economy*, XXXI (1923), esp. 494-504.

[18] In a sense relevant to income measurement, two persons' consumption of, say, strawberries might be very unequal for a period, though the physical quantities involved were identical, provided one consumed them largely in season and the other largely out of season.

the income concept are real and inescapable; but it must suffice here merely to point them out. (Their significance for income taxation will be considered later on.)

Another difficulty with the income concept has to do with the whole problem of valuation. The precise, objective measurement of income implies the existence of perfect markets from which one, after ascertaining quantities, may obtain the prices necessary for routine valuation of all possible inventories of commodities, services, and property rights. In actuality there are few approximately perfect markets and few collections of goods or properties which can be valued accurately by recourse to market prices. Thus, every calculation of income depends upon "constructive valuation," i.e., upon highly conjectural estimates made, at best, by persons of wide information and sound judgment; and the results of such calculations have objective validity only in so far as the meager objective market data provide limits beyond which errors of estimate are palpable. One touches here upon familiar problems of accounting and, with reference to actual estimates of income, especially upon problems centering around the "realization criterion."

Our definition of income perhaps does violence to traditional usage in specifying impliedly a calculation which would include gratuitous receipts. To exclude gifts, inheritances, and bequests, however, would be to introduce additional arbitrary distinctions;[19] it would

[19] The greater part of the enormous German literature on *Einkommenbegriff* may be regarded as the product of effort to manipulate verbal symbols into some arrangement which would capture the essential connotations of *Einkommen* (as something distinct from *Ertrag, Einnahme, Einkünfte,* etc.),

be necessary to distinguish among an individual's receipts according to the intentions of second parties. Gratuities denote transfers not in the form of exchange —receipts not in the form of "consideration" for something "paid" by the recipient. Here, again, no objective test would be available; and, if the distinctions may be avoided, the income concept will thus be left more precise and more definite.[20]

It has been argued that the inclusion of gratuities introduces an objectionable sort of double-counting. The practice of giving seems a perhaps too simple means for increasing average personal income in the community. But philosophers have long discoursed upon the blessings of social consciousness and upon the possibilities of improving society by transforming narrow, acquisitive desires into desire for the welfare of our fellows. If it is not more pleasant to give than to receive, one may still hesitate to assert that giving is not a form of consumption for the giver. The proposition that everyone

---

provide a not too arbitrarily delimited conception, and yet decisively exclude gifts and bequests. It is as though an army of scholars had joined together in the search for a definition which, perfected and established in usage, would provide a sort of "linguistic-constitutional" prohibition of an (to them) objectionable tax practice. For summary of this literature see Bauckner, *Der privatwirtschaftliche Einkommenbegriff* (München, 1921). See also below, chap. iii.

Of course, we must avoid the implication that our definition establishes any decisive presumption regarding policy in income taxation. The case for or against taxation of gratuitous receipts as income ought not to be hidden in a definition. See below, chap. vi.

[20] The force of the foregoing argument is perhaps diminished when one remembers that the distinction creeps in unavoidably on the other side of the transaction—i.e., in the distinction between consumption and expense in the case of the donor. But there remains a presumption against introducing the distinction twice over if once will do.

tries to allocate his consumption expenditure among different goods in such manner as to equalize the utility of dollars-worths may not be highly illuminating; but there is no apparent reason for treating gifts as an exception. And certainly it is difficult to see why gifts should not be regarded as income to the recipient.

The very notion of double-counting implies, indeed, the familiar, and disastrous, misconception that personal income is merely a share in some undistributed, separately measurable whole.[21] Certainly it is a curious presumption that a good method for measuring the relative incomes of individuals must yield quantities which, summated, will in turn afford a satisfactory measure of that ambiguous something which we call social income. This double-counting criticism, in the case of some writers (notably Irving Fisher), carries with it the implied contention that all possible referents of the word "income," in different usages, must be definable or expressible in terms of one another. We have pointed out several different usages of the term in order to show that they represent distinct, and relatively unrelated, conceptions—conceptions which only poverty of language and vocabulary justifies calling by the same name.

[21] Some writers explicitly avoid the implication that social income should be definable in terms of individual incomes or vice versa: Held, *Die Einkommensteuer* (Bonn, 1872), chap. iv, esp. pp. 92 ff.; F. J. Neumann, *Grundlagen der Volkswirtschaft* (Tübingen, 1899), pp. 220–21; Schmoller, *op. cit.*, p. 78; Ammon, *op. cit.*, pp. 21–26; Meyer, *op. cit.*, chap. xii.

Legal

24

In re THE SPANISH PROSPECTING COMPANY, LIMITED.

[No. 80315 of 1909.]

Company—Contract of Service—Cumulative Salary payable out of " Profits "—Winding-up—Payment of Creditors and Shareholders in full—Surplus in Hands of Liquidator—Undrawn Profits—Arrears of Salary.

P. and V. agreed to serve a company at a fixed salary which they were not to be entitled to draw " except only out of profits (if any) arising from the business of the company which may from time to time be available for such purpose, but such salary shall nevertheless be cumulative, and accordingly any arrears thereof shall be payable out of any succeeding profits as aforesaid." The business of the company included the purchase and sale of shares. In the course of and for the purposes of its business the company acquired shares and debentures in another company. The shares were sold for cash and the proceeds brought into profit and loss account. The debentures were included in the yearly balance-sheets of the company as an unvalued asset. In the voluntary liquidation of the company the whole of the assets were sold, the debentures realizing 3072*l.*; all the creditors, except P. and V., to whom about 8000*l.* in respect of arrears of salary was due, were paid in full, and all the subscribed capital was returned to the shareholders, leaving a surplus of 3328*l.* in the hands of the liquidator :—

Held, reversing the decision of Swinfen Eady J., that the surplus in the hands of the liquidator ought to be treated as undrawn profits arising from the business of the company out of which P. and V. were entitled to be paid.

The meaning of the word " profits " explained by Fletcher Moulton L.J.

Frames v. *Bultfontein Mining Co.,* [1891] 1 Ch. 140, and *Rishton* v. *Grissell,* (1868) L. R. 5 Eq. 326, distinguished.

THIS was an appeal from a decision of Swinfen Eady J.

The Spanish Prospecting Company, Limited, was incorporated in 1901 for the objects mentioned in its memorandum of association, which included, inter alia, the acquisition, development, and turning to account of mines and mineral interests in Spain.

By an agreement dated June 4, 1901, and made between W. C. Punchard, J. M. Fleming, and S. Vivian as vendors, and the company as purchaser, it was agreed that the vendor should sell and the company should purchase the benefit of certain options in mining properties in Spain. It was further agreed

that the vendors should during the continuance of the agreement
give to the company the first refusal of all mining properties or
rights in Spain which might be offered to them on sale, lease, or
option.   During the continuance of the agreement the vendors
were to act as technical advisers to the company in connection
with the acquisition, development, or turning to account of any
properties or rights in Spain which it might be interested in or
desire to acquire.   Clause 5 of the agreement was as follows:
"In consideration of the premises the company shall during the
continuance of the agreement pay to each of the vendors a
salary at the rate of 41*l.* 13*s.* 4*d.* per month commencing from
February 15, 1901, provided nevertheless that the said W. C.
Punchard and S. Vivian shall not be entitled to draw their said
salary except only out of profits (if any) arising from the business
of the company which may from time to time be available for
such purpose, but such salary shall nevertheless be cumulative,
and accordingly any arrears thereof shall be payable out of any
succeeding profits available as aforesaid."   The agreement was
to determine ipso facto on the winding-up of the company.

In the course of its business, in June, 1901, the company
acquired through the vendors 6000 shares in a company called
the Spanish Minerals Development, Limited.   Of these shares
the company resold 1200 to Messrs. Punchard and Vivian and
held 4800 until 1906, when the Spanish Minerals Development,
Limited, disposed of the bulk of its property for a large sum
payable in cash, shares, and debentures in the Esperanza Copper
and Sulphur Company, Limited.   The company received for its
4800 Spanish Minerals shares 4040*l.* in cash, 3360 fully-paid
shares of 1*l.* each, and 3840*l.* in debentures of the Esperanza
Copper and Sulphur Company, Limited.   The company afterwards sold the 3360 shares in the Esperanza Company for
4236*l.*, which sum together with the 4040*l.* cash was duly
credited in the profit and loss accounts of the company, but the
Esperanza debentures were not so credited.

The profit and loss account of the company for the year
ended September 30, 1908, shewed a debit balance of 270*l.* 4*s.* 5*d.*
On the credit side of the account appeared a sum of 182*l.* 8*s.* in
respect of interest on the Esperanza debentures, but no value

C. A.
1910
~~
ANISH
PECTING
MPANY,
MITED,
In re.

was placed upon the debentures in the balance-sheet for the same period. In this balance-sheet there was a note to the effect that there was an amount of 7621*l.* 13*s.* 9*d.* due in respect of Messrs. Punchard and Vivian's remuneration under the agreement of June 4, 1901, which sum was only payable out of profits. In previous balance-sheets a note had appeared that there would be a further credit when the Esperanza debentures were realized, but this note was omitted, it was said by a slip, from the balance-sheet for 1908.

At the ordinary general meeting of the company held on December 21, 1908, the directors submitted the accounts above referred to and reported that the interests of the shareholders would best be served by winding up the company and distributing its assets. The report stated that the 3840*l.* debentures in the Esperanza Company were still in the hands of the company.

The company was afterwards wound up voluntarily, and in the realization of the assets by the liquidator the Esperanza debentures were sold for the sum of 3072*l.* The paid-up capital was returned to the shareholders in full, and after all the debts, except the claim of Messrs. Punchard and Vivian, had been satisfied there remained in the hands of the liquidator the sum of 3328*l.* 7*s.* 8*d.*, which was claimed by Messrs. Punchard and Vivian as accumulated profits arising from the business of the company and as such applicable to the payment of the arrears of salary due to them under the agreement of June 4, 1901. The liquidator being prepared to admit their claim, an originating summons was taken out by two contributories asking for a declaration that the applicants were not entitled to prove in respect thereof.

Upon the hearing of the summons Swinfen Eady J. held that at the date of the commencement of the winding-up the debentures formed part of the assets of the company, there being a debit balance of 270*l.* on profit and loss. There was therefore no profit arising in the carrying on of the business of the company, which came to an end with the winding-up. The 3328*l.* in the hands of the liquidator represented the surplus of realized assets over and above the subscribed capital, but it was not, within the authorities, a profit arising from the business of the company, because it was obtained on the ultimate realization of the whole of the property and assets of the company. Under the agreement the claimants had no right to payment of their salary out of surplus assets on the winding up of the company.

From this decision the claimants appealed.

Gore-Browne, K.C., and *Clauson*, for the appellants. The appellants have a contractual right to payment out of the sum in the hands of the liquidator which represents profits arising from the business of the company within the meaning of the agreement. When a partnership concern has to be wound up all debts must be paid, and when each partner has been repaid what he has brought in as capital, then any balance that is left is "profit": *Bishop* v. *Smyrna and Cassaba Ry. Co.* (1) That applies here. The Esperanza debentures might have been realized before the winding-up and the proceeds distributed as profit. The proceeds of sale are none the less "profits" by reason of their having been realized in the winding-up.

Hon. Frank Russell, K.C., and *A. Sims*, for the respondents. This is a service agreement, and "profits" in such an agreement must be restricted to profits realized by the company as a going concern. This item was deliberately omitted from the balance-sheet of 1908.

[FLETCHER MOULTON L.J. Surely these are profits earned or acquired during the life of the company.]

They are not profits arising from the business of the company as a going concern: Buckley on the Companies Acts, 9th ed. p. 652.

Profits realized on a sale in a winding-up are not "profits" within this agreement: *Rishton* v. *Grissell* (2) ; *Frames* v. *Bultfontein Mining Co.* (3) ; *In re Espuela Land and Cattle Co.* (4) The business of a company is at an end when a winding-up takes place: *Bisgood* v. *Henderson's Transvaal Estates, Ld.* (5) The surplus in the hands of the liquidator is not "profits" arising from the business of the company: *Birch* v. *Cropper.* (6)

(1) [1895] 2 Ch. 265.   (4) [1909] 2 Ch. 187.
(2) L. R. 5 Eq. 326.   (5) [1908] 1 Ch. 743.
(3) [1891] 1 Ch. 140.   (6) (1889) 14 App. Cas. 525.

C. A.

1910
~~~
PANISH
SPECTING
OMPANY,
IMITED,
*In re.*
~~~

Clauson in reply. In *Frames* v. *Bultfontein Mining Co.* (1) the business was sold as a whole, goodwill and all. Neither that case nor *Rishton* v. *Grissell* (2) has any application to this case.

The business of the company here resulted in a profit which was kept in specie until the winding-up and realized subsequently. The debentures were properly indicated in the company's balance-sheets though no value was placed upon them. The rights of a creditor are not affected by what the directors may do with reference to the domestic documents of the company.

A. E. Hughes, for the liquidator.

Cur. adv. vult.

Nov. 9. COZENS-HARDY M.R. This appeal turns upon the meaning of the word " profits." The company is in voluntary liquidation. The creditors, except Messrs. Punchard and Vivian, have been paid in full, and all the subscribed capital has been returned, and there is a surplus of upwards of 3000*l.* in the hands of the liquidator, and this sum, less costs, is claimed by Punchard and Vivian under the following circumstances.

By an agreement dated June 4, 1901, Punchard and Vivian were, for the valuable consideration therein mentioned, to receive a salary at the rate of 41*l.* 13*s.* 4*d.* per week each, subject to a proviso that they should not be entitled to draw their salary " except only out of profits (if any) arising from the business of the company which may from time to time be available for such purpose, but such salary shall nevertheless be cumulative, and accordingly any arrears thereof shall be payable out of any succeeding profits as aforesaid." The business of the company included the purchase and sale of shares. In 1901 the company purchased 6000 fully-paid shares of 1*l.* each in the Spanish Minerals Development, Limited, the consideration being the allotment of 6000 fully-paid shares of 1*l.* each in the Prospecting Company. Twelve hundred of the Development Company's shares were sold, leaving 4800 in the company's hands. The Development Company was wound up, and the Prospecting Company received in respect of their holding (*a*) 3840*l.* in cash, (*b*) 3840*l.* debentures of the Esperanza Company, and (*c*) 3360

(1) [1891] 1 Ch. 140.   (2) L. R. 5 Eq. 326.

shares in the Esperanza Company. In the balance-sheet for 1906 the cash was subtracted from the 4800*l.* and the shares were put as an asset at the figure of 960*l.* A note was added that the company had also received items (*b*) and (*c*), but no value was attributed to them in the balance-sheet; and that a further small cash payment would be forthcoming. In 1907 the shares —item (*c*)—were sold, and the proceeds were carried to the credit of the profit and loss account, and it was stated that there would be a further credit when the debentures—item (*b*)—were realized. In 1908 the report of the directors stated that the debentures were still in the hands of the company, and that it was proposed to wind up the company. The debentures were sold by the liquidator shortly after his appointment. There was no goodwill and no fixed capital. The assets consisted solely of cash and loans and shares and these debentures. Swinfen Eady J. has held that at the commencement of the winding-up the debentures formed part of the assets of the company, but that there was still a debit balance on profit and loss account, and that the company's business came to an end with the winding-up, and that the claimants are not entitled to be paid.

With great respect to Swinfen Eady J., I am unable to agree with this conclusion. The proceeds of the 6000 shares from time to time realized by the company were properly entered in the accounts and placed to the credit of profit and loss. This appears from the accounts for 1907. The balance-sheet for the same year recognizes that the company held the debentures which had at present no market quotation, and the directors did not put any estimate of value upon them. The liquidator has, however, realized these debentures, and I can see no reason why the proceeds should not be placed to the credit of profit and loss. The realization of this asset was not new business carried on by the liquidator. If goods are sold and bills given by the purchaser which have not matured at the commencement of the winding-up, the liquidator can collect the bills or discount them without embarking on new business. The language of Lindley L.J. in *In re Bridgewater Navigation Co.* (1) seems to me to **be a** clear authority in support of this view. He

(1) [1891] 2 Ch. 317.

C. A.

1910

ANISH
PECTING
MPANY,
MITED,
In re.

ozens-
dy M.R.

points out that although while the company was carrying on business debts owing to it were underestimated, this was done from motives of prudence, but that when the actual value was known the difference between the estimated and ascertained value really represented undrawn profits. In the present case no estimate was put upon the debentures, and the result is that the entire proceeds realized by the liquidator should be treated as undrawn profits arising from the company's business out of which the claimants are entitled to be paid. It follows that in my opinion the appeal should be allowed and the claimants should be declared entitled to the balance in the hands of the liquidator subject to the costs of the liquidation, including the liquidator's remuneration, and the costs of this summons here and below.

FLETCHER MOULTON L.J. The question for our decision in the present case is of some general interest because it turns upon the legal meaning of the word " profits," and inasmuch as I believe that the decision of the learned judge in the Court below is erroneous and that uncertainty or error in so fundamental a matter may lead to serious confusion, I shall in the first place consider the general question and then proceed to deal with the special facts of the case.

The word " profits " has in my opinion a well-defined legal meaning, and this meaning coincides with the fundamental conception of profits in general parlance, although in mercantile phraseology the word may at times bear meanings indicated by the special context which deviate in some respects from this fundamental signification. " Profits " implies a comparison between the state of a business at two specific dates usually separated by an interval of a year. The fundamental meaning is the amount of gain made by the business during the year. This can only be ascertained by a comparison of the assets of the business at the two dates.

For practical purposes these assets in calculating profits must be valued and not merely enumerated. An enumeration might be of little value. Even if the assets were identical at the two periods it would by no means follow that there had been neither

gain nor loss, because the market value—the value in exchange—
of these assets might have altered greatly in the meanwhile. A
stock of fashionable goods is worth much more than the same
stock when the fashion has changed.   And to a less degree but
no less certainly the same considerations must apply to buildings,
plant, and other fixed assets used in the business, because one
form of business risk against which business gains must protect
the trader is the varying value of the fixed assets used in the
business.   A depreciation in value, whether from physical or
commercial causes, which affects their realizable value is in truth
a business loss.

We start therefore with this fundamental definition of profits,
namely, if the total assets of the business at the two dates be
compared, the increase which they shew at the later date as compared with the earlier date (due allowance of course being made
for any capital introduced into or taken out of the business
in the meanwhile) represents in strictness the profits of the
business during the period in question.

But the periodical ascertainment of profits in a business is an
operation of such practical importance as to be essential to the
safe conduct of the business itself.   To follow out the strict
consequences of the legal conception in making out the accounts
of the year would often be very difficult in practice.   Hence the
strict meaning of the word "profits" is rarely observed in
drawing up the accounts of firms or companies.   These are
domestic documents designed for the practical guidance of those
interested, and so long as the principle on which they are drawn
up is clear their value is diminished little if at all by certain
departures from this strict definition which lessen greatly the
difficulty of making them out.   Hence certain assumptions have
become so customary in drawing up balance-sheets and profit
and loss accounts that it may almost be said to require special
circumstances to induce parties to depart from them.   For
instance, it is usual to exclude gains and losses arising from
causes not directly connected with the business of the company,
such, for instance, as a rise in the market value of land occupied
by the company. The value assigned to trade buildings and plant
is usually fixed according to an arbitrary rule by which they are

H 2   1

C. A.

1910

PANISH
SPECTING
MPANY,
MITED,
In re.

Fletcher
ulton L.J.

originally taken at their actual cost and are assumed to have depreciated by a certain percentage each year, though it cannot be pretended that any such calculation necessarily gives their true value either in use or in exchange. These, however, are merely variations of practice by individuals. They rest on no settled principle. They mainly arise from the sound business view that it is better to underrate than to overrate your profits, since it is impossible for you to foresee all the risks to which a business may in future be exposed. For instance, there are many sound business men who would feel bound to take account of the depreciation in value of business premises (or in the value of plant specially designed for the production of a particular article) although they would not take account of appreciation in the same arising from like causes.

To render the ascertainment of the profits of a business of practical use it is evident that the assets, of whatever nature they may be, must be represented by their money value. But as a rule these assets exist in the shape of things or rights and not in the shape of money. The debts owed to the company may be good, bad, or doubtful. The figure inserted to represent stock in trade must be arrived at by a valuation of the actual articles. Property, of whatever nature it be, acquired in the course of the business has a value varying with the condition of the market. It will be seen, therefore, that in almost every item of the account a question of valuation must come in. In the case of a company like that with which we have to deal in the present case this process of valuation is often exceedingly difficult, because the property to be valued may be such that there are no market quotations and no contemporaneous sales or purchases to afford a guide to its value. It is not to be wondered at, therefore, that in many cases companies that are managed in a conservative manner avoid the difficulty thus presented and content themselves by referring to assets of a speculative type without attempting to affix any specific value to them. But this does not ·in any way prevent the necessity of regarding them as forming a part of the assets of the company which must be included in the calculation by which de facto profits are arrived at. Profits may exist in kind as well as in cash. For instance, if a business is so far as assets and liabilities are

concerned in the same position that it was in the year before
with the exception that it has contrived during the year to
acquire some property, say mining rights, which it had not
previously possessed, it follows that those mining rights represent the profits of the year, and this whether or not they are
specifically valued in the annual accounts.

But though there is a wide field for variation of practice in
these estimations of profit in the domestic documents of a firm
or a company, this liberty ceases at once when the rights of third
persons intervene. For instance, the revenue has a right to a
certain percentage of the profits of a company by way of income
tax. The actual profit and loss accounts of the company do not
in any way bind the Crown in arriving at the tax to be paid. A
company may wisely write off liberally under the head of
depreciation, but they will be only allowed to deduct the sum
representing actual depreciation for the purpose of calculating
the profits for income tax. The same would be the case if a
person had a right to receive a certain percentage of the profits
made by the company. In the absence of special stipulations
to the contrary, " profits " in cases where the rights of third
parties come in mean actual profits, and they must be calculated
as closely as possible in accordance with the fundamental conception or definition to which I have referred.

I would have it clearly understood that these remarks have no
bearing upon the vexed question of the fund out of which
dividends may legally be paid in limited companies. Cases such
as *Verner* v. *General and Commercial Investment Trust* (1) and
Lee v. *Neuchatel Asphalte Co.* (2) shew that this fund may
in some cases be larger than what can rightly be regarded as
profits, and the decisions in these cases depend largely upon the
fact that there is no statutory enactment which forbids it to be
so. In the present case, however, no question as to the
limitations of this fund arises, so that I shall not make any
further reference to these decisions or to the principles on which
they rest, as they do not affect the matter before us.

We have now to apply these principles to the facts of the
present case. The claim of the plaintiffs is under an agreement

(1) [1894] 2 Ch. 239.   (2) (1889) 41 Ch. D. 1.

C. A.
1910
ᴾANISH
ꜱPECTING
ᴍPANY,
ᴍITED,
In re.

Fletcher
ulton L.J.

with the Spanish Prospecting Company, Limited, whereby they were to act as technical advisers to the company in connection with the acquisition, development, or turning to account of any rights or properties in Spain which it might at any time during the continuance of the agreement be interested in or desire to acquire. The clause fixing their remuneration reads as follows : " In consideration of the premises the company shall during the continuance of this agreement pay to each of the vendors a salary at the rate of 41*l*. 13*s*. 4*d*. a month commencing from the 15th day of February, 1901. Provided nevertheless that the said William Charles Punchard and Stephen Vivian shall not be entitled to draw their said salary except only out of profits (if any) arising from the business of the company which may from time to time be available for such purpose, but such salary shall nevertheless be cumulative and accordingly any arrears thereof shall be payable out of any succeeding profits available as aforesaid."

The phrase " profits (if any) arising from the business of the company " gives rise to no difficulty. The memorandum of association was of the widest possible kind, and even if we reject the more general clauses it is evident that the acquisition, development, and turning to account of mineral interests in the kingdom of Spain was in a special sense a business which the company proposed to carry on. It is only to such business that the facts of this case relate.

During the existence of the company it acquired certain shares in a company called the Spanish Minerals Development, Limited. That company sold part of its property to the Esperanza Copper and Sulphur Company, Limited, and subsequently went into liquidation and distributed its assets partly in cash and partly in specie among its shareholders. Inasmuch as the Spanish Prospecting Company, Limited, was a holder of shares in this company at the date of its liquidation, it participated in this distribution of the assets in specie, and accordingly received 8360 shares and 3840*l*. debentures of the Esperanza Company. Nothing here turns on its possession of the shares which were subsequently sold by it at a substantial sum considerably above their face value. The amount so realized was brought into the accounts of the company in the ordinary

C
1·

Spa
Prosi
Com
Lim
I·

Fle
Moul·

way. But the 3840*l.* debentures of that company were retained in specie and formed part of the assets of the Spanish Prospecting Company at the date when it went into voluntary liquidation. The liquidator realized its assets, and amongst them the debentures in question, and after repaying to the shareholders in full their capital and the interest due in respect of it there remained a surplus of 3328*l.* This sum had, no doubt, principally but not entirely arisen from the realization of the debentures in question. It is suggested that these securities were treated as valueless by the company at the date of the liquidation and that this has some legal effect on the status of the money obtained by their realization. I can see no grounds for such a suggestion in fact or law. The shares of the Esperanza Company, which necessarily ranked behind the debentures, had recently been sold for a substantial sum, and there is certainly nothing in the documents of the company which justifies the suggestion that the debentures were thought to be of no value. They were referred to as being in the hands of the company in the balance-sheets for 1906 and 1907 and in the report of the directors in 1908 which was sent to the shareholders with the accounts of that year, and it is plain that they were regarded as assets the value of which it was difficult to fix, but which had some value. I do not, however, propose to go more fully into this question because in my opinion it is immaterial. Whether of much or little value these debentures were unquestionably profits in kind made by the company in its business during the time it was carrying on that business, and when turned into money by realization the sum so realized stood in precisely the same position as the assets which it represented. It follows, therefore, that at the date of the liquidation the company had in its hands " profits " now represented by this sum of 3328*l.* No question arises as to the date at which such profits were earned, because the right of the appellants to payment is independent of any such question. But the respondents contend and have induced the learned judge in the Court below to decide that this sum is not " profits " because it was not in the form of money at the date of the liquidation but was turned into money during the realization. I am wholly incapable of appreciating this argument. It would apply to every asset of

. A.

910

ANISH
PECTING
PANY,
MITED,
n re.

etcher
ton L.J.

the company at the moment of liquidation except the cash in the till or safe. All the other assets exist in the form of land or chattels or rights which have to be realized before they can be treated as money and applied to the payment of liabilities to creditors or returned to the shareholders as capital or paid as profits to the persons entitled to them. What seemed to be mainly relied upon by counsel for the respondents in support of this view was that there would probably have been a difficulty in ascertaining the value of the debentures at the moment of liquidation. But there is nothing in the agreement which necessitates that any such value should be taken. The profits existed in the shape of the debentures; they did not cease to be profits because the company adopted the safer process of actual realization to the more hazardous one of acting on the then views of any person or persons as to the value of these debentures. It was also suggested that this value must have been very precarious because a suit was instituted on behalf of the debenture-holders to protect their interests, which were apparently in jeopardy through some act of the Esperanza Company itself. Even if such considerations were material, which in my opinion they are not, I can attach no weight to an argument which contends that a security must be valueless because its owners think it worth while to bring an action to protect it.

But the main argument on behalf of the respondents was based on certain decisions which are supposed to have established that if assets are realized by means of liquidation they can no longer be counted in the calculation of profits.

The two cases thus relied upon are *Frames* v. *Bultfontein Mining Co.* (1) and *Rishton* v. *Grissell.* (2) In the former case the directors of a company were entitled to be paid in each year as remuneration for their services a sum equal to 3 per cent. on the net profits of the company for such year. The business of the company was sold to another company for a very large sum, and the directors claimed to take that sum into account in calculating the profits of the year in which it occurred for the purpose of ascertaining their remuneration. Chitty J. held that they could not do so, and I cannot see how he could have come to any other

(1) [1891] 1 Ch. 140.   (2) L. R. 5 Eq. 326.

conclusion. The sale included the goodwill of the business of
the company, and therefore they were seeking to take the value
of the goodwill of a company into account in ascertaining its
profits. This is fundamentally wrong. The capital value of
goodwill is an alternative to profits, not part of them It is the
price at which a person renounces his rights to future profits.
Hence the goodwill of a business can never appear in the calculation of its profits. But Chitty J. realized that the company
might have made profits during the time that it was carrying on
its business although those profits could not be ascertained from
the figures of the sale which subsequently took place, because it
was impossible to sever the consideration and ascertain how much
of the price was paid on account of assets and how much on account
of goodwill. He therefore said that the plaintiffs might have an
account of the net profits made by the company during the year.
Such an account must of course have rested on a valuation of the
assets acquired by the company and in its hands at the date of
the liquidation and not on the sum actually realized by those
assets, because there were, as I have said, no means of calculating
what that sum was. The case of *Rishton* v. *Grissell* (1) so far as it
has any application at all illustrates precisely the same point.
Neither of these cases, therefore, gives in my opinion any support
to the contention of the respondents.

I am therefore of opinion that the decision of the learned
judge in the Court below was erroneous and that this appeal
should be allowed.

FARWELL L.J. The appellants are creditors of the company
for a sum of 8000*l.* or thereabouts for arrears of salary under
the agreement of June 4, 1901, but are bound by the proviso in
clause 5 not to claim payment thereof " except only out of profits
(if any) arising from the business of the company which may
from time to time be available for such purpose, but such salary
shall nevertheless be cumulative, and accordingly any arrears
thereof shall be payable out of any succeeding profits available as
aforesaid." I think that the creditors were not during the existence of the company entitled to challenge any valuation or the

(1) L. R. 5 Eq. 326.

C. A.

1910

ᴀɴɪsʜ
ꜱᴘᴇᴄᴛɪɴɢ
ᴍᴘᴀɴʏ,
ᴍɪᴛᴇᴅ,
In re.

well L.J.

amount of a reserve fund or the like fairly made; and accordingly that they cannot now impeach the omission of the Esperanza debentures from the balance-sheet of 1908 or their valuation at nil in that of 1907.   This, however, does not alter the character of the monetary results of the company's business, or affect the rights of the creditors whose claim is cumulative and not confined to the profits of any one year : money which has in fact resulted from the profits made in trading is none the less profit because it is carried over to a suspense account or to a reserve fund : if it is lost in the trading of subsequent years, there is an end of it, but so long as it remains in statu quo it remains as undistributed profits: see Lindley L.J.'s judgment in *In re Bridgewater Navigation Co.* (1)   The first question then is, are these Esperanza debentures profits arising from the business of the company ?   I am of opinion that they are.   The business carried on by the company was that of speculators and dealers in mining properties, and these are amongst the objects included in their memorandum of association.   The profits arising from the business of a company are not necessarily the same as the profits of that company.   A company may have fixed capital as well as circulating capital (as I have endeavoured to explain in *Bond* v. *Barrow Hæmatite Steel Co.* (2)), and in that case the profits of its business would be those arising from the use of its circulating capital excluding its fixed capital.   For instance, the profits arising from a draper's business would not include the increase over cost price of a freehold warehouse used in the business and afterwards sold.   But in this case the company acquired in the course and for the purposes of its business certain shares and debentures in the Esperanza Company.   The shares were sold in 1907, and the proceeds thereof duly and rightly brought into the profit and loss account of that year.   The debentures appear in the same account, but have no value set against them and for the purposes of that account are treated as of no value, and in 1908 are mentioned in the directors' report as still in the hands of the company, but do not appear at all in the balance-sheet annexed to that report.   Before any further report or balance-

(1) [1891] 2 Ch. 317.   (2) [1902] 1 Ch. 353.

sheet was issued the company went into voluntary liquidation, and the Esperanza debentures have been sold by the liquidator for 3072*l.* All the creditors of the company other than the appellants have been paid in full, the shareholders have received back all their share capital, and there remains a net balance of 3328*l.* 7*s.* 8*d.*, which the appellants claim as profits arising from the business of the company. Now it is not suggested that the company had anything that could be called fixed capital. The liquidator's account shews the realization of divers assets, and all are such as formed the general stock in trade with which the company dealt. The liquidator has simply wound up the business by realizing that stock in trade. The learned judge has decided against the appellants on two grounds—(1.) because the "profits" mentioned in clause 5 are confined to "profits" arising while the business of the company is being carried on. But assuming this to be so, it does not preclude the creditor from obtaining payment out of profits made but not realized during the continuance of the business. When a company is wound up its assets are applied in paying debts and liabilities irrespective of the nature and origin of such assets; but when all debts and liabilities have been paid and contributories have rights which depend on the nature and origin of the assets, it becomes necessary to analyze them and ascertain their origin. The question usually arises between preference and ordinary shareholders, but creditors with a claim against profits only are in at least as good a position as preference shareholders. (2.) The second ground on which the learned judge decided the case was that, on the authorities, the surplus of realized assets on winding up over and above the subscribed capital is not a profit arising from the business of the company. This, in my opinion, depends on the nature of the company's business and assets and cannot be predicated as universally true of all companies, and the authority of *Frames* v. *Bultfontein Mining Co.* (1), on which the learned judge relies, is really an authority against his decision. In that case the whole of the assets of the company were sold, including goodwill; the directors were entitled to 3 per cent. of the "net profits" of the company in each year. The company owned and

(1) [1891] 1 Ch. 140

C. A.

1910

PANISH
SPECTING
NPANY,
LMITED,
In re.

well L.J.

worked a diamond mine : the assets shewn on the balance-sheet included the value put on this mine (less a sum for depreciation) and diamonds sold and the like. The plaintiff was paid down to May 31, 1887. The company went into liquidation in April, 1888, and Chitty J., while rejecting the claim to any part of the profit made by the sale of the mine and goodwill, directed an inquiry as to the net profits made by the company down to May, 1888. He could not have directed such an inquiry if there was no right at all to any profits after winding-up. In the present case all the profits arise from the sale of part of the stock in trade after liquidation. There is no need for an inquiry because the amount is ascertained. I am of opinion that the judgment should be reversed.

Solicitors : *Slaughter & May ; Pemberton, Cope, Gray & Co.*

G. A S

C. A.

1917

PETERSON
J.

May 21, 22,
23, 24 ;
June 5, 6, 7 :
July 10.

C. A.
Oct. 29, 30,
31 ;
Nov. 1, 2, 5, 7.

AMMONIA SODA COMPANY, LIMITED v. CHAMBERLAIN.

[1916 A. 624.]

*Company—Director—Misfeasance—Payment of Dividends out of Capital
—Lost Capital on Revenue Account—Appreciation of Capital Assets
—Subsequent Profits—Liability to recoup lost Capital before Payment
of Dividends—Fixed Capital—Floating Capital.*

The Companies (Consolidation) Act, 1908, does not, nor does the
general law, prohibit a company from distributing the clear net
profit of its trading in any year unless its paid-up capital is intact
or until it has first made good all trading losses incurred in previous
years.

There is no rule of law which forbids a company from setting off
an appreciation in the value of its capital assets, as ascertained by
a bona fide valuation, against losses on revenue account.

A manufacturing company carrying on a newly-established
business incurred losses on its trading account for some years after
its incorporation and subsequently made profits. The directors
set off the losses against an appreciation of the company's capital
assets as ascertained by a valuation made by two of their number
who were not expert valuers and approved by the company in
general meeting, and paid dividends out of the subsequent net
profits without any further provision for replacing the losses.
Depreciation of buildings, machinery, and plant had been charged
in revenue account to an amount exceeding the losses :—

Held by Peterson J. : (1.) that in considering whether or not the
dividends were paid out of capital the sums charged for depreciation
could be written back to capital ;

(2.) that as the valuation was in fact made bona fide, and was
approved by the company in general meeting, the appreciation in
value could properly be set off against losses.

Held by the Court of Appeal and Peterson J. : (1.) that there was

(1) And see *Herbert* v. *Torball* (1663) 1 Sid. 162.—F. E.

C. A.
1917

AMMONIA
SODA
COMPANY
v.
CHAMBER-
LAIN.

no objection in law to such a revaluation and such a treatment of the appreciation in value ascertained thereby ;

(2.) that, apart from any question as to the depreciation allowed for buildings, &c., and whether or not the revaluation could be justified, the dividends were not in fact paid out of capital but out of current profits.

Lee v. *Neuchatel Asphalte Co.* (1889) 41 Ch. D. 1, 15 ; *Verner* v. *General and Commercial Investment Trust* [1894] 2 Ch. 239, 266 ; *In re National Bank of Wales* [1899] 2 Ch. 629, 669, considered and applied.

The observations of the Lords in *Dovey* v. *Cory* [1901] A. C. 477 cannot be considered as having overruled or qualified the previous decisions of the Court of Appeal in the above-mentioned cases.

Per Swinfen Eady L.J. : The fixed capital of a company is what the company retains in the shape of assets upon which the subscribed capital has been expended, and which assets either themselves produce income independent of any further action of the company, or, being retained by the company, are made use of to produce income or gain profits. The circulating capital of a company is a portion of the subscribed capital intended to be used by being temporarily parted with and circulated in business in the form of using goods or other assets which, or the proceeds of which, are intended to return to the company with an increment and to be used again and again and always return with accretions. When circulating capital is expended in buying goods which are sold at a profit or in buying raw materials from which goods are manufactured and sold at a profit the amount so expended must be charged against or deducted from receipts before the amount of any profit can be considered.

WITNESS ACTION.

This was an action by the plaintiff company claiming that the defendants, Mr. Arthur Chamberlain and Mr. Cocking, ought to make good the sum of 8203*l.* 18*s.* 4*d.*, the amount of the dividends paid on September 30, 1912, March 31, 1913, September 30, 1913, and April 4, 1914, and also the sum of 4264*l.* 12*s.*, part of the dividend of 4912*l.* 10*s.* 1*d.* paid on March 31, 1915 (a total of 12,468*l.* 10*s.* 4*d.*), or so much thereof respectively as was paid out of capital.

The material facts were as follows :—

In July, 1908, the plaintiff company was incorporated as a private company with a capital of 10,000 shares of 10*l.* each, subsequently increased to 15,000 shares of 10*l.* each, making a total of 150,000*l.*, for the purpose of acquiring, developing, and working as brine land the Holford Hall Estate, Cheshire, containing about 260 acres,

C. A.
1917
AMMONIA
SODA
COMPANY
v.
CHAMBER-
LAIN.

with underlying beds of rocksalt. This property was conveyed to the company in consideration of 55,000*l.* in shares and the liability under a mortgage of the property for 46,086*l.*, making a total of 101,086*l.*, of which 15,281*l.* was attributed to property passing on delivery, thus leaving 85,805*l.* for land, buildings, and fixtures.

The company then proceeded to erect works and sink another bore-hole and shaft with the object of developing the land as a brine field and utilizing the brine for manufacturing purposes, and until the early part of 1911 was not in a position to show profits. In April, 1911, one of the directors, Mr. Arthur Chamberlain, sen. (since deceased), suggested that the company should be converted into a public company and raise the additional 150,000*l.*, which the company needed, by the issue of preference shares to that amount. The difficulty in the way was that the company then owed the bank 10,000*l.*, and in addition there were debentures for 18,000*l.* and the mortgage debt of 46,000*l.* The balance-sheet for December 31, 1910, showed a loss of 19,028*l.* 5*s.* 4*d.* up to that date, comprising a sum of 10,601*l.* 16*s.* 7*d.* representing depreciation on buildings, machinery, and plant. This depreciation fund was increased to 13,702*l.* 15*s.* 7*d.* by July 31, 1911, and to 16,293*l.* 14*s.* 5*d.* by January 31, 1912. In these circumstances it was desirable, before inviting applications for preference shares, to be able to produce a balance-sheet which did not on the face of it show a loss of this description, and it appeared possible to do this if the land were of sufficient value to cancel the debit to profit and loss account.

At a board meeting on July 12, 1911, it was resolved that, having regard to the various boreholes that had been made and the amount of knowledge that had been acquired of the brine and salt land, it was desirable to make a revaluation of the land, and Mr. Chamber-lain, sen., and the defendant Mr. Cocking were requested to report to the next board meeting what sum would represent, in their opinion, the value of the land in accordance with the knowledge which the company then possessed. Neither Mr. Chamberlain, sen., nor the defendant Mr. Cocking had had any previous experience in valuing salt or brine lands. They ultimately advised that the land should be valued at 79,166*l.*, taking no account of its surface value but adding to that amount the expenses incurred in sinking shafts and other items already expended on it and charged against it in

C. A.

1917

AMMONIA
SODA
COMPANY
c.
CHAMBER-
LAIN.

the books. They based this valuation of the land upon the practically inexhaustible supply of brine and upon the solid beds of rocksalt, both of which had been proved to exist as the result of the works executed by the company since the purchase of the land.

The value of the land having been increased in this way, the balance-sheet for July 31, 1911, was prepared : "This balance-sheet " [the following statement of the facts is taken from the judgment of Peterson J.] " showed the land as of the value of 83,788*l.* 9*s.*, being the aggregate of 63,246*l.* 6*s.* 5*d.* and 20,542*l.* 2*s.* 8*d.*, the additional value on revaluation by the directors. On the other side of the account this additional value appeared under the heading of ' Reserve Account,' and from it were deducted the balance to the debit of profit and loss account (19,028*l.* 5*s.* 4*d.*) less the profits for the seven months up to July 31 (5682*l.* 3*s.* 2*d.*) and income tax recouped (375*l.* 3*s.* 11*d.*), and also the item of 1500*l.* for goodwill which had appeared in the previous balance-sheet and a premium on redemption of debentures (1980*l.*), leaving a balance to reserve account of 4091*l.* 4*s.* 5*d.* The object of the revaluation was thus achieved, the debit balances were wiped out, and the way was open for the conversion of the company into a public company and for inviting subscriptions for preference shares. The balance-sheet was signed by Mr. Chamberlain, sen., and by Mr. Cocking, and the auditors, Messrs. Thomas Johnston & Co., certified the balance-sheet, adding a special note which called attention to the fact that the directors had revalued the land, increasing the value by 20,542*l.* 2*s.* 8*d.*, which had been placed to a reserve account, against which had been written off loss on trading to date 12,990*l.* 18*s.* 3*d.*, goodwill 1500*l.*, and premium on redemption of debentures 1980*l.*, and contained the statement that ' subject to the foregoing in our opinion the balance-sheet is properly drawn up so as to exhibit a true and correct view of the state of the company's affairs.' It is to be observed that while the auditors called attention to the revaluation and to the application of the increase they do not appear to have advised the directors that it was improper to apply the increase in value to the writing off of the various items to which they referred. The balance-sheet was presented to and approved by a board meeting held on September 27, 1911, at which Mr. Chamberlain, sen., and the two defendants were present.

C. A.
1917

AMMONIA
SODA
COMPANY
v.
CHAMBER-
LAIN.

" On October 31 an extraordinary general meeting of the company was held, when seven members were present, including Mr. Arthur Chamberlain, sen., and the two defendants. At this meeting it was resolved that the company should be converted into a public company, that the capital should be increased by the creation of 150,000 preference shares of 1*l.* each, and that the accounts for the seven months ended July 31, 1911, and the directors' and auditors' reports thereon be received and approved of, and that the revaluation of the salt land therein referred to should likewise be approved. The company therefore in general meeting sanctioned and approved of the valuation which had been made by Mr. Cocking and Mr. Chamberlain, sen.

" In March, 1912, a balance-sheet and a profit and loss account were prepared as of January 31, 1912. The balance-sheet showed an additional value upon revaluation by the directors 16,450*l.* 18*s.* 3*d.*, this figure being the result of deducting from the original 20,542*l.* 2*s.* 8*d.* the balance of 4091*l.* 4*s.* 5*d.* remaining at reserve in the balance-sheet of July 31, 1911, while the profit and loss account showed a balance of profits for the year of 7348*l.* 13*s.* after deducting the sum of 5682*l.* 3*s.* 2*d.* which had been passed to reserve in the balance-sheet of July 31, 1911. A prospectus was then issued in May, 1912, inviting applications for the preference shares and resulted in the allotment of a considerable number of shares. On these preference shares dividends were paid amounting in the aggregate to 13,116*l.* Neither of the defendants held any of these preference shares. In the early part of 1916 Brunner, Mond & Co., Limited, purchased the bulk of the ordinary shares and a large portion of the preference shares at par, and appointed their nominees as directors, and in due course the new board instituted this action."

The action was tried before Peterson J. on May 21, 22, 23, 24, and June 5, 6, 7, 1917, when a considerable amount of evidence was given, the result of which is stated by his Lordship in his judgment.

Gore-Browne, K.C., *Sir John Simon*, K.C., and *J. H. Stamp*, for the plaintiff company.

Clauson, K.C., and *D. D. Robertson*, for the defendants.

Cur. adv. vult.

C. A.

1917

AMMONIA
SODA
COMPANY
v.
CHAMBER-
LAIN.

1917. July 10. PETERSON J., after stating the facts above set out, continued : It will be convenient if at this stage I state the conclusion at which I have arrived with respect to the revaluation. In my judgment the directors were not guilty of any mala fides in the matter. Mr. Chamberlain, sen., was obviously the master spirit in the company, and admittedly he was a man who had a high reputation for integrity and capacity. It was said that the object of this revaluation was to enable the company to obtain further capital by the issue of preference shares. I think that this was so ; but there is nothing unlawful or reprehensible in that object. The only ground on which complaint could be made is that the object was achieved by improper means. The directors no doubt would have been better advised if they had obtained a revaluation from some expert valuer, although, if one may judge by the evidence on the subject which I have heard, the margin of difference between the views of valuers on the subject is very great. But there is no rule of law which requires directors to obtain outside assistance in such matters or prevents them from valuing the property themselves, provided, of course, that they act honestly in doing so. In this case the directors requested two of their number to revalue the land ; and unfortunately the two who were selected were not really competent to deal with the problem. As I view the evidence, the directors, not being adequately conversant with the salt business, entertained inflated ideas of the value of the large deposit of rocksalt which had been discovered, and the members of the company who attended the extraordinary general meeting on October 31, 1911, all of whom seem to have been business men, appear to have held the same mistaken belief. In my judgment, the valuation, whatever may be its demerits, was honestly made, and I exonerate the directors from any charge of mala fides in connection with it. While this method of revaluation is clearly open to animadversion—and, indeed, no serious attempt was made to justify the basis on which it was constructed—it still may be that the result is approximately correct, and I have therefore to consider whether the land in August, 1911, was approximately of the value of 83,788*l.* The evidence which was adduced on this point was more than usually divergent. [His Lordship then reviewed the evidence in detail, and continued :]

I do not propose to attempt to say what in July, 1911, was the real value of the land as part of a successful undertaking. On the evidence before me I think that it was less than 80,000l. and considerably in excess of 60,000l. Nor do I think that it is necessary for me to arrive at a more definite or precise conclusion. The directors of the plaintiff company in my view honestly entertained the view that the land in 1911 had largely increased in value, and the plaintiff company in general meeting adopted their views knowing that the valuation had been made by the directors, and knowing, as they must have known, that the directors who had made the valuation were not professional valuers or men who had had a long experience in the salt business.

There is not any ground for suggesting that any facts were concealed from the shareholders by the directors. In these circumstances it is not, in my opinion, open to the company to attack the directors for an honest, though it may be erroneous, estimate which has been expressly adopted by the company in general meeting after the attention of its shareholders had been pointedly called to the resolution by the auditors' certificate which was attached to the balance-sheet.

It was contended, however, that there was no justification for the payment of the dividends in question, even if the valuation was honest and even if in its result it was correct. Mr. Gore-Browne said that the essential question was whether or not capital assets could be written up so as to justify payment of a dividend ; that the valuation, however careful and however thorough and satisfactory to the Court, was not a justification for paying dividends ; that the profit and loss account was a continuous account which was always open, and that there was no profit on it until all past losses had been worked off. My attention was directed to a long series of cases which dealt with the method in which a company's accounts ought or ought not to be kept, but it is not altogether easy to reconcile them. I have before me, however, the warning of Lord Halsbury and Lord Macnaghten in *Dovey* v. *Cory* (1), and I propose to lay to heart as far as possible the example of Lord Macnaghten when he declined to formulate precise rules for the guidance or embarrassment of business men in the conduct of business affairs.

(1) [1901] A. C. 477.

There is one distinction which should, I think, be remembered for the purposes of the present case. A dividend may be improper because it is paid out of capital, or it may be open to objection because it is paid when there are no profits available for the purpose. If during the year there is no balance to the credit of profit and loss account, any dividend which is paid must be provided out of the paid-up capital, and any such payment must reduce the paid-up capital. This is exemplified in one of the early cases in which interest was paid on share capital before the company had reached the stage when its receipts on trading exceeded its outgoings : *In re National Funds Assurance Co.* (1) Such a payment is clearly a reduction of the paid-up capital and is ultra vires. But where a company has made losses in past years and then makes a profit out of which it pays a dividend the question is a different one. Such a dividend is not paid out of paid-up capital. If it were, the paid-up capital would be still further reduced by the payment. In fact the assets representing the paid-up capital remain the same or of the same value as before the payment of the dividend. It may be that the balance to the credit of profit and loss account ought to be applied in making up lost capital, and it may be that the directors are liable for neglecting to apply it in this way. But such a payment does not involve a reduction of capital ; it involves a failure to make good capital which has already been lost : see *Bond* v. *Barrow Hæmatite Steel Co.* (2) If payment of dividends out of the balance to the credit of profit and loss is open to attack, it is, I think, on the ground (omitting any question of dishonesty) that the course adopted is one which is contrary to the practice which governs all competent business men in the keeping of their accounts. This is possibly another aspect of the distinction on which stress has sometimes been laid between the two propositions that dividends must not be paid out of capital and that dividends can only be paid out of profits.

In the present case the dividends in question were not paid out of capital, if the word " capital " is used as meaning assets which at the time in fact represented paid-up capital. They were in fact paid out of the balance standing to the credit of profit and loss account for the years in which they were paid. The question in this case, therefore, is whether any profits which were made had to be applied in

(1) (1878) 10 Ch. D. 118.   (2) [1902] 1 Ch. 353, 364.

C. A.
1917

AMMONIA
SODA
COMPANY
v.
CHAMBER-
LAIN.

Peterson J.

C. A.

1917

AMMONIA
SODA
COMPANY
v.
CHAMBER-
LAIN.

Peterson J.

making good any losses of previous years, and whether an increase in the value of the fixed capital could be taken into consideration for the purpose of wiping out previous losses of paid-up capital.

On the first question the decisions are such that any business man who consulted them for the purpose of ascertaining whether he could frame his accounts in a particular way might easily find that his difficulties had not been diminished. As the law stands at present losses of circulating capital must be made good before there are any profits out of which dividends can be declared ; but having regard to the observations of Lord Davey in *Dovey* v. *Cory* (1), the question whether a similar rule applies in the case of fixed capital appears to be still open. At the same time Lord Halsbury in *Dovey* v. *Cory* (1) expressed some doubt whether an abstraction of this kind, however proper in economic treatises, is applicable to the concrete realities of business life. What is circulating capital and what is fixed capital is a question which in many cases may well embarrass the business man and the accountant as well as the lawyer. According to some of the definitions, the same asset may be fixed capital in one company and circulating capital in another. It has, for instance, been suggested that investments are fixed capital when they are bought for permanent retention, while they are circulating capital if they are bought for the purpose of reselling them at a profit. One economist has argued that houses and lands if purchased for resale are circulating capital, but that if land is bought with a view to retention as a permanent investment it is fixed capital. In *Lee* v. *Neuchatel Asphalte Co.* (2) asphalte mines held for a term which were exhausted by working them were treated as being fixed capital : see *In re National Bank of Wales* (3) ; while in *Bond* v. *Barrow Hæmatite Steel Co.* (4) Farwell J. considered that iron ore mines of leasehold tenure which had been acquired for the purpose of providing the company with ore for smelting and buildings used in connection with them were circulating capital, and the reasoning would seem to indicate that if the tenure had been freehold the same conclusion would have been reached. I have, however, come to the conclusion that it is not necessary for me to attempt to determine what is the true view on these vexed questions.

(1) [1901] A. C. 477.   (3) [1899] 2 Ch. 629, 670.
(2) 41 Ch. D. 1.   (4) [1902] 1 Ch. 353.

C. A.

1917

AMMONIA
SODA
COMPANY
e.
CHAMBER-
LAIN.

Peterson J.

The plaintiffs in substance allege that the debit to profit and loss account, amounting to 19,028*l*., or, after deducting the profits up to July 31, 1911, and return income tax, 12,960*l*. 18*s*. 3*d*., ought to have been made good out of profits before there were any profits available for dividend. The greater part (13,722*l*. 15*s*. 7*d*.) of this debit of 19,028*l*. represented a depreciation of 2½ per cent. on buildings and 7½ per cent. on plant and machinery which had been written off as representing a diminution in value of these assets. The question is whether it is prohibited to utilize an increase in the value of the fixed assets for the purpose of wiping out this deficiency in the value of the capital assets. Sir Woodburn Kirby and Mr. Gibson both expressed the view that it could not. Sir Woodburn's opinion was that it was contrary to all principles of commercial accountancy to write up the value of a fixed asset and apply the surplus so obtained to meet a deficit on trading, and Mr. Gibson stated that such a course was absolutely wrong and " illegal." Sir Woodburn also accepted the proposition that it is a recognized and accepted principle of commercial accountancy that nothing should be taken into profit unless it is first realized. This, however, goes too far, for stock and book debts are habitually brought into profit and loss account before being realized, and probably Sir Woodburn intended to confine his statement to fixed assets. I am not satisfied that the proposition that it is contrary to all principles of commercial accountancy to utilize an increase in the value of a fixed asset for the purpose of getting rid of a debit which represents loss of paid-up capital is not too wide. It may be a precept of prudence and yet be far removed from the sphere of the categorical imperative. Assuming that a company ought to keep the value of its assets up to the amount of the liabilities and paid-up capital, or, in other words, to see that its paid-up capital is intact, why should it be absolutely precluded from stating the true value of its assets ? If an agricultural company has land under which valuable coal measures are discovered, it is difficult to see why it should not be allowed to show in its balance-sheet the increased value of its lands. If it is necessary or proper that a company shall maintain its assets at the amount of its paid-up capital and liabilities, there would not appear to be anything illegitimate in showing that the assets are equal to the paid-up capital and liabilities. Nor for this purpose can it matter that the

C. A.

1917

AMMONIA
SODA
COMPANY
v.
CHAMBER-
LAIN.

Peterson J.

increased value is due to the fixed assets. The paid-up capital is represented by both fixed and circulating capital, and it seems somewhat arbitrary that circulating capital may be shown at its true value while fixed capital must not. Take the case of a depreciation fund. The effect is that the value of the assets as shown in the account is diminished by the amount of the depreciation fund. If the assets in fact increase in value to the extent of the depreciation fund, there is no rule which prohibits a company from wiping out the depreciation fund from the liabilities side of the account. In *Bond* v. *Barrow Hæmatite Steel Co.* (1) Farwell J. held that if a sum is carried from profits to reserve account to meet an estimated deficiency of capital assets, and the assets subsequently increase in value to the necessary amount, the sum which has been carried to reserve account is not part of the capital, or, in other words, the subsequent increase in value may be utilized for the purpose of wiping out the previous estimated loss. To my mind it seems hardly logical to say that while this may be done in the case of an estimated loss it is necessarily illegitimate in the case of one which has been ascertained.

It would be a strange result if directors were prohibited from showing that the assets, fixed and circulating, were of a value equal to the liabilities and paid-up capital and yet, on a petition for reduction of capital, were required to show that the value of the assets was less than the amount of the paid-up capital and liabilities : see *In re Barrow Hæmatite Steel Co.* (2) If the present value of the assets were such that, notwithstanding previous losses, the paid-up capital was intact, the company would fail on a petition for reduction of capital and would, on the plaintiffs' contention, be bound to apply future profits for the purpose of making good past losses on the hypothesis, which had been proved to be false, that the paid-up capital was not intact. It is also to be observed that in *Lee* v. *Neuchatel Asphalte Co.* (3) the decision both of the Court of Appeal and of the Court of first instance proceeded upon a finding that the value of the assets, ascertained by valuation, was greater than it was when the company commenced its business. This was a case in which the question was whether dividends could be paid, and the Courts which dealt with

(1) [1902] 1 Ch. 353.　　　(2) [1900] 2 Ch. 846.
(3) 41 Ch. D. 1.

C. A.

1917

AMMONIA
SODA
COMPANY
v.
CHAMBER-
LAIN.

Peterson J.

it did not see any impropriety in ascertaining whether the capital assets had in fact been increased or diminished in value. Directors would no doubt not be justified in ascribing to a fixed asset a value which is the result of purely temporary fluctuations. It is one thing to treat an unrealized increase in value of a fixed asset as profit and to pay dividends out of it as profits ; but it appears to me to be a different question whether in considering whether there is a deficiency in paid-up capital owing to past losses, which ought to be made good out of future profits, the real value of the assets can be ascertained with the object of discovering if in fact there is a deficiency in the paid-up capital.

As Lindley L.J. said in *Lee* v. *Neuchatel Asphalte Co.* (1), " You must not have fictitious accounts. If your earnings are less than your current expenses, you must not cook your accounts so as to make it appear that you are earning a profit, and you must not lay your hands on your capital to pay dividend." In saying this the learned judge plainly meant that you must not pay a dividend out of your paid-up capital. In *Bond* v. *Barrow Hæmatite Steel Co.* (2) Farwell J. summarized the result of the authorities in this way : " there is no hard and fast rule by which the Court can determine what is capital and what is profit." The mode and manner in which a business is carried on, and what is usual or the reverse, may have a considerable influence in determining the question : per Lord Halsbury in *Dovey* v. *Cory.* (3) It may be safely said that what losses can be charged to capital and what to income is a matter for business men to determine, and it is often a matter in which the opinion of honest and competent men will differ : *Gregory* v. *Patchett.* (4) " There is no hard and fast legal rule on the subject " : per Lindley M.R. in *In re National Bank of Wales.* (5) A similar view was expressed by Warrington J. in *Hinds* v. *Buenos Ayres Grand National Tramways Co.* (6)

In the present case the business men who were the directors and shareholders of the plaintiff company, of whom some at least were very competent, were of opinion that it was, in the circumstances, quite proper to apply the increase in the value of the fixed assets

(1) 41 Ch. D. 1, 25.   (4) (1864) 33 Beav. 595.
(2) [1902] 1 Ch. 353, 364.   (5) [1899] 2 Ch. 629, 670.
(3) [1901] A. C. 477.   (6) [1906] 2 Ch. 654, 659.

C. A.

1917

AMMONIA
SODA
COMPANY
v
CHAMBER-
LAIN.

Peterson J.

in cancelling the previous deficiency of capital assets, and that, as the company's assets were equal to the liabilities and paid-up capital, there was no adequate ground for contending that the balance to the credit of profit and loss account ought to be applied in making up paid-up capital which had been lost. Even if the increase in the value of the fixed assets ought not to have been applied in this way, I should not be inclined to hold the directors liable for the dividends which were paid. The problem is not by any means a simple one. I am satisfied that the directors acted honestly. What they proposed to do was clearly shown in the balance-sheet and the auditors' report which were submitted to the general meeting of the company in October, 1911. Most, if not all, of the shareholders who attended that meeting were commercial men, and they unanimously approved of the proposal. The auditors, while they properly called attention to the revaluation by the directors and to the way in which it was proposed to apply the increase in the value of the land, do not appear to have advised the directors or the shareholders that there was any impropriety in dealing with the increase in this way ; and the same firm of auditors and an additional firm of auditors, both of whom were admittedly experienced chartered accountants, certified the balance-sheet of January 31, 1912, without suggesting any doubts as to the correctness of the course which had been pursued. " Directors are not liable for all the mistakes they may make, although, if they had taken more care, they might have avoided them. . . . . Their negligence must be, not the omission to take all possible care ; it must be much more blameable than that : it must be in a business sense culpable or gross " : per Lindley M.R. in *In re National Bank of Wales.* (1) In a case where there is no question of an ultra vires act it would be difficult for the company to make directors liable for following a course which had been approved by the shareholders, with full knowledge of the facts, in general meeting.

In my judgment, then, the present action fails, and must be dismissed with the usual consequences.

R. M.

The plaintiff company appealed. The appeal was heard on October 29, 30, 31, and November 1, 2, 5, 7, 1917.

(1) [1899] 2 Ch. 629, 672.

26

A. A. BERLE & F. S. FISHER JR.

ELEMENTS OF THE LAW OF BUSINESS
ACCOUNTING*

INTRODUCTORY

A business account is a hybrid document. It is an attempt to unite in two statements (the balance sheet and the income statement) at least four separate types of information, and to do this in a form which will be intelligible at once to persons who may be intimately connected with the business and to persons who may know little, if anything, about it.

(1) *Proprietary Interests*

Historically, a statement of account is designed to show the proprietor of the property (which in accounting language means the owner of an equity interest) what happened to property interests which were placed in the hands of someone else. The legal idea of accounting largely derives from this theory. Thus, a ward on coming of age would request an accounting from his guardian, the theory being that at one time the property of the ward had been deposited with the guardian, that through a period of years the guardian had handled this property, and that he now is called upon to make a showing that he still has this property in his hands or that he has undertaken some legally authorized operation with the property and has the proceeds in his hands. Slightly later this was enlarged to cover the idea of a showing not merely as to

---

* A word as to the history of this study is appropriate.

The Columbia Law School has for several years been experimenting with the subject of accounting as a part of its legal curriculum; it has given a course in accounting since 1929. The technique of treating accountancy as a field of law has been a matter of serious consideration.

Obviously, an attempt merely to teach the details of technical bookkeeping lies outside the Law School field. Equally, however, the well-equipped lawyer is obliged to know underlying accounting principles. This has led to an attempt to compare the recognized principles of accounting with that part of the decided case law which necessarily involves some accounting premise, with a view to determining how far an interweaving process has taken place;—how far, in a word, rules of accounting have become rules of law. The preliminary conclusions appear in this essay. The interweaving process seems to have gone so far that in some measure rules of accounting and rules of law are almost indistinguishable. The tentative conclusion seems warranted that the subject of accounting can be handled in large measure, not as an outside technique of incidental

the location of the property or its proceeds, but also as to the results of the operations with such property—that is, a distinction between what may be called "capital" and what may be called "income." Accounting for the purposes of trustees, guardians, executors, and fiduciaries generally, still proceeds primarily on this principle. It is both as old as the parable of the ten talents and as new as the elaborate endeavors to determine whether stock dividends are principal or income.

(2) *Result of Operations—Gain or Loss*

This necessarily brought into action a second principle. Not only was the accountant to show a state of affairs regarding property and proceeds but he was also supposed to show the distribution of this property properly among those interested in it. For it was never necessarily true that the property in his hands belonged in all its attributes to one individual or interest alone. Often, it was split, the principal to belong to a remainderman, the income to a life tenant; or any variation on this theme.

Out of this grew the second great division of accounting—a division which may be called in Professor Ripley's words a "dynamic pic-

---

advantage to the lawyer, but as an actual body of law, susceptible of being systematized, digested and taught as is any other field of law (insurance, for instance) in which a body of cases has grown up around a frame of commercial practice.

This essay does not purport to do more than give a background and bare outline of part of such a field of law. A number of other areas come readily to mind: *e.g.*, the growth of law in the accounting field distinctly influences the law of corporations, the law of trusts, and the law of taxation; it plays an important part in the development of that portion of the law of torts (deceit, *etc.*) which revolves around the law of corporation finance; it is of paramount importance in the law of public utilities. And these by no means exhaust the list.

On its farther borders, accountancy impinges upon the field of pure economics; it *is* the medium whereby various accepted economic conclusions find their way into practice. As the accounting conclusion is adopted into the law as a basis for imposing or withholding liability, the economic concept at length attains the dignity of a more or less obligatory rule of conduct.

The cases cited in support of this article almost without exception involve corporate accounts. However, we feel that the principles and rules here set forth are equally applicable to other forms of business enterprise. It is of course true that change and variation becomes apparent when we leave the corporation. For example, interest on invested capital must be accounted for in ascertaining partnership profits and an enterprise may have no need to distinguish between operating and non-operating income or expenses. Yet this accumulated mass of authority in the corporate field represents a force, perhaps still unapplied, which will undoubtedly in many instances be utilized with advantage and persuasion in other, non-corporate, situations. It is for these reasons that this article is entitled elements of "business" rather than of "corporate" accounting.

For assistance in the preparation of this essay and for many ideas in its development, we are indebted to Messrs. Mark R. Briney, Spencer Byard, Paul J. Kern, LL.B., John P. Ohl, Roger V. N. Powelson, P. Warren Roberts, LL.B., and Orson L. St. John of the Columbia Law School and to Professor Shaw Livermore of the University of Buffalo. Save for the fact that it is unfair to hold them responsible for the form of presentation and for certain of our conclusions, this essay might be regarded as a joint adventure.

ture" of what has occurred. Segregation of interests so often followed the line between "income" and "principal" (whatever that may have been) that it became necessary to work out some test as to the difference between an original fund, its proceeds and accretions, and the fund which would be recorded as payable to a person or interest entitled to the "income." This posed for the accountant a problem involving a question of economics (the economic theory never having been settled), a further question of business practice, and ultimately, a puzzle in legal theory as courts endeavored to wrestle with varying business problems and to reach what they considered the appropriate result.

It is true that the owners of a fund in a business, particularly a fund representing an equity, may be entitled both to the fund and to all accretions from it. Nevertheless, they wish to know the result of operations—that is, to know whether there are accretions or whether there are losses. And in the modern business structure it by no means follows that the same individuals are entitled to both funds. A corporation, for example, having an income bond or non-cumulative preferred stock outstanding, may find that the owner of such bonds or stock has rights directly dependent on the existence of earnings; and an accounting process may be required in order to determine whether and to what extent such earnings actually exist.

(3) *Valuation*

With this was bracketed a third principle, that of valuation. Technically speaking, this is not an accounting problem though the accountant has to reckon with it so often that it necessarily becomes a part of his practice. Specifically, the accountant has to check up on other peoples' valuations. For instance, a trustee who holds a particular piece of land in trust, paying the rents and profits to *A* during his life and delivering the land to *B* on *A*'s death, has no primary interest in the problem of valuation. He may, for the sake of convenience, assign the land an inventory value at the beginning of his trust. It does not greatly matter whether he assigns $10 or $10,000 as its value. For the question asked of him is not, "What is this land worth?" but "Where is and what has happened to this particular piece of land?" The business man, however, and even the modern trustee, has long since gone beyond this phase. Property does not remain static. The chance that a trustee will have at the close of the trust the same piece of property that was presented to him at the beginning of his relationship is relatively small. Even a trust in land is today subject to the chance that a portion of it will be condemned, and that in lieu of a part of the property, the trustee will have proceeds for which he must account. A trust with a power of sale definitely contemplates not only the possibility but the likelihood of a change in the property and reinvestment. In this event, in place of the original piece of property, the accountant must show proceeds. As soon as there is such change, the question arises as to whether there has been a profit—which involves first valuing the original piece of property, then valuing the proceeds, and then setting up a difference. The law will then, using the accounting process as a test, determine to whom this difference belongs.

In business, the valuation problem is even more acute. For while part of the property in a business enterprise may remain relatively static (*e.g.,* fixed assets), another large part of the property is usually in process of being turned over, often with high speed. Earnings, profits or income, as the case may be, may largely turn on the difference in valuation of this property, or its proceeds, at the end of an accounting period as compared with its valuation at the beginning of the period; the computation of income, return, accretion, or gain of any sort depends directly upon this calculation. Thus, it is essential that there be an ascertainment of value at both ends.

(4) *Quality of Assets or Liabilities*

For many business purposes (peculiarly for the banker who proposes to lend money at short term), interest is focused on the business position of the body of assets or property. Can any of it be swiftly turned into cash? What proportion is fixed and non-liquid? Conversely, the same banker may be interested in the quality of a liability. Is it likely to fall due shortly and thus become a draft on the assets? The enterprise may be worth many millions of dollars, but if all of it is in non-liquid real estate it is a poor risk for a bank loan. Again, a corporation may have a considerable amount of liquid assets, may likewise be heavily in debt, but still may be a perfectly good short term credit risk if the debt is in the form of a long term bond issue which does not become due for some years. Again, what assets are mortgaged? What liabilities have priority? In a word, the accounts should show not only the existence, amount and operating results of the property, and the amount of the claims against it, but also the quality of the property and of the corresponding claims.

The latest phase of the combination of these issues is a striking one. When business property is introduced into the modern corporation, and the aggregate of interests are represented at least in part by bonds or shares of stock, the financial machinery whereby liquidity is attained becomes increasingly important. Much of our industrial life is built upon this assumption of liquidity. On analysis (a process not germane to this essay), liquidity turns in part upon a constant series of appraisals of the shares—appraisals which in turn reflect in a measure the ability of the business enterprise to make earnings or profits—and in part the value (on some basis which varies with the views of the community at any given time) of the underlying enterprise. These appraisals are necessarily based on the showing which the company makes, that is, on its published accounts varied up or down by more fleeting information. The accounting problem thus becomes a matter of serious concern not only to owners and stockholders, but to every portion of the business world in which the values thus arrived at enter as a business consideration.

The basic diversity of the various theories thus combined in the normal business account becomes obvious. If we were to endeavor to make the whole process extremely clear we would have at least four separate and distinct sets of documents. The first would be a careful history of each piece of property of any sort entering into the business organism and running through the accounting period. This might be expressed in figures; ideally, it might be a matter of narrative. Second, there would be a series of running appraisals or values made up according to the best appraisal theory in respect of each piece or type of property exactly paralleling the narrative as to what happened to the property. The third would be an analysis of the set of values at the beginning of the accounting period and at the end of the accounting period with a view to determining the result expressed in terms of appraisal. A fourth document would take the properties and liabilities as they stood at the close of the accounting period and would analyze each piece of property and each liability with a view to determining its quality—which, in general, means its relative convertibility into cash in the case of assets, and its relative priority in the case of liabilities.

This diverse quality of the business account is due primarily to the diverse uses to which it is put. It is in a sense all things to all men. It should tell the owner what has been done with his property and where such property or its proceeds are. It should tell the different interests in the property what may be considered as an accretion or gain, what loss, and what merely replacement of property used up. It should tell the intending lender or investor the nature of the various properties and obligations. It should tell all of these people the values or amounts in respect of each item. It may furnish the test upon which interests are distributed between the proprietors.

Like any other ideal, this is not wholly obtainable in any mundane sphere, because of the limitation on documents and because no process of scientific accounting or economics can state any of these conclusions with complete accuracy. The process is perhaps simplest where it concerns merely the history of property. In determining values, opinion plays a very large part. When we come to the distinction between original assets or capital, and income, gain or accretion, a question of legal theory enters, since what is "income" (for legal purposes) and what is other accretion, gain or profit, turns very largely on a more or less arbitrary and conventional pre-judgment which the accountant must follow rather than fix. And when the quality of assets or liabilities is concerned, business practice, commercial probabilities and legal obligation must all be considered.

These questions (and many others) have in lump been referred to the accountant. Yet, day by day, lawyers and courts predicate legal effects on the results of accounting. It may fairly be said that rules of accounting are for many purposes rules of law; or, conversely, that rules of law entail rules of accounting. The respective tasks of a lawyer and accountant here intermingle so closely that neither can proceed without the other. To a much larger degree than perhaps either profession realizes this intermingling has already taken place. Courts have in fact and in form laid down rules which bind the accountants, or they have themselves adopted accountants' conventions. The accountant, once his rules have found their way into the body of law, becomes legally obliged to follow them in his further work. This essay is an endeavor to work out in a few of the simpler business problems the interrelation of accountancy and law. The accounting rules and conventions set forth are for the most part axiomatic but the extent to which they have been applied by the courts is not generally known.

I.

The Balance Sheet

The balance sheet is generally described as an instantaneous photograph of the state of the assets and liabilities of an enterprise at a given instant of time. It aims to show

(1) The *quality* of the assets and liabilities—current assets, current liabilities; deferred assets, accrued liabilities (items not "current"); fixed assets, long term indebtedness; contingent assets, contingent liabilities.

(2) The *interests*, ownership or otherwise, in the enterprise (always shown, conventionally, on the liability side)—secured as against unsecured indebtedness; priorities of indebtedness; equity ownership (conventionally shown by capital liabilities and by surplus).

(3) The *value* of the assets of various classes and the amount of the liabilities of various classes—the latter running all the way from a

note which necessarily has a fixed amount, through a debit claim which can only be estimated, to the equity interests, whose amounts turn entirely on the valuation of all the preceding items as set against the assets.

(4) Certain *margins for adjustment*—reserves against contingencies; depreciation reserves; amortization funds, *etc.* These reflect themselves in the description under which the respective assets and liabilities appear on the balance sheet.

The pertinent case law is not as easily categorized. The decisions which bear upon these aspects of the balance sheet are more conveniently noted in a discussion of what constitutes, A. Current Assets—Current Liabilities, and B. Fixed Assets—Fixed Liabilities. The margins for adjustment are treated in more detail in the consideration of the Income Statement below.

A. *Current Assets—Current Liabilities*

Conventionally, and also because of their supreme importance in short term credit transactions, balance sheets usually concern themselves first with assets and liabilities known as "current." The underlying idea is that current assets are assets which can rapidly be turned into cash within some assumed business term (conventionally six months); set against these are liabilities which will represent an assumed draft on the assets of the corporation within a relatively short term, conventionally one year. It will be noticed at once that these items raise primarily two of our four questions: that of quality—are these assets or liabilities properly placed in this category?, and that of value—how much of each actually exists?

(1) *The Cash Item*

Even the item of cash yields to some analysis, though valuation is not normally an issue. It includes legal tender actually in the till. It also seems to include bank notes, checks, postal and bank money orders, as well as I.O.U.'s.[1]

Any peculiar ownership factors in connection with the cash must likewise appear. Thus, cash to which the enterprise has title but which is actually subject to a trust in favor of someone else, apparently must be separately itemized.[2] A loan made merely for the purpose of creat-

---

[1] KESTER, ACCOUNTING THEORY AND PRACTICE (2d ed. 1922) 13; United States v. Smith, 152 Fed. 542 (W. D. Ky. 1907). The cases cited in this and the following footnotes are commented upon at length in the Appendix. It is sought to avoid repetition by limiting the footnotes to the body of this essay, in the main, to citation of the cases alone.

[2] American Life Ins. Co. v. Ferguson, 66 Ore. 417, 134 Pac. 1029 (1913).

ing a cash balance, the lender intending to withdraw it immediately, as soon as the account has been looked at, must be separately listed,[3] and where there is an agreement that the cash cannot be drawn upon except to pay losses after all other assets of the company are exhausted, it is a false representation to state the sum as a cash asset.[4] Both of these cases raise a double problem of quality and ownership. Quality, because though apparently it is cash in the till, in fact the asset is immobilized by an underlying understanding; ownership, because the appropriate liability against the specific asset must be properly recorded.

(2) *Notes Receivable*

Notes receivable are defined to include acknowledgments of a definite obligation for a sum certain which may be realized within the conventional current period.[5]

Again, the two questions of quality and value arise. The notes must be notes for a sum certain due not only at a stated period, but from a debtor who may reasonably and in commercial practice be expected to pay. Thus, a note due from a subsidiary or from an officer probably does not come within the definition (a subject discussed hereafter), and a short term note renewed from time to time for a debtor who, it is known, cannot pay on time, or taken under an agreement that the debtor need not pay on time, is likewise excluded.[6] Similarly, there must be a reasonable belief that the notes are worth their face, else deduction must be made. Notes of irresponsible persons carried through a need to increase the apparent amount of notes receivable fail to satisfy the requirements either of quality or of value and their inclusion in a balance sheet is a false representation,[7] although, where as a practical matter the note was given by an outsider solely for the purpose of swelling the assets and there was every reason to believe that the outsider would pay on time, both requisites were met.[8] If a corporation desires to rid itself of any notes on hand, it must do so by a valid transfer; a transaction by which the legal title is merely colorably divested, in that there is an agreement for subsequent reacquisition, is of no legal effect—title remains in the corporation, and failure to indicate the fact is fraudulent.[9]

---

[3] Otherwise, the representation of the amount of cash is considered false for the purpose of insurance law. American Life Ins. Co. v. Ferguson, *supra* note 2; *cf.* United States v. Peters, 87 Fed. 984 (C. C. D. Wash. 1898).
[4] Russell v. Bristol, 49 Conn. 251 (1881).
[5] KESTER, *loc. cit. supra* note 1.
[6] United States v. Smith, *supra* note 1.
[7] *Cf.* Hayes v. United States, 169 Fed. 101 (C. C. A. 8th. 1909).
[8] Dykman v. Keeny, 16 App. Div. 131, 45 N. Y. Supp. 137 (2d Dept. 1897).
[9] People *ex rel.* Hegeman v. Corrigan, 195 N. Y. 1, 87 N. E. 792 (1909).

(3) *Accounts Receivable*

Accounts receivable represent the liquidated claims of the business against its trade customers for goods sold on open account and not paid for.[10] They sometimes include all claims against debtors except those which are in the form of notes.[11] They are segregated from notes receivable on the theory that they are of somewhat different quality. A note receivable is readily transferable by endorsement, an account receivable is not. The quality here turns mainly on the legal attribute of negotiability.[12] Qualitatively, an account receivable must be of some use to the company—there is a lower limit to the probability of payment, below which any inclusion of accounts is improper. Accounts realizable only after protracted litigation are not properly included.[13] A distinction is drawn between the prospective performance of an obligation by an outsider and the prospective performance of the corporation itself—the latter is presumed to perform its obligation and may therefore include money paid to insure such performance as an account receivable.[14] In general, any known impairment of the probability of collection must be indicated and allowed for.

The valuation of the account depends upon the amount which could be obtained on a present liquidation—face value is merely a factor to be taken into consideration.[15]

(4) *Merchandise Inventory*

In this account there are involved at least three of our four problems. Not only must we determine whether or not a particular item is a part of the current merchandise inventory (and not a fixed asset), but we must also determine the interest which the company has in the article and its proper value. Merchandise inventory represents the stock-in-

---

[10] KESTER, *op. cit.*, at 12.

[11] ACCOUNTING TERMINOLOGY (Preliminary Report of Special Committee on Terminology, N. Y., 1931) 5. The Report goes on to say that accounts receivable are those amounts which are continually being converted into more liquid and more available assets, such as cash, from which liabilities may be met.

[12] American Life Ins. Co. v. Ferguson, *supra* note 2.

[13] *In re* Commonwealth Lumber Co., 223 Fed. 667 (W. D. Wash. 1915); First National Bank v. Wyoming Valley Ice Co., 136 Fed. 466 (M. D. Pa. 1905); Pettibone v. Toledo Ry. Co., 148 Mass. 411, 19 N. E. 337 (1899); *In re* Cooper, 12 F.(2d) 485 (D. C. Mass. 1926); *cf.* Adams v. Burke, 102 Ill. App. 148 (1902) and Brown v. DeYoung, 167 Ill. 549, 47 N. E. 863 (1897), in which cases illegal salaries were treated as assets because in the eyes of the law they had never left the possession of the corporation!

[14] Majestic Theatre Co. v. Keith-Orpheum Circuit, 21 F.(2d) 720 (C. C. A. 8th, 1927).

[15] *Cf.* Gaines v. Yates, 61 Neb. 100, 84 N. W. 596 (1900); Hubbard v. Weare, 79 Iowa 678, 44 N. W. 915 (1890); Cameron v. First Nat. Bank, 194 S. W. 469 (Tex. Civ. App. 1917); *In re* Rome Planing Mill Co., 99 Fed. 937 (N. D. N. Y. 1900); Plymouth Cordage Co. v. Smith, 18 Okla. 249, 90 Pac. 418 (1907).

trade in which the business deals;[16] it indicates any movable object of trade or traffic specifically the object of commerce.[17] This test thus involves the intent of the owner, accompanied by a reasonable basis for belief that the intent can be carried out.

Assuming that a given article is of the defined quality, of what nature must be the "interest" of the corporation to justify the appearance of the item on the balance sheet? A rule of thumb often used is to determine whether or not legal title has passed—if it has, the item is included; if not, then excluded. The test is applied to determine the propriety of including in merchandise inventory such items as goods held under a conditional sales contract, goods in transit at the time of inventory, or goods in excess of the normal stock of the company.

Merchandise inventory is commonly valued at "cost or market, whichever is lower."[18] This rule does not, however, answer all of the questions which may be raised. Merchandise is presumably intended for sale. It is consequently argued that the real valuation ought to be the selling price at the time of accounting. This might be a fair guide for the owner; but since the selling price represents a hope rather than a fact, accountants commonly discard it as a basis of valuation. Present market value seems (though in fact it rarely proves) much closer to actuality; the real reason for not accepting it probably is that it so frequently cannot be realized. There is, indeed, a fine distinction drawn here. Unrealized appreciation (discussed below) is not normally included in an account. Hence, where an excess of market value over cost price appears, it can be said to be realized only after sale. On the other hand, appreciation in value due to a manufacturing process is permitted to appear,—the theory being, apparently, that there has been a change in the quality of the property, or else that there is an added element of cost. At all events, the rule of "cost or market, whichever is lower" seems fairly well established in law as well as in accounting;[19] unrealized appreciation of merchandise is not sanctioned,[20] while unrealized appreciation due to manufacturing or processing is allowed.[21]

(5) *Investments*

Unissued stock of a corporation universally is not and ought not be included among its current assets. The majority of accountants con-

---

[16] KESTER, *op. cit.*, at 12.

[17] ACCOUNTING TERMINOLOGY, *op. cit.*, at 83. It is said that items of merchandise are proper current assets when they are in a condition to be convertible into cash within one year. MONTGOMERY, FINANCIAL HANDBOOK (1925) 729.

[18] HATFIELD, ACCOUNTING (1928) 199.

[19] Branch v. Kaiser, 291 Pa. 543, 140 Atl. 498 (1928); Davenport v. Lines, 72 Conn. 118, 44 Atl. 17 (1899).

[20] *In re* Kingston Cotton Mill Co., [1896] 1 Ch. 331; Hill v. International Products Co., 129 Misc. 25, 220 N. Y. Supp. 711 (1925).

[21] Hutchinson v. Curtiss, 45 Misc. 484. 92 N. Y. Supp. 70 (1904).

sider that treasury stock as well has none of the qualities requisite to an "asset."[22] There is some accounting authority in opposition, however, and the only case found on this point in effect requires treasury stock to be treated as an asset.[23]

No such difficulty arises as to securities of other enterprises (see, however, the discussion below of investments in other enterprises included within the same economic unit). The same principles of valuation apply here as in the case of merchandise inventory, and the same result should follow, assuming our premise that a balance sheet is the representation of a condition extant at one, and only one, point of time. In accord with these principles, where an investment has more than one "value"—that is, a value at maturity and a value on present liquidation, the present value is apparently the only proper one which the law recognizes in ascertaining the correctness of a balance sheet entry.[24] A quotation in the open or public market is, however, under some circumstances, disregarded in favor of a higher figure.[25]

(6) *Deferred Charges*

This class of items is defined as "that portion of expense items which is applicable to the period subsequent to the closing date" of the balance sheet.[26] It would seem that the quality requisite to justify the inclusion of such an expense is measured in terms of an active benefit to the corporation. That is, can the corporation make some use or recovery of the results of the prepayment? Thus, prepaid taxes are not proper "current assets," for their quality is similar to a condition precedent to engaging in business, which, once satisfied, contributes no further to the ease or profit of carrying on the enterprise.[27] On the other hand, prepaid rent and insurance are proper deferred charges.[28] Accrued interest, because it is definitely beneficial to the corporation, has been held to be a current asset, though it must be properly isolated.[29]

---

[22] MONTGOMERY, *op. cit.*, at 560, 1590.
[23] *Cf.* Morse v. U. S., 174 Fed. 539 (C. C. A. 2d, 1909).
[24] *In re* London Bank, [1895] 2 Ch. 673; Dovey v. Cory, [1901] A. C. 481 (1901) (*dictum*).
[25] *In re* Cleveland Discount Co., 9 F.(2d) 97 (D. C. Ohio 1924). The practice of disregarding market quotations in view of peculiar circumstances has been sanctioned during the 1929-1932 depression by the Insurance Commissioner of New York. But this necessarily involves a departure from the test of present realizable value.
[26] HATFIELD, *op. cit.*, at 126.
[27] Cox v. Leahy, 209 App. Div. 313, 204 N. Y. Supp. 741 (3d Dept. 1924).
[28] Majestic Theatre Co. v. Keith-Orpheum Circuit, *supra* note 14; Cox v. Leahy, *supra* note 27; HATFIELD, *op. cit.*, at 127.
[29] HATFIELD, *op. cit.*, at 255. *Contra:* Southern Cal. Home Builders v. Young, 45 Cal. App. 679, 188 Pac. 586 (1920); People v. San Francisco Savings Union, 72 Cal. 199, 13 Pac. 498 (1887). *Cf.* Badham v. Williams, 86 L. T. R. 191 (Chan. 1902) (accrued interest considered an asset, but not one capable of being distributed as a dividend). This subject is discussed at greater length, *infra.*

(7) Notes Payable

Here the question asked of the accountant is relatively simple: Is any debt owed in the form of a note? How much is owed? The accountant appears to follow the strict legal line. Thus, prior to maturity, accommodation liability is not a "note payable," within the meaning of a statute involving liability for debts incurred.[30]

(8) Accounts Payable

Both in law and accounting, accounts payable turn on the existence of a debt, i.e., an obligation to pay cash,[31] and apparently they must be liquidated.[32]

(9) Contingent Liabilities

Liabilities whose qualities are such that they may or may not become payable need not be included among the "debts" of a corporation in a report required by statute. But, if a balance sheet is supposed to indicate the condition of the enterprise, the existence of a known possibility which may translate itself into a liquidated cash liability is certainly a factor fairly to be considered. Otherwise, the accuracy of the picture is impaired. The law, however, does not recognize a "debt" until the condition creating liability has occurred;[33] and the accountants have had difficulty in passing this technical line. The problem is commonly solved by an appropriate notation on the foot of the balance sheet. Since such liabilities should be indicated at some point in the balance sheet if a true disclosure of the state of the enterprise is to be achieved, it is held to be a false entry entirely to omit from a financial report an obligation as a guarantor of an unmatured note.[34]

---

[30] Witherow v. Slayback, 11 Misc. 526, 32 N. Y. Supp. 746 (1895).

[31] Wing v. Slater, 19 R. I. 597, 35 Atl. 302 (1896); U. S. Smelting Co. v. Hopkins, 261 Fed. 546 (E. D. Pa. 1919); Whitney Arms Co. v. Barlow, 68 N. Y. 34 (1876).

[32] Victory Webb Printing Co. v. Beecher, 26 Hun 48 (N. Y. Sup. Ct. 1881).

[33] Witherow v. Slayback, supra note 30. [But cf. Byers v. Franklin Coal Co., 106 Mass. 131 (1872)]. Cf. Wing v. Slater, supra note 31; U. S. Smelting Co. v. Hopkins, supra note 31 (listed in Appendix under Accounts Payable); Whitney Arms Co. v. Barlow, supra note 31 (same); Spilman v. Parkersburg, 35 W. Va. 605, 14 S. E. 279 (1891) (same); Saleno v. City of Neosho, 127 Mo. 627, 30 S. W. 190 (1895).

[34] Cochran & Sayre v. U. S., 157 U. S. 286, 15 Sup. Ct. 628 (1894). The Federal Reserve Board also recognizes endorsements as contingent liabilities and requires them to be shown on the balance sheet as notes received, discounted, or sold with endorsement. But cf. People v. Grout, 174 App. Div. 608, 161 N. Y. Supp. 718 (2d Dept. 1916). See also Scott v. Eagle Fire Co., 7 Paige 198 (N. Y. 1838); DePeyster v. Amer. Fire Ins. Co., 6 Paige 486 (N. Y. 1837) (reserves for future losses must be set up out of unearned premiums before surplus can be determined for purposes of preference in the distribution of assets of insolvent companies).

(10) Accrued Expenses

Accrued expenses represent the accumulating but unpaid claims against the business for services rendered it, as distinguished from accounts payable, which usually represents purchases of assets (either current or fixed).[35] These items must appear on the balance sheet, especially if the corresponding accrued assets are carried as assets;[36] if not listed, there is a material misrepresentation of financial status.[37]

B. Fixed Assets—Fixed Liabilities

(1) Capitalized Expenses

The first item to be considered is organization expense. Accountants generally allow this to be capitalized, provided there is an early write-off.[38] Any expense of this nature, not represented by tangible property, must be clearly designated as an organization expense when it appears on the balance sheet.[89]

While capitalization of organization expense may be justified on the theory that it was the *sine qua non* of the corporation, and that without such expense there would be no business enterprise, the capitalization of early development expenses cannot be so rationalized. Such development expenses are more properly a part of the general cost of operating the business (discussed later); hence accountants disapprove of their capitalization,[40] and it has been held that interest paid on bonds during the period of development may not be capitalized to show a surplus available for dividends.[41] But it has likewise been suggested that such expenditures by an insurance company, when evidence of good business management, is "like sowing seed for a future sure harvest."[42] This might indicate that the courts test the validity of the capitalization of development expenses in the light of subsequent events; in the first case, the company's subsequent operations proved highly unprofitable, while in the latter case, a very substantial insurance business was built

---

[35] Hatfield, *op. cit.*, at 19.

[36] Hubbard v. Weare, *supra* note 15.

[37] *In re* Lustgarten, 289 Fed. 481 (C. C. A. 2d, 1923), aff'd, 266 U. S. 321, 45 Sup. Ct. 107 (1924); *cf. In re* Bloch, 109 Fed. 790 (C. C. A. 2d, 1901).

[38] MONTGOMERY, AUDITING, THEORY & PRACTICE (4th ed. 1927) 620; HATFIELD, *op. cit.*, at 66. *Cf.* CLASSIFICATION OF INVESTMENT IN ROAD AND EQUIPMENT OF STEAM ROADS (I. C. C. 1914) 3637 (allowing capitalization of such expenses without any write-off).

[39] KESTER, *op. cit.*, at 365; Bowe v. Provident Loan Corporation, 120 Wash. 574, 208 Pac. 22 (1922). See also ENGLISH COMPANIES ACT (1929) § 124, subsection 2; OHIO GENERAL CORPORATION ACT (1927) § 29, both of which require this item to be separately stated.

[40] HATFIELD, *op. cit.*, at 115.

[41] Hill v. International Products Co., 129 Misc. 25, 220 N. Y. Supp. 711 (1925).

[42] *Cf.* Kingston v. Home Life Ins. Co. of America, 11 Del. Ch. 258, 101 Atl. 893 (1918).

up by moneys spent during the early period of the corporation's existence. The test of subsequent benefit to the enterprise has in fact been used to determine whether or not costs of research and experimentation might properly be considered as capital assets.[43] This would seem to be good practice, when we consider that fixed assets, unlike current assets, have a primary value which in large extent may be characterized as a "value-in-use," as distinguished from a "value-in-exchange."[44]

There seems to be some doubt as to whether or not interest on borrowed capital may be capitalized as an asset; on principle, under ordinary circumstances, it should not be so treated. Accrued interest represents no property; it detracts from the accuracy of the item of "borrowed capital" on the right hand side of the balance sheet. Money borrowed is for the purpose of running a business and producing profit. To pay interest for the use of such money and, at the same time, to consider such interest as an asset would seem to be a clear contradiction in analysis.[45]

There is little authority allowing capitalization of dividends paid during the period of construction.[46]

Wherever items which may fairly be considered payments are in process of capitalization, the vital question before the corporation is that of quality. Rephrased, it may be said that a particular expense is justifiably included among fixed assets when it results in a concrete and tangible benefit to the corporation and there is no available fund or account (*e.g.*, operating expense account, or non-operating expense account, as to which, see *infra*[47]) to which such expense should be allocated.

(2) *Tangible Assets*

In dealing with tangible assets, the most important problem is that of valuation. As it is beyond the scope of this paper to discuss the

---

[43] GREENDLINGER, FINANCIAL BUSINESS STATEMENTS (1923) 183; HATFIELD, *op. cit.*, at 71; MONTGOMERY, *op. cit. supra* note 38, at 224; KESTER, *op. cit.*, at 345.

[44] *Cf.* Lincoln Chemical Co. v. Edwards, 272 Fed. 142 (S. D. N. Y. 1921), where an excess profits tax was levied on royalties received from a secret process; it would seem that this indicated the process to be a legitimate capital asset. So in Hubbard v. Weare, *supra* note 15, money spent in developing a machine of no demonstrated worth was held not a profitable asset, but, on the contrary, a loss.

[45] See MONTGOMERY, *op. cit. supra* note 17, at 1320. *Contra:* HATFIELD, *op. cit. supra*, at 63 *et seq.*; KESTER, *op. cit.*, at 541; Hinds v. Buenos Aires Grand Int'l Tramways Co., Ltd., [1906] 2 Ch. 654 (where interest on income bonds was held earned, although only because interest on bonds was capitalized, the capitalization being held proper as part of the cost of construction).

[46] See ENGLISH COMPANIES ACT (1929) § 54 which apparently allows such capitalization.

[47] P. 593 *et seq.*

technique of valuation, an analysis of the methods employed is all that may be attempted. In discussing these methods of valuation, the divergent interests of the accountant, the appraiser and the economist must be distinguished; historically, the accountant in valuing fixed assets looks to the past, the appraiser to the present, and the economist (depending on his purpose) to the future. Thus, the accountant is primarily interested in how much a certain property cost, and will reach a present value by means of an "adjustment account" ("cost-less-depreciation"); the appraiser is primarily interested in the present or re-sale value ("present value"); and the economist is, or at least may be, primarily interested in how much society at the present moment values property which has a capacity for producing a given "income stream" ("replacement value"). The Supreme Court of the United States has said,[48]

> "There is a logical incongruity in entering upon the books of a corporation as the capital value of property acquired for permanent employment in its business and still retained for that purpose a sum corresponding not to its cost but to what might be realized by sale in the market. It is not merely that the market value has not been realized or tested by sale made, but that sale cannot be made without abandoning the very purpose for which the property is held, involving a withdrawal from business so far as that particular property is concerned."[49]

Whether or not an unrealized appreciation or depreciation in the value of a fixed asset should be reflected in the income account is discussed later.

The other important problem involved in the "fixed assets" account is that of "adjustment." As has been pointed out above, adjustment is primarily connected with valuation, but in any attempt to portray a true picture of the corporation's condition, such adjustment must be clearly labeled, so that one examining a balance sheet may know its exact method and quantity. So, depreciation (a device used to amortize capital outlay over the various accounting periods during which it becomes continuously less valuable) should be identified with the particular property involved. And in keeping with our theory, whatever the technique used in computing depreciation, the quality of the figure ascertained should in some manner be indicated. While the early cases at first ignored the necessity of depreciation and allowed capital replace-

---

[48] LaBelle Iron Works v. U. S., 256 U. S. 377, 41 Sup. Ct. 528 (1921) (the court used "cost" rather than "market" as the basis for valuing fixed assets).
[49] See also HATFIELD, *op. cit.*, at 74-77, 282-283. *Contra:* State v. Bray, 323 Mo. 562, 20 S. W. (2d) 56 (1929) (current reproduction cost allowed to support the declaration of a stock dividend).

ment to be charged to operating expense,[50] such practice is of recent years no longer tolerated.[51]

(3) *Intangibles*

This group of assets includes good will, patents, trademarks and the like. The preliminary problem is whether or not such items should be shown on the balance sheet at all—that is, have they enough of the qualities of an asset to justify such an inclusion. If patents, trademarks or good will have been bought for value, it is thought that there is a justification for the appearance of such an item on the balance sheet. There is a similarity in quality between these "intangible assets" and the capitalized expenses discussed above. An intangible asset bought is a real expense, for which perhaps nothing is received, and, as shown below, if the intangible asset is worth nothing,—if it produces no benefit to the corporation,—then there is not a sufficient quality to justify an inclusion on the balance sheet.[52]

Assuming that an item of patents or the like is properly included, the important problems of valuation and adjustment then arise. Patents and trade-marks, at least, should be carried at cost, with amortization dependent on the measurable life of the asset, or as quickly as possible if there be no definite point of expiration.[53] It is safe to say that if such an asset is valued at a figure greater than either cost or "fair market value," there is a misrepresentation.[54]

Good will may be defined as the source of earnings unattributable to other assets. It is a device used for a multitude of purposes—a judicious padding of accounts, a justification for buying stock at a premium over book value (holding companies sometimes do this), a means of increasing compensation paid a dissenting stockholder, and the like.

---

[50] Kansas Pac. R. R. Co. v. U. S., 99 U. S. 455 (1878); Union Pacific R. R. Co. v. U. S., 99 U. S. 402 (1878).

[51] Cameron v. First Nat'l Bank, 194 S. W. 469 (Tex. Civ. App. 1917); United Oil Co. v. Eagle Transportation Co., 173 N. E. 692 (1930).

[52] KESTER, *op. cit.*, at 344.

[53] HATFIELD, *op. cit.*, at 129. In Bond v. Barrow, Haematite Steel Co., [1902] 1 Ch. 353, 367, the court said: "For instance I cannot think that it would be right for the defendant company to purchase out of capital the last two or three years of a valuable patent and distribute the whole of the receipt in respect thereto as profits without replacing the capital expended in the purchase. It is for the court to determine on evidence in each case whether the particular company ought or ought not to have a depreciation fund." *Cf.* Larson Co. v. Wrigley Co., 20 F.(2d) 830 (C. C. A. 7th, 1927): "It might well have been the case that the patents did not depreciate in value, but that, in fact, they appreciated depending quite wholly upon conditions other than the expiration of a portion of the period of their grant." (Deduction from profits for depreciation on patents on ground patent was expiring refused.) And see Matter of Dupignac, 123 Misc. 21, 204 N. Y. Supp. 273 (Surr. Ct. 1924).

[54] Heard v. Pictorial Press, 182 Mass. 530, 65 N. E. 901 (1903).

It is invariably said that good will should not be indicated except when purchased, and then only at cost price.[55] Whether or not it should be periodically "adjusted" or written off, is not as clear.[56] It would seem that if good will has been lost or rendered negligible in value it should of course be written off.[57] The value of good will is generally ascertained, in accordance with our definition above, by a consideration of the excess of the profits over the income derivable from the investment of the capital of the enterprise in some other enterprise. Such excess is then capitalized for a number of years, the number depending upon various factors.[58]

Items such as good will must be separately stated and clearly indicated so that an appraisal of their quality is apparent upon inspection, thus preventing an apparent over-valuation of some other item.[59]

II.

THE INCOME STATEMENT

Representation of the condition of an enterprise at a particular moment is of little help without an indication of the events propelling the corporation to that point. The income statement is an endeavor to give a summarized presentation of the material events and transactions occurring during a period immediately preceding the dates covered by

---

[55] KESTER, *op. cit.*, at 359; HATFIELD, *op. cit.*, at 113; SALIERS, ACCOUNTANTS' HANDBOOK, 586; GREENDLINGER, *op. cit. supra* note 43, at 175. *Cf.* Coleman v. Booth, 268 Mo. 64, 186 S. W. 1021 (1916); Stapley v. Read Bros., Ltd., [1924] 1 Ch. 1.

[56] Thus, Kester advocates a periodic write-off of purchased good will (*op. cit.*, at 359), while Hatfield (*op. cit.*, at 113) does not agree.

[57] *Cf.* Washburn v. National Wall Paper Co., 81 Fed. 17 (C. C. A. 2d, 1895) (plaintiff failed to prove overvaluation and accordingly was denied relief in suit to enjoin defendant on the ground a proposed dividend would impair the capital).

[58] Matter of Dupignac, *supra* note 53; *In re* Bijur's Estate, 127 Misc. 206, 216 N. Y. Supp. 523 (Surr. Ct. 1926) (court refused to use income from years 1917-1919 because they reflected abnormal war profits); White & Wells Co. v. Commissioner of Internal Revenue, 50 F.(2d) 120 (C. C. A. 2d, 1931); *In re* Hall's Estate, 94 N. J. Eq. 398, 119 Atl. 669 (1923), modified, 99 N. J. L. 1, 125 Atl. 246 (1923), aff'd, 100 N. J. L. 405, 126 Atl. 924 (1924); *In re* Welch, 137 N. Y. Supp. 941 (Surr. Ct. 1912); *In re* Schlossman's Adm'x, 136 Misc. 893, 242 N. Y. Supp. 417 (Surr. Ct. 1930) (non-operating income excluded in ascertaining net profits); Matter of Seaich, 170 App. Div. 686, 156 N. Y. Supp. 579 (1st Dept. 1915) (deduction of reasonable return on net capital must be made); *In re* Flurscheim's Estate, 107 Misc. 470, 176 N. Y. Supp. 694 (Surr. Ct. 1919) (deduction should be a reasonable return on *net* invested capital only and not on *gross* invested capital). The following factors are used in the evaluation of good will: length of time the corporation has been in business, position of the company in the trade, the amount of recent advertising, reputation of the firm, the trend of sales, the contracts held by the company and the trend of profits. See Pett v. Spiegel, 202 N. Y. Supp. 650 (Sup. Ct. Sp. T. 1923).

[59] HATFIELD, *op. cit.*, at 125; MOODY, 1921 MANUAL OF INDUSTRIALS, vii; Galloway v. Schill, Seebohm & Co., [1912] K. B. 354.

the balance sheet. While the problem of valuation of necessity must run through every item on the income statement, the most important consideration is that of quality—that is to say, a determination of the proper classification of each item on the statement.

Care must be taken in defining the terms used.

Gross sales is the aggregate value of the goods or services delivered or rendered within a given period without regard to the collection of the proceeds.[60]

Gross earnings comprises those items properly included within "operating income."[61]

Gross receipts is generally considered to comprise all receipts arising from the employment of the corporation's capital, whether in its principal business or not.[62]

Gross income includes accruals, as distinguished from cash receipts, from all sources.[63]

Net income is the balance remaining after the deduction from gross income of charges, costs, expenses and loss which have accrued during the given period, together with the amount of reserves which may have been set up.[64]

Profits describes the balance that remains after all items of income and all items of expense have been considered.[65]

A. *Operating and Non-Operating (Recurrent and Non-Recurrent) Income*

Operating income is defined as "the income derived from the general operation of the business."[66] It is at once seen that quality is primarily in issue.

Dividends may be paid to an investor out of any "income." But in determining the prosperity of an enterprise over a period of years, careful allowance must be made for any gain to the corporation which

---

[60] MONTGOMERY, *op. cit. supra* note 38, at 355.
[61] State v. N. W. Telephone Exch. Co., 107 Minn. 390, 120 N. W. 534 (1909).
[62] State v. Central Trust Co., 106 Md. 268, 67 Atl. 267 (1907); Commonwealth v. Brush Electric Light Co., 204 Pa. 249, 53 Atl. 1096 (1903); People v. Comptroller, 157 N. Y. 677, 51 N. E. 1093 (1898).
[63] MONTGOMERY, *op. cit. supra* note 38, at 354; ACCOUNTING TERMINOLOGY, *op. cit.*, at 69. Note that the Interstate Commerce Commission uses gross income as the aggregate of operating income (operating revenues less the operating expenses and taxes) and non-operating income.
[64] ACCOUNTING TERMINOLOGY, *op. cit.*, at 70; MONTGOMERY, *op. cit. supra* note 38, at 360.
[65] HATFIELD, *op. cit.*, at 241. *Accord:* Price Bros. v. Cushing, 135 Iowa 457, 110 N. W. 1030 (1907); Hubbard v. Weare, *supra* note 15; Carter v. Phillips, 88 Okla. 202, 212 Pac. 747 (1923); Park v. Grant Locomotive Works, 40 N. J. Eq. 114, 3 Atl. 162 (1885), *aff'd*, 45 N. J. Eq. 244, 19 Atl. 621 (1885). Obviously the term "gross profits" is a contradiction in terms.
[66] ACCOUNTING TERMINOLOGY, *op. cit.*, at 70.

may be in the nature of a windfall. Consequently, "non-recurring" or "non-operating" income is to be carefully differentiated. Two considerations urge this. First, the corporation is engaged in a particular line of endeavor, and an accurate portrayal of its progress in such line may be had only when the profit (*i.e.*, operating income or operating revenues less operating expenses) from the endeavor may be calculated, irrespective of chance earnings. Second, if non-recurring and incidental income are to be taken into account in calculating operating income or profit, a wholly misleading picture of the enterprise's success in operations may result. The law in most respects supports the accountant in requiring the two classes of income to be segregated and separately labeled.[67]

B. *Realized and Unrealized Change in Asset Valuation*

Whether a particular item be classified as operating or as incidental, non-operating income, a primary question arises: to what extent must the value of a particular item be reduced to cash before it may properly be included in the income statement? We have met the problem before in considering the balance sheet—as, *e.g.*, where it is desired to reflect changes in value of fixed assets or inventory.

The first problem is one of properly segregating and labeling the item. Where a corporation is primarily engaged in trading in fixed assets, an increase in value, if realized, might properly be included as an item of operating income. Realized appreciation of current assets is commonly so labeled and segregated, since most enterprises are operated primarily to realize appreciation of current assets either through a rise in market value or through a process of manufacture.

The art of accounting has proceeded much farther than the case

---

[67] See BELL, ACCOUNTANT'S REPORTS (1921) 101: "Profit from operations is the profit from the regular operation of the business before deducting the cost of procuring capital with which to operate the business and any extraordinary loss or losses over which the management has had no control—other income credits should represent income from sources *other* than the *regular* operation of the business." So in a utility company, operating income is the sale of gas or other commodity or service dealt in. Municipal Gas Co. v. Public Service Commission, 113 Misc. 748, 186 N. Y. Supp. 541 (Sup. Ct. 1920); Boston Elevated R. R. Co. v. Commonwealth, 199 Mass. 96, 84 N. E. 845 (1908); People *ex rel.* Joline v. State Board of Tax Commissioners, 145 N. Y. Supp. 226 (Sup. Ct. 1912); Detroit G. R. & W. R. Co. v. Commissioner of Railroads, 119 Mich. 132, 77 N. W. 631 (1898); State v. Minn. & I. R. R., 106 Minn. 176, 118 N. W. 679, 1007 (1908).
The following items have been held not to fall within the "operating income": interest on bank balances, N. Y. & Queens Gas Co. v. Prendergast, 1 F.(2d) 351 (S. D. N. Y. 1924); receipts from sale of worthless judgments, Livingston County Bank v. First State Bank, 136 Ky. 546, 121 S. W. 451 (1909); receipts from the sale of leasehold by furniture corporation, *In re* Schlossman's Adm'x, *supra* note 58; receipts from advertising in cars, People v. State Board, *supra*.

law. So far as the decided cases go, appreciation in value, when realized, is apparently a proper fund out of which to pay dividends,[68] although one old case goes so far as to recognize that if the rise in value of an asset is incidental or unusual, the realized increase should be treated as non-operating income and separately labeled.[69]

Unrealized increase in asset value presents the problem in a more difficult form. The difficulty is twofold. In the first place, does the increase in value really exist? The conservative view (probably justified in view of the human tendency to record hopes as facts) is that there can be no profit or income until the increase in values has been consummated by a sale or a reduction to cash.[70] It may well be argued that in case of a "conservative" appreciation of an asset (*i.e.*, an appreciation which probably will remain permanent), a corporation should be allowed to indicate such an increase, either on its balance sheet or income statement, in order that further commercial credit may be secured. In the second place, assuming that some account should be taken of the unrealized appreciation, should it be included in the "income statement" or directly transferred to a special reserve account? The difference in quality between a fixed and a current asset suggests that more liberty ought to be allowed the practice of depicting the unrealized appreciation of a fixed asset than of a current asset, on the theory that the very nature of a current asset contemplates its convertibility into cash within a limited period. Accordingly, there would seem little ground for giving any indication whatsoever of an unrealized appreciation to current assets—let the deed of conversion tell its own story,—whereas in the case of a fixed asset, the increase may well be the result of the community's revaluation of the potential productivity and utility of the property, which, as it is not designed for sale, may escape record indefinitely. In such case, the recognition on the balance sheet of an unrealized appreciation of a fixed asset, while excluding it from the income statement (though not from a proper surplus or profit and loss account), presents a somewhat truer picture of the present worth of the company. However, inasmuch as the accountant is concerned primarily with the "historical" value of fixed assets, it may well be argued that his only duty is

---

[68] Lubbock v. British Bank of South America, [1892] 2 Ch. 198; Lapham v. Tax Commissioner, 244 Mass. 40, 138 N. E. 708 (1923); People *ex rel.* Mercantile Safe Deposit Co. v. Sohmer, 158 App. Div. 110, 143 N. Y. Supp. 313 (3d Dept. 1913); *In re* Spanish Prospecting Co., [1911] 1 Ch. 92; see HATFIELD, *op. cit.*, at 280.

[69] State v. Bank of Louisiana, 5 Mart. (N.S.) 327 (La. 1827).

[70] HATFIELD, *op. cit.*, at 282; Kingston v. Home Life Ins. Co., 11 Del. Ch. 258, 101 Atl. 898 (1917); Jennery v. Olmstead, 36 Hun (N. Y.) 536 (3d Dept. 1885); Sexton v. Percival Co., 189 Iowa 586, 177 N. W. 83 (1920); People *ex rel.* Kings Co. Lighting Co. v. Willcox, 210 N. Y. 479, 104 N. E. 911 (1914). And see also (1921) 31 JOURNAL OF ACCOUNTANCY 389.

to reflect such an unrealized appreciation of a fixed asset in a marginal note.[71] One cannot avoid the impression that the real reason (and a sound one) for completely excluding unrealized appreciation from income statements, and for admitting it grudgingly, if at all, to balance sheets, is the fear of human frailty. Revising values upward is unduly easy, where the revision is put to no pragmatic test such as a sale. This feeling seems to run through the legal decisions as well as through accounting technique. On this aspect, the experience of both professions tends to converge.

---

[71] Thus Hatfield, *op. cit.*, at 283, quoting Dickinson (ACCOUNTING PRACTICE & PROCEDURE, at 81) and Leake (GREAT BRITAIN ROYAL COMMISSION ON INCOME TAX, at 3605) questions the validity of including unrealized appreciation for credit purposes. Holding that unrealized appreciation is not profit, see U. S. v. Phellis, 257 U. S. 156, 42 Sup. Ct. 63 (1921); Southern Cal. Home Builders v. Young, *supra* note 29. The following statutes expressly forbid cash dividends from surplus created by unrealized appreciation: THE UNIFORM BUSINESS CORPORATIONS ACT [adopted in Idaho (IDAHO BUSINESS CORPORATIONS ACT § 20 IVa) and, Louisiana (La. Laws, 1928, Act 250, § 26, IIIa); OHIO GENERAL CODE (1924) §§ 8236-38; INDIANA GENERAL CORPORATION ACT § 12. Vermont [VERMONT GENERAL LAWS (1917) § 4939] and Wisconsin [WISCONSIN STATUTES (1929) § 182.19], however, seem to permit dividends from such a source. For authority requiring the surplus created by unrealized appreciation to be descriptively labeled and physically isolated, see Moss, TREATMENT OF APPRECIATION OF FIXED ASSETS (1924) 36 JOURNAL OF ACCOUNTANCY 161; IDAHO BUSINESS CORPORATIONS ACT § 20 II; Burmingham v. Burke, 67 Utah 90, 245 Pac. 947 (1926) (*dictum*). That there is no duty to indicate the fact of an appreciation, see Newton v. Birmingham Small Arms Co., [1906] 2 Ch. 378; and see Young v. Brownlee, [1911] S. C. Cases 677.

RECENT
CONTRIBUTIONS

G. EDWARD PHILLIPS

THE ACCRETION CONCEPT OF INCOME

ACCOUNTING theory and practice have long suffered from diversity and controversy. There is wide agreement that it must be possible to greatly increase the usefulness of accounting and that the key to achieving this lies in improving accounting theory as a foundation for accounting practice.

This article is an attempt to demonstrate: (1) that progress in accounting theory must begin with income concepts, (2) the appropriateness of a single concept, accretion, rather than a variety of concepts, (3) that the accretion concept is an all-purpose concept, relevant to taxation and other areas as well as accounting, and (4) that general acceptance of this concept would have significant effects on accounting practice as well as "theory."

The accretion concept is neither complex nor difficult but has far reaching implications for accounting theory and practice. The accretion concept defines income as an increase in economic power which can be measured with reasonable objectivity. For an individual, income for a period equals the change in economic power during the period plus the value of goods and services consumed. For other entities, income is the change in economic power adjusted for capital contributions and distributions.

The requirement of objectivity of measurement imposes limitations on the concept, but also is the source of its usefulness. Because the concept does not tell us when a change in economic power is reasonably measurable, it leaves room for disagreement as to whether a wide range of items constitute income. This may appear to be a weakness in the concept but actually is an advantage, since it forces us to focus attention on measurability as the critical question in controversies over income.

In emphasizing objective measurability, the accretion concept differs from the economic concept of income, as usually conceived, and also from the concept implicit in conventional accounting practice. In many discussions of "economic income," present worth of future receipts is stressed as the basis for valuation. The inherent subjectiveness of estimates of future receipts and appropriate discount rates is overcome in the accretion concept by emphasizing market values as value measures. Conventional accounting, rather than being too subjective, sets objectivity standards unreasonably high in insisting on transactions before recognizing many value changes.

Progress in Accounting Theory. The widespread dissatisfaction with the present state of accounting "principles," and also the belief that improvement requires a solid conceptual base, are reflected in the establishment of the Accounting Principles Board and the research program of the American Institute of Certified Public Accountants. The accounting profession urgently needs, and apparently believes in the possibility of obtaining, a basis for determining the soundness of accounting practices.

A critical issue is the question of uniformity versus diversity. Few accountants are willing to advocate achieving uniformity by arbitrarily requiring all firms to follow identical practices. But if comparability is to be attained, the alternative is

* G. Edward Philips is Assistant Professor of Accounting in the University of California at Los Angeles. He has published previously in the *National Tax Journal* and in the *NAA Bulletin*.

to have each company follow sound practices, with general agreement as to what is "sound." Anyone familiar with the controversies among reputable theorists as to the propriety of such things as variable costing and income tax allocation may conclude that reaching agreement on soundness is a hopeless cause, but the Institute's actions clearly indicate that hope has not yet been given up.

If this hope is justified, then it must be possible to develop a theoretical basis for judging the soundness of alternative accounting practices. The development of this theoretical basis requires central attention to income concepts. Almost all of the significant controversies in accounting can be traced to differences as to what should be recognized as affecting income. A distinction can be made between differences as to what, in theory, constitutes income and what, in accounting practice, we can measure with reasonable objectivity. This distinction cannot be absolute, but it is important that accountants clearly recognize when their differences are theoretical, being differences as to what income is, and when their differences are practical in being differences as to whether or how a given item can be measured with reasonable objectivity.

Progress in accounting theory has been handicapped by two ideas which have caused much confusion. These are (1) that there must be different concepts of income for different purposes and (2) that the "matching principle" constitutes, or provides a basis for, a theory of income. Both ideas need to be re-examined and clarified, and perhaps should be ceremoniously discarded.

It is true that different data are relevant for different purposes and even that individuals and groups have reasonable differences in what they hope to learn from financial statements. But it is a mistake to conclude that there must be as many concepts of income as there are uses or purposes of data related to income. If accounting principles are to be arrived at deductively, we cannot avoid the necessity of starting from some concept of what constitutes income. So long as we accept many concepts of income we will have many theories of accounting. The importance of a single concept of income is discussed in some detail below, under the heading "An All Purpose Concept."

The concept of matching costs with revenues has been, and should continue to be, useful in achieving consistency (in the sense of reporting costs in the period in which revenue is recognized), but it is an error to conclude that sound accounting principles can be deduced from matching. Any income concept involves periodic matching—that is, assignment of the recognition of value changes to time periods. The objection is not to this general notion, but rather to the idea that a theory of income can be constructed around the association of specific costs with specific revenues. Matching is necessary because of the currently accepted concept of realization, not because matching itself is a concept of income. When we recognize revenue only when "realized" it is desirable that we recognize costs as expenses in the corresponding periods if a relationship can be identified. Matching is more aptly described as an expedient necessitated by our arbitrary definition of realization than as a basis for a theory of income.

The first accounting research study under the new American Institute research program[1] is meant to be a foundation for "developing a co-ordinated system of postulates, principles and rules for accounting."[2] In this writer's opinion, that study is an excellent beginning toward a

---

[1] Maurice Moonitz, *The Basic Postulates of Accounting,* American Institute of CPA's, 1961.
[2] *Ibid.,* p. 55.

foundation, but is no more than a beginning. The study fails to deal decisively with the most vital question—income concepts. Moonitz correctly points out that the measurement of income involves measuring changes in wealth,[3] but admits to "the absence of a theory of valuation or of pricing of assets and liabilities, and

cipal problem in the search for a satisfactory measurement of wealth and income. The conflict between "reality" and objectivity is illustrated in the list of five "concepts" of income given below. From the first to the last of the five, objectivity increases at the expense of conceptual reasonableness.

Concepts	Characteristics
Psychic income	Purely subjective. Income is what you think it is—based on "utility" and inseparable from consumption.
Economic present value income	Gains objectivity by omitting "non-economic" factors. Values are dependent on future receipts.
Accretion income	Income is an increase in economic power which can be verified with reasonable objectivity. Relies primarily on market values as measures of economic power.
Accrual accounting income	Mixed. Some use of forecast and market values but generally requires an outside transaction before recognizing value changes.
Cash basis accounting income	Strictly objective. Requires realization in cash.

their related concepts."[4] A theory of valuation, however, is essential to a definition of income, and accounting theory can hardly exist without it.

The Accretion Concept. Terminology is important, but not vital, in accounting theory. The argument here is not for the term "accretion" or even "income," but rather for a concept which is essential as a foundation for accounting principles. The accretion concept is not a revolutionary new concept originating with this paper. Indeed, among the major merits of the concept are its age and the fact that it is consistent with views widely expressed in economic and accounting literature. A revolution is needed, however, in the sense that the accounting profession needs to give recognition to the value of this concept as a normative standard or directional guide in dealing with the problems of financial reporting.

An income concept that is to be useful outside of ivory towers must be measurable with reasonable objectivity. The inevitable conflict between the needs for objectivity and for conceptual soundness is the prin-

Any notion of income must ultimately rest on a concept of subjective well-being or utility and therefore only "psychic" income can claim to represent true income. The distinction between psychic income and economic income is often overlooked, but is of vast importance. When we take the step from psychic to economic income we have already made a large sacrifice of reality for the sake of objectivity. Instead of defining income in terms of satisfactions (psychic income) economic concepts define it in terms of economic power, i.e., command over goods and services which are capable of a money measure.

Although economists have not reached universal agreement on a definition of income, it seems fair to describe economic income as being based on the present value of future receipts.[5] Thus the theoretically correct way to place a value on an asset

---

[3] *Ibid.*, pp. 15–16.
[4] *Ibid.*, p. 55.
[5] Sidney S. Alexander, "Income Measurement in a Dynamic Economy" in *Five Monographs on Business Income*, published by the Study Group on Business Income, American Institute of Certified Public Accountants, 1950, p. 59.

(or on a business as a whole) is to compute the present value of the expected net receipts (dividends) that will be derived from it. Income for a period is equal to the net receipts of the period adjusted for the change in asset values (economic power). This concept of income clearly defines the relevant factors, but any attempts to measure income on this basis must be highly subjective because of uncertainty. We cannot ordinarily predict future receipts and select an appropriate discount rate with much objectivity.

In contrast to this economic concept, the accretion concept bases its measure of economic power on market values, rather than discounted receipts. This can be viewed as a concession of some conceptual soundness in order to gain greater objectivity of measurement. It seems obvious to this writer that the superiority as to objectivity of the accretion concept over economic present value income much more than offsets any loss in conceptual soundness. A more critical question is whether the gain in objectivity of present practice (accrual accounting income) over accretion income justifies the accompanying loss of conceptual soundness.

The principal differences among economic, accretion, and accrual concepts of income relate to realization. Economic present value income has no realization requirement; income arises with an increase in the "true" value of an asset. Accretion recognizes income if the increase in value is reasonably measurable; e.g., reflected in increased market value. This is equivalent to a realization requirement; income is "realized" when objectively measurable market values of assets rise. Present accounting practice has a much stricter realization requirement; generally income is recognized only with an actual market transaction. These differences may be illustrated by considering the income of a corporate shareholder. Economic income

for a given year would be the dividends received adjusted for the change in value of the share, this value measured by computing the present value of expected future dividends. Accretion income would be dividends adjusted for the change in market value. Accrual accounting would ordinarily include only current dividends in income and would recognize the value change when and if the share is actually exchanged. The case for the accretion concept rests on the proposition that market values are sufficiently more objective than computed present values to justify their use despite the loss of conceptual soundness and that the further gain in objectivity does not justify waiting for "realization" as presently defined.

It is perhaps obvious that much objectivity is gained when values are measured by looking to market figures rather than by discounting expected future receipts. It is not so obvious that a serious conceptual loss results from using market values rather than discounted receipts. If everyone in the market made the same forecast of future receipts and applied the same discount rate, market values would equal present values and there would be no difference between accretion income and economic present value income. Market values may be viewed as reflecting various estimates and discount rates. Furthermore, economic power does not exist without market values. For example, an investor may perceive that the present value of future receipts from a given security exceeds market value, but he has no corresponding economic power until the market value rises or the receipts are realized.

The use of the phrase "with reasonable objectivity" in our definition of accretion income might be considered unsatisfactory, since it leaves room for judgment as to what constitutes reasonable objectivity. A principal merit of the concept, however, is that, while it does not solve all accountants' problems in deciding how to measure income and economic position, it does force a consideration of these problems as being primarily problems of objectivity of measurement rather than of conceptual soundness. This can be illustrated by considering the continuing controversies over inventory valuation, including LIFO and variable costing. Insofar as financial reporting is concerned, these controversies involve "proper" measurement of income. But there are always two aspects to the problem: (a) what is income? and (b) given the necessity for objectivity, how can we best measure it? The second aspect might be phrased differently as: "How greatly must we depart from income as we would like to measure it because of the necessity of being objective in our measurements?" It is neither possible nor desirable to put an end to controversy as to this question. Indeed, the answers can be expected to change with new developments in institutional structures and record keeping techniques. On the other hand, it should be possible to reach wide agreement as to the first aspect. Unless we can agree what it is we are trying to measure, there is little hope that we will agree how to do it.

LIFO, FIFO, and variable costing are all inventory valuation methods based on costs. If our concept of income is that income is a result of matching costs and revenues, then it is proper to discuss the merits of these alternatives in terms of which does the best job of matching. But if our concept of income is in terms of economic power (e.g. accretion income) the question becomes which, if any, of these methods of valuation gives the best balance between objectivity of measurement and portrayal of economic reality.

Under the accretion concept, any change in inventory value (or value of any other asset or liability) which can be measured with reasonable objectivity would be reflected in the accounts. If this concept is accepted, whether cost or market values should be used is not a question of theory but a question of practicability. Market should be used unless not measurable with sufficient objectivity. If market is rejected, choice of cost method requires a balancing of objectivity with degree of approximation to the "ideal" concept. The argument here is that accretion income should be accepted as the ideal—a normative standard or directional guide to be used in evaluating the merits of alternative practices.

Accrual accounting income is income as measured by present generally accepted practice. This is a mixture of arbitrary rules and concessions to economic reality. It is difficult to see what could fairly be described as an income concept in this practice, but it is common to refer to income as the excess of revenues over costs. In fact, important attempts have been made to demonstrate that the concept of matching costs with revenues is the accounting concept of income.[6] It appears more appropriate to this writer to view matching not as a concept of income but as a practice which is necessitated (to obtain internal consistency) by our insistence on a rather arbitrary definition of realization. If we did not insist on realization, we would not need to be concerned about matching. It might be maintained that the accretion concept is a realization concept in the sense that a change in economic power is recognized (realized) whenever it is reasonably measurable. But the difference between accretion and accrual accounting with respect to realization is important. In the accretion concept both revenue and expense are recognized when they are reasonably measurable and this alone deter-

---

[6] See especially W. A. Paton and A. C. Littleton, *An Introduction to Corporate Accounting Standards*, American Accounting Association, 1940.

mines the time periods in which they are reflected. There is nothing sacred about transactions.

The accretion concept is of great potential value to accountants as a standard or guide but is not a pat formula or prescription for practice. Those who advocate emphasis on valuation are often accused of failing to see the difficulties of valuing assets or wanting to make accountants into appraisers. Acceptance of the accretion concept implies neither. It does imply recognition of the fact that to the extent that we can measure values objectively we can measure income realistically. Our problem, therefore, is to seek out reasonably objective realistic measures of value rather than to construct a "theory" of income based on matching. The likely effects on accounting practice of general acceptance of the accretion concept are discussed in another section of this article.

Cash basis accounting income carries realization to an extreme. The gain in objectivity is substantial—on a strict cash basis you need not be concerned about depreciation and bad debt estimates—but accountants are agreed the loss in portrayal of economic reality it too great to give useful results in most cases.

Limitations on the Accretion Concept. There are three problem areas in the measurement of income and economic position which are not resolved by the accretion concept. These are (a) defining the entity, (b) adjusting for changes in the value of money, and (c) distinguishing income from "operations" from total income.

The accretion concept assumes that the entity for which income is being measured has been defined. In most instances the entity is quite clear-cut, but serious conceptual problems sometimes arise. For example, it is clear that children often have economic power, but it is not obvious that they, or an individual husband or wife, should be considered an entity separate from the family. This poses income tax problems, as does the question of whether a corporation is a proper taxable entity apart from its owners. The problems of determining when it is appropriate to consolidate the financial statements of related corporations are familiar to accountants. The accretion concept does not contribute directly to solving these problems. That it would, however, help clarify some aspects of them is illustrated by the fact that accretion would require a parent corporation to include in income any objectively measurable increase of equity in a subsidiary.

Changes in the value of money are ignored in the accretion concept. This departure from "reality" is perhaps largely made up for by the fact that accretion reduces the significance of this problem. Much of our difficulty with price level changes is due to our strict adherence to realization. The effects of gradual changes in price levels on asset values are often realized all at once, with a resulting large distortion of income. To the extent that assets can be revalued periodically, the "bunching" effect is eliminated. This would not make any more "real" an increase in value which corresponds to a rise in the price level, but the distortions caused by delayed realization are eliminated.

The problem of price level changes is related to that of distinguishing operating from non-operating income. Accretion is an all-inclusive concept which makes no distinction between a gain which results from efficient management and one which is a "windfall." It is obvious that such a distinction is useful to many users of financial statements and even that accountants should do their best to provide data that can be used for this purpose, but it does not follow that "operating" income should be the underlying concept of accounting income. Although accountants can often segregate such unusual value changes as fire losses from other data, the possibility of reasonable objectivity is lost long before all significant "non-operating" events are taken into account. For example, a large rise in inventory values (whether recognized now or later, when realized) might result from astute management planning, non-operating factors, such as unusual market fluctuations, or even poor management if the company was overstocked but hit a fortunate price rise. If we accept the accretion concept and report as income the over-all economic progress of the entity, we can be somewhat more objective than if we attempt to separate out operating income.

An All-Purpose Concept. Proponents of a variety of income concepts, as opposed to a single "all-purpose" concept, emphasize that there are many purposes for which income is measured or that there are many possible approaches to measuring the concept. Although this variety of purpose and possible approach creates complexities, it is not conclusive evidence that a number of concepts must be accepted.

While it is certainly true that different users of accounting data will find different figures relevant to their purposes, it does not follow that there must be many concepts of income. On the contrary, whenever the relevant figure is "income" for a period of time, there is ideally only one figure that is appropriate. A distinction can be made between two tasks of accountants. One of these is the measurement of the economic progress and status of an entity (income and financial position), the other is the collection and interpretation of relevant data for decision making. This distinction is useful even though income and financial position are the relevant data for some decisions. It is often appropriate for accountants to supply data on such things as cash and funds flows, differential costs, and variable

costs. This need for a variety of data does not, however, imply a need for variety of income concepts. Agreement on a meaningful concept of income is essential to improvement of the financial reporting function of accountants, and there is no inherent reason for this concept to interfere with the collection, analysis, and interpretation of data relevant to particular decisions.

Much has been written on the similarities and differences of appropriate income measurement for tax purposes and financial reporting purposes. There is substantial evidence that improvement of both taxation and accounting practice requires an income concept as a directional guide and that the same concept is appropriate for both. The term accretion was chosen for the income concept which appears most satisfactory for accounting because of this similarity between tax and accounting needs—the term has been used by some students of tax problems.[1] The same general concept has often been called the "Haig-Simons" income concept after Robert Murray Haig and Henry C. Simons.[2] This concept is particularly relevant to the growing concern about the need for income tax reform. The objectives of taxation include fairness or equity, desirable economic effects, and administrative feasibility. There is frequently a conflict between fairness and administrative feasibility which is closely related to (and often identical with) the accounting conflict between economic reality and objective measurability. In both accounting and taxation there is a need for a basic concept of income to be used as a direc-

[1] E.g. Robert Murray Haig, "The Concept of Income: Economic and Legal Aspects," in R. M. Haig (ed.), *The Federal Income Tax* (New York: Columbia University Press, 1921), p. 17, and Richard A. Musgrave, *The Theory of Public Finance* (New York: McGraw-Hill Book Company, Inc., 1959), p. 165.

[2] Robert Murray Haig, *op. cit.* and Henry C. Simons, *Personal Income Taxation*, (Chicago: The University of Chicago Press, 1938).

tional guide. General acceptance of such a concept would greatly clarify the issues in both tax and accounting controversies by separating the question of what is income from the question of how can we objectively approximate income.

The fact that income taxation is often modified in an attempt to bring about certain social or economic effects perhaps makes it hopeless that tax and accounting income will ever be identical. Whether or not it is *desirable* to use income taxation for such purposes is an issue which is not related to this article. In any event, it seems clear that insofar as we wish simply to tax income, the same need for soundness of concept and objectivity of measurement exists both for taxation and accounting. Academic and practicing public accountants face a real challenge in this area. If they take the lead in improving the soundness of accounting practice this not only will increase the fairness of taxation but also will reduce the danger of governmental regulation of accounting practices.

Much support can be found for rejecting the argument that measuring national income requires a different basic concept of income than measuring income of a business or other entity. It is reasonable to conclude that (a) the accretion concept is quite consistent with the general concept of national income and (b) the closer we can come to measuring accretion income of various entities, the more easily and accurately will we be able to measure national income.

The measurement of national income involves conceptual difficulties and also problems of using accounting figures to compute national income data. The most significant conceptual problems include aggregation and real versus money measurements.

Conceptually, aggregation is not a serious problem, though it is sometimes taken to be so. The problem arises from the fact

that what is true of the parts may not be true for the whole. For example, changes in relative prices result in real gains and losses to various entities but not to the entire economy and an exchange between a parent company (or a proprietor) and a subsidiary can change the economic position of each, but not that of the consolidated entity. This is a conceptual problem because of conceptual difficulties of defining the relevant entities, not because the data are inherently nonadditive. If we could, for example, measure the effects on each entity of relative price changes we would find that they could meaningfully be algebraically summed and that the total would always be zero.

Distinguishing real from mere money income when price levels change poses more serious conceptual difficulties. As noted in the preceding discussion of the accretion concept, accretion income (as defined here) does not deal directly with this problem. Accretion avoids the bunching of unreal gains that results from postponing recognition until realization, but does not attempt to measure the amount of unreal gains. It is probably more appropriate to attempt to make the necessary price level adjustments in computing national income than in computing entity income. The need for objectivity is perhaps less strict for the large aggregates being dealt with in national income computations, and the fact that the effects of relative price changes cancel each other perhaps eliminates the necessity of separating these from the effects of price *level* changes. Of course, the difficulty of defining and measuring the general price level is a problem which cannot be avoided.

The basic notion of the accretion concept is that income is any change in economic power that can be measured with reasonable objectivity. This does not appear essentially different from what we have in mind when we attempt to measure national income. To the extent that we are able to approximate this for every entity in the economy we can measure national income by summing entity income. In this respect, progress toward the accretion concept would contribute to the improvement of national income data as well as entity income data.

Many controversies about income measurement stem from divergent interests of various parties. In addition to taxpayers versus the government there are, for example, unions versus management, utility shareholders versus consumers, and even management versus shareholders on occasion. In controversies of this type, the special interests of each party can be expected to lead to a bias in favor of methods of computation which will give desired results. This, however, does not justify a variety of income concepts but rather adds to the urgency of the need for a single concept as a standard. Income and financial position data are typically not the only factors relevant to necessary decisions in these controversies. Insofar as the decision hinges on a measurement of income, agreement on a concept of income is a necessary preliminary.

The accretion concept is very close to the concept of profit implied in the phrase "attempt to maximize profits." Though there has been a good deal of controversy about the objectives of businessmen, there can hardly be any doubt that it is usual and appropriate for a manager to be concerned about changes in the economic well-being of the entity for which he has responsibility. To the extent that businessmen attempt to maximize the economic position of their firms, as opposed to altruistic or social objectives, they are forced to use a concept such as accretion. Uncertainties as to the future (and even as to such things in the present as the shape of demand curves) make it generally impossible to measure income and economic position in terms of present value of future receipts. To the extent that accountants can approximate accretion income, they can provide a measure of the things in which businessmen are interested. Further, if there is truth in the contention that businessmen often (irrationally, it would seem) attempt to maximize income as reported rather than economic income, then coming closer to the accretion concept would lead to an improvement in management decisions.

Implications for Accounting Practice. Acceptance of the accretion concept does not necessarily imply radical changes from present accounting practice. The concept itself does not tell us specifically what changes should be made, rather it provides a foundation for the decision by defining the income and economic position which we are attempting to measure. The definition does not state exactly when a change in economic position is measurable with "reasonable objectivity." This is inherently a matter of judgment on which we can never hope to achieve unanimity. We can expect such judgments to vary and to change as changes in markets and other institutions take place. The accretion concept requires us to face squarely the question of how much we are willing to depart from economic reality in order to attain objectivity and uniformity of method. The following discussion of possible changes in accounting practice reveals that in the present writer's judgment, significant changes in accounting practice ought to be made. These would result in a more realistic portrayal of income and economic position without serious loss of objectivity —in some cases both realism and objectivity can be increased. Disagreement with the judgments made does not necessarily invalidate the accretion concept nor make it less useful in distinguishing controversies over what is income from those over what is reasonable objectivity.

The asset cash does not pose serious income measurement problems. Its value is ordinarily measurable with a high degree of both objectivity and economic reasonableness.[9] In the case of receivables it might be said that accountants already follow the accretion concept in their present practice. Because receivables are generally fixed in money amount, there is no problem of unrecognized increases in value. Decreases in value are possible and are recognized, as soon as they reasonably can be measured, by deducting allowances such as for bad debts and cash discounts. This is simply and appropriately a matter of asset valuation, not of matching costs and revenues.

Short-term investments in marketable securities can be valued at market with relative ease, and commonly are so valued when market is below cost. The accretion concept would require that market values be used whenever they are reasonably measurable regardless of cost. Whether market values are measurable with sufficient objectivity in a particular case is the critical question for income recognition rather than "realization." If the present usual practice of not recognizing gains until realized through an arm's length transaction is to be preferred, it is because market values are not reasonably measurable rather than because true income does not exist until so realized. The accretion concept requires the accountant to exercise judgment (as to objectivity) in each particular case while present practice avoids some of these decisions by relying on the (inconsistent) broad judgment that increases in value above cost are never measurable with sufficient objectivity while decreases generally are. The accretion concept will have significant effects on accounting for marketable securities, then, to the extent that it is decided that market values can be measured with reasonable objectivity. Very likely the change from usual practice would be considerable.

Much of the same reasoning applies to inventories. Whenever values different from cost can be measured with reasonable objectivity they should be reflected in the accounts. The accretion concept, if accepted, could be expected to result in major changes in balance sheets and reported incomes even if objectivity requirements were quite severe. This can be demonstrated by showing that there are many circumstances in which market values can be measured with greater objectivity than costs.

Any attempt to assign a dollar amount to inventories, whether the amount is meant to represent cost or value, involves estimates and is subject to a margin of error. A conclusive demonstration that in a particular circumstance the margin of error is less for value than for cost would require research and analysis beyond the scope of this article. Such research should be encouraged. The possibility of this result can be shown by pointing out some of the inherent weaknesses in cost measures and relative strengths of value measures.

The principal difficulty in attempting to measure inventory cost is the problem of allocation. It is not an overstatement to say that common costs pervade all types of businesses and industries. The problem is perhaps most obvious in the case of joint products, but similar problems of allocating overhead and selling and administrative expenses are nearly universal. Allocation difficulties have caused accountants generally to refrain from including any "operating expenses" in inventory values and many advocate going further and not inventorying any fixed costs. The growing support for variable costing can be inter-

[9] The problem of price-level change effects on real income is disregarded. In this writer's judgment, even a fairly severe inflation or deflation would not justify an attempt to come closer to "real" income than is accomplished by the accretion concept.

preted as evidence of the lack of reasonable objectivity in attempts to allocate fixed overhead to production and inventories. The most effective argument against variable costing is not that fixed overhead can be reasonably allocated but rather that variable costing inventory figures are not likely to be a reasonable approximation to value and therefore will result in a poor measure of income.

Another inherent weakness in attempting to measure costs is the problem of deciding which costs are appropriate. This is most strikingly demonstrated by the LIFO controversy. The failure of the concept of matching costs and revenues to constitute a concept of income is revealed by the fact that matching does not tell us which costs to match. The LIFO method can result in an artificial smoothing of income because it fails to reflect the real gains and losses resulting from fluctuations of inventory values, not because it matches costs and revenues improperly.

The basic reason for the non-objectivity of cost measurements is that cost allocations cannot be proved to be sound without reference to values. On the other hand, the difficulty of objectively measuring market values is often exaggerated. Vast amounts of inventory consist of materials and merchandise for which a market price is readily measurable. The difficulties are probably greatest for partly finished manufactured goods and for finished goods or merchandise when the time and terms of sale are somewhat uncertain. But in these cases the difficulties of reasonable cost allocations are also likely to be serious, and it is not obvious that costs can be more objectively measured than values. Extensive research into these problems should prove valuable.

The case for using cost on grounds of objectivity is much stronger for fixed assets than for inventories. Because fixed assets are relatively unique and infre-

quently exchanged, market valuations are typically subject to considerable uncertainty. This undoubtedly justifies generally adhering to cost as the most reasonable approximation to value. It might be argued that even when significant changes in value can be measured with reasonable objectivity, cost should be retained in order to achieve consistency or uniformity of method. This is not convincing. Even when every entity reports fixed assets on a cost basis, comparability is not achieved because different entities acquire assets at different times and prices. Universal adherence to the cost basis thus achieves neither reasonable measures of income nor comparability. Freedom to reflect objectively measurable value changes, even if permitted only in highly restricted circumstances, would conceptually improve both income measures and comparability.

The accretion concept might not have a great effect on accounting practice in recording intangibles, such as patents and research and development, because we are already pretty close to this concept for these items. Thus, insofar as research and development costs exceed the reasonably measurable value of the resulting assets, we are forced to use an "accretion" measure of the asset, unless we plead conservatism and record a nominal amount. In the latter case we cannot also claim to be attempting to measure income fairly. Where the reasonably measurable value of intangible assets exceeds cost, the accretion concept calls for a change from usual present practice.

Another area in which accounting practice could be affected is the recording of lease obligations and corresponding assets. Again, the question becomes one of judging reasonable measurability of the asset and liability (and any corresponding effects on income) rather than a question of whether the asset or obligation exists.

On the whole, general acceptance of the

accretion concept, and the corresponding relegation of matching to a minor role as an occasionally useful technique rather than a concept of income, would have significant effects on accounting practice. On balance, the result might well be a gain rather than a loss of objectivity, and improved comparability as well as economic reasonableness would certainly result.

Conclusions. Needed improvement of accounting theory and practice is unlikely to be achieved unless accountants are able to reach general agreement on a concept of income which both conforms well to economic reality and is measurable with reasonable objectivity. The accretion concept meets these requirements. The failure of the concept of matching costs and revenues as a concept of income is reflected in both the present diversity of practice and in theory controversies.

The claim that we must accept a variety of purposes is not convincing. Whenever the purpose is such as to require a measure of economic position and income, a single concept is appropriate. This is not the same as to say that measurements of economic position and income provide all data relevant to all decisions. On the contrary, management, investors, and others often require quite different data for various purposes. Insofar as accountants attempt to report financial position and income, it is necessary to have a meaningful single concept of income.

Although the accretion concept does not serve all needs for data, it has a striking degree of universality of applicability in many areas including taxation, national income measurement, and management decision-making. Acceptance of the accretion concept would not require a sudden overturning of most of what accountants now do. It would significantly affect practice, but this could be brought about by a gradual transition accompanied by gains in both comparability and reasonableness.

D. A. CORBIN

COMMENTS ON "THE ACCRETION CONCEPT OF INCOME"

DONALD A. CORBIN*

Introduction. The recent article on the "accretion" concept of income by Professor G. Edward Philips calls for a reporting revolution—the recognition of a new, single concept of income for financial reporting by public accountants.[1] Several recommendations for improving accounting theory and closing the gap between theory and practice are also timely, coming on the heels of the Sprouse and Moonitz Accounting Research Study No. 3— "A Tentative Set of Broad Accounting Principles For Business Enterprises." Although this writer finds himself in general agreement with the objectives and approach suggested by Professor Philips, his *accretion* concept of income must be significantly modified in one important respect if it is to be theoretically sound and generally useful in practice.

The main purposes of the following short comments are: (1) to encourage widespread acceptance of Professor Philips' objectives and general approach, (2) to suggest the necessity for measuring net income in real rather than in absolute dollar terms, except when price levels do not change significantly, and (3) to present a few comments on the income-tax and goodwill problems which arise in this context.

The accretion concept. The Philips article demonstrates quite well that progress in accounting theory should begin with developing a single income concept, rather than a variety of income concepts; and that this single income concept should also aid various interested parties in making a variety of decisions. His point that simply because accountants must supply varied data for many different uses, does not imply a need for more than one concept of income is well taken. He says: "Agreement on a meaningful concept of income is essential to improvement of the financial reporting function of accountants, and there is no inherent reason for this concept to interfere with the collection, analysis, and interpretation of data relevant to particular decisions."

After discarding the "psychic" and "economic present value" concepts of income, because of their subjectivity (a reasonable approach at this juncture in history), Professor Philips chooses the *accretion* concept of income, defining it as "an increase in economic power which can be measured with reasonable objectivity." Economic power refers to net assets; reasonable objectivity of measurement means reporting objectively determined market values of assets. Further, the measurements are to be made in dollar, rather than real (or purchasing-power) terms. This accretion concept is called the "ideal concept."

Measurement in real terms. The suggestion to use *objective* market value changes for the realization of profit or loss is a significant step forward, but material changes in the value of the dollar should *not* be ignored. Price level changes could readily have been included in the definition simply

---

* Donald A. Corbin is Associate Professor of Economics and Accounting in the University of Hawaii, Honolulu, Hawaii. He has taught at the University of California, Berkeley and Riverside, has contributed frequently to accounting journals, and has recently completed an elementary accounting text.
[1] THE ACCOUNTING REVIEW, January, 1963, pp. 14-25.

by inserting the economic term "real." Then, income would be the increase in *real* economic power which could be measured with reasonable objectivity.

This change is required if the concept is to be theoretically sound. A yardstick of changing size is unsound. Past experience with inflation and deflation indicates that measurement in real terms is often required if income statements are to be useful for decision-making. We are all familiar, for example, with the fallacy of the home-owner who bought a house in 1945 for say $10,000, sold it for $19,000 in 1950, and believed that his $9,000 dollar "gain" was real until he searched for new housing.

Professor Philips does not ignore the price-level problem in his paper, but concludes that even a severe inflation or deflation would not necessitate eliminating unreal gains or losses from income statements. He also states that his suggested accretion concept eliminates the "bunching" effect of realizing periodic accretion gains all at one time, as is presently done. The following current illustration, which is probably realistic for assets in general, shows that he is probably in error on the first count, but correct on the second.

Consider a $100,000 investment in a listed security whose value can be determined objectively. It rises 10 percentage points a year for ten years, during a period when the general price level rises 5 percentage points a year. At the end of the tenth year the investment is sold for $200,000. The income determined under three concepts, the conventional "cost" concept, the accretion concept, and the purchasing power (or real) concept is compared for the 9th and 10th years in Table I below.

It is of course true that some assets recently have risen much more rapidly than has the general price level; these cases illustrate Professor Philips' contention, but are extreme cases. If, for example, an investment in Waikiki or Palm Springs land rose 80% (from $40,000 to $72,000) during a year when the general price level rose 5%, the accretion concept would show income of $32,000; whereas, the real income concept would reveal $30,000 income. This difference of $2,000 probably is not significant; but again, this is not the usual case. Although prices in the economy vary widely, giving rise to extremes such as the land cases, prices generally follow a central tendency. Most prices cluster near the 5% general price level average change. The first illustration is the more typical. Thus, many accretion "gains" will be unreal, and

TABLE I. INCOME COMPARISONS

Year 9:	Conventional "Cost" Concept	Accretion Concept	Real Income Concept	
Value-ending	$100,000	$190,000		$190,000
Value-beginning	100,000	180,000	$180,000	
Price Level Increase			5,000*	185,000
Income	None	$ 10,000		$ 5,000*
Year 10:				
Sales Price	$200,000	$200,000		$200,000
Value-beginning	100,000	190,000	$190,000	
Price Level Increase			5,000*	195,000
Income	$100,000	$ 10,000		$ 5,000*

* Of the $10,000 increase in value each year, $5,000 is an asset and owner's equity revaluation, and $5,000 is a real gain.

economic decisions based thereon may be in error.

Income tax. The problem of income taxation is a case in point. Assume that the first illustration of the $100,000 investment represented a business inventory (rather than common stock). The accretion concept would subject the company to $10,000 taxable income each year, whereas the real income concept would report only $5,000 taxable income. The firm's owners are really not $10,000 wealthier each year if $5,000 of this amount is required merely to maintain the original purchasing power of their investment in the business.

Some businessmen will go further, arguing that none of the annual $10,000 accretion should be taxed, because it now takes $10,000 more to replace the specific asset. They argue that a specific index of purchasing power should be used for each asset, rather than a general purchasing power index. This approach appears to go too far; it asks for too much. All capital gains would be 100% tax free. *Any* business investment which rose in value while it was held, even speculative investments in oil wells, patents, securities, or land would completely escape income taxation. It seems that although taxation of the full accretion gain would be unrealistic and unfair, taxation of the gain in purchasing power (real "economic power") is reasonable. This might necessitate business borrowing to pay taxes, but the collateral then would exist, and this practice is not at all new.

Goodwill. A final comment. As mentioned earlier, Philips chose the accretion concept as his "ideal" concept. If we eliminate psychic income measurement as being too far out at the present state of knowledge, economic present value income probably is a better candidate for the "ideal" concept. Market values of assets are approximations, based on estimates of future revenues and discount rates by various participants in the market. As Philips implies they would equal discounted values were it not for individual differences and errors. Therefore, market values may be regarded as approximations or estimates of present values.

In order for economic present value income to be determined, it would be necessary to calculate the discounted value of all assets each period, including the asset goodwill. Then the sum of the values of the net assets would equal the discounted value of all future net receipts for the entire business. This is another reason why the economic present value income concept is usually rejected in practice—the difficulty of assessing goodwill.

Since the accretion concept requires objective measures of asset values, goodwill changes would not be included as a part of accretion income. This means that the accretion concept loses more of its claim to being "ideal." It also means that unless goodwill always remained constant, accretion income would not equal present-value income, even if all people in the market evaluated individual assets alike.

Conclusion. It must be concluded that Philips' accretion concept of income, when *measured in real terms,* is a realistic and practical, single, general-purpose concept of income. It has theoretical validity, as well, if changes in the value of goodwill may legitimately be ignored. It represents a significant improvement over the conventional historical-cost-basis concept of income, since the latter is both theoretically unsound and practically misleading whenever prices change significantly.

R. J. CHAMBERS

ACCOUNTING FOR INFLATION

Exposure Draft

**Department of Accounting (H04)
The University of Sydney
N.S.W. 2006.**

September 1975.

ACCOUNTING FOR INFLATION
EXPOSURE DRAFT

Conventional (historical cost based) accounting is almost universally recognized to be defective under inflationary conditions. Experience under these conditions has prompted the search for a dependable alternative.

There are at present in circulation in Australia "preliminary exposure drafts", prepared by the Australian Accounting Standards Committee,entitled

"A Method of 'Accounting for Changes in the Purchasing Power of Money" (issued December 1974), and
"A Method of 'Current Value Accounting'" (issued June 1975).

Notwithstanding the express need of a method of accounting for inflation, neither of these statements is, or claims to be, a method of accounting for inflation. The first deals with ways of taking account of some of the effects of changes in the purchasing power of money, but disregards the effects of changes in the prices of particular assets. The second proposes the use of the replacement prices of assets in financial statements, but disregards the general effects of changes in the purchasing power of money. As both types of change occur concurrently during inflationary periods, both of the above methods are partial or incomplete, and therefore potentially misleading.

The object of the publication of the preliminary exposure drafts was to encourage discussion and comment, preparatory to the publication of an "accounting standard". But discussion of two quite different and incomplete methods can scarcely be well-informed, if there is also a method which does not suffer from their defects.

This Exposure Draft deals with a method of accounting -continuously contemporary accounting - which takes into account both changes in particular prices and changes in the general level of prices. It is thus more comprehensive than the two methods previously mentioned. And the financial statements it yields are up-to-date, more realistic and more readily comprehensible.

R. J. Chambers
Department of Accounting (HO4)
The University of Sydney
N.S.W. 2006

ACCOUNTING FOR INFLATION

CONTENTS

APPENDIXES

270

PART I — ACCOUNTING GENERALLY

1. The discussion and conclusions to be presented will have reference to business firms generally.

Any method of business accounting should be expected to be serviceable in substantially the same ways, no matter what the form of ownership of the business to which accounts relate. However, the most extensive array of uses of accounting information is exemplified by the relationships between companies and their shareholders, creditors and others. For this reason much of the discussion will relate to companies and company accounting. But, because the principles or rules which emerge are equally pertinent to companies and other types of business ownership, the general term "business firm" or simply "firm" will be commonly used. Also the terms "net profit" and "net income" will be used interchangeably, as synonyms.

2. Financial statements are expected to represent fairly and in up-to-date terms the financial characteristics of firms.

The products of the accounting process are dated balance sheets and income (profit and loss) statements. These are expected, by the laws relating to companies, to give a true and fair view of the financial positions and of the results of companies as at the dates and for the periods to which they relate. They are put to use by a variety of parties; by actual and potential investors and creditors; by investment advisers and underwriters and trustees for creditors; by tribunals concerned with wages and prices; and by governmental authorities for fiscal and other regulatory purposes. The decisions and actions of all of these parties are taken in the light of what they know, at the time, of the past results and present financial positions of companies (or of firms generally). Unless the financial statements of companies correspond fairly well with their actual positions and results, actions based upon them may affect adversely, and quite unexpectedly, the interests of companies or of other parties related to them.

3. The survival and growth of firms depends on their command of money and money's worth.

The actions of all the above mentioned parties are directly related to money receipts and payments of a company - receipts by way of sales income, loans or credits, subsidies or bounties, and the proceeds of new share issues; payments by way of purchases, wages, taxes, interest, and loan repayments. The capacity of a company to grow or to change its operations, on a small or large scale, as new opportunities arise and present operations become less attractive, depends on its command of money or money's worth. In the ordinary course of events, companies are expected to pay their debts to others when they fall due. In some circumstances they may find it worth while, or be forced, to repay debts before they fall due. Generally, then, the ability to meet debts owed is a condition of survival. For all these reasons, it is a matter of importance that the managers of companies, and that other parties having financial interests in companies, shall know from time to time the money and money's worth at the command of companies and their outstanding financial obligations.

4. Financial position is a dated relationship between assets and equities.

The money and money's worth at the command of a company at a point of time is given by the sum of its holdings of cash and receivables and the market (resale) prices of its other (non-monetary) assets. The resale price of an asset at a given date is its money equivalent at that date. Possession of the asset is financially equal to possession of the sum of money representing its resale price. It is therefore possible to add amounts of cash and receivables and the money equivalents of other assets to obtain a financially significant aggregate. The total amount of liabilities to short and long term creditors represents money claims against the aggregate money's worth of assets. The difference between total assets and total liabilities is a genuine money amount, since the amounts of total assets and total liabilities are genuine money amounts. This difference represents the residual interest of shareholders or owners in the total assets, or the total investment at risk in the business of the company. It also represents the amount of net assets, or assets financed otherwise than by credit.

5. The amount of income is deduced from changes in dated financial positions.

A balance sheet in which assets are represented at their money equivalents gives to all users of it an up-to-date indication of the total wealth of a company at a point of time and total claims against or interests in that wealth. Given two such balance sheets, in the absence of inflation, the increment in the amount of net assets represents the retained profit of the intervening period (provided there has been no new share issue). The sum of retained profit and the dividends paid in the period is the net profit or net income of the period. Net income may be calculated by setting out the several classes of gain or loss of a company in a period. But the amount so obtained is necessarily equal to the difference between the opening and closing money amounts of net assets. It is a genuine increment in money's worth, since the net assets figures are genuine money amounts (para. 4)

6. Financial positions and results are aggregative; their elements must satisfy the rules of addition and relation.

Total wealth, total liabilities, the amount of net assets, the calculation of net profits, all entail addition and subtraction. Other calculations made by investors and creditors, such as rates of return and debt to equity ratios, are relations between aggregates. All particular elements of financial statements must therefore be capable of proper addition and relation. The money amounts and money equivalents referred to in the two previous paragraphs satisfy this condition. By contrast, no logical or financial significance can be assigned to the sum of an amount of money and the purchase price, past, present or future (including replacement price) of any good. No such sum can properly be related to any debt outstanding, or to any plan to purchase goods or services, or to pay taxes and dividends.

7. Financial positions and results are both the consequences of past actions and the bases of future actions.

The financial position of a firm is a consequence of past (historical) events up to the date for which it is ascertained. No future event or expectation of a future event has any bearing on it. But given an ascertained financial position (and other information and expectations), choices may be made among the courses of action available to the firm. If at a given date the liquidity of a firm is strained, action to restore its liquidity is necessary. If at a given date a firm is heavily in debt, liquidity cannot readily be restored by further borrowing. If the results of the immediately past period are unsatisfactory in any sense, action must be taken to improve the result in the following period. All deliberate actions having financial consequences must be considered in the light of the aggregative financial characteristics of the firm at the time of choice. And all estimations of the probable financial consequences of future actions must be based on the position of the firm at the time of choice of future courses of action. Financial position as described is the one common element in all calculations relating to choices of future actions.

8. **The money equivalents of assets, the purchase prices (replacement prices) of assets and the user-values of assets are used in conjunction; none is a substitute for the other.**

If a prospective course of action entails the "replacement" of an asset, it is necessary to know the money equivalent of the present asset and the purchase price of the new asset. If a prospective action entails the purchase of additional assets, their purchase prices must be known. Whether or not any such course is financially "feasible" can only be ascertained by comparison of those purchase prices with the money equivalents of present assets, or some selection of present assets. Which is to be preferred of the feasible courses of action is indicated, inter alia, by comparisons of the expected net proceeds of the alternative projects or investments in assets. Expected net proceeds, or present (discounted) values, are user-values. They are personal estimates based on expectations of the future; they are therefore subjective. They represent the expected outcomes of specific possible future actions. They cannot therefore be used in balance sheets as indicative of the financial feasibility of *any* course of action, even of those courses to which they relate. In short, the money equivalents of assets, the purchase prices of goods not presently held, and user-values of assets or projects are used when considering specific possible courses of action. But each is used for its own purpose and in its own way. None is a substitute for the other. None of them may properly be added together. Only the money equivalents of assets are properly useable for the representation of financial position at a given date.

PART II — THE EFFECTS OF INFLATION

9. **Changes in the structure and in the general level of prices occur concurrently but not equally.**

In an inflationary period two things occur which affect the positions and results of companies. The prices of particular goods change relatively to one another. There is a change in the *structure* of prices. Such changes may occur at any time as the wants of consumers change, technology changes or the policies and outputs of companies change (collectively, supply and demand conditions). There is also a change in the general *level* of prices. "Inflation" is descriptive of a rise in the general level of

274

prices, or of its counterpart, a fall in the general purchasing power of money. When inflation occurs all prices do not rise to the same extent or at the same time. Some may fall as rises in others force business firms and consumers to change their spending habits. Inflation may thus cause changes in the structure of prices, to the benefit of some firms and to the detriment of others. The beneficial or detrimental effects may arise from changes in the money equivalents of assets held, or from changes in the profit margins obtainable for goods and services sold.

10. The effects on a firm of changes in the structure and level of prices can only be ascertained in the aggregate.

When changes in the structure of prices and changes in the general level of prices occur in the same period, it is not possible to say that any particular price change is caused by inflation, or by the shift in the relation between the supply and demand conditions, or partly by the one and partly by the other. All that is known is that prices and the level of prices are different from those of an earlier date. Nevertheless, it is possible to calculate the aggregate effects of changes in prices and the general level of prices on the positions and results of firms. Because changes in particular prices and changes in the general level of prices influence one another, the effects of both should be brought into account. One cannot be considered as isolated from the other. Whatever the outcome, it cannot be said whether any part of the result is due solely to managerial judgements or solely to accidental or unforeseeable factors. Managers may be expected to use their best judgements at all times. Only the results in aggregate will indicate with what effect firms have been able to meet the conditions through which they have passed.

11. The conventional money unit, in terms of which financial positions are represented, is equally service-able for that purpose in inflation.

Financial position has been described as the dated relationship between amounts of assets and equities (para 4). The dating of a financial statement represents both (a) that the money unit used in it has reference to that date and (b) that the number of money units appearing beside any item is the appropriate money equivalent of that item at that date. To suppose otherwise would be anachronistic, and confusing. The money unit is by its nature the unit of general purchasing power and debt-paying power at any specified date whatever, and the unit in which the money equivalents (resale prices) of assets are expressed. That the same nominal money unit may have a different general purchasing power at some other date is of no consequence when determining a dated financial position.

12. The increment in the nominal amount of net assets during a year is not serviceable as indicating net income in an inflationary period.

Calculation of net income in the manner described in para 5 brings into account the effects of all changes in the money equivalents of assets, in the absence of inflation. If particular assets have risen or fallen in price during a year, for whatever reason, these changes in the structure of prices will be captured by taking the resale prices of assets at the opening and closing dates of the year. Since, in the absence of inflation, there is no change in the general purchasing power of money, the net income so calculated will represent a genuine increment in the general purchasing power or debt-paying power of the net assets of a firm. Part of it will be the resultant of trading costs and revenues, and part the resultant of rises and falls in the money equivalents of assets since the beginning of the period or since (the subsequent) date of purchase. The rises and falls during the year in the money equivalents of assets held at the end of a year may be described as *price variation adjustments.* But if the purchasing power of the money unit has changed during the year, the difference between the opening and closing amounts of net assets will not represent a genuine increment in general purchasing or debt-paying power.

13. Provision must be made for the loss of purchasing power in an inflationary period of the amount of net assets (or capital employed) at the beginning of the accounting period.

Money holdings and claims to fixed amounts of money may be described as monetary assets. Their money equivalents at any date may be discovered directly. All other assets are non-monetary assets. Their money equivalents at any date must be discovered by reference to market resale prices at or near that date. Monetary assets held during an inflationary period lose general purchasing power. Likewise every dollar representing the money equivalent of non-monetary assets at the beginning of a period loses general purchasing power. And likewise every dollar owed during an inflationary period loses general purchasing power; borrowings thus constitute a "hedge" against losses in the purchasing power of money. By subtraction, the amount at risk of loss in general purchasing power during inflation is the amount of net assets (total assets less liabilities) at the beginning of the accounting period. The amount of the loss thus sustained must be made good out of other surpluses before it can be said that a surplus in the nature of net income has arisen. This amount may be described as a *capital maintenance adjustment,* since its object is to secure that, in calculating net income, provision is made for the maintenance of the general purchasing power of the opening amount of net assets (or capital employed).

It may be noted that, across a whole community, the aggregate amount of price variation adjustments might be expected to correspond with the aggregate amount of capital maintenance adjustments, since the general price index is indicative of the average of changes in specific prices. But particular firms are affected differentially by changes in prices and in the price level. Rises in the prices of particular goods do not correspond with or offset falls in the general purchasing power of money. That is why the aggregates of both should be taken separately in the accounts of firms.

14. Net income is the algebraic sum of trading surpluses, price variation adjustments and the capital maintenance adjustment.

The amount of the capital maintenance adjustment is the opening amount of net assets multiplied by the proportionate change in the general level of prices. Thus, if a firm begins a period with net assets of $1,000 and an index of changes in the general level of prices rises from 130 to 143 in the period, the amount of the capital maintenance adjustment is $1,000 x 13/130, or $100. A general price index is used because the amount of net assets is a genuine dated money sum, irrespective of the composition of assets, and because the firm is considered to be free to lay out any part of its assets or the increment in its assets in any way it pleases. The index to be used would be chosen on the basis of competent statistical advice. From the two preceding paragraphs, net income will be the algebraic sum of trading surpluses, price variation adjustments and the capital maintenance adjustment. The amount charged as capital maintenance adjustment will be credited to a capital maintenance reserve. If any part of this reserve were appropriated as a dividend, it would impair the general purchasing power of the opening amount of net assets. (See also para 34).

277

PART III — GENERAL PRINCIPLES OF
CONTINUOUSLY CONTEMPORARY ACCOUNTING

15. The method of accounting described is called continuously contemporary accounting (C.C.A.).

Asset valuations are brought up-to-date, at least at the end of each accounting period, by reference to independent sources of information. Those valuations are in terms of the purchasing power unit at the time. That the balance sheet is a dated statement implies that the amounts stated in it relate to that date and that the dollars in which those amounts are expressed are dollars of dated purchasing power (see para 11). C.C.A. satisfies this requirement. Shareholders' equity amounts are augmented by the capital maintenance adjustment periodically and the balance of net income is a sum also expressed in dollars of the same dated purchasing power as other items in the balance sheet. All reported balances of a given date are therefore contemporary with that date. There are no prices of different dates nor purchasing power units of different dates in the balance sheet of any date. Hence the description "continuously contemporary accounting".

16. Accounts may be brought up to date periodically or more frequently.

The price changes affecting a firm may be occasional or frequent, and individually large or small. As up-to-date information on a firm's assets and liabilities is the only dependable basis for managerial action, the accounts may be continually adjusted for changes in the prices of assets. In principle this is the most desirable mode of accounting. But for external reporting it is sufficient to bring the account balances to their money equivalents at the end of each reporting period. Accounts could be kept just as they are presently kept during the accounting period. But at the end of the period all account balances are adjusted to their current money equivalents. The variations of money equivalents from book balances are summarized and charged or credited, as price variation adjustments, in the income account. And of course the capital maintenance adjustment is computed and charged. The method may be called "continuously contemporary" because, in principle, accounts can be kept continuously up-to-date, even though in practice adjustments may be made less frequently than price changes occur. Under either process the results will be exactly the same.

278

17. **C.C.A. conforms with the established principle of periodical, independent verification of account balances (the objectivity principle).**

To verify the physical existence of, and legal title to, assets at balance date is a well established principle. Independent checking of cash balances and receivables balances has long been regarded as a necessary safeguard against misrepresentation. But the same process of verification is not applied, under traditional historical cost accounting, to the money amounts assigned to other assets. The mere checking of physical existence and legal title is inconsistent with the fact that financial statements relate to the *financial* characteristics of firms, not to physical or purely legal characteristics. The financial characteristics of assets should be independently verified, no less than other characteristics. C.C.A. applies this principle uniformly to all assets.

18. **C.C.A. conforms with the well-established accrual principle.**

The accrual principle entails accounting for changes in the financial characteristics of a firm independently of the conversion of assets and obligations to cash. Revenue is brought into account when customers are billed; earlier, that is, than cash is received from customers. Depreciation is brought into account periodically; that is, long before the diminution in value of an asset is discovered on its resale. Applications of the principle pervade current practice. Yet there are also numerous cases in traditional practice where the principle is not applied. Changes in the prices of assets are not accrued usually, unless they are downward changes. And quite generally the effects of advantageous changes are not accrued but the effects of disadvantageous changes are accrued; thus depreciation is charged, but appreciation is not brought into account. These inconsistencies cannot yield realistic and up-to-date statements of financial position and results. C.C.A. avoids inconsistency by applying the accrual principle uniformly to all assets and liabilities, and hence also to shareholders' equity.

19. **C.C.A. conforms with the well-established going concern principle.**

The going concern principle entails that the financial position as represented in a balance sheet shall be indicative of the position of a firm as a going concern. The significant financial characteristics of a going concern are its ability to pay its debts when due, to pay for its supplies of goods and labour service, to change the composition of its assets, liabilities and operations if the present composition hinders its survival or growth, and the ability to earn a rate of profit consistent with the risks of the business. The ability of a firm to pay its debts, to pay for its necessary inputs, to borrow on the security of its assets, and to change the composition of its assets and operations, is indicated only if assets are shown at their money equivalents, since all the matters mentioned entail receipts and payments of money. The ability of a firm to earn an adequate rate of profit may be judged only if the profit earned is a genuine increment in purchasing power and the amount of net assets (or shareholders' equity) to which it is related is a genuine money sum. The use of market (resale) prices in C.C.A. has nothing to do with liquidation of a business; it is simply the only way to find the present money equivalents of non-monetary assets from time to time.

20. C.C.A. satisfies the requirements of stewardship accounts.

As financial statements indicate in general terms the disposition of assets and increments in assets from time to time they are regarded as the basis upon which the performance of a company and its management may be judged. Such judgements must be supposed to be made periodically in respect of the year recently past; their formal expression lies in the resolutions of annual general meetings. It is necessary, therefore, to know the amount of the assets available for use and disposition by the management at the beginning of each year, if a satisfactory account is to be given of the use, disposition and increase of assets in that year. If the amounts of assets from time to time were stated on any basis other than their money equivalents, there would be no firm and satisfactory basis for determining the use and disposition of assets. Since all uses and dispositions in a period entail movements of money or money equivalents, financial statements based on the money equivalents of assets provide information on which periodical performance may fairly be judged.

21. C.C.A. adheres closely to the principle of periodical accounting.

Financial statements generally purport to represent dated positions and the results of defined periods. But the effects of events in one period are frequently allowed to influence what is reported of another. This occurs whenever some future event or outcome is anticipated (as in the usual calculation of depreciation charges), or whenever some actual effect on results or position is "deferred' for recognition in a later period. C.C.A. makes no such concessions, on the ground that reports which do not represent the effects of events in a defined period cannot properly be interpreted, singly or in series, by reference to the dated context of business events and circumstances. It may be objected that to base accounts on a dated selling price could be misleading if the price were anomalous. But exactly the same can be said of dated purchase prices which are used in other forms of accounting. In any such case the anomaly might be expected to be explained rather than concealed.

PART IV — THE DETERMINATION OF MONEY EQUIVALENTS

22. Any asset for which there is not a present resale price cannot be considered to have a present financial significance.

A company may have assets for which there is no present resale price. They may have a high user-value (see para 8), but they cannot be considered to have financial significance in the sense of purchasing or debt-paying power or as security for.loans. Investors, creditors, suppliers and others would be misinformed of the financial capacity for action by balance sheets in which money amounts were assigned to assets having no current money equivalents. The assets to which this rule applies include some work in progress, and specialized plant and equipment for which there is no market in the ordinary course of business. The same rule applies to expenditures on exploratory or developmental work which has yielded no vendible product or asset. The notion of conservatism in traditional accounting would tend to have the same effect as the treatment suggested. But that notion is vague and loosely applied, whereas the principle here stated is definite and it yields information which is relevant to the judgements and decisions of parties financially interested in companies. If it is desired, on any ground, to indicate that a company has assets, or has incurred costs and outlays, having no present money equivalent, parenthetical or footnote information may be given.

23. The determination of the money equivalents of assets at a stated date is necessarily approximate.

Prices may vary from place to place for the same goods on any given day. What is required is a fair approximation to the current money equivalent of each asset. This may require the exercise of judgement, but abuse of judgement is constrained by the necessity of approximating a definite characteristic of the asset and by the prices discovered at or about the balance date. In any case, no form of accounting escapes the use of dated prices; even historical cost accounting uses dated prices which may or may not have been the only prices, or representative prices, at dates of purchase. Any attempt to distort results and positions by the choice of prices which are not fair approximations to money equivalents is constrained by the independent inspection and judgement of auditors. It is also constrained by the fact that the whole of the asset balances of one year determine the amounts of the price variation adjustments, and hence the income, of the following year. There are no alternative permissible rules by resort to which this constraint may be avoided.

24. Resale prices are accessible to most firms for most assets.

All proposals considered in anticipation of purchases and the settlement of debts include at some point sums of money which are presently available, or which could shortly become available by the sale of assets (inventory or other assets), or which could be borrowed on the security of assets. In the latter two cases some approximation to the money equivalent or resale price of non-monetary assets is required. Changes in the prices of goods and services used and in the markets for a firm's products may at any time force its management to reconsider the costs of its present mode of operations. And if it is assumed that one of the functions of management is the pursuit of efficiency or economies, the possibility of changes in its operations and assets will be under examination from time to time. It follows that some person or persons will be acquainted with the approximate market prices of the assets the firm presently holds, and with changes in those prices from time to time. It is possible for any firm to draw on its purchasing officers, salesmen, engineers and project evaluation officers for information on the prices of assets; and to have recourse to prices published in trade journals and the general press as well as direct inquiry. A great deal of information of this kind is readily available without recourse to specialist valuers. But valuations by specialists on an asset resale basis may also be obtained, where necessary of themselves, or as a check on the information available otherwise.

25. Receivables: The amount to be reported will be the amount deemed, on the evidence available, to be recoverable from debtors in the ordinary course of business.

Generally this will be the face value or book value of debtors' accounts, for that is the amount of the claims against debtors at balance date. There is no need to speculate about the possibility that some debtors may take advantage of discounts offered for prompt settlement. Whether they do so or not, the consequence will lie in the following period and will be then reported. Where there is evidence that the full amount of a debt will not be recovered, the amount of the debt may be reduced or written off according to the evidence then available. The amount of receivables yielded by these rules will be the best approximation to the money equivalent of receivables in the light of the information then available, without speculative allowances for what may subsequently occur.

26. Inventories will be valued consistently on the basis of their present market selling prices in the parcels or quantities in which they are customarily sold by the firm.

In the ordinary course of events, raw materials will have a somewhat lower money equivalent than their recent purchase prices, since the user is not a trader in those materials. Work in progress inventories may have a substantially lower money equivalent than their costs, for such work in progress may not be salable in its then state and condition. Finished goods inventories will generally have higher money equivalents (current selling prices) than their costs.

To report inventories at market resale prices is not novel. Nor is it novel that work in progress may appear at a low or zero value; for the traditional rule, "lower of cost and market", should produce the same result. By comparison with the recorded costs, the higher money equivalents of finished goods will to some extent "offset" the lower money equivalents of raw materials and work in progress. But whether the resulting aggregate differs much or little from a cost-based aggregate is less important than the fact that a uniform rule - market price - is used throughout, and that the aggregate has a definite, dated money significance which "cost" and the "lower of cost and market" do not have.

27. Plant and equipment will be valued at market resale prices, in the units or combinations in which, in the ordinary course of business, they are bought, sold, or put out of use.

The object of the traditional method of accounting for plant is to record its cost and to provide out of periodical revenues sufficient to reduce that cost to its market resale price, or scrap value, by the time it is put out of service. The method of C.C.A. has exactly the same object; but it is attained by direct reference to market prices year by year, rather than by relying on an arithmetical formula and disregarding the actual changes, up or down, in market prices from time to time. Market resale prices may be estimated from information obtained by the methods mentioned in para 24. The prices sought are not prices obtainable on liquidation or under duress. They are to be the best approximations to the money equivalents of assets in the ordinary course of business. To determine the best approximation entails skill and judgement; but judgement is to be applied to the information obtainable on prices, not to construct imaginative valuations. Checks on the possibility of manipulation are (i) that auditors must be satisfied that the assigned market values are based on current price information, (ii) that excessive understatement reduces the profit of the year and the asset backing of shares and debt at the end of the year, and (iii) that excessive overstatement reduces the profit of a subsequent year and improperly boosts the asset backing of shares and debt. The use of market resale prices may entail heavy charges, due to the sharp drop from cost to money equivalent of some plant, in the early years of use. Some assets may have virtually no resale price, but high user-value. Such occurrences necessarily reduce the adaptive capacity of firms, their command of money and money's worth. The reduction is made explicit in the amounts by charges against revenues, or against other shareholders' equity accounts if the amounts are extraordinary. (See also para 22 above).

28. Land and buildings will be valued at market resale prices, or approximations based on official valuations, prices of similar property and expert valuations.

The same considerations apply to land and buildings as to plant and equipment. Local government valuations (for taxing or rating purposes) provide evidence additional to that from other sources. No single valuation or price need necessarily be taken as a proper approximation to money equivalent; but the chosen valuation must be justifiable in the circumstances. The checks mentioned in para 27 tend to limit arbitrary or unusual valuations.

29. **Investments in the shares of other companies will be valued at net market prices where the shares are publicly traded; otherwise at the proportionate interest in the net assets of the investee company.**

Holdings of listed shares are readily priced by reference to stock exchange quotations (i.e. "buyer"). Allowance may be made for commissions payable on sale, to obtain the net money equivalent of the investment. There is no readily available and dependable price for non-listed shares. An alternative is required which yields the best approximation to the money equivalent of the investment. If C.C.A. is used uniformly, the proportionate interest in the net assets of the investee will provide an approximation; for the accounts of the investee will represent assets at money equivalents. Strictly the amount so calculated will not be the same as a share price; but it is a better approximation than the original cost, or a valuation related to user-value (e.g. based on capitalized prospective earnings).

30. **Liabilities will be represented by the amounts owed and payable to creditors in the ordinary course of business.**

No amount shall be shown as a liability unless it represents an amount owed to and legally recoverable by a creditor. Whether the due date is near or distant is immaterial. Long-dated obligations may become due and payable if any circumstance threatens the security of creditors.

PART V — OWNERS' EQUITY ACCOUNTS

31. **All transactions of a period will be recorded at their actual effective prices, and so charged in the income (profit and loss) account.**

All transactions have determinate effects on balances of cash or receivables and payables. The general purchasing power of the cash receipts and payments during an inflationary period will change from time to time. But the aggregate effect of changes in the purchasing power of the money unit is brought into account by way of the capital maintenance adjustment at the end of the accounting period. By showing the actual amounts of receipts and payments, all such amounts are traceable, and identical with their counterparts elsewhere in the accounts.

32. **Price variation accounts will be credited with all increases in the book values of assets, and debited with all decreases, during the period.**

The book balances of accounts, other than monetary item accounts, may be adjusted for changes in asset prices during the year. The valuation of all assets at the end of the year at their resale prices gives effect to all variations in prices which have not previously been brought into account. The amounts by which the book values of assets are increased (decreased) during the year to correspond with market resale prices will be debited (credited) to the asset accounts and credited (debited) to the price variation accounts. There may be price variation accounts for as many separate asset classes as is deemed necessary. Under C.C.A., the depreciation account, representing a fall in the market resale price of an asset or class of assets, is a price variation account. The price variation accounts are closed by transfer of their balances to the income account.

33. **The capital maintenance adjustment will be calculated by applying to the opening amount of net assets the proportionate change in the index of changes in the general level of prices.**

The net amount of price variations will tend to be (but will not necessarily be) positive during inflation. But these are gross increments, and the resulting asset balances are in units of year-end purchasing power. The full effect of the change in the purchasing power of money on the results of the year is given by the calculation of the capital maintenance adjustment. The calculation is a mathematically proper calculation, since under C.C.A. the opening amount of net assets is a genuine, dated money sum to which a change in the index may legitimately be applied. The capital maintenance adjustment is debited in the income account (in inflationary years).

34. **The amount of the capital maintenance adjustment will be credited proportionately to the opening balance of undistributed profits and to other opening balances of owners' equity accounts.**

The amount of net assets at the beginning of a year is equal to the sum of the balances of the owners' equity accounts. The object of crediting the amount of the capital maintenance adjustment to owners'equity accounts is to restate the aggregate of the opening balances in units of purchasing power at the end of the year. Part of the capital maintenance adjustment may therefore be credited directly to the retained profits account, a part equal to the opening balance of retained profits multiplied by the proportionate change in the index of changes in the general level of prices. The remainder of the adjustment will be the appropriate amount to credit to a capital maintenance reserve. Where the amount subscribed by shareholders is required to be shown in balance sheets, this money amount may be carried indefinitely in the accounts. Following the above rules, the sum of the amount subscribed and the balance of the capital maintenance reserve at the end of any year will be the purchasing power equivalent at that time of all sums deemed to have been subscribed by shareholders.

35. Where there are outstanding issues of preference shares, these shall be treated as equivalent to outstanding debt, for the purpose of calculating the capital maintenance adjustment.

Preference shares are, like debts, redeemable at fixed, contractual money amounts. Therefore, like debts, they provide a hedge against the effects of changes in the general purchasing power of money. The amount of outstanding preference shares will therefore be deducted (together with all other liabilities) from total assets to obtain the amount of net assets to be used in the calculation of the capital maintenance adjustment.

36. Net income of a year will be the algebraic sum of transaction surpluses (para 31), price variation adjustments (para 32), and the capital maintenance adjustment (para 33).

The balance of the income account after incorporating the consequences of transactions and the price variation and capital maintenance adjustments will be the net income in units of year-end purchasing power. The whole of it may be paid out without impairing the purchasing power of the opening amount of net assets. Or if it or any part of it is transferred to a retained profits account, the whole of the balance of that account could be paid out (as dividends) without impairing the purchasing power of the amounts subscribed or deemed to have been subscribed by ordinary shareholders.

PART VI — SOME FEATURES OF THE SYSTEM

37. All original entries relate to the amounts of transactions; all adjustments are based on information from sources external to the firm.

These features ensure that all amounts represent actually experienced or accrued effects on a firm's position and results. Doubts about the magnitudes of accrued effects are resolved by recourse to external information, not to internal formulae. There are no arbitrary apportionments, no questionable assumptions about future events or uniformities, and no arbitrary demarcations between outcomes which are and which are not controllable, in some sense, by firms and their managements. The accounts and financial statements may be audited, therefore, with reference to independent sources of information; and the representations they make will be pertinent to the financial relations of the firm with the rest of the world.

38. C.C.A. applies a single valuation rule throughout, avoiding the addition of different kinds of magnitudes in balance sheets.

There are no optional rules for asset valuation, as there are in all other systems. There is no possibility, therefore, that the significance of aggregates will be distorted by the addition of magnitudes of different kinds. Although the transactions figures and price variation adjustments are magnitudes expressed in money units of different purchasing powers, the combined effect of them and the capital maintenance adjustment is a net income in units of the same purchasing power as other items in a closing balance sheet.

39. C.C.A. entails uniform valuation rules for all companies, making possible comparison of the financial features of companies.

Under accounting systems which allow optional valuation rules, the financial significance of the resulting figures is always open to doubt, and strictly no direct comparison of financial magnitudes, rates and ratios is possible. Financial statements based on market resale prices, on the other hand, yield technically proper and practically significant indications of the composition of assets, of current ratios, debt to equity ratios, and rates of return - all of which may be directly compared with corresponding features of other companies and with corresponding features of the same company in prior years.

40. Some of the figures yielded by C.C.A. may seem unusual by contrast with traditional accounting; they should be considered, not separately, but as parts of the whole system.

To value finished goods inventory at market price, when higher than cost, may seem unusual; and to value raw materials and work in progress at current market price, when lower than cost, may also seem unusual. It may appear that to calculate net income on such a footing is to "anticipate profits". But in the first place, the use of one valuation rule yields a comprehensible aggregate. Second, the "unusual" effects are to some extent offsetting. And third, the overriding charge for the capital maintenance adjustment is built-in protection against the overstatement of periodical net income. The same reasoning applies to the bringing to account of changes in the market prices of other non-monetary assets.

41. No right or advantage which arises only on disposal of the company as a whole is brought into the accounts.

C.C.A. is strictly concerned with a company as a going concern. No value is assigned to such things as developmental costs, goodwill and specialized plant having no resale value, which are realizable only on liquidation or disposal of part or whole of the company. Insofar as any amount has been paid out in respect of these items, it constitutes a sunk cost, and is not available as such for any financial purpose in the ordinary course of business. Such amounts may be charged against shareholders' equity directly, or treated in the manner of the "double account" system, above the balance sheet proper. This treatment is in accordance with the practice of financial analysis, and avoids the impression that the company has assets which are convertible to cash in the ordinary course of business. The mixing of subjective user-values with objective financial values has led, in many cases, to serious misdirection of investors and other financial supporters (see also para 8).

289

42. The information given by C.C.A. is consistent with that demanded by lenders and analysts of business affairs, and with the sense of the legislation relating to financial disclosure.

Lenders on the security of property are concerned with the up-to-date market values of assets; they alone constitute effective cover for debt. Press discussion of company affairs has drawn attention repeatedly to the differences between "accounting values" and market values - both when specific prices have been rising and when they have been falling. The statutory requirements relating to financial disclosure have increasingly stipulated the publication (by footnote or otherwise) of market values, or have indicated that realisable value is important information to users of financial statements. Examples are the disclosure of the market values of listed securities, general provisions relating to the valuation of current assets, provisions relation to the valuation of property charged as security by borrowing companies, and the U.K. provision requiring directors to comment on differences between market values and book values of interests in property. C.C.A. does systematically what all these practices, in piecemeal fashion, imply.

43. The financial statements yielded by C.C.A. constitute, in series, a continuous history of the financial affairs of a company.

Because the method of C.C.A. embraces the consequences of actual transactions and of external changes which affect the wealth and results of companies, the statements for any period and at any date are all-inclusive. Taken in series, they represent a continuous record of shifts in wealth, solvency, gearing or leverage and achieved results. They are historical, avoiding the defects of dated speculation about the future; they are fully historical, avoiding the defects of partial representation of what has occurred up to any date or between any two dates.

PART VII — SUMMARY

44. The rules of continuously contemporary accounting are:

(a) All assets should be stated at the best approximation to their money equivalents, in their then state and condition, at the date of the balance sheet.

(b) All transactions shall be accounted for in the amounts at which they occurred.

(c) All variations from the costs or book values of assets, which are not already brought into account by the sale of assets in the period, shall be brought into the income account at the end of the period as price variation adjustments.

(d) There shall be charged against total revenues, in calculating net income, the amount of a capital maintenance adjustment, so that the amount of net income is a surplus by reference to the maintenance of the general purchasing power of the opening amount of net assets.

(e) Net income is the algebraic sum of the outcomes of transactions, price variation adjustments and the capital maintenance adjustment.

APPENDIXES

APPENDIX A

ILLUSTRATION OF METHOD OF CONTINUOUSLY CONTEMPORARY ACCOUNTING

The simplified example which follows traces the recording of transactions, the making of closing adjustments and the derivation of the final statements. All transactions are recorded at their cost throughout the year. The closing price adjustments convert closing book balances to their ascertained money equivalents, represented in the final two columns of the Work Sheet. The workings are shown fully in the Work Sheet. The transactions and adjustments are alphabetically keyed, in the following description and in the Work Sheet, so that the counterparts of all entries may be traced. The figures in the columns headed "Balances" are the money equivalents at the respective dates.

The paragraph numbers in the right hand column of the table of data are the paragraphs in the text of this Draft where the accounting treatment is described.

		$	Para.
Transactions of the year			
A	Credit sales	410	31
B	Receivables collected	390	31
C	Raw materials purchased (on credit)	160	31
D	Suppliers on credit paid	140	31
E	Wages and other costs (to Work in progress)	90	31
F	Raw materials to Work in Progress	145	
G	Work in progress to Finished Goods	225	
H	Cost of finished goods to Income Account	270	
J	Administrative and other cash costs	60	31
K	Interest paid	4	31
L	Taxes paid	20	31
M	Dividends paid.	14	31
N	Dividends received	2	31
P	Plant purchased	25	31

Year-end adjustments	$	Para.
Price variation adjustments (differences between book values and ascertained money equivalents at year-end)		
Q - raw materials	10	32
R - work in progress	15	32
S - finished goods	-55	32
T - plant and buildings	20	32
U - land	-6	32
V - shares	3	32
W Provision for taxes	30	30
X Provision for dividends	26	30
Capital maintenance adjustment (assuming the general price index rose by 10 per cent in the year). Apply this to the opening balance.		
Y - undistributed profits (71 x 10/100)	7	34
Z - capital maintenance reserve (150 x 10/100)	15	34
AA Net profit transferred to Undistributed profits	39	36

WORK SHEET FOR YEAR ENDED 31 DECEMBER 19x4

	Balances 31 Dec. 19x3 Dr	Cr	Transactions and Adjustments Dr	Cr	Balances 31 Dec. 19x4 Dr	Cr
Assets						
Cash	20		390 (B), 2 (N)	140 (D), 90 (E), 60 (J), 4 (K), 20 (L), 14 (M), 25 (P)	59	
Trade debtors (receivables)	40		410 (A)	390 (B)	60	
Inventories — raw materials	25		160 (C)	145 (F)	30	
— work in progress	30		145 (F), 90 (E)	10 (Q), 225 (G)	25	
— finished goods	80		225 (G), 55 (S)	15 (R), 270 (H)	90	
Investments in listed shares	15			3 (V)	12	
Plant and buildings	80		25 (P)	20 (T)	85	
Land	40		6 (U)		46	
Equities						
Trade creditors (payables)		30	140 (D)	160 (C)		50
Provision for taxes		20	20 (L)	30 (W)		30
Provision for dividends		14	14 (M)	26 (X)		26

Long-term creditors (10% p.a.)	25	25
Preferred shareholders (10% p.a.)	20	20
Ordinary shareholders		
— paid in	120	120
— capital maintenance reserve	30	45
— undistributed profits	71	91
Totals	**330**	**407**

Income (profit and loss) items

Sales		410 (A)
Finished goods sold — book value	270 (H)	
Price variation adjustments		
— raw materials	10 (Q)	
— work in progress	15 (R)	
— finished goods	20 (T)	55 (S)
— plant and buildings		6 (U)
— land	3 (V)	
— shares	60 (J)	
Administrative and other cash costs	4 (K)	
Interest paid	26 (X)	
Dividends received		2 (N)
Provision for taxes	30 (W)	
Capital maintenance adjustment		
— undistributed profits	7 (Y)	7 (Y)
— capital maintenance reserve	15 (Z)	15 (Z)
	39 (AA)	39 (AA)
Net profit		
Totals	**2,181**	**2,181**

INCOME [PROFIT AND LOSS] ACCOUNT FOR THE YEAR ENDED 31 DECEMBER 19x4

Sales		410
Dividends received		2
		412
Finished goods sold (book value)	270	
Inventory price variation adjustments (net)	(30)	
Depreciation, plant and buildings	20	
Price variation adjustment, land	(6)	
Price variation adjustment, shares	3	
Administrative costs	60	
Interest paid	4	
Capital maintenance adjustment		
-undistributed profits	7	
- capital maintenance reserve	15	343
Profit before tax		69
Provision for taxes		30
Net income		39

BALANCE SHEETS AT 31 DECEMBER

	19x3	19x4
Assets		
Cash	20	59
Trade debtors	40	60
Inventories	135	145
Investments in listed shares	15	12
Plant and buildings	80	85
Land	40	46
	330	407
Equities		
Trade creditors	30	50
Provision for taxes	20	30
Provision for dividends	14	26
Long term creditors (10%)	25	25
Preferred shareholders (10%p.a.)	20	20
Ordinary shareholders		
- paid in	120	120
- capital maintenance reserve	30	45
- undistributed profits	71	91
	330	407

Note: All assets are shown at the best available approximations to their money equivalents at the respective balance dates.

APPENDIX B

COMPARATIVE EVALUATION OF
PRICE LEVEL ADJUSTED HISTORICAL COST
ACCOUNTING [C.P.P.]
REPLACEMENT PRICE ACCOUNTING [R.P.A.]
AND CONTINUOUSLY CONTEMPORARY
ACCOUNTING [C.C.A.]

If a choice is to be made from the above alternatives to historical cost accounting, it must be based on the respective capacities of the systems to provide information which is unambiguous and significant for the purposes of investors, creditors, managers and others. There are many particular calculations and comparisons which these parties, and others concerned with the regulation and assistance of business, may make. The three systems may therefore be ranked according to their capacities to give reliable, significant and readily understandable figures. That system should be considered as the best which satisfies these tests.

The following assessment indicates whether or not each system satisfies the listed "test" points. For its preparation the three systems have been analyzed in detail, on the basis of the Australian Exposure Drafts, "A Method of 'Accounting for Changes in the Purchasing Power of Money'" and "A Method of 'Current Value Accounting'" and the present Draft. The analyses are lengthy and cannot be reproduced here. They are given in the related publication, *Accounting for Inflation - Methods and Problems*. But each of the assessments can be substantiated by reference to the source materials. The three systems are described briefly in terms of their salient features.

Price level adjusted historical cost accounting has been given its popular description "current purchasing power accounting". "Replacement price accounting" is used here of the method of current value accounting expounded in the second exposure draft above. The "current cost accounting" proposal of the U.K. Sandilands Committee is of the same family. With few exceptions, it would score similarly to R.P.A. in the following evaluation.

Current purchasing power accounting (C.P.P.) The general basis of asset valuation is, for monetary assets their face values, for non-monetary assets, original cost "indexed" by changes in an index of the general level of prices. Discretionary variations from the rule for non-monetary assets are permissible. Periodical charges against gross revenues in respect of non-monetary assets are based on the "indexed" cost figures. Gains or losses of purchasing power in respect of monetary items are brought into account in income calculation.

Replacement price accounting (R.P.A.). This is the variety of "current value accounting" dealt with in the abovementioned exposure draft. The general basis of asset valuation is, for monetary items their face values, for non-monetary assets the current replacement prices of assets expected or intended to be replaced; for non-monetary assets not intended to be replaced, their net market selling prices. Periodical charges against gross revenues in respect of non-monetary assets are based on replacement prices.

Continuously contemporary accounting (C.C.A.). The general basis of asset valuation is the money's worth, or money equivalents, of assets, which in the case of non-monetary assets means the best approximation to their resale prices at balance date. Charges against (or credits to) gross revenues are based on changes in the money equivalents of assets. Gains or losses of purchasing power are brought into account in respect of the whole of the opening amount for the year of net assets (or net owners' equity) by use of a readily calculated capital maintenance adjustment.

There are possible tests beside those listed below. There is, for example, the cost of doing the accounting. As C.P.P. and R.P.A. require numerous calculations to be made additional to the processing of original entries, and C.C.A. requires only one additional calculation, the last is the least costly. There is the cost of getting the closing balance sheet valuations. Under C.P.P. (taking the historical cost accounts and supplementary C.P.P. accounts together), there are costs of getting several valuations and choosing between alternative valuation rules. Under R.P.A., there are the costs of getting replacement prices and choosing between alternative valuation rules. Under C.C.A., there are the costs of getting values according to only one valuation rule; and, as para 24 of the main text indicates, most of the valuations required are generally accessible. It could also be shown that C.C.A. is superior in respect of most of the general "principles" of accounting; consistency of method, application of the accrual principle, representation of the facts of a company as a going concern, periodical matching of revenues and costs, and so on.

However, as financial statements are expected to be serviceable to their users, all the tests which follow relate to the usefulness of the products of the three systems.

300

EVALUATION

	CPP	RPA	CCA
1. Are assets shown at their money (or purchasing power) equivalents at each balance date?	No	No	Yes
2. Does net income, as calculated, represent a genuine increment in purchasing power up to balance date?	No	No	Yes
3. Can particular figures in balance sheets properly be added and related?	No	No	Yes

Monetary items are, in all systems, represented by money equivalents. It is logically improper and practically misleading to add to these figures any others which are not money equivalents. Hence the answer to (3). From (1), (2) and (3) flow the following consequences:

	CPP	RPA	CCA
4. Does the balance sheet yield a proper current ratio?	No	No	Yes
5. Does the balance sheet yield a proper debt to equity ratio?	No	No	Yes
6. Do the statements yield a proper rate of return?	No	No	Yes
7. Does the aggregate of asset values fairly represent gross wealth?	No	No	Yes

To make certain judgements or decisions it is necessary to compare the positions and results of different companies as at a given time and of the same company in successive years. Comparisons of the first kind are invalid unless all companies use the same valuation rules; comparisons of the second kind are invalid unless a given company uses the same rules from year to year and those rules embrace all types of change in financial position and results. Therefore:

		CPP	RPA	CCA
8.	Is the rate of return technically comparable with the rates of return on other types of investment?	No	No	Yes
9.	Are the aggregates and ratios yielded comparable from year to year and fair indicators of trends?	No	No	Yes
10.	Are the main ratios comparable as between firms?	No	No	Yes

The information in financial statements is used by managers and by outsiders in a variety of settings. The particulars and aggregates must be understandable by and useful to those parties.

		CPP	RPA	CCA
11.	Are the figures free of ambiguity and equally interpretable by and useful to managers and others?	No	No	Yes
12.	Do particular asset figures represent amounts of money accessible for alternative use?	No	No	Yes
13.	Are the figures a firm basis from which to calculate prospective results and positions?	No	No	Yes
14.	Does the net asset figure suggest a minimum acceptable takeover bid?	No	No	Yes
15.	Are the statements fair and serviceable for negotiations and other relations with public and other bodies?	No	No	Yes
16.	Are the statements complete as statements of results and position, needing no supplementary inform – ation or statements?	No	No	Yes
17.	Are the statements a fair basis for periodical "stewardship" evaluation?	No	No	Yes
18.	Do the statements give a true and fair view of financial results and position?	No	No	Yes
19.	Are the amounts representing assets and liabilities verifiable independently of the company's internal calculations?	No	No	Yes

No specific reference has been made above to inflation or its effects, except by references to purchasing power (1), (2), and to supplementary statements (16). There are several specific tests, however, which should be satisfied.

	CPP	RPA	CCA
20. Are retrospective corrections or adjustments to previously reported figures avoided?	No	No	Yes
21. Are any adjustments made in respect of changes in the prices of particular assets?	No	Yes	Yes
22. Are any adjustments made in respect of changes in the purchasing power of money?	Yes	Yes	Yes
23. Are adjustments made for the gain or loss of purchasing power during each period in respect of all assets and liabilities?	No	No	Yes
24. Is the method of accounting a method of accounting for inflation?	No	No	Yes

Two further points might be made. Although C.P.P. accounting makes reference to current purchasing power, a C.P.P. balance sheet does *not* represent assets by amounts which are in fact their current purchasing power (or money) equivalents. The point is covered in (1) above; but it may escape notice because of the description of the system.

Secondly, although replacement price accounting purports to provide for the replacement of assets by charges against gross revenues, the figures it yields do *not* indicate whether or not a firm could in fact replace those assets; a replacement price valuation does not represent purchasing power at the command of the firm, yet purchasing power is the only means of buying a "replacement" asset.

These inconsistencies with their apparent or avowed aims score against the two systems mentioned.

The practical superiority of C.C.A. is demonstrated.

M. C. WELLS & S. J. GRAY 30

Corporate Liquidity and the Disclosure of Financial Position: A Comment on European Developments and a Counter Proposal.

Dr. *Gray* is a lecturer in Accounting and Finance at the University of Lancaster, England, and Professor *Wells* is a Professor of Accounting at the University of Sydney, Australia.

Minimizing Differences

There has recently been considerable activity in Europe, aimed at improving the quality of company accounts. This activity has taken place both within individual nations, and at the level of the European Community of nine nations. In respect of the latter, the European Commission in Brussels has brought forward a number of proposals relating to company accounts, the most important being contained in the fourth directive proposal[1] (hereafter referred to simply as the 4th Directiv) on annual accounts (content, classification, presentation and valuation) and in the seventh directive proposal[2] on the special problems of group accounts.

The aim of those proposals is to eliminate, or at least minimize, the differences between Member States in 'the legal requirement governing both the structure and content of companies' annual accounts' (4th Directive, p. 35). The elimination of differences is thought to be necessary to encourage both commercial ties between companies in the Member States, and capital investment in the Community generally:

> Persons who intend to establish relations with companies in other Member States, or who have already done so, have the greatest interest in being able to obtain sufficient and comparable information concerning the assets, financial position and results of companies (4th Directive, p. 35).

One aspect of the 'comparable information' contained in the 4th Directive proposal is that the assets in the balance sheet be classified according to 'their degree of liquidity'. This is said to be 'the principle underlying the classification and subdivisions' and it is to be applied consistently with the assets which.

> 'are generally the most difficult to convert into liquid funds, and the valuation of which is the least precise, being shown at the top of the balance sheet' (4th Directive, p. 41).

Notice that the 'valuation' of assets is directly linked to the notion of liquidity. This may or may not have been a deliberate attempt by those framing the directive to ensure that the 'persons who intend to establish relations with the companies' are

---

1 Commission of the European Communities. *Amended Proposal for a fourth Council Directive for Co-ordination of national legislation regarding the annual accounts of Limited Liability Companies* (Brussels, 1974). See also the original *Proposal for a fourth directive on the Annual Accounts of Limited Liability Companies* (Brussels, 1971) which contains a full „Statement of Grounds" on which the proposal is based.
2 Commission of the European Communities. *Proposal for a Seventh Council Directive concerning Group Accounts* (Brussels, 1976).

able to assess the capacity of those companies to engage in transactions and pay their debts. But whether deliberate or not the implication is clear, and we may conclude that the balance sheet is intended to disclose the company's financial position — that is, where the company stands in relation to other participants in the market at a stated date.

This order of presentation is consistent with the model layouts prescribed in France (1971, Article 1)[3], Germany (1965, S. 151)[4], and Italy (1942, Article 2424)[5] though in Denmark (1973, S. 102)[6] the reverse order is suggested. However, in other European Community Countries, including the U.K., 'flexibility' prevails and they have no specific requirements on this aspect. Despite that lack, it is interesting to note that a survey of reporting practices ascertained from the 1972/73 accounts of the 100 largest European industrial companies[7], revealed that 85% of the companies surveyed listed assets in the order of fixed assets/current assets as required in the fourth directive proposal. The different legal requirements would also explain a statistically significant difference at the 5% level (using the Chi-Square test) as between UK and Continental companies in this respect with only 71% of UK companies following this order compared with 96% of continental companies.

Some Curiosities.

The European Commission's intention to reveal the liquidity and exchangeability of assets is certainly consistent with the need to evaluate a company's liquidity and solvency at least to the extent of disclosing the situation at a point in time.[8] But it is curious that its method of doing so, though supported to some degree by existing legal requirements and company reporting practice, negates the purpose stated. This is so for two reasons; first the primary method of asset measurement proposed is patently contrary to any indication of liquidity or exchangeability and second the conventional categories of "fixed" and "current" are unrelated to those factors. They depend upon managerial intentions of how the assets are to be used and not upon the degree to which they are liquid. The 4th Directive proposal states, in fact, that the classification of assets is to "depend on the purpose for which they are intended" (Article 12 (1)). Moreover, items to be treated as fixed assets are those which "are intended to be used on a continuing basis to enable the undertaking

to operate" (Article 12 (2)) whilst current assets are those which do not satisfy this criterion. This is a necessarily personal and subjective classification which completely denies the earlier reference to the market determined factors of liquidity and exchangeability. It raises particular problems when like items, such as securities, appear in both the fixed and current assets categories and are therefore valued following different conventions. The consequent detriment to the additivity within and comparability between financial statements is obvious. Moreover, the criterion of liquidity would suggest that even if it is management's purpose to retain an asset indefinitely, that asset may well be readily realisable (that is, liquid) regardless of its classification — the example of securities classified as fixed assets is an obvious anomaly.

Another curiosity is the repeated use of the word 'value' in the 4th Directive. All references to assets and how they are to be disclosed in the accounts are in terms of 'asset values'. This is, of course, conventional, but it sits oddly with the liquidity and exchangeability criteria. Those criteria do not relate to values at all. Values, like intentions, are essentially personal and subjective. But a company's 'actual' financial position is a matter of fact, and not a matter of someone's intentions or values. A financial position, as for any physical or geographic position, is a matter of calculation based on measurements. For the calculation of physical or geographic positions we measure distances from identified points of reference. Similarly with financial position. We base

---

3 *Decree No. 71—86 of 6th January 1971* (which amends *Decree No. 65—968 of 28th October 1965*) which is made applicable to commercial compnaies in some respects by *Decree No. 67—236 of 23rd March 1967* which amends the *Law on Commercial Companies No. 66—537 of 24th July 1966.*
4 The *Stock Corporation Law (Aktiengesetz, 1965).*
5 *Civil Code (Codice Civile of March 16, 1942).*
6 *Companies Act. No. 370 of 13th June 1973* (as amended by Act No. 287 of 14th June 1974).
7 As ranked in *Fortune* magazine in 1973. Note that State owned and unquoted companies were excluded from the survey. A full report on the survey which covered many aspects of European Financial Reporting can be found in *S. J. Gray, Company Financial Reporting Standards and the European Community.* Ph. D. Thesis. International Centre for Research in Accounting, University of Lancaster, 1975. Appendix C.
8 A full evalution of a company's liquidity situation would also, of course, entail the compilation of ex funds flow and cash flow statements together with statements of budgeted and forecasted cash flows.

305

our calculations of the position on measurements of the financial relationship of the company through its assets with the markets in which it conventionally deals.

A balance sheet, or statement of financial position is, accordingly, a statement of certain financial measures. If those measures are to be useful in the calculation of financial position, and an assessment of the company's liquidity, then they will be measures of the monetary equivalents of the company's assets and liabilities. For monetary and for liabilities the monetary equivalent is given by the face value of the instruments evidencing the obligation. For non-monetary assets the best indication of their monetary equivalent is given by the current market selling price of similar goods in the markets in which the firm usually deals.

The Nature of Liquidity.

It is, of course, no coincidence that the best indication of liquidity is also given by the face value of monetary assets and the availability of market selling prices of non-monetary assets. If market prices are readily ascertainable in respect of a particular asset, and if that asset is actively traded in the market, then as a general rule, that asset would be highly liquid. That is, it is readily convertible into cash. If, on the other hand, prices are not readily ascertainable, and the market is 'thin', then that asset is not easily converted into cash and it is not liquid.

Notice again that the indications of liquidity are quite independent of managerial intentions. They are market determined because it is the market to which the company must turn if it needs to convert its assets into cash for the purposes of paying its debts and meeting its obligations. The managers may well have intentions about which assets, and in which order the assets will be liquidated. But the purpose of gaining an indication of liquidity is to gauge the company's capacity to pay its debts and meet its obligations. For that purpose, all the assets must be considered because if the managers are prevented from carrying out their intentions (for whatever reason) then all or any of the company's assets may be called upon to help meet pressing claims.

There is a further reason why conventional classifications are no longer useful as indicators of liquidity. The notions of fixed and current do not indicate the ease with which assets may be used in

various ways to raise amounts of cash required in the normal course of business, or to stave off insistent creditors. The sale and leaseback of land and buildings is but one example of the ease with which a major asset (normally classed as 'fixed') may be converted into cash without losing possession or disrupting normal business activities.

Notice also that none of the 'valuation' methods specifically referred to in the 4th Directive are capable of yielding any indication of liquidity or exchangeability. Articles 29, 33 and 36 refer to the 'purchase price or production cost' of assets, while Article 30 allows Member States to "authorize valuation on the basis of replacement value for tangible fixed assets with a limited life, and/or stocks". As there is no necessary relationship between the acquisition cost (whether by purchase or production) or the current replacement price of an asset and the current monetary equivalent of that asset, the valuation rules are clearly at odds with rules for presentation. The two are, in fact quite incompatible, and their juxtaposition within the 4th Directive is likely to mislead the reader of a balance sheet rather than enable him 'to analyse the annual accounts of companies in other Member States' (p. 35).

An Alternative Presentation

Reference is made above to the nature of the amounts shown for assets and liabilities. If these are to show the financial position of the company, then they will be financial measures. It follows that the balance sheet, or more correctly, the statement of financial position, should be regarded as a statement of measures, and the classificatory system employed should follow the kinds of measures employed.

In the 4th Directive the use of a 'current value' method other than 'replacement value' is permitted, at the discretion of individual member countries ,by means of a continuous 'valuation' process or by occasional revaluation, under Articles 30 and 31. It is, therefore, possible to propose a system which could be implemented under the existing articles of the proposed Directive. The following system is hence advocated as a way of better satisfying the intention of the 4th Directive.

The system is based on the financial measures described above — the statement of assets and liabilities at, or at the best approximation of, their current monetary equivalent.[9] For monetray assets and liabilities, their current monetary equivalent is, generally, their face value. The best indication of the current monetary equivalent of non-monetary assets will be given by their current market selling price. As there will be great variability in the availability of evidence of those prices, we propose that the assets be classified according to the availability of that evidence. An illustration is given in Exhibit A.[10] The classes provided are for assets which will be shown at 1. Their current monetary equivalent; 2. Approximations of current monetary equivalent; 3. Estimates of current monetary equivalents; and 4. Those that have no current monetary equivalent. The equities follow the conventional short-term and long-term liability classification, and an estimate of shareholders' equity.

The first class of assets will be those that have an easily identifiable current monetary equivalent — cash, collectible debtors, and goods which are the subject of a continuing open offer. This is likely to only a limited number of goods. More commonly, a good approximation of the measure will be given by the prices of similar goods traded in active and representative markets accessible to the company. Where the goods are traded only sporadically or where the market is thin, an estimation of the measure will be made on the basis of what evidence is available. Finally there will be some assets which are unsalable and which do not therefore contribute to the company's current financial position or its liquidity. They will be listed, but with no monetary equivalent shown.

Exhibit A

STATEMENT OF FINANCIAL POSITION

A. *Assets*

A. 1. *At Current Monetary Equivalent*
A. 1. 1.	Cash	X	
A. 1. 2.	Debtors	X	X

A. 2. *At Approximation of current monetary equivalent*
A. 2. 1.	Listed shares in other companies	X	
A. 2. 2.	Debentures in other companies	X	
A. 2. 3.	Debtors	X	
A. 2. 4.	Inventory of finished goods	X	
A. 2. 5.	Motor vehicles	X	
A. 2. 6.	Land and buildings	X	X

A. 3. *At estimate of current monetary equivalent*
A. 3. 1.	Inventory of raw materials	X	
A. 3. 2.	Plant-General	X	X

A. 4. *No current monetary equivalent*
A. 4. 1.	Inventory of work in progress	—	—
A. 4. 2.	Plant-specialized		X

B. *Equities*

B. 1. *Short-term Liabilities*
B. 1. 1.	Creditors	X	
B. 1. 2.	Dividends proposed	X	
B. 1. 3.	Taxation due	X	
B. 1. 4.	Short-term loans	X	X

B. 2. *Long-term liabilities*
B. 2. 1.	Debentures	X	
B. 2. 2.	Unsecured notes	X	X

B. 3. *Estimate of Shareholders Equity*
B. 3. 1.	Issued Share Capital	X	
B. 3. 2.	Capital Maintenance Reserves	X	
B. 3. 3.	Retained Profits	X	X
			X

The measure of the interests of shareholders is a derived measure insofar as it is a consequence of the measures determined for all assets and other equities. It must therefore be ranked in an equivalent manner to the least certain of the classes of measures used for the other items listed. For although the contributed capital of the shareholders may be determined accurately (albeit subject to adjustment for changes in the general price level), the retained income can be no more certain than its least certain component. As it is the whole of the interest of the residual equity holders that determine their rights relative to other equity interests, the stockholders' equity is summed and included under the class heading of an "estimate".

Indications of Liquidity.

The proposed classifications follow precisely the nature of liquidity described above. Assets listed at their current monetary equivalent are more or less immediately convertible into cash. Those classed as 'approximations' are readily convertible, 'estimations' are somewhat more difficult, and those with no current monetary equivalent do not contribute in any

9 The underlying theory of this system, and details of its practical application are set out in R.J. Chambers, *Accounting, Evaluation and Economic Behavior.* (Prentice-Hall, 1966); „Second Thoughts on Continuously Contemporary Accounting", *Abacus* (September 1970); and 'Accounting for Inflation: Exposure Draft' (University of Sydney, 1975).
10 An illustration of this form of presentation was first given in M. C. Wells, „Costing for Activities", *Management Accounting* (USA) (May 1976), p. 36.

307

way to the company's liquidity. The measures thus provided can be compared directly with the liabilities which are also listed in the order of required liquidation.

The indication of liquidity given by this proposal is not just that related to a company in financial distress. It also indicates the financial viability of the company, at least in the short term. The measures of assets are, of course, the financial resources which the company has, or can call upon, to enable it to continue to trade in markets, pay salaries and wages, meet its debts, pay interest and dividends, and so on. The financical aspects of the company are therefore more directly relevant to the interests and concerns of the readers of balance sheets with which the 4th Directive is concerned.

Conclusion.

If the European Commission's aim of disclosing corporate liquidity and exchangeabiltiy is to be achieved then a reassessment of its proposed classification and measurement requirements are necessary. An approach which is directly useful to the readers of balance sheets is a system of measurement and classification based on the ease with which assets can be exchanged and the order in which liabilities will have to be discharged. Such an approach is consistent with the purpose of discovering corporate liquidity and is more likely to provide useful insights into the capacity for business survival. It should be considered by the European Commission as a matter of urgency if the proposed Fourth Directive is to achieve its stated purpose.

"Companies Are Reporting Useless Numbers"

Tremors of reformation- if not revolution -have been disturbing the once placid pro-fession of accounting. Bedeviled by inflation, the merger wave, and new reporting require-ments imposed by the Securities and Ex-hange Commission, more and more accoun-ants have concluded that their arcane rules -dating back to the fifteenth century, when double entry bookkeeping was invented- pro-vide investors with deplorably little informa-ion that is of practical value in making financial decisions.

The profession's rule-making body, the Financial Accounting Standards Board, has been soliciting proposals for reform. One of the most radical answers has come from Rob-rt Sterling, dean of the Jesse H. Jones Graduate School of Administration at Rice University. He argues that what accountants should be measuring is "exit" values–that is, the market prices at which a company could sell its assets and (in theory at least) go out of business. Accountants would make these empirical observations the basis of statements bout the company's net worth–and changes n net worth from year to year–ignoring the myriad rules that are now being used.

Not surprisingly, Sterling's background is different from most accountants'. In addition o being a professor of accounting, he has tudied and taught economics and the phi-osophy of science. While his views are a long vay from generally accepted accounting prin-iples, some recent developments, like the SEC's requirement that oil and gas compa-ies disclose the present value of their re-erves, suggest that financial reporting may e moving in his direction. Sterling recently iscussed the shortcomings in present ac-ounting methods and his proposals for hange with FORTUNE's Mary Greenebaum.

Q. There has been a lot of talk lately bout how financial statements are being istorted by inflation. Do you see this s being the main problem?

A. The problems caused by inflation are only a symptom. The fundamental issue is that companies are reporting useless numbers. Take the oil-company profits that have been attracting so much attention. The big earnings gains are meaningless be-cause the cost numbers that are being used are meaningless. We have producers here in Texas who are pumping oil at a report-ed cost of a nickel a barrel, but that's a num-ber that doesn't refer to anything in the real world. In reality the company is dis-posing of valuable assets. But when the wells were drilled, accountants took the cost of drilling each well and capitalized it and then divided it by the number of bar-rels they expected the well to produce to get a depletion figure. As long as you use a whole set of fictions called depreciation and amortization to determine income, you are going to get irrelevant information.

Q. Irrelevant in what way?

A. You can't use it to make decisions. I'll give you a simple example. You buy a car for $5,000 this year and you decide it's going to last for five years, so you take straight-line depreciation of $1,000 a year. Next year your financial statements tell

Robert Sterling

309

you that the value of your car is **$4,000**. There is not a single decision you can make with that information. It won't help you figure out whether you should keep the car, sell it, or scrap it. Those are the kinds of decisions managers have to make.

Q. Well, what information do they need?

A. They need to know the market value of the car. Maybe you can make money selling that car and replacing it with a leased car.

That's why I say let's base accounting on exit—or market—values. That's the only way to give an accurate picture of a company's status. For an oil company, the major economic event occurs when it hits a wet hole instead of a dry hole—not when it sells the oil. Many of the oil profits reported this year were earned twenty years ago when the reserves were discovered.

Q. But don't managers really know this already and take it into account when making decisions?

A. When they are assessing a new investment, managers know better than to rely on the figures they report in their accounts. They make projections of a cash flow and compare them with current market prices. That's what the capital-budgeting model does: it compares your required sacrifice for a project with the cash flows you expect the project to generate. And the required sacrifice for a new asset is its purchase price. But managers usually don't extend this analysis to the assets that the company already owns. They should be comparing the cash flow from these assets with what they could *sell* them for. They may be underutilizing their assets, based on what they could get for them in the marketplace.

Q. But why would they do this? Are they trying to hide their inefficiency?

A. I don't think there's any conspira involved. It's a mental set. People have g used to figuring companies' results a ce tain way. Besides, historic-cost accounti is a cheap way to report. All you have do is gather costs and then allocate the If you were actually trying to measure t market value of your assets, that would more expensive to do.

Cost isn't the whole explanation, thoug Somehow, a long time ago, managers ar accountants got the idea that accounti could not be an empirical science. Y could not measure things. Instead, th took a legalistic approach and based repo ing on conventions. If you want to show building on your balance sheet, you car call a few brokers and find out how mu someone would pay for the building. I stead, you have to follow a bunch of a bitrary rules for valuing the buildin We're going to keep on doing this as lo as we define our subject matter as som thing totally abstract called unexpir costs. I've been looking for an unexpir cost for a long time so I could measure but I haven't found one yet.

Q. Still, there is an impressive body evidence saying that the financial marke are efficient, even if accounting is de cient. Don't investors already take the things into account?

A. The market may, but many indivi ual shareholders don't. They have to re on historic-cost numbers because that's they get. And this irrelevant informatie is preventing them from making goo judgments about their investments. Tak overs are the prime example—or at lea the most easily understood example. In perial Group recently made a tender off for Howard Johnson. What Imperial real wants is Howard Johnson's real-esta holdings, but the shareholders have idea what that real estate is worth. It's n reported in the financial statements. I' not saying that the shareholders could g the full market value per share if they kn what that full value was, but they coul get a lot closer. They could hold out f more if they thought an offer was too low. At least they could make their decision on the basis of accurate information.

Q. Would the accounting system you're advocating boost stock prices?

A. Theoretically it would, because shares are claims on a company's assets, and assets are generally understated. I say theoretically, though, because no one has been reporting market values, so there's no way to test the effect of this kind of accounting on stock prices.

But the implications are a lot broader than the effect on stock prices. I mentioned investors because they are the most visible victims of poor information. But really it's the whole economy that suffers. We talk a lot about the problem of low productivity. Our financial statements are a restraint on productivity. Managers aren't being forced to look at the opportunity cost of what they're doing. They can go right on running the business they've been running, regardless of whether it's a good use of resources. Maybe peddling twenty-eight flavors of ice cream is not a very productive use of Howard Johnson's real estate. If we had a realistic measure of assets, the company's return on equity would show that. We're living in an economy that's underutilizing its assets because it doesn't know what their value is.

Q. How practical is it to think that companies could report market values? It may be easy enough for a car-rental company to measure the value of its fleet, but how do you get the market price of an electric utility's nuclear plant?

A. I'm not saying I have all the answers. What I have found is that there are a lot more prices out there than people realize —not just for cars and tractors but for lathes and airplanes. There's a market for oil and gas reserves because people buy and sell leases and participations in drilling partnerships. Factoring companies and banks buy accounts receivable. Obviously there are cases where there is no market. But accountants could learn how to develop synthetic prices through regression analysis, using prices for similar assets. In the sciences, sometimes you have to infer from like objects when you run into a measurement problem.

Every business has at least some assets that can be valued in the marketplace. I'm not one who believes we have to solve all the measurement problems before we can make any changes. Right now, we're not even showing marketable securities at what they're worth.

Q. I can visualize a balance sheet with market values for the assets and liabilities. But how do you get at income from market values?

A. Income would simply be the difference between balance sheets from one year to the next. The main change from what you see in annual reports now is that there would be no allocations. I would get rid of this arbitrary slicing up of costs. Depreciation would be the change in market value of an asset from year to year. The value doesn't have to decline—it could go up.

Q. Won't a lot of the increase in values be just the result of inflation?

A. You can get around that problem by multiplying the beginning balance sheet by the C.P.I. and taking your differences after you've made that adjustment. One of the big arguments in accounting these days is that people are saying that we ought to do *either* look at current values *or* make a price-level adjustment. I say we ought to do both. The information we really need is current market values *adjusted* for inflation.

Q. Another effect of inflation is to push up interest rates, reducing the value of a company's debt. Would you include that as a gain in income?

A. The relevant thing to look at for debt is discharge value. If bonds with a face value of $1,000 are selling for $600, the manager has to choose between paying $1,000 ten years from now or going into the market and discharging his obligation for $600. And it's truly a gain for the firm to pay back only 60 percent of what it borrowed.

Q. What about taxes? How would they be figured?

A. The government can base taxes on anything it wants. The French government once taxed people on the number of windows they had in their houses. A lot of managements would like to base taxes on replacement-cost income because then their companies would pay less. I think we should assess taxes on annual changes in value because that's the most equitable and neutral method. The oil companies' windfall profits that are causing so much controversy wouldn't exist if the income had to be booked when it was earned.

Q. You mentioned that replacement-cost accounting would generally lower pretax income—and taxes. What effect would your approach have on the level of companies' income?

A. It's impossible to generalize. It all depends on the real change in market values at each company. In some cases, like the computer companies, the value of the assets is falling. In others, it's rising. Wine vats appreciate with age.

Q. Your method of accounting would provide plenty of information about the values of assets and liabilities, but isn't cash flow really more important for assessing a company's prospects?

A. I would never argue that cash flow is not important, but advocates of cash-flow analysis come perilously close to saying that cash stocks are irrelevant. Surely if you have a million dollars in the bank, that is as relevant as knowing how much your cash flows are going to be. Once you admit cash stocks are important, then it's a small step to considering other stocks, because ultimately everything can be converted to cash. That's

what market values are: cash equivalents.

Stocks and flows are inextricably entwined. It's a mistake to say that the balance sheet or the income statement or the funds-flow statement is the most important. All three are equally important for making decisions.

Q. How would these financial statements you envision be prepared? Who would set the standards?

A. No one. That's the whole difference between the scientific and the legalistic approach to accounting. If accounting became an empirical science, the F.A.S.B. could wither and die. You wouldn't need this barrage of regulations and interpretations of regulations. You would just go out and measure what you saw in the real world. You need laws in astrology to tell you when Mars is on its cusp. You don't need laws in astronomy. You can observe where Mars is. Setting rules to determine the location of Mars would be as ludicrous as the Indiana legislature's famous attempt to change the value of pi in geometry to three to get rid of the decimals. Right now accounting is more like astrology.

Q. Would auditors be eliminated too?

A. No, but they would have to come out of their ivory tower. They would have to become experts in market values instead of experts in allocations. Reserve recognition accounting is a step in that direction, but only a small one.

Actually, until the 1930's, auditors did nothing but check the arithmetic in people's ledgers. Then came the McKesson & Robbins scandal. A company reported inventory in warehouses that didn't exist —let alone the inventory. That got accountants in white shirts and ties out into the warehouses. They started putting sticks in oil tanks and climbing to the top of grain elevators. And they've become pretty good at verifying quantities. The approach I'm proposing would do for asset values what McKesson & Robbins did for honest quantities. ∎

T. A. LEE

32

Reporting Cash Flows and Net Realisable Values *

T. A. Lee

Several arguments have been advanced for financial reporting to be based on cash flow accounting (CFA).[1] The literature also contains many items explaining the case for net realisable value accounting (NRVA).[2] Typically, however, these systems of reporting have been examined and presented separately, and rarely has any detailed attempt been made to link them.[3] The purpose of this paper is to make such a connection, in the hope of revealing to the interested reader that CFA and NRVA are parts of a single system of

reporting which concentrates on the importance and accessibility of cash in business enterprise activity. As such, it is concerned particularly with describing how CFA and NRVA data can be brought together in a series of articulating financial statements which provide more relevant information for the report user about cash and cash management than can be given in either a CFA or NRVA system on its own.

It is not concerned with advancing individual arguments for the reporting of either CFA or NRVA data. These have already been well rehearsed in the accountancy literature, and should be familiar to the interested reader. Equally, it is not concerned with demonstrating that CFA is a particular sub-set of NRVA, or vice versa. Such artificial distinctions are futile if, as is suggested in this paper, both are parts of a single cash-orientated system of financial reporting. In other words, the writer is concerned that advocates of CFA and NRVA have been working separately, and may well have ignored the possibility that their arguments and recommendations are similar but incomplete without each other, and could be strengthened through unification.

Points of similarity

Before proceeding to the main part of the paper, it would appear to be relevant to describe briefly the main points of similarity in CFA and NRVA as they are presently and separately constituted. These are made in order to demonstrate that linking the two systems within one reporting framework is not a casual *ad hoc* exercise, and that they are compatible.

1. CFA and NRVA are both based firmly on the importance of cash as a business resource. CFA describes in detail cash flows to and from various sources, and NRVA describes the adaptability of the reporting enterprise in terms of its command over money (resources being valued using net realisable values, or 'current cash equivalents').

---

*This paper is based on an earlier one presented to the annual conference of the European Accounting Association, Amsterdam, March 1980. It has benefited considerably from comments on the earlier paper by Professors R. J. Chambers and M. C. Wells and an anonymous referee.

[1] For a summary of CFA arguments, and a full bibliography on the subject, see T. A. Lee, 'Cash Flow Accounting and Corporate Financial Reporting,' *Discussion Paper 6*, University of Edinburgh, 1980.

[2] For a full bibliography on the case for NRVA, particularly as expounded by R. J. Chambers and R. R. Sterling, see T. A. Lee, *Income and Value Measurement*, Nelson, 2nd. ed. 1980, pp. 185–7.

[3] Only in a casual way has it been attempted before: see R. Edwards, 'The Nature and Measurement of Income,' in *Studies in Accounting*, W. T. Baxter and S. Davidson (eds.), Institute of Chartered Accountants in England and Wales, 3rd. ed. 1977, pp. 126–38; H. C. Edey, 'Accounting Principles and Business Reality,' *Accountancy*, December 1963, p. 1087; T. A. Climo, 'Cash Flow Statements for Investors,' *Journal of Business Finance and Accounting*, Autumn 1976, pp. 11 and 13; T. A. Lee, 'The Cash Flow Accounting Alternative for Corporate Financial Reporting,' in *Trends in Managerial and Financial Accounting*, C. van Dam (ed.), Martinus Nijhoff, 1978, p. 84; and T. A. Lee, 'The Simplicity and Complexity of Accounting,' *Accounting for a Simplified Firm*, in R. R. Sterling and A. Thomas (eds.), Scholars Book Co., 1979, pp. 47–50. Edwards' contribution was originally published in 1938 and appears to have been the first, although it must be noted that his recommendations relating to cash flow and net realisable value were effectively limited to what he described as merchanting businesses (that is, retail concerns). In fact, he specifically excluded total valuations for industrial businesses, with a recommendation that only individual assets ought to be valued where this would produce relevant information. Additionally, his cash flow recommendations were vague, being based on cash receipts and expenditures with certain unspecified adjustments, and lacking any illustration or numerical example. The cash flow accounting recommended appears to have been based for industrial businesses on the nineteenth century double-account system of accounting and reporting.

2. CFA and NRVA are both allocation-free systems. Neither contains arbitrary allocations due to short-term periodic reporting, and thus both are free of such accounting interference.

3. The condition of enterprise survival is greatly emphasised in CFA and NRVA—the former being concerned with the way in which cash has been generated to meet its obligations and requirements, and the latter with the availability and accessibility of cash for future activity and needs.

4. Both systems concentrate on reporting on the activity of the enterprise and its management. Neither assumes continuity of this activity, and both appear capable of providing essential information on the financial management of the reporting entity (particularly that pertaining to its liquidity).

5. Cash, current cash equivalents, and cash flows are matters which appear to underlie most of the decision models to which financial reporting is directed—for example, shareholders concerned about dividends; lenders, bankers and creditors concerned about interest and capital repayments; employees concerned about wages and security of employment; and so on. Both CFA and NRVA would therefore appear to be of relevance to these potential report users.[4]

Linking CFA and NRVA

In its historic form, CFA describes the realisation and utilisation of cash—that is, the conversion of non-cash resources into cash, and the use of cash funds generated from various sources to acquire resources and meet obligations. NRVA, on the other hand, describes, within aggregate totals, a mixture of both the realisation and utilisation of cash (as in CFA), and the pre-realisation changes in the net realisable values of non-cash resources and the amounts due on various obligations. The 'linking' of the two systems can be achieved relatively easily by the segregation of NRVA data into realised cash flows and unrealised cash flows—the former described in detail in CFA terms, and the latter represented by the aforementioned changes in the net realisable values of reported assets, and changes in the amounts of reported obligations. In this way, it can be argued that CFA-based financial statements would thereby cease to be incomplete because of their

[4]This has been recognised in at least one major study of financial reporting: Accounting Objectives Study Group, *Objectives of Financial Statements*, American Institute of Certified Public Accountants, 1973, pp. 17-20.

present failure to deal with unrealised cash flows (and thus with statements of financial position); and NRVA-based statements would provide much greater information on the realised cash flows which presently are contained, but not separately identified, in its measures of realisable income. The exact formulation required for the 'linking' can be described as follows:

$$\Delta C + \Delta N = \Delta O$$

where ΔC represents the net realised change in the total cash resources of the reporting enterprise for a defined period—that is, sales revenues received minus total operational payments, minus total payments for new and replacement investment, minus loan interest, taxation, and dividend payments, plus or minus cash transactions relating to long-term financing (such as loans and share capital).

ΔN is the total unrealised net cash flow representing the periodic change in the net realisable value of the non-cash assets of the reporting enterprise (including those assets which are readily-realisable, those which are not-so-readily realisable, and those which are non-realisable). ΔO is the total change in the various obligations or liabilities of the reporting enterprise (including its short, medium and long-term debts, and its owner's capital measured in net realisable value terms). This aggregation of periodic realised and potential cash flows from the use and holding of assets provides the report user with a total cash flow figure which is equivalent to the net increase (or decrease) during the period in taxed and undistributed, actual and potential, cash funds in the enterprise. It is an expression of the change in its total measured command over money, and reveals the increment (or decrement) in the enterprise's potential for repaying its financial obligations, maintaining and changing its operations and activities, meeting wage claims and making distributions. In other words, it represents financial information which ought to be of interest to most report users.

Because of the flow nature of this data, they should be contained within a statement which reconciles with position statements at the beginning and end of the period concerned. Thus, using assumed figures for purposes of demonstration, the overall reporting system described above could be summarised as in Figure 1.

This outline contains several features which ought to be described at this stage before proceeding further:

1. The opening and closing position statements

Figure 1

Opening Cash Resources Statement		Total Cash Flow Statement		Closing Cash Resources Statement	
	£000		£000		£000
Realised cash	5	Realised cash flow	39	Realised cash	44
Readily-realisable assets	43	Increase in potential cash flow	17	Readily-realisable assets	60
Not-readily-realisable assets	18	Increase in potential cash flow	12	Not-readily-realisable assets	30
Non-realisable assets	–	Increase in potential cash flow	–	Non-realisable assets	–
	66		68		134
Short-term obligations	32	Additional credit received	18	Short-term obligations	50
Long-term obligations	10	Additional borrowings received	8	Long-term obligations	18
Indefinite obligations	24	Additional funds accruing	42	Indefinite obligations	66
	66		68		134

are described as 'cash resources' statements rather than as conventional balance sheets. They treat all measurable assets of the enterprise as cash or potential cash—through the use of net realisable values. Thus, its command over money is emphasised by measuring its assets in current cash equivalent terms.

2. The assets are ordered for purposes of the position statements in order of realisability—from the already-realised to the non-realisable. This provides the user with some idea of the degree of certainty associated with the enterprise's command over money (such command being more absolute with certain assets than with others). It also means a rethinking of asset classification from either the traditional fixed and current or monetary and non-monetary categories.[5] If a system of reporting is being advocated which emphasises the realisation or potential realisation of the reporting enterprise's resources, it appears only sensible to ensure that the latter are described in a way which accords with the notion of realisability. The above formulation does this; the traditional classification, although intended originally to do so in terms of fixed and current assets, does not.

3. The liabilities of the enterprise (including its ownership interests) are also ordered—in this case in terms of order of potential repayment (from the most to the least immediate obligation). Again, this will require rethinking as to classification, but should provide report users with some impression of the timing of repayments of obligations for which cash resources will be required (and are available as described in the earlier part of the cash resources statement).

4. The total cash flow statement reflects all actual and potential cash flow changes affecting the assets and obligations of the enterprise over a defined period—that is, the total net increase or decrease in its command over money. The separate parts of this total cash flow are attributable to the various actual and potential cash and cash equivalent resources and obligations in the cash resources statement. Thus, the entire emphasis in the system is on cash flow and cash resources (actual and potential). It is essentially one concerned with the cash management function within the enterprise although, as will be seen later, it can also be used for purposes of income assessment as a means of evaluating the success or failure of enterprise management in terms of returns on capital employed, etc.

5. It is possible to derive a measure of income from the reported data, this being based on net realisable values. The datum describing additional funds accruing to indefinite obligations forms the basis for this, as it represents (assuming no new

[5]This is not entirely a new idea—a somewhat different variation of it can be seen in M. C. Wells, 'Costing for Activities,' *Management Accounting* (USA), May 1976, pp. 35–6; and in S. G. Gray and M. C. Wells, 'Corporate Liquidity and Disclosure of Financial Position: A Comment on European Developments and a Counter Proposal,' *Journal UEC*, 3/1977, pp. 156–8.

capital issued or capital repayments) the income retained for the period after taxation and distribution. Thus realisable income (Y_r) could be formulated as follows:

$$Y_r = \Delta R + t + d \pm 1$$

where ΔR represents the additional funds accruing to capital in net realisable value terms; t represents taxation provided for the period; d represents dividends provided for the period; and 1 represents capital repayments (+) or new capital (−).

6. The non-realisability of certain specialised assets, and therefore their lack of potential in providing cash from sale as distinct from use, is recognised in this scheme with nil values and value changes being attributed to these items.

Outline financial statements

The above outline is obviously insufficient for financial reporting purposes. It requires to be expanded and presented in such a way as to be comprehensible and meaningful to its readers. Thus, as a first step, the undernoted outline statements have been prepared—that is, a Statement of Realised Cash Flow; a Statement of Total Cash Flow Movements (realised and potential); a Statement of Net Cash and Cash Equivalent Resources (again, realised and potential); and a Statement of Realisable Income (see Figures 2, 3, 4 and 5).

Figure 2 provides its reader with a portrayal of the actual cash inflow and outflow for the defined period. It could be supported by detailed schedules analysing the composition of individual figures given in it. As such, it describes the cash flow underlying the retained income measure based on net realisable values, and represents the factual and incontrovertible part of the latter datum (although the ordering and presentation of data are open to debate). The next statement looks beyond the point of realisation, and describes potential increases and decreases in cash resources which, with varying degrees of certainty, could be converted into actual cash movements.

If reported, Figure 3 would provide an explanation of the total potential increase in the reporting enterprise's command over money during the period. It is a general statement of the cash management exercised within the enterprise, resulting in a net realisation of cash flow and a net increase in potential cash flow. In particular, it reveals the incremental changes in cash and cash-equivalent resources available to cover the incremental changes in financial obligations—in the case of resources, highlighting the range of potential realisability; and, in the case of obligations, the range of possible repayment timing.

As such, it provides more information concerning the realisability of assets, and repayment of obligations, than does the equivalent NRVA-based income statement. The latter does not

---

Figure 2
CF Ltd.
Statement of Realised Cash Flows
Period $t_1 - t_2$

	000
Cash receipts from customers	187
Less: cash payments for materials, wages and overheads	124
Cash Operating Margin	63
Less: loan interest paid	2
Pre-tax Cash Flow	61
Less: taxation paid	13
Distributable Cash Flow	48
Less: dividends paid	10
Operating Cash Flow Available for Investment	38
Add: long-term loans received	8
Total Cash Flow Available for Investment	46
Less: cash payments for new buildings	7
Total Increase in Cash Resources	39

Figure 3
CF Ltd.
Statement of Total Cash Flow Movements
Period t_1-t.

	£000	£000
Realised Cash Flows		
Net realised cash flow for the period (as per Statement of Realised Cash Flows)		39
Readily-Realisable Cash Flows		
Potential cash flows represented by an increase (decrease) in the net realisable values of readily-realisable assets:		
Amounts due by customers	7	
Stocks of finished goods	8	
Motor vehicles	(6)	
Land and buildings	8	17
		56
Not-Readily-Realisable Cash Flows		
Potential cash flows represented by an increase (decrease) in the net realisable values of not-readily-realisable assets:		
Work-in-progress	15	
Plant and machinery	(3)	12
Total Potential Increase in Cash Resources		68
Change in Short-Term Obligations		
Potential cash outflows in the near future resulting from increases in:		
Amounts due to suppliers	9	
Taxation due to Inland Revenue	7	
Distributions due to owners	2	18
Change in Long-Term Obligations		
Potential cash outflows in the long-term resulting from increases in:		
Borrowings from merchant bank		8
Change in Indefinite Obligations		
Indeterminate future cash outflows resulting from increases in:		
Funds pertaining to owners (see Statement of Realisable Income)		42
Total Potential Increase in Obligations		68

reveal specific details of cash or cash equivalent movements in individual asset categories, and it also fails to report changes in many of the obligations of the reporting enterprise. In other words, the Statement of Total Cash Flow Movement is effectively a funds statement based on net realisable values; its data are rearranged to be compatible with the position statement—the Statement of Total Net Cash and Cash Equivalent Resources—which is based on a reasoned ordering of the enterprise's assets and liabilities.

The next statement supporting these descriptions of cash flow is the end-of-period 'cash resources' report—the Statement of Net Cash and Cash Equivalent Resources (Figure 4). Together with corresponding figures relating to the begin-

ning of the period, it contains descriptions of the total resources of the enterprise in cash or cash equivalent terms. As such, it provides a total reporting of the actual and potential cash resources and obligations of the reporting enterprise. Thus, it not only describes the assets and liabilities of the enterprise in current value terms which are understandable and not subject to the arbitrariness of periodic data allocations; it also reveals the financial resources currently available to management to meet existing financial obligations and future commitments. The uniqueness of this 'balance sheet' is that it is a statement of financial position which attempts to reflect the liquidity of the reporting enterprise in reasonably clear and understandable terms which do not

Figure 4
CF Ltd.
Statement of Net Cash and Cash Equivalent Resources
as at t_1 and t_2
Resources

	t_1 £000	t_2 £000
Realised Cash Resources		
Bank, cash and deposit balances	5	44
Readily-Realisable Non-Cash Resources		
Amounts due to customers	11	18
Stocks of finished goods	10	18
Motor vehicles	10	4
Land and buildings	12	20
	43	60
Not-Readily-Realisable Non-Cash Resources		
Work-in-progress	9	24
Non-specialist plant and machinery	9	6
	18	30
Non-Realisable Non-Cash Resources		
Specialist plant and machinery		
	66	134
Obligations		
Short-Term Obligations		
Amounts due to suppliers	9	18
Taxation due to Inland Revenue	13	20
Distributions due to owners	10	12
	32	50
Long-Term Obligations		
Borrowings from merchant bank	10	18
Indefinite Obligations		
Funds pertaining to owners (see Statement of Retained Income)	24	66
	66	134

Figure 5
CF Ltd.
Statement of Retained Income
Period t_1 to t_2

	£000
Realisable income	74
Less: taxation provided	20
Distributable Income	54
Less: dividends provided	12
Retained Income for Period	42
Add: retained income of previous periods	24
Total Retained Income (as per Statement of Net Cash and Cash Equivalent Resources)	66

adhere to the rather misleading fixed and current asset categories of traditional accounting, and are compatible with the cash flow analysis contained in the previous cash-based funds statement. It is therefore a rearranged NRVA-balance sheet, and provides a position statement which has for so long been missing from CFA systems of reporting.

The final Statement of Retained Income (Figure 5) also provides a means of filling a gap in CFA—in this case, the lack of a measure of income in the latter.

This statement thus completes the combined CFA and NRVA system by providing the NRVA-based measure of income which reconciles with the equivalent position statement. Thus the complete system comprises a realised cash flow statement, a cash-based funds statement, a realisable income statement, and a net realisable value position statement.

Advantages of the combined system

The above outline statements contain the following advantageous features which appear to strengthen the case for reporting in such a way:

1. The two cash flow statements clearly separate and identify the objectively measured realised cash flow data from the far more subjective potential cash flow data described by the unrealised movements in the enterprise's assets and liabilities. The idea of distinguishing factual from judgmental data in accounting statements in this way should be capable of aiding their users in assessing the varying degrees of credibility inherent in such information. In addition, the 'ranking' of actual and potential cash flows in order of realisability and repayment provides them with indications of what cash is or will be available for future activities and commitments of the enterprise.

2. Although it can be argued that there is no need to ensure the articulation of the 'surplus' and 'position' statements, the above scheme of reporting ensures a proper reconciliation of actual with potential cash flows. It is thus intended as a complete cash-orientated system with all reported data being capable of being matched, compared and justified. In this way, these cash-based statements are available for an assessment of the extent and quality of the reporting enterprise's cash management. If the managing of cash flow is regarded as a vital ingredient in the survival of the enterprise in both the short-term and long-term, it appears to be sensible to report on such matters.

Thus, it can be anticipated that these statements would be useful primarily for, for example, (a) bankers, lenders and suppliers concerned with evaluating the liquidity of the enterprise in connection with the amount and risk associated with their existing and potential cash claims on it; (b) investors anxious to predict the amount and risk associated with the future cash distributions by the enterprise which are such a vital ingredient in their investment decisions; (c) employees desiring to assess the financial position of the enterprise in connection with future job and pay prospects; and (d) government monitoring the effects of its taxation policies and procedures on the cash flow of business enterprises. Each of the decision models inherent in the above descriptions of users relies to a considerable extent on the short or long-term availability of cash within the reporting enterprise. The recommended system provides information likely to meet these requirements. Income is there as well, but this system destroys the notion of the all-embracing importance of income in relation to such matters as interest and capital repayments, credit settlements, dividend distributions and wage claims.[6] With respect to each of these matters, cash appears to be just as, if not more, important.

In addition, it does not appear unreasonable to presume that enterprise management would find such statements useful when involved in the process of managing cash flow and resources—for example, when comparing with previously forecast activity, determining distribution levels, and deciding on borrowing requirements. Indeed, as has been recently suggested, the aims of enterprise management should be compatible with those persons interested in its financial reports, and thus the information needs of management and external interests should be just as compatible.[7]

3. The accounting practices used in the above statements are simple and straightforward—no complex data allocation procedures have been undertaken, and no extensive explanation of such procedures is necessary to the report user.

4. The combined system ought to satisfy the advocates of both CFA and NRVA. It contains all the data normally required in each of these systems, but in such a way as to highlight the crucial feature of both—cash and its accessibility.

[6]This was originally suggested by Edwards, op. cit, p. 135, and more recently implied in H. C. Edey. 'The Logic of Financial Accounting.' The Deloitte, Haskins and Sells Lecture, Cardiff University College Press, 1980, pp. 8–11.
[7]This idea has been most elegantly explored in Edey, op cit, pp. 6–7.

Conclusion

The above points have been put forward as matters for debate by those who regard improvements to the financial reporting function to be essential. In particular, they are presented as a means of extending CFA and NRVA to the point at which it can be said that the reported data are complete so far as liquidity management assessment at least is concerned. It is not a case of adding CFA and NRVA data together; it is an admission that each is incomplete without the other, and that financial reports are irrelevant without both. Finally, it might be suggested that this cash-orientated system may only have a limited application to certain types of enterprise whose asset structure is mainly composed of readily-realisable assets (such as banks, property and insurance companies).[9] To limit the system in this way is to deny that liquidity matters, generally, and cash flow and cash accessibility, particularly, are of no concern to industrial organisations. The non-realisability of assets in the latter due to their specialised nature is recognised in the system outlined in this paper—they have no sale value, and therefore do not add to the reporting entity's command over money until such time as they generate cash flows from use.

---

[9]As suggested in Edwards, *op cit*, pp. 132-3.

For Product Safety Concerns and Information please contact our EU
representative GPSR@taylorandfrancis.com
Taylor & Francis Verlag GmbH, Kaufingerstraße 24, 80331 München, Germany